AF352565

THE CATHOLIC UNIVERSITY OF AMERICA
CANON LAW STUDIES
No. 130

CANONICAL NORMS GOVERNING THE DEPOSITION AND DEGRADATION OF CLERICS

A HISTORICAL SYNOPSIS AND COMMENTARY

A DISSERTATION

*Submitted to the Faculty of Canon Law of the
Catholic University of America in Partial
Fulfillment of the Requirements for the
Degree of Doctor of Canon Law*

BY THE

REV. STEPHEN WILLIAM FINDLAY, O.S.B., A.B., J.C.L.

THE CATHOLIC UNIVERSITY OF AMERICA PRESS
WASHINGTON, D. C.
1941

TO MY MOTHER
AND
IN MEMORY OF
MY FATHER

CHAPTER II

CHAPTER III

CHAPTER IV

PART II

CANONICAL COMMENTARY

CHAPTER V

CHAPTER VI

FOREWORD

It is the purpose of this dissertation to trace the historical development of the canonical penalties of deposition and degradation as well as to present a commentary on the present legislation of the Church governing these penalties. Throughout their history deposition and degradation have been closely related. Indeed, during the first twelve centuries they were synonymous terms for one and the same penalty. After the twelfth century deposition and degradation became two distinct penalties and as such they appear today in the Code of Canon Law. In view of their intimate relation in the past as well as in the present law of the Church it has been deemed expedient for a proper consideration of either penalty to make a study of both penalties. In undertaking this work it is the hope of the writer to bring about, especially by contrast, a clearer understanding of each penalty.

The dissertation accordingly has been divided into two parts. In the first section consideration is given to the development of these penalties from their earliest use in ecclesiastical law to their present constitution in the Code of Canon Law. Of necessity this history will be synoptic rather than discursive. It has been divided into four chronological periods within which the important or significant developments of the penalties transpired. Since many phases of the penalties remained unchanged throughout these succeeding periods, the interests of clarity and coherence necessitate in their presentation a certain amount of repetition. The consequent unity, however, renders the history helpful for an understanding of the present discipline of the Church which is considered in the second part of this work.

Throughout the dissertation the emphasis is placed on the canonical norms which govern the establishment of the penalties and not on their application in particular instances. A study of cases is obviously impossible in a work of this type. Canonical procedure has its own fascinating history and its principles today comprise the whole fourth book of the Code. Nevertheless, a glimpse of this apparatus devised by the Church to secure justice and to safeguard rights must be incorporated in this work in order to determine within the various periods of history the ecclesiastical authority vested with the right to pronounce a sentence of deposition or degradation. A consideration of the changes in the discipline governing this competency leads to a better understanding of the penalties themselves. However, this objective will be attained if the question of the competent tribunal is viewed solely in relation to the penalties as affecting bishops, priests and lesser clerics, for it was on the basis of holy orders that the significant changes developed.

This study, moreover, considers only the canonical norms instituting and regulating the deposition and degradation of clerics. Hence it does not consider the unjust intrusions of the civil power in these matters. Neither does it take up the deposition of lay rulers by ecclesiastical authority, nor the application of these penalties by analogy to other ecclesiastical persons who are not clerics.

The work is concerned only with the canonical provisions for the deposition and degradation of clerics, that is, of all who have been dedicated to the divine ministry at least by first tonsure.[1] While clerics by divine ordinance are distinct from the laity in the Church,[2] they are not all of the same rank for they form a sacred hierarchy in which some are subordinate to others.[3] They are constituted within different degrees of the power of orders by sacred ordination and in the divers degrees of jurisdiction by canonical appointment, except for the Roman Pontiff, who in the very act of his election and acceptance thereof receives jurisdiction by the divine law itself.[4] As only clerics can obtain the power either of orders or ecclesiastical jurisdiction, and as they alone can be given ecclesiastical benefices and pensions,[5] they alone are properly the subjects of the canonical penalties of deposition and degradation which, as punishments for grave crimes, deprive the delinquent of his rank and dignity in the Church, of his orders, of his offices, benefices and pensions.

---

[1] Cf. canon 108.
[2] Cf. canon 107.
[3] Cf. canon 108.
[4] Cf. canon 109.
[5] Cf. canon 118.

In the order of clerics, then, from those who have received first tonsure to the superior prelates in the Church, cardinals not excluded, no one is exempt from these punishments if he commits a crime warranting their application. The Roman Pontiff alone cannot be truly and properly the subject of these penalties since he is the judge of all within the Church but can be judged by no one on earth.

In the preparation of this work the author has contracted many obligations which it is his great pleasure now to acknowledge. In the first place he wishes to express profound gratitude to his superior, the Right Reverend Patrick M. O'Brien, O.S.B., Abbot of St. Mary's Abbey in Newark, N. J., whose abiding interest and generosity have made possible the pursuit of graduate studies at the Catholic University of America. He likewise acknowledges his indebtedness to the Dean and Faculty of the School of Canon Law for their kind interest and generous assistance throughout his course and especially in the preparation of this dissertation. He also expresses his gratitude to all his confreres, and particularly, to the Very Rev. Anselm Kienle, O.S.B., of happy memory; to the Very Rev. Vincent Amberg, O.S.B., Prior of St. Mary's Monastery in Morristown, N. J.; to the Very Rev. Dr. Albert Hammenstede, O.S.B., S.T.D., Prior of the Abbey of Maria Laach in the Rhineland; to the Rev. Dr. W. Hugh Duffy, O.S.B., S.T.D., pastor of Notre Dame Parish of Cedar Knolls, N. J. Finally, the author wishes to voice anew his sincere thanks to all his relatives and friends, for their helpful co-operation and generous assistance during his years spent at the University.

INTRODUCTION

According to the classical definition given by St. Paul the priest
is indeed a man "taken from amongst men," yet, "ordained for men
in the things that appertain to God."[1] Commissioned as the official
mediator between God and man, the priest has a dignity and consequent duty exceedingly great, as is summarily indicated by the
Apostle of the Gentiles when he writes: "Let a man so account of us
as of the ministers of Christ and the dispensers of the mysteries
of God."[2]

The august powers of the priesthood are conferred in a special
sacrament instituted by Christ for this purpose. They are not
"merely passing or temporary in the priest, but are *stable* and *perpetual,* united as they are with the indelible character imprinted on
his soul whereby he becomes 'a priest forever,'[3] whereby he becomes
like unto Him in Whose eternal priesthood he has been made a
sharer."[4]

It is through the office of the priesthood that the faithful are
sanctified, not through the personal virtues of priests. Nevertheless,
priests are the channels carrying that life of grace which springs
from Him Who is the Head of all the members.[5] Consequently, the
Church has ever urged on priests their dignity as intermediaries between Christ and souls as a solid reason for cultivating personal
holiness.[6] So, too, it is quite natural for the laity to look upon the
priest "not merely as a guide, but as a model also of Christian life
and of Apostolic virtue."[7]

[1] Heb., V: 1.

[2] I Cor., IV: 1.

[3] Cf. Ps., 109: 4.

[4] Pius XI, litt. encycl., *Ad catholici sacerdotii,* 20 dec. 1935—*Acta Apostolicae Sedis,* XXVIII (1936), 15; Vatican Press Translation: *The Catholic Priesthood* (Washington, D. C.: The National Catholic Welfare Conference, 1936),
p. 14.

[5] St. Thomas, *Summa,* Suppl., P. III, Q. 35, A. 1.

[6] Cf. canon 124.

[7] Pius XI, litt. encycl., *Ad catholici sacerdotii, AAS,* XXVIII (1936) 36;
Vatican Press Translation, p. 43.

Ever conscious of the fundamental importance of the priesthood
to her sublime mission, the Church down through the ages has shown
a maternal solicitude for its well-being and the preservation of its
lofty dignity. This loving care, while acknowledging that "even
the most lamentable downfall, which, through human frailty is possible to a priest, can never blot out from his soul the priestly character," [8] nevertheless, has been constrained at times to separate forever from the service of the altar clerics whose lives became con-
taminated with crime.

The welfare of the Christian religion, the salvation of souls and
the dignity of the Christian priesthood all combined to induce the
Church, early in her history, to exercise her own inherent right and
remove forever from her ministry clerics who by their crimes had
proved themselves unworthy of their sacred charge. This expulsion
from the ranks of the clergy, at first variously designated, gradually
came to be known as deposition or degradation.

From early times this punishment was usually accompanied with
a ceremony in which the delinquent cleric was publicly and solemnly
stripped of all the insignia of his clerical rank.[9] A perusal of this
ceremony as it appears even today in the Roman Pontifical [10] indicates that it was designed not only to increase and manifest the
debasement incurred by the delinquent cleric, but also to strike fear
into the hearts of witnessing clerics, who might thereby take heed to
avoid such a catastrophic conclusion to their own clerical careers.

Thus, it is proper to observe at the very outset of this study
that the penal sanction itself, whether of deposition or of degradation, was very often added to laws not exclusively with the practical
view of meeting violations with these penalties, but also with the
intent to manifest the horror of the Church for such crimes and to
instruct her clergy with a similar terror for them. In this way,
moreover, the Church supplemented the love of virtue ordinarily

---

[8] Pius XI, litt. encycl., *Ad catholici sacerdotii*, *AAS*, XXVIII (1936), 15;
Vatican Press Translation, p. 15.

[9] Cf. Martène, *De Antiquis Ecclesiae Ritibus* (Rotomagi, 1702), III, c. 2.

[10] Cf. *Pontificale Romanum* (Ratisbonae, 1908), III, tit. III. *Ordo suspensionis, reconciliationis, depositionis, dispensationis, degradationis, et restitutionis sacrorum ordinum.*

possessed by her clergy with an added deterrent from crime, so that in any case wherein the love of virtue through human frailty had perhaps declined, the fear of these grave punishments could supply the needed motivation to safeguard a cleric against involving himself in crime.

PART I

HISTORICAL DEVELOPMENT

CHAPTER I

DEPOSITION AND DEGRADATION FROM THE FIRST TO THE SIXTH CENTURY

ARTICLE 1. CIVIL AND MILITARY PRECEDENTS

THE natural law, perceived by man through the use of reason, prescribes substantially the same devices for every society to restore its public order when it is deranged by crime and to serve as a fitting punishment for its disturbance. The common element running through all penalties is to be found in the restriction or privation of the rights and privileges formerly enjoyed by the offender either as a person or as a member of society.[1]

In the Roman Republic, as early as the fifth century before Christ, the public official charged with guarding the economic and moral integrity of the state punished delinquents with reduction of their civil status which, in turn, involved serious economic and political losses. In this degradation a citizen was deposed from a place in the senate, or from the rank of knighthood, or from one tribe of higher rank and greater political power to another of lesser power and prestige.[2] The Romans described this diminution of civil ca-

---

[1] This is as true today as at any time in the past. Hence, in the United States human and civil rights are guaranteed by the Constitution, Amendment XIV, section 1: " . . . No State shall make or enforce any law which shall *abridge* the privileges or immunities of citizens of the United States; nor shall any State *deprive* any person of life, liberty, or property, *without due process of law;* nor deny to any person within its jurisdiction the equal protection of the laws."—*The Story of the Constitution,* United States Constitution Sesquicentennial Commission (Washington, D. C., House Office Building, 1937), p. [84.] A similar prohibition is placed on the Federal Government by Amendment V to the Constitution.—Cf. *op. cit.,* pp. [81]-[82].

[2] Cf. *Enciclopedia Italiana* (Milano-Roma: Instituto Treccani, 1929 1936), *s. v.* "Censore," IX, 739-741; Daremberg-Saglio, *Dictionairre des Antiquités Grecques* (Paris, 1873), *s. v.* "Censor," I, 995-997.

pacity as *capitis deminutio,* defined by Gaius as a change of former status *"prioris status permutatio."* [3]

When the delinquent held a position of trust or importance in the state, punishment often accompanied or followed a procedure in which the rank or dignity possessed by the offender was removed from him in order, on the one hand, to preserve the dignity of the office and, on the other, to increase the opprobrium of the penalty. Thus, in the Roman army punishments included dishonorable discharge, degradation, reduction in rank, and transfer to a lower branch of the service.[4] When a soldier, because of disgraceful conduct, was degraded and dismissed from the army, the insignia of his rank were stripped from him and by that very act he became infamous before the law.[5]

In the pagan society of ancient Rome the vestal virgin held an esteemed position because of her important sacred office. This daughter of Vesta vowed herself to celibacy for thirty years. A violation of this vow brought terrible punishment. After conviction she was deprived of her sacred office by the Pontifex Maximus, beaten with stripes and then led through the city to be buried alive at the Colline Gate. "All make way in silence and accompany her passage with downcast looks. There is no more fearful sight than this, nor any day when the city is plunged into deeper mourning." [6]

The Catholic Church, established by her Divine Founder as a juridically perfect society, enjoys in her own right the power to punish delinquent members. How and when she must proceed in the punishment of the excesses of clerics was clearly deduced not merely from the precedents of civil law but, as the Fathers of the

[3] G. 1, 159; cf. Buckland, *A Textbook of Roman Law from Augustus to Justinian* (2. ed., Cambridge: At the University Press, 1932), p. 135.

[4] Cf. D. (49, 16) 3, 1; Major Brand, *The Military Laws of Ruffus*—Bulletin of the Riccobono Seminar of Roman Law in America, No. 39 (Washington, D. C.: The Catholic University of America, School of Law, 1940), p. 7.

[5] D. (3, 2) 2, 2.

[6] Plutarch, *Life of Numa,* §§ IX, X—*Plutarch's Lives,* translated from the Greek by Stewart and Long (London and New York, 1889-1892), I, 108-110. Cf. Dionysius Halicarnassensis, *Antiquitates Romanae,* lib. II, par. 67—*Opera Omnia,* ed. Henricus Stephanus (Lipsiae, 1774-1777), I, 379; lib. IX, par. 40— *op. cit.,* III, 1853.

IV Lateran Council (1215) have declared,[7] "from the authority of the New and Old Testaments from which the canonical decrees were afterward drawn. For we read in the Gospel that the steward who was accused to his master of wasting his goods, heard him say: 'How is it that I hear this of thee? Give an account of thy stewardship, for now thou canst be steward no longer'; [8] and in Genesis the Lord said: 'I will go down and see whether they have done according to the cry that is come to Me.' "[9]

In the following pages it will be seen how the Church in restricting or even withdrawing the rights and privileges of the clerical state from gravely delinquent clerics established and developed the canonical penalties of deposition and degradation.

ARTICLE 2. EARLIEST USE OF THE CANONICAL PENALTY OF DEPOSITION

Universal legislation governing the deposition or degradation of clerics is lacking during the early ages of the Church and especially, as could be expected, during the era of the persecutions. Nevertheless, there is not wanting in this period some historical evidence to indicate an early use by the Church of a penalty by which gravely delinquent clerics were punished with perpetual privation of their orders, ecclesiastical rank and offices, a penalty at first variously designated but eventually properly named deposition or degradation.

The first century had not closed before a Roman Pontiff had occasion at least to express a fundamental and perennial canonical norm in regard to the penalty of deposition. Pope St. Clement of Rome, a disciple of the Apostle St. John, in terminating a dispute in the Church at Corinth, instructed the faithful there that priests who had blamelessly and religiously fulfilled their duties could not *justly* be dismissed from the ministry.[10]

---

[7] C. 8—Schroeder, *Disciplinary Decrees of the General Councils* (St. Louis: Herder Book Co., 1937), pp. 248-249. Hereafter this work will be referred to as *Disciplinary Decrees*.

[8] Luke, XVI: 2.

[9] Genesis, XVIII: 21.

[10] I *Ep. ad Corinth.*, c. 44—Gebhart, Harnack, Zahn, *Patrum Apostolicorum Opera* (Lipsiae, 1876-1877), I, 135.

At the end of the second century Tertullian records the deposition of a priest in Asia who had been convicted of composing the *"Acta Pauli et Theclae"* and of falsely ascribing it, even though in devotion, to the Apostle Paul.[11] Baronius also cites this case as an example of deposition in the early Church, which he explains as the ejection of a minister of the Church from the office and orders to which he had been raised.[12]

Another indication of the early existence of this penalty may be found in the life of Origen. He was ordained priest, in 228, at Caesarea in Palestine, by a bishop other than his own. About the year 231 the diocesan bishop of Origen, Demetrius of Alexandria, convoked a synod which deprived Origen of his sacerdotal dignity.[13] Kober mentions this case as an early example of deposition but adds that it was accomplished without sufficient reason.[14] Hefele, however, maintains that the penalty was in order,[15] for Origen was uncanonically ordained by a bishop of another diocese; he had mutilated himself; and he had held erroneous opinions in his works *"De principibus"* and *"Stromata."*[16]

St. Cyprian, who was bishop of Carthage during the years 248 to 258, often refers to the penalty of deposition.[17] Indeed, in one

---

[11] *De Baptismo,* c. 17: "Quod si quae Paulo perperam adscripta sunt exemplum Theclae ad licentiam mulierum docendi tinguendique defendunt: sciant in Asia presbyterum, qui eam scripturam construxit, quasi titulo Pauli de suo cumulans, convictum atque confessum id se amore Pauli fecisse, *loco decessisse.*"—Migne, *Patrologiae Cursus Completus, Series Latina* (Parisiis, 1858-1864), I, 1219. Hereafter this work will be designated by the use of the letters *MPL.*

[12] *Annales Ecclesiastici* (Barri-Ducis, 1864-1883), I (an. 57), 400, n. 22.

[13] Cf. Hefele, *A History of the Christian Councils,* translated from the German and edited by William Clark (2. ed., Edinburgh, 1883), I, 87-88. Hereafter this work will be referred to as Hefele-Clark.

[14] *Die Deposition und Degradation nach den Grundsätzen des kirchlichen Rechts, historisch-dogmatisch dargestellt* (Tübingen, 1867), p. 2. Hereafter this work will be referred to simply as *Die Deposition und Degradation.*

[15] Hefele-Clark, I, 87.

[16] Cf. Eusebius, *Historia Ecclesiastica,* VI, 23—Migne, *Patrologiae Cursus Completus, Series Graeca* (Parisiis, 1856-1866), XX, 584. Hereafter reference to this work will be made by the letters *MPG.*

[17] Cf. e.g., *Ep. LXV—MPL,* IV, 396; *Ep. LXVIII—MPL,* IV, 400.

of his letters he supplies the first technical use of the term deposition.[18] In this letter to Rogation, a bishop in Mauretania, St. Cyprian assures the prelate that he is acting within his rights if he decides to depose a rebellious deacon.[19]

At the beginning of the fourth century history records the infliction of this penalty on Meletius, Bishop of Lycopolis in Egypt. This prelate was deposed by Peter of Alexandria on various charges, the most grievous of which was his denial of the faith during the Diocletian persecution.[20] Shortly thereafter, in 320 or 321, Alexander, Bishop of Alexandria, convoked in that city a synod in which the heresiarch Arius was deposed.[21] As a matter of fact, the history of the fourth and subsequent centuries is so replete with instances of the employment of this ecclesiastical penalty that it is needless to restate them. The examples here cited sufficiently make clear the early existence of deposition in the Church. It remains to consider the canonical expressions of this penalty as well as its nature and effects during the first five centuries.

ARTICLE 3. VARIED TERMINOLOGY OF THE PENALTY

As it is certain that the penalty of deposition was employed in the early Church, so, too, it is beyond question that this punishment was expressed in a varied terminology. It has already been observed how the term *"deposition"* was introduced during the third century in the writings of St. Cyprian.[22] The technical term *"degradation"*

---

[18] Cf. Kober, *Die Deposition und Degradation*, p. 5, note 9; Aichner, *Compendium Iuris Ecclesiastici* (6. ed., Brixinae, 1887), § 220, p. 747, not. 8.

[19] *Ep. LXV*, III: "Quod si ultra te contumeliis suis exacerbaverit et provocaverit, fungeris circa eum potestate honoris tui, ut eum vel *deponas* vel abstineas."—*MPL*, IV, 397.

[20] Concilium Alexandrinum (306), *Depositio Meletii* — Mansi, *Sacrorum Conciliorum Nova et Amplissima Collectio* (Parisiis, 1901-1927), II, 407-408. Hereafter this work will be cited simply as Mansi.

[21] Synodus Alexandrina, *Depositio Arii*—Hardouin, *Acta Conciliorum et Epistolae Decretales ac Constitutiones Summorum Pontificum* (Parisiis, 1715), I, 310. Hereafter this work will be referred to simply as Hardouin.

[22] Cf. *Ep. LXV*, III—*MPL*, IV, 397; *supra*, note 19.

appeared in canonical usage only later, in Spain, at the Council of Elvira in 306.[23]

With their appearance, however, these terms were not at once universally or exclusively employed. Many centuries were to elapse before the nomenclature of the developing penal legislation attained such clarity and precision. Indeed, a study of the early canonical provisions sanctioning deposition or degradation leads to the conclusion that there existed originally no clear distinction between them: both terms were used synonymously and designated one and the same penalty until the end of the twelfth century.[24]

In this connection it is helpful to note that in the early Church the clear distinction of the present law between the power of orders and the power of jurisdiction did not exist. Offices and orders were closely interwoven as is evidenced by the fact that until the twelfth century no cleric could be ordained without obtaining at the same time an appointment to a specific office. Ordination practically meant appointment to a particular office.[25] Hence, it is not surprising that it was only in the twelfth century that a distinction was

[23] C. 20: "Si quis clericorum detectus fuerit usuras accipere, placuit eum *degradari.*"—Hardouin, I, 252; in Gratian, c. 5, D. XLVII; cf. Aichner, *Compendium Iuris Ecclesiastici*, § 220, p. 747, not. 8.

[24] Cf. Du Cange, *Glossarium ad Scriptores Mediae et Infimae Latinitatis* (ed. nova, Parisiis, 1937-1938), *s. v. "Degradatio"*; Kober, *Die Deposition und Degradation*, p. 130; Chelodi, *Ius Poenale et Ordo Procedendi in Iudiciis Criminalibus iuxta Codicem Iuris Canonici* (Tridenti, 1925), p. 66; Devoti, *Institutionum Canonicarum Libri IV* (editio prima Romana post quintam, Romae, 1825), § XIX, n. 2, p. 389 (hereafter this work will be referred to simply as *Institutiones*); Lega, *De Delictis et Poenis* (2. ed., Romae, 1910), p. 281; Wernz, *Ius Decretalium* (2. ed., Prati et Romae, 1906-1913), VI, p. 121, n. 119; Benedictus XIV, *De synodo dioecesana* (Parmae, 1764), lib. IX, cap. 6, n. 3. Hence, either term could be used to designate this penalty during the first twelve centuries. In this work deposition is usually preferred in view of the later and distinct meaning of degradation.

[25] Cf. Council of Chalcedon, c. 6—Hardouin, II, 603; Schroeder, *Disciplinary Decrees*, p. 95; also Rainer, *The Suspension of Clerics* (Catholic University of America, Canon Law Studies, No. 111: Washington, D. C., 1937), p. 16. "It was the Third Council of the Lateran (1179) that brought into bold relief the distinction and separability of the two powers of the keys."—Miaskiewicz, *Supplied Jurisdiction According to Canon 209* (Catholic University of America, Canon Law Studies, No. 122: Washington, D. C., 1940), p. 43.

established between deposition and degradation for, properly considered, according to the Roman Pontifical, one is deposed from dignities and honors but is degraded from orders.[26]

Moreover, this obscurity in the distinction and separability of the powers of orders and of jurisdiction undoubtedly contributed to the varied terminology of this penalty. Simultaneously with the terms deposition and degradation, other words were employed to express the punishment. This fact is amply demonstrated by the conciliar legislation of the Church both in the West as well as in the East. While briefly indicating the use of this varied terminology one may helpfully mention some of the crimes for which the penalty was incurred. This will show, at least in a general way, that although there was diversity in expression, there was unity in purpose; namely, clerics guilty of grave crimes were to be removed from ecclesiastical offices and forever barred from returning to them.

In Spain, the Council of Elvira (306), presenting the first written law on a much earlier practice, namely, ecclesiastical celibacy, ordained that a cleric who violated this law should be *expelled from the honor of the clergy*.[27] Another canon of this council decreed that clerics convicted of usury *be degraded*.[28] Finally, a third canon employs the term deposition. It decrees that a layman who is a heretic is not to be ordained; if any former heretics have been ordained in the past, *they are to be deposed*.[29]

In Gaul, the Council of Arles, celebrated in 314, decreed that clerics who were publicly known to have delivered up to the persecutors the Sacred Scriptures, holy vessels or the names of the

---

[26] *Pontificale Romanum* (Romae, 1908), Pars III, tit. VII, *Degradationis forma*, § II.

[27] C. 33: "ab honore clericatus exterminetur."—Mansi, II, 11; Hefele-Clark, I, 150. This law imposed clerical celibacy only on bishops, priests and deacons. If they continued to live with their wives and begot children after their ordination, they were to be deposed. Cf. Schroeder, *Disciplinary Decrees*, p. 193, n. 19.

[28] C. 20: "Si quis clericorum detectus fuerit usuras accipere, placuit eum degradari."—Mansi, II, 9; Hardouin, I, 252; Hefele-Clark, I, 145; in Gratian c. 5, D. XLVII; cf. Aichner, *Compendium Iuris Ecclesiastici*, § 220, p. 747, not. 8.

[29] C. 51: "sine dubio deponantur."—Mansi, II, 14; Hefele-Clark, I, 159.

brethren, were to be *removed from the clerical order*.[30] This council also ruled that one ordained should remain in the place of his ordination.[31] Priests and deacons who violated this law and took up their ministry in another place were to be *deposed*.[32]

In Africa, a Council convoked at Carthage in 398, among other provisions, decreed that a cleric who idled in the markets, or dealt in flattery and treachery, or spoke evil, especially against priests, should be *degraded from office*;[33] a clergyman who, during persecution, abandoned his post or discharged his duties negligently should be *removed from office;*[34] and one who incited schism in the Church was to be *removed from his rank*.[35]

The councils of the East likewise display a variety of expressions in sanctioning the penalty of deposition. A council held at Neocaesarea (314-325) in Pontus ruled that a priest who married should be *removed from his order*.[36] The First Ecumenical Council of the Church, celebrated in 325 in Nicaea (now Isnik), a city of Bithynia in Asia Minor, provided that any cleric in sound health who had castrated himself had to *resign from the ministry*.[37] It was also decreed that if in the future a grave sin be discovered in a

[30] C. 13: "ab ordine cleri amoveatur."—Mansi, II, 472; Hardouin, I, 265; cf. Hefele-Clark, I, 191; Kober, *Die Deposition und Degradation*, p. 4.

[31] C. 2: "Ubi quisque ordinatur, ibi permaneat."—Schroeder, *Disciplinary Decrees*, p. 45; Hefele-Clark, I, 185.

[32] C. 21: "De presbyteris aut diaconibus . . . placuit ut eis locis ministrent, quibus praefixi sunt; quod si relictis locis suis ad alium se locum transferre voluerint, deponantur."—Mansi, II, 473; Hardouin, I, 266; Hefele-Clark, I, 195.

[33] Cc. 48, 56, 57: "ab officio suo degradetur."—Hardouin, I, 982; cf. Hefele-Clark, II, 414-415.

[34] C. 50: "ab officio suo removendum."—Hardouin, I, 982; cf. Hefele-Clark, II, 414.

[35] C. 105; "si clericus fuerit, cadat de proprio gradu."—Hardouin, I, 986; cf. Hefele-Clark, II, 418.

[36] C. 1: "Presbyter si uxorem duxerit: ordine suo moveatur" (text of Gentianus Hervetus), "ab ordine deponatur" (Dionysius Exiguus, "ab ordine suo illum deponi debere" (Isidorus Mercatoris).—Mansi, II, 540; Hardouin, I, 281.

[37] C. 1: "cessare debet"—Hardouin, I, 323; cf. English translation in Fulton, *Index Canonum* (4. ed., New York, 1892), p. 121; Hefele-Clark, I, 376-377; in Gratian c. 7, D. LV.

cleric and he be convicted by two or three witnesses, he must *lay aside his clerical office.*[38] Clerics were forbidden to take interest or devise other schemes of dishonest profit; those who violated this prohibition were to be *ejected from the clerical state.*[39]

Among the disciplinary enactments of the Council of Antioch (341), in Pisidia, it was decreed that clerics who obstinately persisted in celebrating Easter contrary to the law of the Church should be *deposed from the priesthood and ministry.*[40] A priest or deacon who persistently refused to heed the summons of his bishop to return to his own parish,[41] or who, despising his bishop, separated himself from his church, gathered a private assembly and raised an altar, should be *wholly deposed.*[42]

The *Canons of the Apostles,*[43] in the Greek text, consistently employ the term καθαιρείσθω to express the penalty of deposition.[44] In the Latin texts the term is rendered "deponatur"[45] and is translated in the English versions by the clause *"let him be deposed."*[46]

The *Canons of the Apostles* inflict this penalty (*a.*) *on a bishop*

---

[38] C. 2: "cesset a clero."—Hardouin, I, 330; cf. Schroeder (*Disciplinary Decrees,* p. 21), who, adverting to the obscurity of the expression "a grave sin" (ψυχικόν τι ἁμάρτημα), offers the reasonable interpretation that it included "all such crimes for the expiation of which there was formerly enjoined a public penance, as apostasy, adultery, homicide, which then as now were regarded as capital sins." The penal sanction of deposition points to such an interpretation. Cf. Hefele-Clark, I, 378.

[39] C. 17: "abiiciatur a clero"—Mansi, IV, 413; cf. English translation in Schroeder, *Disciplinary Decrees,* p. 48; Hefele-Clark, I, 424.

[40] C. 1: "deponit a sacerdotio et ministerio"—Hardouin, I, 594; cf. English translation in Fulton, *Index Canonum,* p. 233; Hefele-Clark, II, 67.

[41] C. 3—Mansi, II, 1310; Hardouin, I, 593; Hefele-Clark, II, 68.

[42] C. 5: "omnino deponatur."—Mansi, II, 1310; Hardouin, I, 595; the Greek text has παντελῶς καθαιρείσθαι, translated by Fulton (*Index Canonum,* pp. 234-235, 236-237) "wholly deposed"; so also Hefele-Clark, II, 68.

[43] Attributed by most modern authorities to the early fifth century.—Cf. Lijdsman, *Introductio in Ius Canonicum* (Hilvershum in Hollandia, 1924-1929), I, 99.

[44] Cf. Hefele-Clark, I, 458-492.

[45] Cf. Hardouin, I, 9 sq.; Mansi, I, 30 sq.

[46] Cf. Hefele-Clark, I, 458-492; Fulton, *Index Canonum,* p. 233 sq.

who has obtained his church through secular rulers (c. 30, 28),[47] or who ordains outside his territory without the consent of the local bishop (c. 36, 34); (*b.*) *on a bishop or priest,* who offers anything other than wine at the altar (c. 3); who will not receive one who turns from his sins, but rejects him (c. 52, 51); who, persisting in negligence and self-indulgence, neglects the clergy or people and does not teach them religion (c. 58, 57); who cannot be persuaded to abandon public business and occupy himself with the affairs of the Church (c. 81, 80); who shall rebaptize one who has true baptism (c. 47, 46); or who does not employ the prescribed form of baptism (c. 49, 48 and c. 50, 49); (*c.*) *on a bishop, priest, or deacon* who engages in worldly business (c. 7, 6); celebrates Easter before the vernal equinox (c. 8, 7); is convicted of fornication, perjury or theft (c. 25, 24); strikes any of the faithful who sin or any unbelievers who have acted wrongfully (c. 28, 26); has obtained his office for money (c. 30, 28); is given to dice or drunkenness and does not desist (c. 42, 41); persistently exacts usury from debtors (c. 44, 43); persistently fails to supply what is necessary when one of the clergy is in need (c. 59, 58); receives from anyone a second ordination (c. 68, 67); desires while serving in the army to retain both the Roman command and the priestly ministry (c. 84, 83); (*d.*) *on any cleric* who joins in prayer with a deposed clergyman (c. 10, 11); who becomes security for anyone (c. 20, 19); who mutilates himself (c. 23, 22); who denies the name of clergyman (c. 62, 61); who enters a synagogue of Jews or heretics to pray (c. 64, 63); who strikes a man and kills him (c. 65, 64); who treats with insolence his bishop (c. 55, 54), the emperor or magistrates (c. 84, 83); who does not fast in the holy forty days of Lent, or on Wednesdays and Fridays, unless he be hindered by bodily weakness (c. 69, 68); who fasts on the Lord's day, or on any Sabbath, except one only (i. e. on the eve of Easter) (c. 66, 65); who fasts with the Jews, or observes festivals with them, or receives from them gifts such as unleavened cakes, or the like, from their feasts

---

[47] The first number refers to the enumeration of Dionysius Exiguus: in Hardouin, I, 33 sq., Mansi, I, 49 sq., Hefele-Clark, I, 458 sq.; the second number refers to the collection of Gentianus Hervetus: in Hardouin, I, 9 sq., Mansi, I, 30 sq. Cf. English translation in Fulton, *Index Canonum,* p. 233 sq.

(c. 70, 69); who abstains from marriage, or flesh, or wine, not for discipline, but because he abhors them, blasphemously slandering God's work, forgetting that all things are very good, and that God made man male and female (c. 51, 50).

In the fifth century, diversity continued to mark the canonical expressions of deposition. Two ecumenical councils of the period amply demonstrate this fact. The Council of Ephesus (431), which condemned the doctrines of Nestorius, issued an encyclical letter declaring that the holy synod had by one common decree *deposed from all ecclesiastical communion* and *deprived of all priestly power* those bishops who refused to join in the decree against Nestorius and preferred to promote the opinions of Nestorius and Celestius.[48] Attached to this synodal letter were six canons, three of which sanctioned the penalty of deposition for clerics who in the future united themselves with these heretics. A metropolitan was to be *degraded from his episcopal rank*;[49] provincial bishops were to be *deposed from the priesthood and forfeit their rank*;[50] in fact, if any of the clergy fell away, and publicly or privately presumed to maintain the doctrines of Nestorius or Celestius, it was declared just by the holy synod that these also *should be deposed*.[51] If any clerics had been condemned for evil practices by the synod, or by their own bishops, and if with his usual arrogance, Nestorius should attempt uncanonically to restore such persons to communion and to their former rank, the council decreed that they would not be aided thereby but would remain nonetheless *deposed*.[52] Finally, any

---

[48] C. Ephesinum, *Epistola Synodica*: " . . . quos sancta synodus communi decreto ab omni ecclesiastica communione alienos esse statuit et omnem sacerdotii functionem illis ademit."—Hardouin, I, 1622; cf. Fulton, *Index Canonum*, p. 151.

[49] C. 1: "omnino deiectus sit a sede episcopatus"—Hardouin, I, 1622; cf. Fulton, *Index Canonum*, p. 153.

[50] C. 2: "penitus alienos esse sacerdotio et a gradu cecidisse"—Hardouin, I, 1622; cf. Schroeder, *Disciplinary Decrees*, p. 76.

[51] C. 4: "istos quoque depositos esse"—Hardouin, I, 1623; cf. Fulton, *op. cit.*, p. 153.

[52] C. 5: "istos censuimus nihil profecisse, et manere et esse nihilominus depositos."—Hardouin, I, 1623; cf. Fulton, *loc. cit.*

clerics who aimed to undo the work of this great council would *absolutely forfeit their rank.*[53]

The General Council of Chalcedon (451) employed three different phrases to express the one penalty of deposition: a bishop who conferred ecclesiastical orders or positions for money *forfeited his own rank* (*periclitabitur de suo gradu*); the one who received orders or positions for money was to be *removed from his charge or dignity* (*alienus sit a dignitate vel cura*), and the cleric who negotiated these disgraceful and unlawful transactions was to be *deposed from his rank* (*de suo excidat gradu*).[54]

ARTICLE 4. NATURE OF THE PENALTY

The various terms employed to designate this penalty, and particularly deposition, degradation, καθαίρεσις, especially when viewed in the light of other information gleaned from the sources of this period,[55] indicate that the punishment substantially consisted in the complete privation of the power and authority committed to the cleric in his ordination and in the consequent reduction of the delinquent clergyman to the lay state. "As the Church had the power," observes Bingham,[56] "to grant this authority and commission at first, so she had the power to resume and withdraw it again upon great misdemeanors and just provocation. And then a clergyman whatever character he sustained before, was totally divested both of the name and dignity, and power and authority belonging to his former order and function."

A. Deposition Differed from Mere Privation

Even in these early centuries indications are not lacking that deposition was marked with a special character by which it was dis-

---

[53] C. 6: "eos omnino a proprio cadere gradu."—Hardouin, I, 1623; cf. Fulton, *loc. cit.*

[54] C. 2.—Hardouin, II, 601; Mansi, VII, 393; cf. English translation in Fulton, *Index Canonum*, p. 175; Schroeder, *Disciplinary Decrees*, p. 87.

[55] Not to mention again the lack of a clear distinction during these centuries between the powers of orders and jurisdiction; *q. v. supra*, p. 6.

[56] *The Antiquities of the Christian Church* (reprinted from original edition, London, 1865), II, 1030. Hereafter reference to this work will be made as *Antiquities.*

tinguished from mere privation: deposition involved the complete *ineligibility* for any ecclesiastical office. The deposed cleric not only lost his office without any hope of return, but he also became radically incapable of obtaining another office or ecclesiastical dignity.[57]

This privation of the power of orders and jurisdiction involved in deposition is revealed already in certain cases treated during the episcopacy of St. Cyprian at Carthage. The question had arisen as to whether or not a bishop or priest who had lapsed from the faith under persecution and then after his repentance had obtained reconciliation was to be restored, not only to his place among the faithful, but also to his place in the hierarchy. This question seems to have received everywhere practically the same answer. The bishop or priest could be received among the faithful, but could not again exercise his ministry.[58]

In one of his letters St. Cyprian relates such a case in the affair of Trophimus, a bishop in Italy, who had been a *thurificatus* (i. e., one who lapsed from the faith by offering incense in pagan worship). He had been restored, after penance, by Pope Cornelius, but only as a layman. He was forever deprived of the powers and prerogatives of the priesthood.[59]

In the year 258 the fourth council held at Carthage under Cyprian was convoked to examine the cause of two bishops, Basilides and Martial, who had been deposed in Spain as *libellatici* (i. e., persons who, in persecution, privately denied the faith but avoided public denial by bribery). With the restoration of peace these two bishops contrived to regain their sees from Pope Stephen. The assembled bishops at Carthage, however, approved the sentence of deposition passed by the synod in Spain and declared that *"libel-*

---

[57] Cf. Wernz, *Ius Decretalium*, II, n. 233, p. 336; VI, n. 118, p. 120; Kober, *Die Deposition und Degradation*, p. 5; Hinschius, *Das Kirchenrecht der Katholiken und Protestanten in Deutschland* (Berlin, 1869-1897), IV, 726-727. Hereafter reference to this work will be made as *Kirchenrecht*.

[58] Cf. Watkins, *A History of Penance* (London: Longmans, Green & Co., 1930), I, 211.

[59] *Ep. X, Ad Antonianum*: "Sic admissus est Trophimus ut laicus communicet, non, secundum quod ad te malignorum litterae pertulerunt, quasi locum sacerdotis usurpet."—*MPL*, III, 777.

latici can indeed be admitted to penance but are rightly forbidden clerical ordination and the sacerdotal dignity." [60]

St. Cyprian declares the decision of the Church on this point: "Such men (as Basilides and Martial) strive in vain to claim for themselves the episcopate, since it is manifest that men of this kind *cannot rule over the Church of Christ nor may they offer sacrifices to God*; especially since Cornelius also, our colleague, . . . long ago decreed with us and with all the bishops appointed throughout the whole world, that men of this sort might indeed be admitted to the performance of penance, but were prohibited from the ordination of the clergy and from the sacerdotal honor." [61]

The perpetual loss of the powers of orders and jurisdiction is stated by the Council of Antioch (341). It declared that one who was wholly deposed had no further remedy nor was he capable of regaining his rank. [62] Deposed clerics, the same council decreed, who took their troubles to the emperor would not obtain any pardon or possess any hope of regaining their rank in the future. [63] This provision indicates that while deposition was by its nature perpetual, the one deposed could at least hope to regain his status through the favor of the Church if and when the authorities considered the damage wrought by his crime sufficiently repaired to grant him a dispensation. Again, having established deposition as its penalty for those clerics who persistently refused to obey the summons of their bishops to return to their own churches, this council added that any bishop who received such clerics was to be punished by the synod as one who nullified the laws of the Church. [64]

---

[60] Cf. Baronius, *Annales Ecclesiastici*, III (an. 258), 105, n. 1 sq.; *MPL*, III, 1020.

[61] *Ep. ad Carthaginense Concilium—MPL*, III, 1031; cf. MacKenzie, *The Delict of Heresy* (Catholic University of America, Canon Law Studies, No. 77, Washington, D. C., 1932), p. 5.

[62] C. 5: "omnino deponatur, et non amplius curationem assequi, nec suum possit honorem capere."—Mansi, II, 1310; cf. Fulton, *Index Canonum*, p. 237.

[63] C. 12: " . . . huiusmodi nullam veniam habeat, neque locum affectionis suae, nec spem recipiendi gradus habeat in futurum."—Hardouin, I, 598; cf. Fulton, *op. cit.*, p. 239.

[64] C. 3: "Si autem eum, qui propter hanc causam depositus est, alius

In this way the Council insinuated the permanent character of the loss sustained in deposition.

In the year 385 Pope Siricius wrote in like fashion to Bishop Himerius of Tarragona that incontinent clerics who had been deposed could never thenceforth consider celebrating the holy mysteries, "because present examples [of incontinency] warn us to take care for the future; if any bishop, priest, or deacon (*quod non optamus*) is found to be such hereafter, let him now understand that every avenue of pardon has been closed by us because it is necessary to cut off wounded members that do not respond to medical treatment." [65]   The principle here stated is that deposition with its privation of clerical powers is employed as a last resort, a vindictive penalty, in its effects final.   The pope insinuates that it is within the power of the Church to dispense from such a penalty, but likewise that discipline excludes this dispensation from the intention of the lawmaker who proposes by this disciplinary measure to remove the delinquent forever from the clerical state.[66]

B. Deposition Differed from Suspension

The nature of deposition is further revealed by a comparison between deposition and suspension, which even during the first five centuries appeared as distinct penalties.   By suspension a cleric was deprived of his office and functions for a certain time upon the completion of which he was fully restored to his office and again could exercise all of its functions.[67]   As a temporal punishment it differed from deposition, which punishment was of itself perpetual,

episcopus receperit, ille quoque a communi synodo puniatur, ut qui ritus ecclesiasticos dissolvat."—Mansi, II, 1310; cf. Fulton *Index Canonum*, p. 235.

[65] *Ep. ad Himerium*, c. VII—*MPL*, XIII, 114; in Gratian, c. 4, D. LXXXII.

[66] Cf. Eichmann, *Das Strafrecht des Codex Iuris Canonici* (Paderborn: Ferdinand Schöningh, 1920), p. 7.   Hereafter this work will be referred to simply as *Strafrecht*.

[67] Cf. Kober, *Die Suspension* (Tübingen, 1863), p. 6; Probst, *Kirchliche Disciplin in den drei ersten christlichen Jahrhunderten* (Tübingen, 1873), pp. 404-408.   Hereafter this work will be referred to as *Kirchliche Disciplin*.

rendering a cleric not only incapable of ever returning again to his office but also disqualifying him for any other office in the Church.[68]

The *Canons of the Apostles* attest to this distinction. They speak of two different penalties, one graver than the other. The milder penalty is considered to have been suspension, for only if it proved ineffective in correcting the delinquent did the graver penalty or deposition follow.[69] In stating these penalties the Greek text used the words ἀφορίζεσθω and καθαιρείσθω which Fulton translates as suspension and deposition respectively; as, for example, in canon 59: "If a bishop, priest, or deacon shall not supply what is necessary, when one of the clergy is in need, let him be suspended; and if he persist, let him be deposed, as one who murders his brother." [70] Suspension was primarily concerned with the correction of the delinquent whereas deposition was directly intended for the common good.

Another indication of the distinction between the two penalties is to be found in the enactments of the Council of Antioch (341). Concerning the priest or deacon who abandoned his parish and wholly changed his residence, especially if he did not heed the summons of his bishop to return, the council decreed: "Let him *no longer officiate* . . . and if he persist in his disorder, let him be *wholly deposed* from his ministry, so that no further room be left for his restoration." [71] Thus, by suspension the cleric was forbidden for a time to exercise the functions of his office, whereas by deposition he was forever excluded from the clerical state.[72]

The Council of Ancyra (314) has been adduced as offering a clear distinction between deposition and suspension.[73] The first canon of this council provided that priests who sacrificed to idols during the persecution but afterwards repented, and resumed the

---

[68] Cf. Kober, *Die Deposition und Degradation*, p. 26.

[69] Cf. Rainer, *Suspension of Clerics*, p. 3.

[70] *Index Canonum*, p. 99; cf. also cc. 5, 44, 58, *et al.—op. cit.*, pp. 83, 95, 99 sq.

[71] C. 3: " . . . ne amplius celebret . . . is omnino a sacro ministerio deponatur."—Mansi, II, 1310; cf. Fulton, *Index Canonum*, p. 235.

[72] Cf. Eichmann, *Strafrecht*, p. 7; Probst, *Kirchliche Disciplin*, p. 404.

[73] Cf. Rainer, *Suspension of Clerics*, p. 4.

martyr's combat, not only in appearance but in reality, should continue to enjoy the honor of their office, but could neither offer the sacrifice of the Mass nor preach nor fulfill any priestly office.[74] The council, therefore, distinguished and expressly stated that these priests were to retain their office: hence they could not be considered deposed, that is, deprived of all clerical rights; on the other hand, they were to lose the exercise of certain clerical rights, a characteristic feature of suspension as it developed in the Church.[75]

C. Deposition Differed from Excommunication

Before a further effort be made to analyze the penalty of deposition by comparing it with excommunication, it is imperative to note that in the early Church excommunication was a generic term employed to designate all ecclesiastical penalties.[76] At times it was used to signify the total exclusion of a delinquent Christian from the communion of the faithful (*communio laicalis*), in which case it deprived the affected party of all the rights and privileges of membership in the Church. At other times it was employed to designate only the privation of particular rights and privileges proper to the various grades of communion, either in the ranks of the laity, as in the system of public penance, or in the ranks of the clergy (*communio clericalis, sacerdotalis, episcopalis*). In this relative sense excommunication placed one outside the communion to which his position in the Church entitled him.[77]

According to this relative sense, excommunication for a cleric was equivalent to deposition, for by placing him outside the clerical communion it left him to enjoy only lay communion and deprived him of all his rights as a cleric. It was in this sense that the Council of Nicaea (325) employed excommunication as the penalty for

[74] Mansi, II, 514.

[75] Cf. Rainer, *loc. cit.*

[76] Cf. Ayrinhac-Lydon, *Penal Legislation in the New Code of Canon Law* (New York: Benziger Brothers, 1936), pp. 85-86. Hereafter this work will be referred to simply as *Penal Legislation.*

[77] Cf. Hyland, *Excommunication, Its Nature, Historical Development and Effects* (Catholic University of America, Canon Law Studies, No. 49, Washington, D. C., 1928), p. 19.

priests, deacons and other clerics who deserted their own churches and refused to return.[78] It was also with this restricted signification that the Council of Arles (452) likewise threatened with excommunication clerics who abandoned their churches.[79] In this connection it is also worthy of note that, as a general rule, an offense which was punished with excommunication in the case of a layman was penalized in the case of clerics with deposition.[80] However, this must not be taken to mean that deposition and excommunication were completely synonymous, for while this is true of excommunication in its restricted sense, as just explained, in its fullness of meaning, as the complete privation of all the rights of membership in the Church, excommunication was clearly distinct from deposition.

Deposition was the ordinary penalty for delinquencies among the clergy; but in cases of more flagrant and vicious crimes, two penalties, deposition and excommunication, were inflicted. Through deposition the cleric was removed from clerical communion and reduced to lay communion, that is to say, he was now regarded in all relations with the Church as a layman; through excommunication he was ejected even from lay communion and cut off completely from all participation in the life of the Church.[81]

Thus, St. Cyprian, in writing to Pope Cornelius, stated that Novatus, who was guilty of murder when by means of a blow he caused his wife to miscarry, was not only to be deposed or expelled from the priesthood, but also to be deprived of the communion of the Church.[82] The *Canons of the Apostles* for certain grave crimes

[78] C. 16: "Quodsi non fecerunt, oportet eos communione privari."— Hardouin, I, 330; translation in Schroeder: "In case they refuse, they are to be excommunicated (deposed)."—*Disciplinary Decrees,* p. 46; cf. Balsamon and Zonaras who similarly interpret this penalty as deposition.—Beveregius, *Synodikon sive Pandectae Canonum* (Oxonii, 1672), I, 77. Hereafter this work will be referred to as *Pandectae Canonum.*

[79] C. 13: "No cleric shall under penalty of excommunication (here and frequently equivalent to *deposition*) leave his church."—Hefele-Clark, III, 169. The parenthesis is Hefele's.

[80] Cf. Schroeder, *Disciplinary Decrees,* p. 96; Smith-Cheetham, *A Dictionary of Christian Antiquities* (Hartford, 1880), *s. v.* "Degradatio."

[81] Cf. Probst, *Kirchliche Disciplin,* pp. 405-406; Hinschius, *Kirchenrecht,* IV, 729.

[82] *Ep. VII, Ad Cornelium:* "propter hoc se non de presbyterio excitari

also threatened a twofold penalty. One canon provided that any bishop, priest or deacon who acquired his rank through money was to be deposed *and* excommunicated.[83] Again, if any bishop obtained his church through secular rulers he was to be deposed *and* excommunicated.[84] Another canon decreed that if any bishop, priest or deacon, who had been duly deposed, should presume to exercise the ministry formerly entrusted to him, such a one should be entirely cut off from the Church.[85] These canons show that excommunication was not only a penalty *distinct* from deposition but also more severe,[86] for even lay communion which remained after deposition was lost through excommunication.[87] On the other hand, as a further comparison of these two penalties reveals, deposition was likewise a vindictive penalty.

D. A Perpetual Vindictive Penalty

Ordinarily excommunication was not, as deposition, inflicted forever, but for a greater or lesser period according to the magnitude of the crime and the dispositions of the delinquent.[88] Upon completion of the entire penance admission to full membership in the Church was again granted.[89] After the various grades of public penance were established, in the middle of the third century,[90] admission to the lowest grade involved absolution from the total excommunication, but only in the sense that the penitent was then accepted as a member of the Church in which he could, by ascending the vari-

tantum, sed et communicatione prohiberi."—*MPL*, III, 730. Cf. similar decree of Peter of Alexandria, *Epistola Canonica*, c. 10—Beveregius, *Pandectae Canonum*, II, 15-16.

[83] C. 29 (28)—Fulton, *Index Canonum*, p. 89; Hardouin, I. 15.

[84] C. 30 (29)—Fulton, *loc. cit.*; Hardouin, *loc. cit.*

[85] C. 28 (27)—Fulton, *loc. cit.*; Hardouin, *loc. cit.*

[86] Cf. Benedictus XIV, *De synodo dioecesana*, lib. IX, c. 6, n. 3.

[87] Cf. Lega, *De Delictis et Poenis*, n. 208, p. 281.

[88] Cf. Probst, *Kirchliche Disciplin*, pp. 404-408; Moriarity, *The Extraordinary Absolution From Censures* (Catholic University of America, Canon Law Studies, No. 113, Washington, D. C., 1938), p. 11.

[89] Cf. Moriarity, *op. cit.*, p. 14.

[90] For a detailed description of this system of penance, cf. Hyland, *Excommunication*, pp. 28-29.

ous grades of public penance, successively obtain absolution from the relative excommunications, commensurate with the grades of penance, and thus gradually attain to full participation in the rights and privileges of the faithful.[91]

Clerics in major orders, as already observed,[92] could be admitted, during the third century, after excommunication and deposition, to penance and eventually to lay communion, but not to their former places in the hierarchy. So the Council of Carthage in 258 ordained for apostate clerics.[93] This ordinance was firmly approved by St. Cyprian,[94] who also reported the case of Trophimus, an apostate bishop, who was restored after penance by Pope Cornelius, but only to lay communion.[95] Eusebius likewise testifies that one of the bishops who consecrated Novatian performed public penance and was admitted to lay communion by Pope Cornelius.[96]

An enactment of the Council of Neocaesarea (314-325) also serves to show that penance was efficacious in obtaining pardon for excommunication, but had no such native efficacy in relation to deposition. The first canon of this council decreed: "If a priest marries he shall be removed from the ranks of the clergy (deposed); if he commits fornication or adultery he shall be excommunicated and submit to penance." [97] Hefele explains this canon to mean that if a priest married he was to be deposed from his priestly order and reduced to the *communio laicalis;* if he was guilty of fornication or adultery, he was also to be excommunicated and had to pass through all the degrees of penance in order to regain communion with the Church.[98] The excommunication was removed by penance and absolution. The penalty of deposition, however, remained as a

---

[91] Cf. Probst, *Kirchliche Disciplin,* pp. 406-407; Hinschius, *Kirchenrecht,* IV, 695; Hollweck, *Die kirchliche Strafgesetze* (Mainz, 1899), § 22.

[92] Cf. *supra,* pp. 12-14.

[93] *Epistola Synodica—MPL,* III, 1020; cf. Baronius, *Annales Ecclesiastici,* III (an. 258), 105, n. 1 sq.

[94] *Ep. ad Carthaginense Concilium—MPL,* III, 1031.

[95] *Ep. X:* "sic admissus est Trophimus ut laicus communicet"—*MPL,* III, 777-778.

[96] *Historia Ecclesiastica,* lib. VI, c. XLII—*MPG,* XX, 620.

[97] Hardouin, I, 281; Mansi, II, 540; Fulton, *Index Canonum,* p. 213.

[98] Hefele-Clark, I, 323.

perpetual, vindictive penalty, in itself unaffected by penance and absolution.

The evidences adduced point to the fact that during the first three centuries clerics were admitted to penance, and indeed, public penance. Still it cannot be concluded that this discipline was received by the whole Church. The question as to whether or not clerics performed public penance during the first three centuries may never be answered to the satisfaction of all.[99] After these centuries, however, it is generally agreed, clerics were not allowed to perform public penance.[100] Pope Siricius (384-398) testifies to this fact [101] as does also the V Council of Carthage (401). [102] In the middle of the fifth century St. Leo the Great declared that the admission of clerics in major orders to the performance of public penance was foreign to ecclesiastical custom.[103] Deposed clerics, then, were to perform penance privately to obtain, as Pope Leo stated, the mercy of God and pardon for their grave crimes.[104]

As the reverence of the Church for the clerical order [105] induced her to exclude clerics from public penance, so also it moved her to establish irrevocable deposition as the ordinary penalty for gravely delinquent clerics. It was the will of the Church, as St. Augustine

[99] Cf. Du Cange, *Glossarium Mediae et Infimae Latinitatis, s.v.* "communio laica," II, 457.

[100] Cf. Wernz, *Ius Decretalium,* II, n. 133, pp. 188-189.

[101] *Ep. ad Himerium,* c. XIV: "sicut paenitentiam agere cuiquam non conceditur clericorum."—*MPL,* XIII, 1145; in Gratian, c. 66, D. L.

[102] C. 11: "Item confirmatum est, ut si quando presbyteri vel diaconi in aliqua graviori culpa convicti fuerint, qua eos a ministerio necesse fuerit removeri, non eis manus, tamquam poenitentibus, vel tamquam laicis fidelibus imponatur."—Hardouin, I, 988; in Gratian, c. 65, D. L.

[103] *Ep. CLXVII,* c. II: "Alienum est a consuetudine ecclesiastica ut qui in presbyterali honore aut in diaconii gradu fuerunt consecrati, ii pro crimine aliquo suo per manus impositionem remedium accipiant poenitendi quod sine dubio ex apostolica traditione descendit."—*MPL,* LIV, 1203; in Gratian, c. 67, D. L.

[104] *Ep. CLXVII,* c. II. "Huiusmodi lapsis ad promerendam misericordiam Dei privata est expetenda secessio, ubi illis satisfactio, si fuerit digna, sit etiam fructuosa."—*MPL,* LIV, 1203.

[105] Cf. Martène, *De Antiquis Ecclesiae Ritibus,* III, 421.

(354-430) related,[106] that no one should continue in the clerical state after committing a grave crime or return to it after penance. She followed this policy, not to make any one despair of pardon, but only to insure strict discipline. According to Thomassinus, this severity was required to eliminate simulated repentance performed in the hope of restoration to the clerical state.[107] While it may have been true that some bishops held that clerics, after a worthy satisfaction, should, like the rest of the faithful, regain their former rank in the Church,[108] it can only be said, with Kober, that this mild view never found support in the common law.[109]

E. No Intrinsic Loss of Holy Orders

While a cleric deposed for grave crimes was obliged by the divine law to do penance to obtain peace with God, the performance of penance did not entitle him to return to his former rank in the clerical state. He could, however, be again admitted to his position by the favor of the Church and without any new ordination, for deposition never included in the mind of the Church an intrinsic loss of holy orders. When she willed to do so for grave reasons, the Church relaxed her discipline and allowed deposed clerics to return to the active ministry without any further requirements than her permission. Thus, to promote unity, Pope Cornelius restored the deposed priest, Maximus, who had in an earlier day gone over to the Novatian heresy, with the simple order that he resume his place as a priest.[110] The Fathers assembled at the Council of Nicaea (325)

---

[106] *Ep. CLXXXV*, c. X, n. 45: "Ut enim constitueretur in Ecclesia, ne quisquam post alicuius criminis poenitentiam clericatum accipiat, vel ad clericatum *redeat*, vel in clericatu *maneat*, non desperatione indulgentiae, sed rigore factum est disciplinae."—*MPL*, XXXIII, 812.

[107] *Vetus et Nova Ecclesiae Disciplina* (Venetiis, 1730), pars II, lib. I, cap. LVI, n. 15.

[108] So an Epistle of Calixtus I in Gratian c. 14, D. L. declares. This epistle, however, has been attributed to Pseudo-Isidore. Cf. Hinschius, *Decretales Pseudo-Isidorianae et Capitula Angilramni* (Lipsiae, 1863), p. 141.

[109] *Die Deposition und Degradation*, p. 35; cf. also Wernz, *Ius Decretalium*, II, n. 233, p. 336.

[110] *Ep. VI*, n. 3: "Credimus autem fore, quinnimo pro certo iam confidimus, ceteros quoque qui in hoc errore sunt constituti in Ecclesiam brevi reversuros cum auctores suos viderint nobiscum agere."—*MPL*, III, 725.

did not require a new ordination for the deposed clergy who returned to the unity of the Church.[111]   St. Augustine testified that it was the practice of the African Church, in the interests of unity, to receive the Donatist clergy back again into their former rank and without a new ordination.[112]

Indeed, during this period reordinations were formally proscribed by the III Council of Carthage (397).[113]   Moreover, any bishop who would reordain, or any bishop, priest or deacon who would submit to reordination, was to be punished with deposition.[114]   Thus, the constant teaching of the Church was manifested that the character impressed on the soul by the sacrament of orders was indelible and could not be taken away [115] even by the greatest crimes or by the severest penalties inflicted by the Church for such deeds.[116]

ARTICLE 5. EFFECTS OF THE PENALTY

A. Lay Communion

The penalty of deposition, not only excluded the delinquent from his office but even expelled him from the ranks of the clergy, and in consequence juridically reduced him to the legal status of the laity.[117]   Delinquent clerics in the fourth century, as St. Basil testifies, were cast out of their rank but were not forbidden lay com-

---

[111] Cf. Hefele-Clark, I, 411-412.

[112] *Contra Ep. Parmeniani,* lib. II, n. 28: "Si visum est opus esse ut eadem officia gererunt, quae gerebant, non sunt rursus ordinati, sed sicut baptismus in eis, ita ordinatio manent integra."—*MPL,* XLIII, 70.

[113] C. 38—Hardouin, I, 968.

[114] *Canones Apostolorum,* c. 68 (67)—Fulton, *Index Canonum,* p. 101; Hardouin, I, 26.

[115] Denzinger-Bannwart-Umberg, *Enchiridion Symbolorum* (ed. 21-23, Friburgi Brisgoviae: Herder and Co., 1937), n. 960.

[116] From this it is evident how false is the explanation given by Sohm (*Kirchenrecht* [2 ed., München and Leipzig: Dunker and Humblot, 1923], footnote 39, pp. 303-307) of the canonical penalty of deposition in the early Church which, according to him, declared void the ordination of the delinquent cleric. Denying the existence of a visible Church, Sohm interprets canon law accordingly and subjects all external elements of religion to human caprice, valid today, invalid tomorrow.

[117] Cf. Hinschius, *Kirchenrecht,* IV, 728-729; Eichmann, *Strafrecht,* p. 7.

munion for "Thou shalt not punish twice for the same crime." [118] Deposition alone was a sufficient penalty. When St. Basil ruled that a deacon who was found guilty of adultery should be deposed but not barred from lay communion, he explained that if a layman was excommunicated he could again, after repentance, be received into lay communion, but that a deacon once deposed remained so and could not be restored to the diaconate. And this held true of all clerics in major orders.[119] The *Canons of the Apostles* prescribed that if a cleric in fear of Jews or heretics denied that he was a cleric he was to be deposed, but if he repented he might be received as a layman.[120] The deposed cleric could still maintain relations with the Church, but only as a layman, *"ut laicus communicet,"* an effect of the penalty expressly recognized as early as the time of St. Cyprian.[121]

Since this effect embraced all others a word of explanation is in order. For laymen lay communion was a great privilege, in fact, as Christians it was their greatest prerogative for it signified their complete participation in the goods of Christ's Church. For the clergyman, however, lay communion was a punishment, involving as it did in his case a reduction from a higher degree of participation or communion. Hence the penalty as early as the fourth century was aptly termed degradation,[122] for it meant the diminution of

---

[118] *Ep. (CXCIX), ad Amphilochium,* c. 32: "Peccatum ad mortem peccantes clerici de gradu deiiciuntur a laicorum communione non arcentur. 'Non enim vindicabis bis in idipsum.'" (Nahum, I, 9)—*MPG,* XXXII, 727; cf. Beveregius, *Pandectae Canonum,* II, 91.

[119] *Ep. (CLXXXVIII), ad Amphilochium,* c. 3: "Diaconus post diaconatum fornicatus, diaconatu eiicietur quidem, sed in laicorum detrusus locum, a communione non arcebitur."—*MPG,* XXXII, 671; cf. Beveregius, *Pandectae Canonum,* II, 53.

[120] C. 62 (61)—Fulton, *Index Canonum,* p. 101; Hardouin, I, 23; cf. also c. 15 (14)—Fulton, *op. cit.,* p. 85; Hardouin, I, 14.

[121] *Ep. X—MPL,* III, 777; *Ep. LXVIII,* n. 6—*MPL,* III, 1030. Cf. Kober, *Die Deposition und Degradation,* p. 56 ff.; Hinschius, *Kirchenrecht,* IV, 729, footnote 1.

[122] In the Council of Elvira (306), c. 20—Hardouin, I, 252; in Gratian, c. 5, D. XLVII; and the IV Council of Carthage (398), c. 48—Hardouin, I, 982; in Gratian, c. 4, D. XCI; cf. Aichner, *Compendium Iuris Ecclesiastici,* p. 747.

the cleric's status in the Church, a reduction in his degree of communion.

The real meaning of lay communion was lost to some scholars of a later day who, as Cardinal Bona observed, no sooner heard of lay communion than they interpreted it, overlooking the ancient notion, as the reception of holy communion in one species. The fallacy of this opinion is obvious when it is recalled that clerics were reduced to lay communion at a time when even laymen communicated in both species.[123] Others erred in thinking that lay communion for delinquent clerics implied their reception of holy communion outside of the altar rail with laymen.[124] While this is indeed a manifestation of lay communion, it does not express its essential meaning, for a sick priest could receive holy communion outside the sanctuary, in his home, and yet not be reduced to the lay state.[125] The full and essential import of reducing a cleric to lay communion is correctly stated by Chamier when he says "it was called lay communion neither from the place of communicating nor from communicating the laity after the clergy, but from the condition and quality of the person communicating; namely, because he that before was a clergyman, or in the roll and nomenclature of the clergy, is now become a layman, and considered as one in the order of laymen only." [126]

B. Loss of Revenues

The deposed cleric, then, except for the indelible character of orders, was in all things considered a layman.[127] As such he was no longer entitled to support from church funds [128] which during the first five centuries were generally centralized in the church of the bishop who employed them partly for the maintenance of the

---

[123] *Rerum Liturgicarum Libri Duo* (Augustae Taurinorum, 1753), lib. IX, c. XIX, § III.

[124] Cf. Bona, *loc. cit.*

[125] Cf. Kober, *Die Deposition und Degradation*, pp. 57-58.

[126] Quoted by Bingham, *Antiquities*, II, 1031; cf. also Du Cange, *Glossarium, s. v.* "communio laica," II, 457; Bona, *Rerum Liturgicarum Libri Duo*, lib. IX, c. XIX, § III.

[127] Cf. Aichner, *Compendium Iuris Ecclesiastici*, p. 746.

[128] Cf. Hinschius, *Kirchenrecht*, IV, 726.

clergy.[129] St. Cyprian supplied an indication that deposed clerics lost their title to partake of these revenues when he directed that certain subdeacons be deprived of the monthly distribution until their case had been decided.[180] Obviously St. Cyprian held that their right to a share depended on the decision as to their status.

Similar conclusions may be drawn from the case of Paul of Samosata. In the year 268, a successor, Domnus, was named to the see of Antioch which had been canonically vacated by the deposition of Paul. The latter, however, confident in the support of Zenobia, then ruler of Antioch, refused to leave the church or rectory. With the return of Antioch to Roman rule, in the victory of Emperor Aurelian in 272, the case for Paul's dispossession was again introduced. The decision was duly given by the emperor that Paul had lost his rights for "the bishop of Antioch was the man whom the bishops of Italy and Rome acknowledged to be such." [181]

Again, in the Acts of the Council of Chalcedon it is recorded how Maximus, the Bishop of Antioch, generously requested the council to have pity on his deposed predecessor and grant him sustenance.[182] This request for maintenance, made *ex caritate* and not *ex iustitia,* argues the lack of a legal title. The fathers of the council, however, readily acceded to this plea for charity.

C. Loss of Clerical Honors and Privileges

The fourth century brings indications of another loss consequent upon deposition. This was the privation of all clerical honors and privileges. Those who were deposed, as the Council of Antioch (341) declared, were deprived of the external honors to which the

---

[129] Cf. Bingham, *Antiquities,* I, 191 ff.

[180] *Ep. XXVIII:* "Interim se a divisione menstrua tantum contineant non quasi a ministerio ecclesiastico privati esse videantur, sed ut integris omnibus ad nostram praesentiam differantur."—*MPL,* IV, 302.

[181] Hughes, *A History of the Church* (New York: Sheed and Ward, 1935), I, 166.

[182] "Deprecor magnificentissimos et gloriosissimos iudices et sanctam hanc et universalem synodum ut humanitatem exercere in Dominum qui fuit Antiochiae episcopus, dignemini et statuere ei certos sumptus de Ecclesia, quae sub me est."—Hardouin, II, 544.

holy canon and the priesthood of God entitled them.[133]   The "holy canon" here mentioned was the register or catalogue kept in each church in which the names of all the clergy were written.   In the East this catalogue was generally called canon (χανών), in the West, *alba, matricula* or *tabula*.[134]   According to the Council of Nicaea (325), the name of a deposed cleric was to be stricken from this list of the clergy.[135]

Upon deletion of his name from the clerical roster in the penalty of deposition, the delinquent was thenceforth deprived of all clerical honors and privileges, such as a special place in liturgical functions and ecclesiastical activities, as well as every title of honor and reverence.[136]   These effects were guaranteed even beyond the limits of the delinquent's own diocese, for wherever he traveled he would be unable to present the testimonial letters required by law to obtain communion with a church and receive the honors due his rank.[137]   Bishops who nullified these laws of the Church by admitting deposed clerics to the honors and privileges of the clergy were to be punished by the synod.[138]

Not only did the deposed cleric lose all the rights, honors and privileges accorded his former rank in the Church, but he lost as well the exemptions and immunities of the clergy as recognized by the civil law with the reign of Constantine.[139]

[133] C. 1: "Depositos autem etiam honore qui extrinsecus est privari oportet, quem sanctus canon et Dei sacerdotium promeruit."—Hardouin, I, 594; cf. Fulton, *Index Canonum*, p. 233.

[134] Cf. Bingham, *Antiquities*, I, 115.

[135] C. 17: "e clero deponatur et fit alienus a canone."—Hardouin, I, 330; Fulton, *Index Canonum*, p. 131; Schroeder, *Disciplinary Decrees*, p. 48.

[136] Cf. Wernz, *Ius Decretalium*, II, n. 233, p. 336.

[137] Cf. Council of Chalcedon, c. 13—Fulton, *Index Canonum*, p. 183; Council of Antioch, c. 7—Hefele-Clark, II, 69; Synod at Rome under Innocent I (402), c. 14—Hefele-Clark, II, 430; *Canones Apostolorum*, c. 33 (32)—Fulton, *op. cit.*, p. 91; Hardouin, I, 15; Bingham, *Antiquities*, I, pp. 32, 164; Schroeder, *Disciplinary Decrees*, pp. 102, 105.

[138] Cf. Council of Antioch, c. 3—Hardouin, I, 593; Mansi, II, 1310.

[139] For example, exemption from personal services: C. Th. (16, 2), 24: "Presbyteros, diaconos, subdiaconos, exorcistas, lectores, ostiarios etiam et omnes perinde qui primi sunt, personalium munerum expertos esse praecipimus."   The Code of Justinian (1, 3), 6, lists the same privilege, but instead of

ARTICLE 6. TESTIMONY OF ROMAN LAW

While the sources of ecclesiastical law clearly demonstrate that deposition was an established penalty in the early Church, confirmaiton of its existence as well as an insight into its nature and effects may also be derived from Roman law. In 408 the Emperors Honorius and Arcadius issued a decree authorizing the *curia* to claim for its offices deposed clerics.[140] The primary purpose of this decree was to build up membership in the *curia*, the municipal government.[141] While two hundreds years earlier the honor of being a *curialis* was eagerly sought, in the declining prosperity of the empire it became an increasingly unenviable position because of the mounting financial burdens imposed on it by the imperial government. What was once a prized distinction had become a sort of official slavery.[142]

The decree is significant here because of the testimony it affords concerning the canonical penalty of deposition at the beginning of the fifth century. It is a public, imperial acknowledgment of the right and power of the bishop to remove from the ministry of the Church those clerics who by their crimes had proved themselves unworthy of their sacred offices.[143]

the words "omnes perinde qui primi sunt" it reads "acolythos." Another was the exemption from curial offices: C. Th. (16, 2), 2: "Qui divino cultui ministeria religionis impendunt, id est, hi qui clerici appellantur, ab omnibus omnino muneribus excusentur: ne sacrilego livore quorumdam a divinis obsequiis avocentur." Cf. Boak, *A History of Rome to 565 A.D.* (2. ed., New York, The Macmillan Company, 1938), p. 371.

[140] C. Th. (16, 2), 39: "Quemcumque clericum indignum officio suo episcopus iudicaverit et ab ecclesiae ministerio segregaverit . . . *continuo eum curia sibi vindicet,* ut liber illi ultra ad ecclesiam recursus esse non possit, et pro hominum qualitate et quantitate patrimonii vel ordini suo vel collegio civitatis adiungatur: modo ut quibuscumque apti erunt publicis necessitatibus obligentur, ita ut colludio quoque locus non sit."

[141] Cf. Gothofredus, *Commentarium in Codicem Theodosianum* (16, 2), 39.

[142] Cf. Jolowicz, *Historical Introduction to the Study of Roman Law* (Cambridge, University Press, 1932) pp. 357-358; Boak, *A History of Rome to 565 A.D.,* pp. 309, 371; Stephenson, *Medieval History* (New York, Harper and Brothers, 1935), p. 26.

[143] "Quemcumque clericum indignum officio suo episcopus iudicaverit et ab ecclesiae ministerio segregaverit . . ." C. Th. (16, 2), 39.

Moreover, it is to be noted, the command in the decree is imposed on the curia,[144] not on the bishop or delinquent cleric. The execution of the decree depends upon the canonical infliction of the penalty of deposition. Only then is the *curia* empowered to act and make a legal claim to the services of the former cleric. In view of later developments it should also be noted that this power to apprehend the deposed cleric is derived from a law of the state and not of the Church.

With deposition, then, the delinquent lost the clerical privileges and became subject to all the obligations and duties of citizenship, even to the most unwelcome assignments of the *curia*. Moreover, upon his incorporation into the *curia* the perpetual character of deposition received an added quality of exclusion: both the civil law here stated as well as the canons of the Church excluded from the clerical ranks those who served in the *curia*.[145]

Article 7. Partial Deposition

It was only in the course of centuries that the developing penal law of the Church reached that stage of perfection in which each of the various canonical penalties received a precise definition and a proper name. Hence, it is not surprising to find in the early Church the employment of a penalty best described in this era as a partial deposition, but in a later age clearly recognized as suspension, interdict, privation, disqualification, or even irregularity *ex delicto*. A consideration of these partial depositions serves to clarify by contrast the complete deposition or degradation, for the former, above all, reveal themselves as an alleviation of the latter, manifesting thereby the benignity of the Church in relaxing her discipline as the occasion warranted.

Thus, there was employed a partial deposition by which a cleric was reduced from a higher rank to a lower one.[146] Examples of the

---

[144] "continuo eum curia sibi vindicet"—C. Th. (16, 2), 39.

[145] Cf. C. Th. (16, 2), 39: "liber illi ultra ad ecclesiam recursus esse non possit"; *Ep. Innocentii ad Victricium*, c. XII—*MPL*, XX, 477; in Gratian, c. 3, D. LI; Bingham, *Antiquities*, I, 148, 180.

[146] Cf. Aichner, *Compendium Iuris Ecclesiastici*, p. 746; Kober, *Die Deposition und Degradation*, pp. 120-125.

use of this penalty may be found in the decrees of the Council of
Neocaesarea (314-325) which provided for the reduction of un-
chaste deacons to the rank of subdeacons,[147] and in the I Council
of Toledo (400) which reduced subdeacons who remarried to the
rank of porters or lectors.[148] The Acts of the Council of Chalcedon
(451) report the legates of the Roman Pontiff as being adverse
to the idea of reducing a bishop to the rank of a priest.[149] Previously, however, the I Council of Nicaea (325) had acted in this
fashion when it conceded to a bishop who returned to the unity of
the Church from the Novatian schism only the sacerdotal dignity
providing the diocesan bishop deemed it best not to permit him to
take part in the dignity of the episcopal title.[150] In a later day,
moreover, the Trullan Council (692) also ordained that bishops who
preached unlawfully in another diocese be reduced to the rank of
priests,[151] and the Council of Rheims (1049) deprived a bishop of
Nantes, who was guilty of simony, of his episcopal office but permitted him the sacerdotal office.[152]

There is also to be found during the first five centuries a partial
deposition which took from the cleric the powers of his rank but
allowed him to retain its dignity.[153] Thus, the Council of Ancyra
(314), in deciding the status of clerics who had sacrificed to idols,
but who afterwards resumed the combat in persecution and became
confessors of the Faith, allowed those who were priests to retain their
places of honor among the clergy, but forbade them to offer Mass,
to preach or to perform any sacerdotal office.[154] St. Basil provides

---

[147] C. 10: "Similiter et diaconus, si in idem peccatum (corporale) inci-
derit, ministri ordinem habeat."—Mansi, II, 541; Fulton, *Index Canonum*, p.
215; cf. Devoti, *Institutiones*, I, tit. IV, § 19, not. 2.

[148] C. 4—Hardouin, I, 990.

[149] Actio IV: "Episcopum in gradum presbyterii redigere sacrilegium est.
Si vero et causa quaedam iusta illos ab actu episcopatus amovet, nec presbyterii locum retinere debent."—Hardouin, II, 441.

[150] C. 8—Hardouin, I, 326; Schroeder, *Disciplinary Decrees*, p. 8.

[151] C. 20—Hardouin, III, 1670.

[152] Acta Concilii—Hardouin, VI, 1006.

[153] Cf. Devoti, *Institutiones*, I, tit. IV, § 19, not. 2; Chelodi, *Ius Poenale*,
n. 52, p. 70.

[154] C. 1: ". . . visum est eos cathedrae quidem honoris esse participes, non
licere autem ipsis offerre, seu sermonem conferre vel omnino sacerdotale ali-

another example of this type of partial deposition. He allowed a priest who unwittingly (*insciens*) became involved in unlawful nuptials to retain the honor of his rank but deprived him of his priestly powers.[155] The Council of Tours (461) employed the same penalty for priests who persistently violated celibacy.[156]

At times only certain offices pertaining to his order were taken from a cleric while the others were left to him. Thus, the Council of Neocaesarea (314-325) decreed that if any priest confessed that he had been guilty of unchastity before his ordination, he should not offer Mass but might continue in the exercise of all his other offices.[157] And the IV Council of Carthage (398) provided that if a bishop knowingly ordained anyone who had performed public penance, he should, for this transgression of the canons, be deprived of his episcopal power of ordaining. With this limitation, the law allowed him the exercise of all other episcopal powers.[158]

There also existed a partial deposition involving only a reduction in seniority without any deprivation of office or hierarchical rank. Such a partial deposition could have great consequences, particularly in Africa where, as Bingham rightly observes, the designation of the primate depended on seniority, the oldest bishop in ordination regularly succeeding to the primacy. To punish a bishop there

quod munus obire."—Mansi, II, 514; in Gratian, c. 32, D. L.; cf. Kober, *Die Deposition und Degradation,* p. 115. Although this canon has already been adduced in evidence as illustrating an early, incipient distinction between suspension and deposition, it is applicable also to the point under consideration here, for suspension as a penalty only evolved gradually from the severer penalty of deposition. Cf. Rainer, *Suspension of Clerics,* p. 15.

[155] *Ep. ad Amphilochium,* c. 27: ". . . nec publice nec privatim benedicat, nec corpus Christi distribuat aliis, nec quodvis aliud sacrum munus obeat, sed honorifica sede contentus."—*MPG,* XXXII, 723. This provision was repeated in the Trullan Council of 692 in canon 26.—Hardouin, III, 1670.

[156] C. 2: ". . . id decrevimus, ut sacerdos vel levita coniugali concupiscentiae inhaerens, vel a filiorum procreatione non desinens, ad altiorem gradum non ascendat, neque sacrificium Deo offerre, vel plebi ministrare praesumat. Sufficiat his tantum, ut a communione non efficiantur alieni."—Hardouin, II, 794.

[157] C. 9—Mansi, II, 541.

[158] C. 68: "Si sciens episcopus ordinaverit talem [penitentem] etiam ipse ab episcopatus sui ordinandi dumtaxat potestate privetur."—Hardouin, I, 983; cf. Kober, *Die Deposition und Degradation,* p. 118.

with loss of seniority was tantamount to depriving him of his right to the primacy by rendering him incapable of ever attaining it.[159]

The nature of these partial depositions as well as an insight into the part they played in the development of the penal law of the Church is expressed very well in a letter of St. Augustine.[160] Briefly, he relates the case of one Antonius, a bishop in Africa, who had been deprived of his jurisdiction over a section of his people. Antonius had complained that this was an infringement of his rights; either a bishop should be deposed or be left in the full exercise of his jurisdiction. St. Augustine shows that this penalty was neither new nor unreasonable, for a bishop may be guilty of some misdemeanors which cannot be left wholly unpunished, but which do not, on the other hand, warrant such severity as to deprive him completely of his episcopal rank and jurisdiction. This explanation of St. Augustine bespeaks the mind of the Church as is evidenced by the records of history which show how various milder penalties gradually evolved from the severer penalty of deposition.

ARTICLE 8. INFLICTION OF THE PENALTY

Having explained the penalty of deposition or degradation as it existed in the early Church up to the beginning of the sixth century, one must still consider the canonical authority competent to inflict this penalty when such an action was warranted. The one who enjoys this right is usually designated by canonists as the active subject of deposition, while the recipient of the penalty is described as the passive subject. Since the terms of this relation vary with the variations of dignity in the clerical ranks, the interests of clarity will be better served by considering the discipline governing the deposition of bishops separately from that regulating the deposition of priests and lower clerics. Hence, in the first section exclusive consideration is given to viewing the right of action against bishops as it obtained during this period. In the subsequent section the right of deposing priests and inferior clerics will be considered.

[159] Cf. Bingham, *Antiquities*, II, 1039.

[160] *Ep. CCIX, ad Coelestinam papam—Corpus Scriptorum Ecclesiasticorum Latinorum* (Editum consilio et impensis Academiae Litterarum caesareae vindobonensis, Vindobonae, 1866-   ), LVII, IV, 357 sq.

A. The Deposition of Bishops

The penalty of deposition was inflicted on a delinquent bishop in the early Church by his fellow bishops assembled in a council. This is evident, even before the fourth century, from the letters of St. Cyprian. One letter relates that two bishops, Basilides and Martial, were deposed by a council in Spain,[161] while another testifies that Privatus, Bishop of Lambesi in Numidia, was deposed by a synod of ninety bishops.[162] A third letter records that when Marcian, Bishop of Arles, fell into heresy, he was tried, convicted and deposed by the bishops of the province.[163]

At the beginning of the fourth century a council convoked at Alexandria (306) by Bishop Peter passed judgment on Meletius, Bishop of Lycopolis, later author of the Meletian schism, and, having found him guilty of sacrificing to idols, deposed him.[164]

The history of the fourth and subsequent centuries records innumerable instances of bishops assembled in council passing the sentence of deposition on a delinquent bishop. Early in the fourth century the Ecumenical Council of Nicaea (325), undoubtedly reflecting the traditional practice, placed such actions within the competence of provincial councils which were to be held twice a year.[165]

Subsequent councils, while regulating appeals to a higher authority, indicate the general law that in the first instance it was the right of the regional bishops to pass a sentence of deposition on one of their fellow bishops. Thus, the Council of Antioch (341) provided

---

[161] *Ep. ad Carthaginense Concilium—MPL*, III, 1029; cf. Baronius, *Annales Ecclesiastici*, III (an. 258), 105, nn. 2, 3, 4.

[162] *Ep. LIX*, n. 10—*Corpus Scriptorum Ecclesiasticorum Latinorum*, III, II, 677.

[163] *Ep. LXVIII*, n. 3—*Corpus Scriptorum Ecclesiasticorum Latinorum*, III, II, 745; cf. Baronius, *Annales Ecclesiastici*, III (an. 258), 107, nn. 8, 9; Lupus, *Synodorum Decreta et Canones* (Venetiis, 1725), V, 176.

[164] Concilium Alexandrinum—Mansi, II, 407.

[165] C. 5—Hardouin, I, 323; Schroeder, *Disciplinary Decrees*, p. 28. Cf. I Constantinople (381), c. 2—Hardouin, I, 810; *Ep. Innocentii ad Victricium*, c. III, n. 5: in conformity with the decrees of the Council of Nicaea, causes of clerics both of the higher as well as of the lower ranks should be decided in provincial councils with due respect for the rights of the Roman Church.—*MPL*, XX, 472.

that a bishop deposed by a synod could appeal to a higher synod.[166]
A synod of Constantinople (382) allowed any bishop who had been
deposed by his provincial council to have recourse to the patriarchal
council.[167] So also the Council of Sardica (343) described the deposition of bishops as originating in provincial councils.[168] The
General Council of Chalcedon (451) decreed that bishops were to
be accused and judged by the provincial council and the metropolitan by the patriarchal council.[169]

In Africa, in order to avoid the difficulties and delays of assembling a provincial council, it was decreed at the Council of Carthage (348) that a court of twelve bishops of the province would
form a competent tribunal to proceed in the deposition of a
bishop.[170]

From all these sources it may be stated as clear law that the
right of deposing a delinquent bishop was vested in the provincial
council. The particular council celebrated at Antioch (341), however, attributed the right of deposing bishops exclusively to the
council of the regional bishops. "If a bishop has been tried by all
the bishops of the eparchy and all have unanimously given sentence
against him, he may not be tried again by others, but the unanimous decision of the bishops of the eparchy must hold good."[171]
A unanimous sentence, then, according to the Council of Antioch,
ruled out all appeals, even to the Roman See.[172] Thus, the council
gave no recognition to the rights of the Roman Pontiff in deciding
causes involving the deposition of a bishop. Rather it transgressed
and invaded these rights. This is not surprising in view of the fact
that this council was convoked by the semi-Arians against St. Athan-

---

[166] C. 12—Hefele-Clark, II, 70.

[167] C. 6—Hardouin, I, 812; cf. Hefele-Clark, II, 366.

[168] C. 4: ". . . cum aliquis episcopus depositus fuerit eorum episcoporum
iudicio qui in vicinis locis commorantur . . ."—Hardouin, I, 639.

[169] C. 9—Hardouin, II, 605.

[170] C. 11—Hardouin, I, 687.

[171] C. 15—Hardouin, I, 599; cf. Hefele-Clark, II, 71; Fulton, *Index Canonum*, p. 241; in Gratian, c. 5, C. VI, q. 4.

[172] Cf. Hefele-Clark, II, 71, footnotes.

asius,[173] who but recently had been restored to his see of Alexandria by Pope Julius I (337-352) to whom he had appealed.

The attempted restriction of the jurisdiction of the Holy See and the destruction of a bishop's right of appeal to Rome had been the Eusebian reply to Pope Julius' Council in Rome and its reinstatement of St. Athanasius. To the Eusebian innovations came a prompt restatement of the old law by the Council of Sardica. This council, convoked at the instance of Pope St. Julius in 343,[174] had for its primary purpose the restoration of peace among the Oriental bishops. Though failing in this, the council left behind a memorable series of disciplinary canons governing, among other matters, the deposition of bishops. The council gave expression to the existing right of the Roman Pontiff to pronounce definitively, when appealed, on a sentence involving the deposition of a bishop. It clearly stated that the provincial council was to decide cases in which bishops were accused. From the provincial council, however, such a bishop, should he be condemned, could appeal and the appeal was to the bishop of Rome. If the Roman Pontiff set aside the decision of the council, he himself could decide the case, or order a new trial and send judges, or appoint the neighboring bishops to investigate and decide the case.[175] The fourth canon of this council was also noteworthy in regulating this discipline. It provided that when a bishop who was deposed by his neighboring bishops appealed his case to Rome, no bishop was to be ordained in his place until the matter had been determined by the bishop of Rome.[176]

After this period, the earlier practice of Eastern bishops to appeal to the Holy See continued unabated. Eustathius of Sebaste, upon being deposed by a semi-Arian synod held at Melitene around 357, appealed to Pope Liberius who reestablished him in his see.[177]

---

[173] Cicognani, *Canon Law*, p. 175.

[174] Cicognani, *Canon Law*, p. 150.

[175] Cc. 3, 7—Hardouin, I, 639, 642; in Gratian, c. 7, C. VII, q. 4 and c. 36, C. II, q. 6.

[176] Hardouin, I, 640; cf. Cicognani, *Canon Law*, p. 176.

[177] Socrates, *Historia Ecclesiastica*, IV, 12—Schaaf and Wace, *Nicene and Post-Nicene Fathers of the Christian Church* (Second Series, New York, 1890), II, 100. (Hereafter this collection is referred to as Schaaf). Sozomen, *Historia*

The successor of St. Athanasius in the see of Alexandria, the Patriarch Peter, fled to the protection of Pope Damasus when he was deposed.[178] Pope Damasus restored him to his see.[179] St. John Chrysostom, deposed and condemned to exile by a local Eastern council in 403, turned to Pope Innocent I to obtain justice. His judges also sent a delegation to Rome in an attempt to win the Pope to their cause. Pope Innocent voided the judgment of the synod and restored Chrysostom to his rights.[180]

The council which is known to history as the Latrocinium of Ephesus assembled in 449. One of its leading figures was the deposed Eutyches. Flavian, Bishop of Constantinople, had presided at the council in which Eutyches was deposed. Now the Latrocinium, a year later, unjustly deposed Flavian and, among others, Theodoret, Bishop of Cyrrhus. Flavian, before he died in prison, managed to send an appeal to Pope Leo who annulled the sentence of deposition pronounced by the Latrocinium.[181] Theodoret of Cyrrhus likewise appealed to Rome and obtained justice.[182]

An incident of the Council of Chalcedon also serves to reveal the attitude of the Eastern Church towards the jurisdiction of the Holy See in matters involving the deposition of bishops. Pope St. Leo had left it to the council to pass judgment on Dioscorus, Bishop of Alexandria, who, among other alleged crimes, had defended the heretic Eutyches and with him arranged the Latrocinium of Ephesus.[183] Having solemnly recited a summary of the crimes of the Bishop of Alexandria, the speaker for the council and papal legate, Paschasinus, declared that the synod had stripped him not only of

Ecclesiastica, IV, 24—Schaaf, II, 320. *Ep. S. Basilii CCLXII, Ad Occidentales*, n. 3—*MPG*, XXXII, 978.

[178] Socrates, *Historia Ecclesiastica*, IV, XXII—Schaaf, II, 106.

[179] Socrates, *Historia Ecclesiastica*, IV, XXXVII—Schaaf, II, 117. Sozomen, *Historia Ecclesiastica*, VI, XXXIX—Schaaf, II, 375.

[180] *Ep. ad Innocentium*—*MPG*, LII, 530 sq.; Palladius, *Dialogus Historicus de vita et conversatione beati I. Chrysostomi*, c. II—*MPG*, XLVII, 8 sq.; S. Gelasius, *Ep. VII, ad Episcopos Dardaniae*—Hardouin, II, 909.

[181] *Ep. Leonis XLV, XLVI*—*MPL*, LIV, 833, 837.

[182] *Ep. CXX, ad Theodoretum*, c. 5.—*MPL*, LIV, 1053.

[183] Cf. Hughes, *A History of the Church*, I, 312.

the episcopal but of all sacerdotal dignity.[184]   As Hughes remarks:
"In 431 Rome had deposed the Bishop of Constantinople and a
general council had carried out her decision.   Now, twenty years
later, Rome had similarly deposed a Bishop of Alexandria and a
second general council had once more, unanimously, accepted the
decision *because of the see* whence it came." [185]

However, it was only in the Council of Trullo (692) that the
canons of Sardica received a legal consecration in as far as this council positively defined the right habitually exercised by the bishops
of the Eastern Church.[186]

In the West the rights expressed by the Council of Sardica had
long been recognized, as has been witnessed in the letters of St.
Cyprian.   Further testimony is offered by St. Augustine (354-430).
In one of his letters he writes about the seventy bishops who condemned Caecilianus, a former Bishop of Carthage.   They had applied to Constantine for judges in a subsequent controversy over
this sentence and were referred to Rome.   There Pope Melchiades,
in 313, acquitted Caecilianus and restored him to his episcopal see.
"This was not a matter concerning priests or deacons or clergy of
inferior order but concerning colleagues who might refer their case
wholly to the judgment of other bishops, especially of the apostol-
ical churches." [187]

When in 445 Bishop Lupicin was threatened with deposition by
an African synod, he appealed to the Holy See.   Pope Leo (440-
461) sent orders for the case to be heard in Africa but reproved
the bishops for installing another bishop in the place of Lupicin before he was finally sentenced.[188]

Earlier, Pope Innocent I (402-417) had written in a similar way
to the clergy and people of Constantinople in connection with St.
John Chrysostom's appeal to the Holy See: "Others were seated in
the places of living bishops, as though any who began from such
discord would be able to possess anything or do anything rightly in

---

[184] Mansi, VI, 1047.

[185] *A History of the Church*, I, 316.

[186] C. 2—Hardouin, III, 1659.

[187] *Ep. XLIII*, n. 3, 4, 7—Schaaf, I, 276-278.

[188] *Ep. XII*, n. 12—*MPL*, LIV, 655.

anyone's judgment. We have never known such audacities to have been done by our fathers. They rather prohibited such innovations by refusing to give power to anyone *to be ordained in another's place* while the occupant was living, since he is unable to be a bishop who is unjustly substituted." [189]

Before the close of the fifth century, Pope Gelasius (492-496) records the traditional use by the Holy See of its right to *restore* bishops whom synods have unjustly deposed and to *depose* bishops for grave cause *even without the action of a council.* Then he adds: "We state only what is known by the whole Church throughout the world, namely, that the See of Blessed Peter the Apostle has the right to loose what has been bound by sentence of any bishops, because it has authority to judge all churches, but can be judged by none. Appeals may be made to it from all parts of the world, but no one may appeal from it." [190]

During this period, then, conciliar legislation as well as pontifical letters indicate that it was the right of provincial councils to depose bishops. However, the deposed bishop had the right to appeal to the Holy See and in this case his sentence was not definitive nor could another bishop be installed in the see until the Roman Pontiff had decided the case.

B. *The Deposition of Priests, Deacons and Inferior Clerics.*

To the bishop it was given "to rule the Church of God." [191] This jurisdiction embraced the clergy as well as the laity. Hence St. Paul advises the bishop to proceed discreetly in judging clerics: "against a priest receive not an accusation but under two or three witnesses." [192]

Canons of the early councils, ordinarily reflecting earlier practices, imply that the bishop alone possessed the right to depose clerics subject to him since they make provision for a cleric who has

[189] Sozomen, *Historia Ecclesiastica*, VIII, 26—Schaaf, II, 146.

[190] *Ep. VII, ad Episcopos Dardaniae*—Hardouin, II, 909; translation in Cicognani, *Canon Law*, p. 143.

[191] Acts, XX: 28.

[192] I Tim., V: 19.

been *deposed by his bishop* to appeal to the synod of the province.[193]

In order to surround with due precautions an act so fraught with such consequences as followed the deposition of a priest or deacon, the Church in early legislation established certain other safeguards besides appeal. Thus, the I Council of Carthage (348) required a bishop when proceeding against one of his priests to be assisted by *six* bishops of the province. In hearing charges brought against deacons, he needed the assistance of *three* provincial bishops.[194] The same law was renewed and confirmed by subsequent councils.[195] The bishop retained more liberty to judge minor clerics. Indeed he could proceed alone to judge and depose clerics in orders below the diaconate.[196]

It is interesting to note that at this time the recourse of priests and lesser clerics to the Holy See was not universally admitted. In Africa, at least, the authorities did not wish to recognize for clerics below bishops the right of appealing beyond the tribunals of its own patriarchs. "If priests, deacons and inferior clerics complain of a sentence of their own bishop, they shall, with the consent of their bishop, have recourse to the neighboring bishops, who shall settle the dispute. If they desire to make a further appeal, it must be only to their primates or to African councils. But whoever appeals to a court on the other side of the sea (Rome), may not again be received into communion by any one in Africa." [197]

The Holy See, however, continued to receive appeals when they were made by priests and lower clerics and, as justice warranted, decided the issue. Pope Leo the Great, in 445, attests to this fact

---

[193] Council of Nicaea (325), c. 5—Hardouin, I, 323; Schroeder, *Disciplinary Decrees*, p. 28; Council of Antioch (341), c. 12—Hardouin, I, 597; Council of Constantinople (382), c. 6—Hefele-Clark, II, 366; Council of Chalcedon (451), c. 9—Hardouin, II, 605; c. 2, C. XXI, q. 5.

[194] C. 11—Hardouin, I, 687; in Gratian, c. 3, C. XV, q. 7.

[195] II Carthage (390), c. 10—Hardouin, I, 953; in Gratian, c. 4, C. XV, q. 7; III Carthage (397), c. 8—Hardouin, I, 962; in Gratian, c. 5, C. XV, q. 7.

[196] III Council of Carthage (397), c. 8: "reliquorum autem clericorum causas etiam solus episcopus loci agnoscit et finiat."—Hardouin, I, 962; in Gratian, c. 5, C. XV, q. 7.

[197] XVI Council of Carthage (418), c. 17—Hefele-Clark, II, 461.

when he writes: "Therefore, your Fraternity should know that the Apostolic See, because of the reverence in which it is held, has also been consulted in numberless cases by the priests of your province, and that upon appeal to us, as the ancient custom required, the judicial sentences of diverse causes were either reversed or confirmed by Us." [198]

[198] *Ep. X, ad episcopos per provinciam Viennensem constitutos*—*MPL*, LIV, 630; cf. translation in Cicognani, *Canon Law*, p. 143.

CHAPTER II

DEPOSITION AND DEGRADATION FROM THE SIXTH TO THE TWELFTH CENTURY

ARTICLE 1. NATURE AND EFFECTS OF THE PENALTY

DURING this period deposition and degradation remained synonymous terms for the one penalty. Kober[1] cites as proof of this fact the legislation of several councils. For example, the Council of Agde (506) threatened clerics guilty of false testimony with deposition,[2] while the III Council of Orleans (538) punished the same crime with degradation.[3] Again, the Council of Agde established deposition as the penalty for clerics unlawfully alienating Church property,[4] whereas the III Council of Orleans punished them with degradation.[5] Moreover, along with the terms *deposition* and *degrada-tion* the penalty continued to be expressed in many other words.[6]

While the nature of the penalty remained unchanged during this period, there was introduced early in the sixth century a significant legal consequence. This was seclusion in a monastery. The Council of Agde, celebrated in the year 506, established this provision when it decreed that if a bishop, priest or deacon committed a capital crime or falsified a document or bore false witness, he should be de-

---

[1] *Die Deposition und Degradation*, p. 130.

[2] C. 50: ". . . ab officii honore depositus."—Hardouin, II, 1003.

[3] C. 8: ". . . ab ordine degradetur."—Hardouin, II, 1425.

[4] C. 49: ". . . ab honore depositi."—Hardouin, II, 1003.

[5] C. 23: ". . . regradetur, communione concessa."—Hardouin, II, 1427.

[6] Thus, for example, in the V Council of Rome (503): "gradu proprio penitus careat."—Hardouin, II, 985; in Gratian, c. 3, C. III, q. 5; III Council of Orleans (538), c. 11: "inter reliquos canonicos clericos nullatenus habeantur."—Hardouin, II, 1425; VIII Council of Toledo (653), c. 4: "loci et ordinis sui dignitate privari."—Hardouin, III, 962; Trullan Council (692), c. 21: "in laicorum locum detrusi."—Hardouin, III, 1670; the Council of Worms (868), c. 9: "ab honore clericatus pellantur."—Hardouin, V, 739; Sigebertus, *Chronica*, ad an. 907: "exordinare."—*MPL*, CLX, 176.

posed and cast into a monastery where, as long as he lived, he could enjoy only lay communion.[7] Eleven years later the Council of Epaon (517) enacted a similar provision.[8] Manifestly it was not the will of these councils to follow the earlier discipline and leave deposed clerics to themselves and in public life, but rather to keep them under the care of the Church, in a monastery, where they were to live as laymen for the remainder of their lives.

Subsequently the III Council of Orleans (538) adopted the same procedure.[9] So also at a synod of North Britain (*ca.* 500-525) it was decreed that "anyone who sins with a woman or with a man shall be sent away to live in a monastery of another country and shall do penance, after he has confessed, for three years in confinement; and afterwards as a brother subject to that altar he shall do penance at the discretion of his director; if he is a deacon, for one year; if a presbyter, for three years; if a bishop or abbot, for four years; each being *deprived* of his order."[10] St. Gregory the Great (590-604) refers often in his epistles to this confinement in a monastery following upon deposition; in fact, he practically considered it to be an ordinary consequence of the penalty.[11] The IV Council of

[7] C. 50: "Si episcopus, presbyter aut diaconus capitale crimen commiserit, aut chartam falsaverit, aut testimonium falsum dixerit, ab officii honore depositus in monasterio retrudatur et ibi quamdiu vixerit, laicam tantummodo communionem accipiat."—Hardouin, II, 1003; in Gratian, c. 7, D. L.

[8] C. 22: "Si presbyter aut diaconus crimen capitale commiserit, ab officii honore depositus in monasterio retrudatur, ibi tantummodo quamdiu vixerit communione sumenda."—Mansi, VII, 561. Note: this canon "lacks the word *laica* to qualify *communio* whilst it stands correctly in the pretended 50th canon of Agde."—Hefele-Clark, IV, 111.

[9] C. 7: "De adulteriis autem honoratorum clericorum id observandum est, ut si quis adulterasse aut confessus fuerit vel convictus depositus ab officio, communione concessa, in monasterio toto vitae suae tempore retrudatur."—Hardouin, II, 1425; in Gratian, c. 10, D. LXXXI.

[10] McNeill, John, and Gamer, Helen, *Medieval Handbooks of Penance*, a translation of the principal *libri penintentiales* and selections from other documents, Department of History, Columbia University: Records of Civilization, Sources and Studies, Number XXIX (New York: Columbia University Press, 1938), p. 170. Hereinafter cited as McNeill, *Penitentials.*

[11] Cf. e. g., *Ep. XXVII*, Epist. lib. III—*MPL*, LXXVII, 624; *Ep. XVIII*, Epist. lib. I—*MPL*, LXXVII, 463; *Ep. XXI*, Epist. lib. XII—*MPL*, LXXVII, 1211.

Toledo (633) likewise ordained that bishops, priests or deacons who were involved in superstitious practices should be deposed and confined to a monastery.[12] In the ninth century the Council of Chalons-sur-Sâone (813), having been informed that canonically degraded priests were living in worldly fashion and neglecting the good work of penance, decreed that they were to be sent into a monastery, either canonical or regular, for the sake of doing penance.[13] A short time later a council in Rome [14] enunciated the same purpose for this confinement in the monastery consequent upon deposition.[15] Even at the end of the twelfth century this practice existed, as is evident from the decretal of Innocent III (1199) to the Archbishop of Sens in which he reminds the prelate not to fail in secluding a deposed cleric in a monastery.[16]

From all the preceding testimony it may be taken as a general rule that during this period deposition was followed by confinement in a monastery or in some other suitable place of penance. This development is significant, for it shows that the Church did not, as formerly, completely abandon the deposed cleric to the lay and civil society, to private penance, and to the secular courts.[17]

The Council of Chalons-sur-Sâone (813), having ordained that deposed clerics be sent to a monastery for repentance, added that if this could not be done then those who were deposed should not desist from penance. If, in these circumstances, they neglected to

---

[12] C. 29: "ab honore dignitatis suae depositus monasterii poenam excipiat ibique perpetuae penitentiae deditus scelus admissum sacrilegii luat."—Hardouin, III, 586.

[13] C. 40—Hardouin, IV, 1038; in Gratian, c. 8, D. LXXXI. An old code of Gratian has this version: "in monasterio iuxta canonicam regulam mittantur"—cf. note to c. 8, D. LXXXI in Richter-Friedberg edition.

[14] In 853 according to Hardouin, V, 66; attributed to Pope Eugene II in Council of Rome (826) by the Decree of Gratian, c. 7, D. LXXXI.

[15] C. 14: ". . . depositus providentia episcopi bene proviso loco constituatur, ubi peccata lugeat, et ulterius non committat."—Hardouin, V, 66.

[16] "Quodsi forsan in purgatione defecerit, ·eum ecclesiasticae disciplinae mucrone percellas, et ab officio et beneficio depositum ad agendam poenitentiam in arctum monasterium detrudere non omittas."—c. 10, X, *de purgatione canonica*, V, 34.

[17] Cf. Benedictus XIV, *De synodo dioecesana*, lib. IX, c. 6, n. 3.

do penance and instead lived in worldly fashion, they were to be further punished with excommunication.[18]

Apart from the provision for subsequent confinement in a monastery or in some other suitable place of penance, the legal sources for this period show no further development in the nature and effects of the penalty. The canonical enactments already quoted, as well as those to follow, show that deposition continued to be the most severe penalty for clerics, completely expelling them from the clerical state and reducing them to lay communion.[19]

When Pope John II (532-535) learned that the Council of Marseilles (533) had sentenced the Bishop of Riez, Contumeliosus, to do penance in a monastery because apart from his other misdeeds he had committed adultery, the Pontiff declared that this bishop should not only be sent to a monastery but that he should also be deposed as the older canons decreed.[20] The III Council of Orleans (538) referred to earlier legislation when it decreed that clerics in major orders who transgressed the law of celibacy should be deposed and reduced to the lay state.[21] Shortly thereafter the V Council of Orleans (549) likewise hearkened back to the canons of an earlier age to threaten with perpetual deposition clerics who violated celibacy.[22]

The III Council of Orleans (538) also states clearly a consequence of deposition already observed in an earlier period: deposition deprives the quondam cleric of ecclesiastical support. The council decreed that clerics who would not fulfill the duties of their office or obey their bishop, should not be counted among the canonical clerics or like them receive support from ecclesiastical funds.[23]

---

[18] C. 40—Hardouin, IV, 1038.

[19] Cf. Hinschius, *Kirchenrecht*, IV, 809; Lega, *De Delictis et Poenis*, n. 208, p. 281; Eichmann, *Strafrecht*, p. 9.

[20] *Ep. Joannis Papae II*—Hardouin, II, 1156; Mansi, VIII, 807.

[21] C. 2: "laica communione contentus, *iuxta priorum canonum statuta* ab officio deponatur."—Hardouin, II, 1425.

[22] C. 4: "usque in diem vitae ab honore accepti ordinis et *sicut habent antiquorum patrum canones*, ab officio deponatur, ei tantummodo communione concessa."—Hardouin, II, 1444.

[23] C. 11: "Si qui clerici ministeria suscepta quacumque occasione agere, sicut et reliqui, detrectant, et excusationem de patrociniis quorumcumque, ne

Pope Gregory the Great (590-604) in his many epistles bears witness to the penalty of deposition in his day. Thus, in one epistle he mentions a certain deposed priest named Marcellus as having been confined to a monastery for penance. The Pope ordains that the necessities of life be provided for him. Then he commands that priests be ordained and installed in parishes vacated by deposed priests, so that the laity may suffer no loss and the deposed clerics may cherish no hopes of returning to their former rank.[24]

In another epistle he explains the nature of vindictive penalties among which deposition is included. When evils which should be washed away with the tears of repentance are on the contrary increased by excesses, then greater correction must be used on the delinquents so that they themselves may recognize, at least by the vindictive penalty, their great crime, and that others, in the fear of ecclesiastical retribution, may be deterred from unlawful conduct.[25] This idea is repeated in another letter when the Pontiff, discussing the case of one Hilary, a subdeacon who had been duly deposed, stated that the penalty of deposition should serve as an example to others, so that by the punishment of this one cleric the correction of many might be obtained.[26]

In the mind of Pope Gregory there was no doubt that deposition was a penalty of perpetual duration. Questioned on this matter by one Bishop Venantius, he replied that a deposed deacon must never

officium impleant, praetendunt, ac sacerdotes suos sub huiusmodi causa aestimant per inobedientiam contemnendos; inter reliquos canonicos clericos, ne hac licentia alii vitientur, nullatenus habeantur, neque ex rebus ecclesiasticis cum canonicis stipendia aut munera ulla percipiant."—Hardouin, II, 1425; cf. Hefele-Clark, IV, 206.

[24] *Ep. XVIII, ad Petrum Subdiaconum*, Epist. lib. I: "Ita enim et locorum ordinatio proveniet, et revertendi lapsus ad gradum priorem, quo melius poeniteat, suspicio non manebit."—*MPL*, LXXVII, 463.

[25] *Ep. XXXI, ad Joannem Primae Justinianae Episcopum*, Epist. lib. XII —*MPL*, LXXVII, 1211. In this epistle the Pope also directs that a deposed bishop be confined to a monastery to do penance: "in monasterium ad agendam poenitentiam retrudendum."

[26] *Ep. LXXI, ad Anthemium Subdiaconum*, Epist. lib. XI: "ut unius poena multorum possit esse correctio."—*MPL*, LXXVII, 1210.

be recalled to his sacred order,[27] and that subdeacons visited with this penalty were likewise irrevocably deposed.[28] The Pope also advised the bishop to warn in writing a deposed priest, Saturninus, never to presume to approach his former ministry.[29] When it was later reported that this deposed priest, Saturninus, had presumed to exercise the priestly ministry, Pope Gregory issued instructions to the bishop to inquire into the truth of the allegation. If the charge proved true Saturninus was to be excommunicated.[30] In a letter to Constantius, Pope Gregory again denied reinstatement to deposed clerics and declared that such severity was simply a part of the penalty fashioned by the Church to preserve the vigor of canonical discipline.[31]

The VIII Council of Toledo (653) described the nature of deposition when it declared that bishops who fail in celibacy know that they are punished with the *irrevocable* sentence of the fathers, that is, they are deprived of the dignity of their rank and order.[32]

Further indications of the nature and effects of deposition at this time are supplied by the Council in Trullo (692) when it refers to deposed clerics as "those who have been guilty of certain crimes and in consequence are subjected to perfect and perpetual deposition, and are degraded to the state of the laity."[33]

---

[27] *Ep. III, ad Venantium Episcopum*, Epist. lib. V: "ad sacrum ordinem non debere vel posse ullo modo revocari."—*MPL*, LXXVII, 725; in Gratian, c. 10, D. L.

[28] "ab officio suo irrevocabiliter depositi, inter laicos communionem accipiant."—*loc. cit.*

[29] "numquam ad sacri ordinis ministerium praesumat accedere."—*loc. cit.*

[30] *Ep. VII, ad Venantium Episcopum*, Epist. lib. V—*MPL*, LXXVII, 728; in Gratian, c. 10, D. L. A similar ruling is found in *Ep. II*, Epist. lib. II—*MPL*, LXXVII, 555.

[31] *Ep. IV, ad Constantium Episcopum*, Epist. lib. V: "Si lapsis ad suum ordinem revertendi licentia concedatur, vigor canonicae procul dubio frangitur disciplinae, dum per reversionis spem pravae actionis desideria quisque concipere non formidat."—*MPL*, LXXVII, 725; in Gratian, c. 1, D. L.

[32] C. 4: ". . . Adeo ut si deinceps episcopi detecti fuerint exsecrabilibus flagitiis cum quibuslibet feminis pollui, aut familiari peculiaritate versari, noverint se irrevocabili sententia patrum ulcisci, id est, et loci et ordinis sui dignitate privari."—Hardouin, III, 962.

[33] C. 21: "Qui canonice quorumdam criminum rei facti, et propterea per-

Although unofficial in character, the Penitentials, which flourished during this age, give further confirmation to what has been said of deposition. *The Penitential of Theodore* (668-690) speaks of different crimes warranting deposition: "If any bishop or deacon or any ordained person has had by custom the vice of drunkenness, he shall either desist or be deposed." [84] "If any priest in his own province or in another or wherever he may be found refuses to baptize a sick person who has been committed to him or on account of the exertion of the journey [declines the duty] so that he dies without baptism, he shall be deposed." [85] "Likewise, he who slays a man or commits fornication shall be deposed." [86] "A bishop, presbyter, or deacon guilty of fornication ought to be degraded and to do penance at the decision of a bishop, yet they shall take communion. With loss of rank, penance dies, the soul lives." [87] Briefly, then, the Penitential of Theodore attests the fact that for stated crimes clerics were to be deposed. They should then do penance, not for the restoration of their clerical status, but for the benefit of their souls, for "with loss of rank, penance dies, the soul lives." This law is stated more directly in the tenth century by the so called *Confessional of Egbert* (*ca.* 950-1000): [88] "If anyone loses his rank, a priest or a bishop, he shall do penance until death *that his soul may live.*" [89] Thus is repeated the traditional teaching that deposition is to be inflicted only for grave, external delinquencies and that penance will restore the deposed delinquent cleric to the grace of God but of itself it will not reinstate him in his rank.

In England, in the eighth century, according to the Archbishop of York in the work entitled *Dialogue of Egbert* (*c.* 750), deposed clerics were subject to public penance. In this work question fifteen

---

fectae ac perpetuae depositioni subiecti, in laicorum locum detrusi sunt."—Hardouin, III, 1670, cf. Hefele-Clark, V, 227.

[84] Book I, title I, canon 1—McNeill, *Penitentials*, p. 184.

[85] Book I, title IX, canon 7—McNeill, *op. cit.*, p. 193.

[86] Book I, title IX, canon 8—McNeill, *op. cit.*, p. 193.

[87] Book I, title IX, canon 1—McNeill, *op. cit.*, p. 192.

[88] McNeill (*Penitentials*, p. 244): "Whatever its origin the *Confessional* is doubtless one of the earliest fragments of penitential material in the language of the English."

[89] C. 8—McNeill, *op. cit.*, p. 245.

asks: "What are the crimes which prevent any man from becoming a priest, or for what (offenses) is one *deposed* who has already been ordained?" The answer to this query states:

"For the following crimes, indeed, we say that no one may be ordained, but that some who have been elevated are to be *deposed*: namely, those who worship idols; those who through soothsayers and diviners and enchanters give themselves over as captives to the devil; those who destroy their faith with false witness; those defiled with murders or acts of fornication, the insolence of perjury. These, moreover, except through *public penance,* must not be admitted to obtain the grace of communion nor to recover the honor of their former dignity, for it is alien to the Church that penitents should minister the sacred things, who were lately vessels of wickedness." [40] However, an English *Penitential* of the same era [41] repeats the prevalent teaching of the Church: "In the *Canons of the Apostles* the judgment is given that a bishop, priest, or deacon who is taken in fornication or perjury, or theft shall be deposed, yet not deprived of communion, for God does not punish twice at the same time." [42]

In the ninth century, Hincmar, Archbishop of Rheims, describes as a novelty the idea of some who maintained that a priest or deacon convicted of crime should not be deposed, but only suspended, and should then be allowed to do penance in order to regain his lost rights. The Archbishop thereupon summons the authority of the fathers and canons of the Church to show that clerics who have been found guilty of certain grave crimes are to be forever deposed.[43]

The ninth century, however, did introduce a new regulation in

[40] McNeill, *op. cit.,* p. 239.

[41] Penitential ascribed to Bede, early eighth century, with later additions. —Cf. McNeill, *Penitentials,* p. 217.

[42] McNeill, *op. cit.,* p. 228.

[43] *Capitula Synodica* (852): "Detecti ergo, sive confessione sua, sive convictione legali ac regulari, de criminibus ad gradus ecclesiasticos non accedant, et in gradibus ecclesiasticis non maneant, vel ad ecclesiasticos gradus non redeant, sicut sacri canones et decreta sedis Romanae pontificum aperte atque expresse decernunt."—*MPL,* CXXV, 786, 789. This was the prevalent doctrine and practice throughout this period despite the fact that a few local councils allowed readmission to the clerical state after the performance of penance. Cf. Hinschius, *Kirchenrecht,* IV, 809.

regard to deposition in what purported to be ecclesiastical legislation. What are now called the Pseudo-Isidorian Decretals appeared at this time,[44] producing among others three false decretals in which provision was made for relegating a delinquent cleric to the *curia*. This mode of action was stated in a decretal assigned to Pope Pius I (142-157) to govern the treatment of a cleric convicted of disobedience, treachery, insults, or malice towards his bishop.[45] Gratian incorporated this chapter in his Decree.[46] A second decretal having the same provision for a similar offense is attributed to Pope Fabian I (236-250).[47] It was also incorporated in the Decree of Gratian.[48] The third time Pseudo-Isidore returned to this subject he attributed the enactment to Pope Stephen I (254-257).[49] This chapter of the decretal ascribed to Pope Stephen I was likewise included in the Decree of Gratian.[50] Thus, in each of these three false decretals a provision was made for delivering over to the *curia* delinquent clerics: *"mox curiae tradatur," "submotus a clero curiae tradatur, cui diebus vitae suae deserviat," "curiae tradi serviendus."*

[44] Modern authorities assign the dates 847-857 as the time of composition and Rheims or the province of Tours as the place of its composition.—Van Hove, *Commentarium Lovaniense in Codicem Iuris Canonici* (Mechliniae-Romae: H. Dessain, 1928), vol. I, tom. 1, *Prolegomena,* n. 164. For a critical text, consult Hinschius, *Decretales Pseudo-Isidorianae et Capitula Angilramni* (Lipsiae, 1863). Hereafter this work will be referred to as *Decretales Pseudo-Isidorianae.*

[45] *Ep. II,* c. 10: "Si quis sacerdotum vel reliquorum clericorum suo episcopo inobediens fuerit, aut ei insidias paraverit, aut contumeliam, aut calumniam, vel convicia intulerit, et convici potuerit, mox curiae tradatur, et recipiat quod inique gessit."—Hinschius, *Decretales Pseudo-Isidorianae,* p. 120.

[46] C. 18, C. XI, q. 1.

[47] *Ep. II,* c. 21: "Similiter statutum est et nos eadem statuta firmantes statuimus, ut si aliquis clericorum suis episcopis infestus aut insidiator fuerit eosque crimineri temptaverit, aut conspirator fuerit, ut mox ante examinatum iudicium submotus a clero curiae tradatur, cui diebus vitae suae deserviat et infamis absque ulla restitutionis spe permaneat."—Hinschius, *Decretales Pseudo-Isidorianae,* p. 165.

[48] C. 31, C. XI, q. 1.

[49] *Ep. II,* c. 12: "Clericus ergo qui episcopum suum accusaverit aut ei insidiator extiterit, non est recipiendus, quia infamis effectus est et a gradu debet recedere aut curiae tradi serviendus."—Hinschius, *op. cit.,* p. 186.

[50] C. 8, C. III, q. 4.

It has been observed that these false decretals were incorporated in the Decree of Gratian. From his *dictum* following the insertion of the purported decretal of Pope Fabian it would seem that Gratian interpreted these clauses concerning delivery to the *curia* as meaning the consigning of the delinquent cleric to the secular court to receive its judgment. This *dictum* concludes with the statement that both canon and civil law forbid a cleric to be brought before a *civil judge* either in criminal or contentious causes.[51] According to Gonzalez-Tellez, canonists turning to the Decree of Gratian commonly understood the term *traditio curiae* to mean delivery of the cleric to the secular arm, committing him to the secular power to be punished, for the *curia* in canon law always implied the secular court.[52]

The clever forger of the Pseudo-Isidorean Decretals, however, derived the expression *curiae tradere* not from ecclesiastical legislation but as Hinschius has pointed out,[53] from the imperial Constitution of Arcadius and Honorius which was received into the Theodosian Code[54] and was renewed in the Code of Justinian.[55] When this constitution was considered earlier in this work[56] it was then pointed out that the deposed cleric was to be taken into the *curia*, the local chancery of the government, to assist in the performance of its manifold duties. Obviously the same meaning should be placed on the term in its use in the false decretals. The letter attributed to Pope Fabian expressly states this: *"submotus a clero curiae tradatur, cui diebus vitae suae deserviat."*[57] The decretal ascribed to Pope Stephen I is no less clear in expressing the purpose of delivering the delinquent cleric to the *curia: "Curiae tradi serviendus."*[58]

When the phrase *curiae tradere* of fifth and sixth century Ro-

---

[51] Cf. *Dictum Gratiani* following c. 31, C. XI, q. 1.

[52] Cf. Gonzalez-Tellez, *Commentaria Perpetua in Singulos Textus Quinque Librorum Decretalium Gregorii IX* (Venetiis, 1699), lib. II, tit. 1, cap. 10, n. 17.

[53] *Decretales Pseudo-Isidorianae,* pp. 120, 165, 185. He traces each of the three decretals to an *Epitome* of the *Breviarium Alarici.*

[54] C. Th. (16, 2) 39.

[55] C. (1, 3) 52, 6.

[56] Cf. *supra,* p. 28.

[57] C. 31, C. XI, q. 1; Hinschius, *Decretales Pseudo-Isidorianae,* p. 165.

[58] C. 8, C. III, q. 4; Hinschius, *op. cit.,* p. 186.

man law reappeared in the Pseudo-Isidore and the Decree of Gratian, its original meaning was lost to a changed society. Very many canonists, unacquainted with antiquity, interpreted the phrase to mean delivery of the delinquent cleric to the *secular court for punishment.* Actually, as Lega maintains, it signified incorporation into the municipal organization responsible for the execution of public offices, burdens which the citizens so abhorred that they assumed them only under coercion, and as it were, in punishment.[59]

While the Decree of Gratian was never approved by the Church as an authentic code of law, nevertheless it did exercise a profound influence on legal thought from its very appearance in the middle of the twelfth century.[60] Along with the traditional law and practice concerning deposition, the Decree incorporated the aforementioned decretals of Pseudo-Isidore which ordered the delivery of the delinquent clerics to the *curia.* Inevitably the meaning of the phrase was controverted. Gradually, as will be seen, it worked its way into ecclesiastical legislation involving deposition until, with Pope Innocent III, in 1209, it was given a definite legal signification in church law.

ARTICLE 2. PARTIAL DEPOSITION

During this period there was also legislation providing for only a partial deposition or degradation. Thus the Council of Agde (506), while admitting that earlier decrees had been more severe, deigned to permit priests and deacons who had married twice or taken a widow in marriage to retain the title (dignity) of their office, but forbade the priests to offer Mass and the deacons to minister at the altar.[61] So too the III Council of Toledo (589) resorted only to a partial deposition as the sanction for one of its

---

[59] *De Delictis et Poenis,* n. 208, p. 282, not. 1; cf. also Gonzalez-Tellez, *Commentaria,* lib. II, tit. 1, cap. 10.

[60] 1140 is assigned by authorities as the date of its composition. Cf. Van Hove, *Prolegomena,* n. 184.

[61] C. 1: "Placuit de bigamis, aut internuptarum maritis, quamquam aliud patrum statuta decreverint, ut qui hucusque ordinati sunt, habita miseratione, presbyteri vel diaconi nomen tantum obtineant: officium vero presbyteri consecrandi, vel ministrandi huiusmodi diacones non praesumant."—Mansi, VIII, 324; cf. Hefele-Clark, IV, 76.

laws: "As the bishops, priests and deacons who have come over from heresy still partly live in matrimony with their wives, this is now forbidden to them. Whoever do so shall be regarded as a lector." [62] Though it did not reduce them in holy orders, the Council of Trullo (692) deposed to the last place within their rank deacons who were proud and assuming, usurping the place of priests.[63]

A similar partial deposition is to be found also in the *Penitential of Theodore* (668-690) under the title: "Of Abbots and Monks or of the Monastery." Canons 12 and 13 state: "Any monk whom a congregation has chosen to be ordained to the rank of presbyter for them, ought not to give up his former habit of life." This admonition is followed with the sanction: "But if he is afterwards found to be either proud or disobedient or vicious, and [if] in a better rank [he] seeks a worse life, he shall be deposed and put in the lowest place, or [he shall] make amends with satisfaction." [64]

The II General Council of Nicaea (787) includes a partial deposition in one of its canons along with other penalties. The canon significantly portrays a gradation and evaluation of these penalties: "Those who boast of having obtained a position in the Church by expenditure of money and who depreciate others who have been chosen because of their virtuous life and by the Holy Ghost without money, these shall, in the first place, *be put back to the lowest grade of their order*, and if then also they still persist [in their pride] they shall be punished by the bishop. But if anyone has given money in order to obtain ordination, the 30th Apostolic canon and the 2nd canon of Chalcedon apply to him. Both the one ordaining and the one ordained shall be deposed and excommunicated." [65]

In the eleventh century the penalty of partial deposition was still employed. The Council of Bourges (1031) reduced to the rank

---

[62] C. 5—Hefele-Clark, IV, 419.

[63] C. 7: " . . . is ex proprio gradu deiectus fit omnium ultimus eius ordinis in cuius est catalago in sua ecclesia."—Hardouin, III, 1664.

[64] McNeill, *Penitentials*, p. 204.

[65] C. 5—Hefele-Clark, V, 379-380; Hardouin, IV, 490; Schroeder, *Disciplinary Decrees*, p. 147. "Zonaras and Balsamon in earlier times, and later, Christian Lupus and Van Espen remarked that the second part of our canon treated of simony, but not the first."—Hefele-Clark, V, 380.

of lectors priests, deacons and subdeacons who would not part from unlawful consorts.[66] In the same year the Council of Limoges (1031), not without reason, outlined the procedure to be followed in deposing a priest to the rank of a deacon.[67] When the Bishop of Nantes confessed in the Council of Rheims (1049) that he had purchased his office, the assembled bishops deprived him of his episcopal ministry, taking from him his ring and pastoral staff, but allowed him to retain the office of priest.[68]

In the thirteenth century partial depositions, as will be seen, were even more clearly established in the law and for definite excesses, as a mitigation of the grave penalty of deposition.

ARTICLE 3. INFLICTION OF THE PENALTY

A. The Deposition of Bishops

In the beginning of this period, as in earlier ages, the right of deposing bishops was exercised by provincial councils. The deposed bishop, however, enjoyed the right of appealing to the Holy See. While this appeal was pending and until the Roman Pontiff delivered a definitive sentence no other bishop could be installed in the see of the deposed bishop.

About the year 546, Fulgentius, a deacon of Carthage, drew up a collection of canons known now as the *Breviatio Canonum of Fulgentius Ferrandus.* This collection, which flourished in the Church up to the twelfth century,[69] contained, among others, two canons, according to which a bishop who had been judged could appeal if he wished to the Holy See,[70] and if he appealed no one else should be ordained in his place.[71]

A similar provision was enacted by the V Council of Orleans

---

[66] C. 5: "Ut presbyteri, et diaconi et subdiaconi, sicut lex canonum praecipit, neque uxores neque concubinas habeant . . . qui vero derelinquere eas noluerint, a proprio gradu et officio cessent et inter lectores et cantores permaneant."—Hardouin, VI, 884.

[67] Hardouin, VI, 884.

[68] Hardouin, VI, 1006.

[69] Cicognani, *Canon Law*, p. 214.

[70] C. 59—*MPL*, LXVII, 952.

[71] C. 60—*MPL*, LXVII, 953.

(549): "No bishop should during his lifetime have a successor given to him or another bishop put in his place unless he had been deposed for a capital offense." [72] Shortly before this council, Contumelious, Bishop of Riez, appealed from a sentence of deposition to the Holy See. Pope Agapetus (535-536) thereupon wrote to the Metropolitan, Caesar of Arles, ordering a new trial and reminding him that no changes were to be made until the appeal from the sentence had been definitively settled by the Roman Pontiff.[73]

An expression of the rights of the Roman Pontiff in regard to the deposition of bishops is to be found in the letters of Pope Gregory the Great (590-604). If a bishop is to be judged who is subject to no metropolitan or patriarch, his cause should be heard and concluded by the Apostolic See, the head of all churches. In like manner an accused bishop may proceed who suspects the prelates who are to pass judgment upon him.[74]

In other letters he restates the customary procedure. The bishops of the province should assemble under the metropolitan and investigate the truth of the charges brought against a provincial bishop. If the charges are found to be true and the crime merits deposition, the council should proceed to this sentence.[75]

When a certain Bishop Januarius appealed to the Holy See, Pope Gregory I sent a delegate to investigate the case, authorizing him to reinstate the deposed bishop if he discovered the sentence to be unjust. Moreover, the bishop who was installed in the place of Januarius while the appeal was pending, *"perverse ac contra canones,"* should be deprived of the priesthood and expelled from the ministry.[76]

When Pope Hadrian (772-795) wrote to Tilpin, Archbishop of Rheims, confirming the privileges of that see, he recalled the affair of a former Archbishop of Rheims, Rigobert, who had been uncanonically deposed without any consent or directions of the Holy See. Hence, he would have it known at Rheims that no authority is com-

---

[72] C. 12—Hefele-Clark, IV, 369.

[73] *Agapetus ep. ad Caesarium Arelatensis*—Hardouin, II, 1179.

[74] *Ep. XLV,* Epist. lib. XIII—*MPL,* LXXVII, 1294.

[75] *Ep. XLVIII,* Epist. lib. II—*MPL,* LXXVII, 589; *Ep. XIV,* Epist. lib. VII—*ibidem,* 869.

[76] *Ep. XLV,* Epist. lib. XIII—*MPL,* LXXVII, 1294; cf. c. 7, C. II, q. 1.

petent to depose a bishop without a canonical process, and no judgment is valid without the consent of the Roman Pontiff if an appeal has been made to the Holy See.[77]

This same Pope Hadrian, in 774, sent to Charlemagne a copy of the Dionysian collection of canons. This collection now known as the *Hadriana* was received and approved by the bishops of the empire at Aix-la-Chapelle (Aachen) in 802.[78] It contained the decrees of the Council of Sardica (343) which provided for the judgment of criminal causes of bishops by provincial councils, reserving to the Holy See, when an appeal had been entered, the definitive sentence. Hence, in regard to these laws the collection merely gave added legal expression to the existing rights and practice.

The ninth century is known for its abundance of documental forgeries. Among such fabrications is the Collection of Capitularies of Benedict the Levite, purportedly the Capitularies of Archbishop Riculf (d. 813) drawn from the archives of the Church of Mainz.[79] Yet this spurious work, appearing in 845, presented no change in existing laws governing the deposition of bishops when it ordained that bishops assembled in a synod form the tribunal of first instance. If a bishop suspected this tribunal, he could be judged by the primate of the province or the Roman Pontiff.[80] It stated that if an accused bishop appealed to the Roman Pontiff what he decided must be followed.[81] Again, a bishop who had been judged by a council could appeal, if he wished, to the Holy See. If he appealed no one was to be ordained in his see until a definitive decision had been rendered.[82]

Shortly after this collection of forgeries another appeared: the Pseudo-Isidorian Collection. Authorities [83] have rightly held that

[77] Hardouin, III, 2026.

[78] Cf. Cicognani, *Canon Law*, p. 217.

[79] Cf. Cicognani, *Canon Law*, p. 238.

[80] *Benedicti Capitularium*, lib. III, c. 314—Pertz, *Monumenta Germaniae Historica, Legum Sectio*, II (pars altera), 122.

[81] *Ibid.*, c. 315—Pertz, *loc. cit.*

[82] *Ibid.*, c. 412—Pertz, *op. cit.*, p. 128.

[83] Van Hove, *Prolegomena*, n. 166; Cicognani, *Canon Law*, p. 247; Lupus, *Synodorum Decreta et Canones*, V, 175; Van Espen, *Ius Ecclesiasticum Universum*, III, 455.

this collection introduced a new law in the discipline under consideration, to wit, the definitive deposition of a bishop pertains exclusively to the Roman Pontiff. Thus, Pseudo-Isidore wrote into the False Decretals not only the earlier law that bishops should be tried by the provincial council [84] and that they may appeal to the Apostolic See to which the case is then reserved along with major causes,[85] but he also fabricated a law which required the authority of the Holy See to convoke a provincial council or to depose a bishop.[86]

Although he may have been influenced by the Pseudo-Isidorian Decretals, Pope Nicholas I (858-867) nevertheless exercised the right he possessed in virtue of the primacy of jurisdiction when he reserved to the Holy See exclusive judgment in causes concerning the deposition of a bishop. When Rothad, Bishop of Soissons, was deposed in his absence by a council held under the authority of Archbishop Hincmar of Rheims, another bishop was installed in his see. Rothad appealed to the Holy See.[87] Pope Nicholas restored Rothad to the episcopacy and decreed that in the future the approval of the Roman Pontiff must be sought in order to proceed against a bishop.[88] Not on appeal alone did the Holy See thereafter decide definitively the deposition of bishops. A decision of a provincial council which pronounced the deposition of a bishop was to have no effect without the confirmation of the Holy See. Thus, Pope Nicholas developed the early law that major causes were reserved to the Holy See. Among such causes must now be considered the definitive deposition

---

[84] Cf. c. 2, C. III, q. 6.

[85] Cf. c. 12, C. II, q. 6.

[86] *E. g., Ep.* ascribed to Pope Julius I; in Gratian, c. 9, C. III, q. 6; c. 1, C. V, q. 4; cf. also cc. 5, 6, 7, C. III, q. 6; cc. 1, 2, 5, 6, D. XVII; Van Espen, *Ius Ecclesiasticum Universum,* III, 455; Van Hove, *Prolegomena,* n. 166; Cicognani, *Canon Law,* p. 247.

[87] Cf. *Libellus proclamationis Rothadi episcopi quem Nicolao Papae obtulit*: "Denique saepefatus archiepiscopus meus (Hincmar) in eodem Concilio tamquam Imperator triumphans et tamquam summus Ecclesiae pontifex decernens . . . iudicium depositionis emisit . . . Interea ordinatur episcopus in cathedra viventis, quamvis ne umquam post appellationem Romani Pontificis hoc fiat, sacri canones evidenter vetare noscantur."—Hardouin, V, 582.

[88] *Ep. Nicolai Papae I ad clerum et plebem ecclesiae Romanae*—Hardouin, V, 584-585; *Ep. XXVIII, XXIX, ad Hincmarum*—Mansi, XV, 294. Cf. c. 13, C. II, q. 6.

of bishops.[89] Nor did Pope Nicholas I hesitate to exercise his right of deposing prelates of the Church when their conduct warranted it. In 863 the Pontiff convoked a council in the Lateran and deposed the Archbishops of Cologne and Treves for their share in the scandal of the Council of Metz (859), wherein the annulment of the marriage of the Emperor's (Louis II) brother, Lothair II, as well as his remarriage were sanctioned.[90]

The new discipline in regard to bishops is also seen in a letter of the Council of Troyes (867) to Pope Nicholas in which the Council stated the necessity of the intervention of the Roman Pontiff in the deposition of bishops.[91] Later, about the year 1050, King Henry I of France proposed a council to judge Bishop Bruno of Angers who was involved in the heresy of Berengarius. Theoduin, Bishop of Liège, informed the king that this could not be done without authorization of the Holy See, *"praeter apostolicam auctoritatem."* [92] Pope Leo IX (1049-1054) restated this discipline in a letter addressed to the primate of Carthage in 1054.[93] According to the report of St. Peter Damian (+ 1072), Pope Victor II (1055-1057), exercised his jurisdiction in this matter at least on one occasion, for he sent Hildebrand, then a cardinal subdeacon, later pope,

[89] *Sermo Nicolai Papae I* (865): "Quamquam etsi numquam provocasset *numquam omnino* praeter scientiam nostram deponi debuerit: quia sacra statuta et veneranda decreta episcoporum causas, *utpote maiora negotia,* nostrae deffiniendas censurae mandarunt."—Hardouin, V, 584. Cf. also Nicolaus I, *Ep. ad universos episcopos Galliae*: "Sed dictis, iudicia episcoporum non esse maiora negotia nec difficiliores causarum exitus . . . Adhuc tamen percontari libet quaenam iudicia vel quorum esse maiora negotia praedicatis si episcoporum causas non inter praecipua computatis negotia."—Hardouin, V, 593. Cf. Lupus, *Synodorum Decreta et Canones,* V, 175, 340. Cf. *infra,* p. 79.

[90] Cf. Hardouin, V, 573-574.

[91] *Ep. Synodica Concilii ad Nicolaum papam*: "nec vestris nec futuris temporibus *praeter* consultum Romani Pontificis de gradu suo quilibet episcoporum deiiciatur . . ."—Hardouin, V, 685.

[92] *Ep. Theoduini ad Henricum Regem.*—Hardouin, VI, 1023.

[93] *Ep. III, ad Thomam Ep. Africanum*: "Hoc autem nolo vos lateat, non debere praeter sententiam Romani Pontificis universale concilium celebrari, aut *episcopos damnari vel deponi,* quia etsi licet vobis aliquos episcopos examinare *definitivam tamen sententiam* absque consultu Romani Pontificis, ut dictum est, non licet dare; quod in sanctis canonibus statutum, si quaeritis, potestis invenire."—Mansi, XIX, 658; Hardouin, VI, 949.

to France and there in a synod at Lyons (1055) he deposed six bishops *"ex Apostolicae Sedis auctoritate."* [94]

In the pontificate of Pope Gregory VII (1073-1085) the reservation to the Holy See of criminal causes of bishops involving deposition is clearly stated. The famous *Dictatus Gregorii VII Pontificis* contains the following canons on this point: The Roman Pontiff alone can depose bishops; [95] Legates of the Pope can pass this sentence; [96] the Pope can depose even those who are not present,[97] and can do so without convoking a council.[98] The reign of Pope Gregory VII shows an application of these principles. He summoned accused bishops to Rome to pass judgment on the charges.[99] At times he sent legates to judge the bishop in a synod and confirmed the sentence of the legates.[100] On other occasions he delegated neighboring bishops to judge their accused colleague or simply to apply the sentence which he had already delivered.[101]

Thus the right of provincial councils to pass a sentence of deposition on gravely delinquent bishops gradually yielded to a higher authority. With the ninth and subsequent centuries the definitive sentence of deposition in the case of a bishop was reserved exclusively to the Roman Pontiff.

B. *The Deposition of Priests, Deacons and Inferior Clerics*

Pope St. Gregory the Great (590-604) repeated the statement of the traditional right of bishops to depose clerics who were subject

---

[94] *Ep. ad Dominicum*—Hardouin, VI, 1040.

[95] C. 3: "Quod Romanus Pontifex *solus* possit deponere Episcopos vel reconciliare."—Lupus, *Synodorum Decreta et Canones*, V, 172.

[96] C. 4: "Quod Papae Legatus omnibus Episcopis praesit in Conciliis, etiam inferioris gradus, et adversus eos sententiam depositionis possit dare."—Lupus, *Synodorum Decreta et Canones*, V, 177.

[97] C. 5: "Quod absentes Papa possit deponere."—Lupus, *op. cit.*, V, 182.

[98] C. 25: "Quod absque Synodali Conventu Papa possit Episcopos deponere et reconciliare."—Lupus, *op. cit.*, V, 375.

[99] *Ep. II, III*, Epist. lib. II—Hardouin, VI, 1261 sq.

[100] *Ep. XI*, Epist. lib. V—Hardouin, VI, 1383; *Ep. XVIII*, lib. VIII—Hardouin, VI, 1466; *Ep. XVI*, lib. I—Hardouin, VI, 1207; *Ep. XXXII*, lib. IX—Hardouin, VI, 1503.

[101] *Ep. VIII*, Epist. lib. V—Hardouin, VI, 1380.

to them. The bishop, however, was not to be quick to believe the charges made against his clerics or to proceed to punishment without hearing the case. Nor was he to inflict the penalty without diligently seeking the facts of the case along with his council (*praesentibus senioribus ecclesiae*). Only then was the canonical penalty to be applied when the charge had been fully established in the presence of the council.[102]

The II Council of Seville (619), held by St. Isidore of Seville, restored to the priesthood Fragitanus, a priest of Corduba, who had been unjustly deposed by his bishop. The council then decreed, in conformity with earlier canons, that no bishop should dare to depose any priest or deacon without a synodal hearing. "For there are many bishops who condemn these clerics unheard, not by canonical authority but by tyrannical power. And just as they elevate some through favor, so through envy and hatred they reduce others and at the faint breeze of opinion they condemn for crimes which they do not prove. A bishop can alone give honors to priests and deacons, but alone he cannot take them away. . . . These clerics then cannot be condemned by one judge, nor by one judge can they be deprived of the privileges of their rank, but in the presence of a synod judgment shall be passed according to the precepts of the canons." [103]

The IV Council of Toledo (633) inferred that, besides the bishops, also priests and inferior clerics could appeal to a synod from a sentence of deposition, since it made provision for the restoration by a later synod of a bishop, priest, or deacon who had been previously unjustly deposed.[104]

The *Breviato Canonum* of Fulgentius required that charges against priests be heard by five bishops together with the bishop of the accused. In the case of deacons the bishop had to be assisted by three other bishops; but in the case of lower clerics he could proceed alone.[105]

---

[102] *Ep. XLIV, Ad Ioannem Panormitanum Episcopum*, Ep. lib. XIII—*MPL*, 77, 1293; in Gratian, c. 23, D. LXXXVI; c. 2, C. XV, q. 7.

[103] C. 6—Hardouin, III, 559; cf. Hefele-Clark, IV, 442; in Gratian, cc. 1, 7, C. XV, q. 7.

[104] C. 28—Hefele-Clark, IV, 453; Hardouin, III, 586.

[105] C. 51—*MPL*, LXVII, 952.

The application of these laws, which originated in Carthage, as already noted, undoubtedly caused the local bishop some inconvenience. Hence the councils of the Middle Ages began to reflect a changing disciplinary procedure. The Council of Fréjus (791) decreed that no bishop should presume to depose a priest, deacon or archimandrite without consulting the metropolitan.[106] The Council of Treves (895) expressly stated that it took its legislation from the councils of Carthage when it decreed that no priest was to be deposed except by six bishops, nor a deacon except by three. The causes of other clerics a bishop could hear and judge alone.[107] Later the Council of Rouen (1072) authorized the bishops who were summoned by an ordinary for the deposition of a priest or a deacon to send, if he himself could not be present, his vicar *"cum sua auctoritate."* [108]

Finally, it should be noted that during this period the right of priests and inferior clerics to appeal, if necessary, to the Holy See was clearly accorded them, especially by Pope Nicholas I. In a letter to the Archbishop of Siena he served a warning that no one should presume to prevent a certain excommunicated priest from approaching the Apostolic See if he so desired.[109] On another occasion he received the appeal of a deposed priest and ordered his restoration, admonishing the Archbishop of Tours to follow canonical procedure in the future.[110]

ARTICLE 4. CEREMONIAL ACCOMPANYING DEPOSITION

Authorities on the history of matters liturgical state that there are no records in the earliest extant pontificals of the manner in which deposition was solemnly performed. However, they are equally positive in their convictions that some form or order was

---

[106] C. 7—Hardouin, IV, 858. It may be noted from this canon that abbots who did not enjoy the privilege of exemption were subject to the jurisdiction of the bishop as much as the clergy of the diocese. Cf. cc. 15, 16, C. XVIII, q. 2; Catalanus, *Pontificale Romanum*, I, tit. XVII, *de benedictione abbatis auctoritate Ordinarii.*

[107] C. 10—Hardouin, VI, 442.

[108] C. 20—Hardouin, VI, 1190.

[109] C. 12, C. III, q. 9.

[110] C. 10, C. II, q. 1; cf. also c. 39, D. L.

observed, that the deposition of a cleric was inflicted not merely by a verbal sentence but by an external and public rite in which the cleric was divested of his clerical robes and insignia.[111]   Early records of this practice show that it was undoubtedly taken over from a custom prevailing in the Roman army, according to which a gravely delinquent soldier, before he was expelled from the army, was publicly stripped of all his military insignia.[112]   In a later day it was to this procedure that Boniface VIII (1294-1303) referred when he established a solemn ceremony for the infliction of real degradation.[113]

Before the sixth century history records a few cases in which a solemn ceremony accompanied the infliction of the penalty of deposition.   At the deposition of Eustachius in the Synod of Antioch (341) all the bishops present mocked and railed the deposed Eustachius and shouted at him "unholy." [114]   A certain Irenaeus (+ *c.* 450) who had fallen into the Nestorian heresy was expelled from the church of Tyre and divested of all his sacerdotal insignia.[115]

Before the end of the twelfth century, however, there was no ceremony required in law for the execution of a sentence of deposition.   On the other hand, the IV Council of Toledo (633) established by decree a formal procedure to be followed in the restoration of a deposed cleric which strongly implies that some ceremony was employed in his deposition: If a bishop, priest, or deacon has been unjustly deposed and is recognized as innocent in a later synod, he must receive back his lost rank before the altar; in the case of a bishop, through reception of the stole, the ring and the staff; in the case of a priest, by reception of the stole and chasuble; a deacon, by reception of the stole and alb; a subdeacon, by reception of the

---

[111] Cf. Martène, *De Antiquis Ecclesiae Ritibus*, III, c. 2, n. 1 sq.; Catalanus, *Pontificale Romanum* (Parisiis, 1852), III, tit. VII, § 1; Maskell, *Monumenta Ritualia Ecclesiae Anglicanae* (London, 1846-1847), III, p. clii.

[112] D. (3, 2) 2, 2; cf. Kober, *Die Deposition und Degradation*, pp. 53, 55; Devoti, *Institutiones*, tit. VIII, § XIX, sec. 4.

[113] C. 2, *de poenis*, V, 9, in VI°.

[114] Eusebius, *Historia Ecclesiastica*, I, c. 24—*MPG*, LXVII, 143.

[115] Cf. Baronius, *Annales Ecclesiastici*, VII (an. 448), n. 6.   For other examples cf. Catalanus, *Pontificale Romanum*, III, tit. VII, § 1 seq.

chalice and paten; and in like fashion the others receive in the restoration of their rank those symbols which they obtained when they
were ordained.[116]   As Hefele [117] points out, this ceremony was not
a reordination,[118] but a restoration.   As such it implied that the
infliction of the penalty of deposition was accompanied with a ceremony wherein the characteristic insignia of orders, according to his
rank, were taken from the cleric.   Where such a ceremony accompanied deposition, at least in the regions affected by the legislation
of this Council of Toledo, a corresponding ceremony as outlined in
its decree was necessary for restoration to his former rank.[119]

The only positive legal requirement of a ceremony in the infliction of the penalty of deposition is to be found in the eleventh
century when the Council of Limoges (1031) established a ceremony for the bishop to follow in the deposition of a priest to the
rank of a deacon.   The bishop, according to this council, was to
order the priest to be vested in all the sacerdotal vestments; then
he was to take from him the maniple and chasuble, and finally cross
the stole on the right side of the cleric.   Thus the bishop deposed
the delinquent cleric from the priesthood to the diaconate.[120]

The indignity and disgrace expressed in these ceremonies of deposition is vividly portrayed in the unjust deposition in the year 858,
of Ignatius, Patriarch of Constantinople (+ 877).   After the sentence of deposition was passed upon him, he was stripped of his vestments and in their place he was clothed in ragged and filthy pontificals.   These were torn from him.   A subdeacon, of unsound mind
and low moral character, whom Ignatius had previously deposed,

---

[116] C. 28—Hefele-Clark, IV, 453; Hardouin, III, 586; cf. Hinschius,
Kirchenrecht, IV, 809.

[117] Hefele-Clark, IV, 453.

[118] Reordination was universally proscribed, as noted above, and was contrary to the common teaching of the Church despite the few historical cases
of this period in which reordination occurred, viz., reordinations performed
by John Scholasticus, Patriarch of Constantinople (564-578); by Pope Sergius
III (904-911); and Pope S. Leo IX (1049-1054)—Cf. Many, *Praelectiones de
sacra ordinatione* (Parisiis, 1905), nn. 18-25, pp. 57-76.

[119] C. 28: "non potest esse quod fuerat, nisi gradus amissos recipiat coram
altari de manu episcopi."—Hardouin, III, 586; in Gratian, c. 65, C. XI, q. 3.

[120] Hardouin, VI, 884.

now approached the Patriarch, struck him and shouted *"indignus."* In this cry the clergy and laity joined.[121]

. In the II General Lateran Council (1139), Pope Innocent II (1130-1143) deposed Peter Leontius and his followers. The Pope called out each one by name and, while the witnesses mocked them, · he took from them their crosiers, pallia and rings.[122]

After the twelfth century, when degradation became a penalty distinct from deposition, its execution involved, as will be seen, a solemn ceremony defined and required by law.

ARTICLE 5. HISTORICAL NOTE ON THE PRIVILEGED FORUM

It has already been noted that deposition or degradation as an ecclesiastical penalty, rests on the judiciary rights of the Church. Inevitably the history of this penalty is colored with the history of the relations between Church and state, but especially with regard to the recognition by the state of the judiciary rights of the Church and the *privilegium fori.*

As soon as the Church, delivered from persecution, began to organize for her conquest of the world for Christ, Christian emperors recognized her rights and privileges and guaranteed them before the state by expressing them in their laws. Constantine was the first emperor who respected the judiciary rights of the Church. St. Augustine relates that this Christian emperor declined to enter a certain controversy to pass judgment on a decision of the bishops.[123] Rufinus (+ 410) testifies that Constantine refused to intervene in a dispute which the bishops, assembled at the Council of Nicaea, submitted to his arbitration: "The Lord has made you priests and given you the power for judging us, and, therefore, we are rightly judged by you. But you cannot be judged by men."[124] Thus, Constantine voiced the perennial mind of the Church that it is inconsistent with the dignity of the clerical state to have the leaders and teachers of the faithful judged by laymen.

---

[121] Cf. Baronius, *Annales Ecclesiastici,* XIV (an. 861), n. 7.

[122] Acta Concilii—Hardouin, VI, 1214.

[123] *Ep. XLIII,* 20—*MPL,* XXXIII, 169.

[124] Rufinus, *Historiae Ecclesiasticae libri duo,* I, 2—*MPL,* XXI, 468.

In 376 the Emperor Gratian decreed that all causes pertaining to religion were to be considered by ecclesiastical tribunals, but he reserved to the civil courts the criminal charges against clerics.[125] Honorius, in 399, gave full recognition to the courts of the bishop in this particular matter when he decreed that clerics could only be accused before the bishop.[126] Justinian likewise recognized the exclusive right of the bishop to judge ecclesiastical crimes.[127]

As regards the *privilegium fori*, however, Justinian was not altogether favorable towards the Church. In this matter he rather restricted the rights of bishops, committing to lay judges the criminal causes of clerics while attributing to the bishop only certain rights in the use of precautions designed to safeguard the dignity of the clerical state.[128] This legislation provided that if a cleric were brought before the bishop in criminal matters the bishop should, if he found the cleric guilty, depose him so that the lay judge would have competence over him; if the cleric were brought directly to the lay judge, this court should communicate the procedural acts to the bishop for his review. If the bishop in this case approved the judgment, he was to relinquish the guilty cleric, deprived of his dignity and office, to the lay court for execution of sentence. If the bishop disagreed, recourse to the emperor was offered.[129]

The course of Roman Law enactments relative to the privileged jurisdictional status of the clergy, not merely in spiritual matters but also in civil and criminal matters, has been aptly expressed in the conclusion of a recent study: [130] "The legislation of the Emperors at times fluctuated, but carried out in ascending degree—although not finally until under Heraclius (A. D. 629)—the thought: *Fas enim*

[125] C. Th. (16, 2), 23.

[126] C. Th. (16, 2), 41: "non nisi apud episcopos accusari convenit." Cf. C. Th. (16, 11), 1.

[127] N. 83, 1.

[128] C. (1, 4), 29; N. (83, pr) 2; N. (123, 21), 1.

[129] N. (123, 21), 1. In virtue of this law Lega (*De Delictis et Poenis*, n. 208) is inclined to believe there were some cases of decreed degradation before the time of Innocent III.

[130] Wenger-Fisk, *Institutes of the Roman Law of Civil Procedure* (revised ed., New York: Veritas Press, 1940), § 36, p. 343.

non est, ut divini muneris ministri temporalium potestatum subdantur arbitrio." [131]

In her synodal decrees the Church again manifested her mind on the subject. At a Council of Mâcon in 581 it was decided that "if a secular judge imprisons or punishes a clergyman without the assent of the bishop, except for criminal causes, that is, murder, theft and fraud, he must be excluded from the Church by the bishop at his pleasure." [132] Only four years later another council assembled at Mâcon (585)—Hefele designates it as a kind of French general council—explicitly reserved all cases involving clerics to the jurisdiction of the Church. The Council declared: "It has happened that clergymen have been dragged by the secular power from their churches and put into public prisons. This must no longer be done; but anyone who has a charge against a bishop must bring his complaint before the metropolitan, who in lighter cases, shall either himself, or with reference to one or two bishops, decide, and in graver cases bring them before a council."[133] "Similarly no one may arrest a priest or deacon or subdeacon, but they must be accused before the bishop." [134]

In the reign of Charlemagne, the civil authorities recognized the *privilegium fori* which was so consistently maintained by the Church in her legislative enactments. In a capitulary of 789 Charlemagne decreed that if clerics committed any faults they were to be tried by ecclesiastical and not by secular judges.[135] The Frankfurt Capitulary of 794 contained a like recognition: "If a priest has been apprehended in crime, he is to be taken to his bishop and punished according to canonical provisions." [136] In 803 the emperor returned

---

[131] Theodosius II and Valentinian III in C. Th. (16, 2), 47, 1—in the year 425.

[132] C. 7—Hefele-Clark, IV, 404.

[133] C. 9—Hefele-Clark, IV, 408.

[134] C. 10—Hefele-Clark, IV, 408.

[135] Cap. 38: "Ut clerici et ecclesiastici ordines, si culpam incurrerint, apud ecclesiasticos iudicentur non apud saeculares."—*Monumenta Germaniae Historica* (Auspiciis Societatis Aperiendis Fontibus Rerum Germanicarum Medii Aevi, Hannoverae, 1835), *Legum Sectio* (Unrevised new printing, ed. Georgius Pertz, Leipzig: Karl Hiersemann, 1925), I, 60.

[136] Cap. 39—Pertz, *Monumenta Germaniae Historica, Legum Sectio,* I, 74.

to this point with insistence. He decreed that neither abbots nor priests, deacons nor subdeacons, nor any member of the clergy could be summoned or tried by secular courts, but were to be judged by their bishops.[137]

This perfect exemption of clerics from the secular court even in criminal causes was at times abused by the clergy.[138] Kober explains this abuse as having its origin in the fact that, as the Church prohibited in her courts the infliction of capital punishment, clerics, subject only to the ecclesiastical court, were therefore practically immune from this penalty. This immunity did not sufficiently coerce criminal clerics. In consequence a few rulers, as Henry II (1154-1189) in England and Frederick II (1212-1250) in Sicily, took action by establishing laws which were contrary to the privileged forum and which were consequently reprobated by the Roman Pontiffs.[139]

In order to meet the abuses of the privileged forum on the one hand, and to satisfy the complaints of the laity on the other, the Roman Pontiffs passed legislation which, while maintaining the privileged forum in principle, made it no longer available for certain classes of incorrigible clerics. This development led to the establishment by the Church of the two penalties of deposition and degradation. This development will be observed in the subsequent chapter.

---

[137] Cap. 12: "Volumus primo ut neque abbates et presbyteri neque diaconi et subdiaconi neque quislibet de clero, de personis suis ad publica vel saecularia iudicia trahantur vel distringantur, sed a suis episcopis adiudicati iustitiam faciant."—Pertz, *Monumenta Germaniae Historica, Legum Sectio*, I, 110.

[138] Cf. Wernz, *Ius Decretalium*, VI, n. 119.

[139] Kober, *Die Deposition und Degradation*, p. 147 ff.

CHAPTER III

DEPOSITION AND DEGRADATION FROM THE TWELFTH CENTURY TO THE COUNCIL OF TRENT

Article 1. Proximate Evolution of the Distinction Between Deposition and Degradation

While Pope Alexander III (1159-1181) was successfully resisting the imperial menace to the freedom of religion as embodied in the Emperor Frederick Barbarossa (1155-1190), St. Thomas à Becket, Archbishop of Canterbury (1162-1170), was zealously defending the rights of the Church in England as regards the punishment of delinquent clerics. The King of England, Henry II (1154-1189), wished to have all accused clerics brought before the bishop, and there, in the presence of a royal officer, to have the bishop pass judgment. If the bishop's court found the accused cleric guilty, he was to be degraded and turned over to the king's court, which would inflict what it considered the just penalty.

The bishops, under the leadership of St. Thomas, did not consent to these demands. They upheld their part in the controversy on two principles of canon law: a lay tribunal is incompetent to try an accused cleric, and secondly, no one is to be condemned twice for the same offense; hence the bishops insisted on protecting from the lay power those clerics whom they deposed.[1]

In the mind of the laity the crimes of the clergy were considered to be only partially punished when the crimes were such as involved in the lay courts mutilation or death, for such penalties were not inflicted in the courts of the Church.[2] Nevertheless, throughout the twelfth century the greatest penalty the Church inflicted on a cleric, apart from excommunication, was deposition with confinement in a

---

[1] Cf. Baronius, *Annales Ecclesiastici*, XIX (an. 1164), 230 sq. "Non vindicabit Dominus bis in idipsum."—c. 12, D. LXXXI.

[2] C. 30, C. XXIII, q. 8; cc. 5, 9, X, *ne clerici vel monachi saecularibus negotiis se immisceant*, III, 50. Cf. Fagnanus, *Commentaria in Quinque Libros Decretalium* (Venetiis, 1697), lib. V, tit. 40, cap. 27, n. 8.

monastery. Confirmation of this may be found in the fact that shortly after the close of the twelfth century Innocent III (1198-1216), replying to a query of the Bishop of London as to how clerics apprehended in robbery or other great crimes were to be punished, directed that they were to be deposed from their orders and cast into monasteries for penance.[3]

A cleric who had been canonically deposed was not, then, to suffer another penalty. Alexander III, first of the lawyer popes, voiced anew this established rule when he stated that a bishop who has deposed a cleric according to the norms of the canons should not deliver him over to the secular judge, for the culprit is not to be punished with a double penalty.[4]

In similar fashion the successor of Alexander III, Pope Lucius III (1181-1185), defended the judiciary rights of the Church over her clergy against any and all encroachments of the civil power, declaring that even though a royal custom held that thieves be judged by secular judges, clerics could not in any case, and especially not in criminal matters, be judged by any other than an ecclesiastical judge.[5]

However, about this time, as already noted, there was much discussion among canonists as to the meaning of the penalty contained in the Decree of Gratian, according to which clerics who were rebellious towards their bishops should be delivered to the *curia*.[6] There was a growing opinion [7] that this provision meant that such incorrigible clerics should be turned over to the secular courts for punishment. This was the common teaching after the time of Pope Innocent III (1198-1216).[8]

Pope Lucius III took a step in this direction when, in 1184, in order to check the ravaging spread of heresy, he decreed that clerics

---

[3] C. 6, X, *de poenis*, V, 37. Cf. Gonzalez-Tellez, *Commentaria*, lib. V, tit. 20, cap. 3, n. 1.

[4] C. 4, X, *de iudiciis*, II, 1: "Non debet [episcopus] quemlibet depositum pro suis excessibus, quum suo sit functus officio, nec duplici debeat ipsum contritione conterere, iudici tradere saeculari."

[5] C. 8, X, *de iudiciis*, II, 1.

[6] Cf. cc. 18, 13, C. XI, q. 1; c. 8, C. III, q. 4.

[7] Cf. Baronius, *Annales Ecclesiastici*, XIX (an. 1164), 230 sq.

[8] Cf. Gonzalez-Tellez, *Commentaria*, lib. II, tit. 1, cap. 10, n. 17.

who persisted in this crime should be stripped of their prerogatives of orders, and, thus deprived of ecclesiastical offices and benefices, should be abandoned to the judgment of the secular power to be punished as it deemed proper.[9] Devoti (1744-1820) stated that this was the first ecclesiastical law in accordance with which a deposed cleric was left to the judgment of the secular power for the reception of a penalty. However, the same author also pointed out that the deposed cleric was abandoned, not delivered, to the judgment of the secular court. The Church by this act only removed the impediment from the state's activity by withdrawing from the individual cleric the privilege of the ecclesiastical court.[10]

The next pope, Urban III (1185-1187), in response to a question concerning the punishment to be. meted out to certain clerics who had committed a civil crime, in no way referred to a judgment of the secular courts. The pope was asked what should be done with certain perverse clerics who had falsified the seal of King Philip Augustus of France (1180-1223). He responded that these clerics were not to suffer any extreme corporal chastisement nor the loss of any bodily members, but were first to be degraded from their orders, and then some character could be imprinted on them as a sign of their evil doing so that they would be thus recognized among men.[11]

Pope Celestine III (1191-1198), however, contributed much towards the distinction developing between deposition and degradation. Indeed, this pope, according to Benedict XIV, introduced the distinction into canon law or at least gave it recognition.[12] Pope Celestine had been asked if it was lawful for the king or any secular person to judge clerics of any rank who were apprehended in theft, homicide, perjury or other crimes. He replied that if a cleric in any rank was apprehended in grave crimes and legitimately convicted

[9] C. 9, X, *de haereticis,* V, 7: "totius ecclesiastici ordinis praerogativa nudetur, et sic omni pariter officio et beneficio spoliatus ecclesiastico, saecularis relinquatur arbitrio potestatis, animadversione debita puniendus."

[10] *Institutiones,* I, tit. IV, § 21, n. 2.

[11] C. 3, X, *de crimine falsi,* V, 20. This was deposition, and not degradation in its proper sense, which as a punishment was inflicted on falsifiers only after the introduction of this penalty by Pope Innocent III. Cf. Gonzalez-Tellez, *Commentaria,* lib. V, tit. XX, cap. 4, n. 10.

[12] *De synodo dioecesana,* lib. IX, cap. 6, n. 3.

he had to be deposed by the ecclesiastical judge. If the deposed cleric remained incorrigible, he was to be excommunicated; then, with any increase in his contumacy, anathemas were to be employed against him. Finally, if entering the depths of evil he was still contemptuous towards ecclesiastical authority—since the Church, unable to do anything more, could not allow the perdition of many— he was to be seized by the secular power so that exile or some other lawful penalty might be inflicted on him.[13]

This response manifested the law and practice towards the end of the twelfth century: laymen could exercise no jurisdiction over clerics, even after they had been deposed for grave crimes. If the clerics persevered in their criminal life after deposition, they were to be excommunicated. Yet they were still subject to the courts of the Church and its greater anathema. It was only after the Church had exhausted her penalties and the deposed cleric had notoriously persisted in his evil way that the state acquired any competence.[14]

While the twelfth century laws and decrees of the Church insinuated the various elements for distinguishing between deposition and degradation, it was left to the thirteenth century to establish, definitely, the distinction. In retrospect it may be noted that Pope Lucius III (1181-1185) merely permitted the case of a cleric who had fallen into heresy *to be left* to the decision of the secular power (*"saecularis relinquatur arbitrio potestatis"*). He did not order the transfer of such a case to the secular court for punishment. Likewise Pope Celestine III (1191-1198) ordained that a criminal cleric be deposed, but he also ordered that such a cleric be kept subject to the jurisdiction of the Church until his manifest incorrigibility warranted his correction by the secular court. Yet, even in this case, no

---

[13] C. 10, X, *de iudiciis*, II, 1: "Si clericus in quocumque ordine constitutus in furto, vel homicidio, vel periurio, seu alio mortali crimine fuerit deprehensus legitime atque convictus, ab ecclesiastico iudice deponendus est. Qui si depositus incorrigibilis fuerit, excommunicari debet, deinde contumacia crescente anathematis mucrone feriri. Postmodum vero, si in profundum malorum veniens contempserit, quum ecclesia non habeat ultra quid faciat, ne possit esse ultra perditio plurimorum, per saecularem comprimendus est potestatem ita, quod ei deputetur exsilium, vel alia legitima poena inferatur."

[14] Cf. Fagnanus, *Commentaria*, lib. II, tit. 1, cap. 10, n. 25.

solemnities surrounded the act wherein the cleric was removed from ecclesiastical to civil jurisdiction. These elements are found only when degradation appears as a unique penalty, distinct from deposition, in the thirteenth century.[15]

The definite distinction in ecclesiastical law between deposition and degradation must be traced to the legislation of the great canonist-pope of the thirteenth century, Innocent III, who ruled the Church for eighteen years (1198-1216). In order to put an end to the malice of forgery and in particular to the falsification of papal documents, Innocent III, in 1202, decreed that clerics who were apprehended in this crime were to be forever deprived of all ecclesiastical offices and benefices, and that those who directly, of themselves, committed this offense of falsification, after they were degraded by the ecclesiastical judge, were to be delivered over to the secular power to be punished according to the lawful constitutions.[16] According to this decree of Pope Innocent III clerics who coöperated in the falsification of papal letters were to be *deposed, "omnibus officiis et beneficiis ecclesiasticis perpetuo sint privati,"* while the forgers themselves were to be *degraded* and turned over to the civil authorities for punishment, *"degradati, saeculari potestati tradantur secundum constitutiones legitimas puniendi."*

Thus, the decree distinguished two separate penalties in deposition and degradation. However, this fact was not immediately realized. Indeed, this constitution, especially in regard to the provision for delivering the cleric to the secular court, must have occasioned doubt and wonder, not to mention controversies, for in 1209 Innocent considered it expedient to render an authoritative exposition of the true intent and meaning of the term *"curiae tradere"* as contained in the ancient canons as well as in his own decree issued against forgers. In explaining this term he referred to the divergent interpretations given to it by his predecessors and then legalized the

---

[15] Cf. Devoti, *Institutiones*, I, tit. IV, § 21, n. 2.

[16] C. 7, X, *de crimine falsi*, V, 20· "clerici qui falsarii fuerint deprehensi, omnibus officiis et beneficiis ecclesiasticis perpetuo sint privati, ita, quod, qui per se falsitatis vitium exercuerint, postquam per ecclesiasticum iudicem fuerint degradati, *saeculari potestati* tradantur secundum constitutiones legitimas *puniendi*, per quam et laici, qui fuerint de falsitate convicti, legitime puniantur."

opinion, approved by many, that a cleric degraded by the ecclesiastical court was thereby deprived of the clerical privileges and, in consequence, was subject to the secular court. Moreover, degradation was to be solemnly carried out with the secular power present. Upon completion of the process of degradation, the ecclesiastical judge had to direct the civil authorities to take over the degraded cleric. The Church, however, was to intercede for the one degraded, so that the civil sentence against him might be moderated to exclude the danger of death.[17]

Thus, says the learned Alteserra, Pope Innocent III adopted in law the error of many who interpreted the term *curiae tradere* as signifying delivery of the delinquent cleric to the secular court to receive the civil penalty for his crime.[18]

All these papal letters, however, which dealt with the distinction between deposition and degradation, were included by Pope Gregory IX in his official collection which enjoyed the force of universal law.[19] From these laws and the later ones in regard to degradation as issued by Pope`Boniface VIII canonists assembled the pertinent legislation of the Church and clarified its meaning with reference to the two distinct penalties instituted by the Church, namely, deposition and degradation. In order to describe this further development properly it will be necessary to consider the two penalties individually.

---

[17] C. 27, X, *de verborum significatione,* V, 40: "Novimus expedire, ut verbum illud, quod (et) in antiquis canonibus, et in nostro quoque decreto contra falsarios edito continetur, videlicet ut clericus, per ecclesiasticum iudicem degradatus, saeculari tradatur curiae puniendus, apertius exponamus. Quum enim quidam antecessorum nostrorum, super hoc consulti, diversa responderint, et quorumdam sit opinio a pluribus approbata, ut clericus, qui propter hoc vel aliud flagitium grave, non solum damnabile, sed damnosum, fuerit degradatus, tamquam exutus privilegio clericali saeculari foro fuerit proiectus; *eius est degradatio celebranda saeculari potestate praesente, ac pronunciandum est eidem, quum fuerit celebrata, ut in suum forum recipiat degradatum, et sic intelligitur tradi curiae saeculari;* pro quo tamen debet ecclesia efficaciter intercedere, ut citra mortis periculum circa eum sententia moderetur."

[18] *Commentarius perpetuus in singulas decretales Innocentii III,* cura et sumptibus Michaelis Marotta (ed. prima Neapolitana, 1780), lib. V, tit. XL, cap. 27.

[19] Cf. Cicognani, *Canon Law,* p. 303.

ARTICLE 2. DEPOSITION

During this period, with the clarification of canonical institutions in general and the definite establishment of the penalties of suspension [20] and degradation in particular, the position and scope of deposition in the penal law of the Church became greatly clarified.

There was no essential change, however, in the penalty itself. The law of the period as well as the expositions of it by canonists indicated that deposition retained its historical character of a vindictive penalty which perpetually deprived the delinquent cleric of his power of orders and jurisdiction, his offices, honors and benefices, leaving him only a vestige of his former state by allowing him to retain certain clerical privileges. Thus the penalty is succinctly described as a removal from clerical dignities, honors, orders, offices, and benefices.[21] It was a perpetual penalty excluding all hope of restoration.[22] The penalty bespoke an irrevocable loss to the deposed cleric of his holy orders and ecclesiastical benefices.[23]

Deposition involved a perpetual suspension from orders.[24] When a cleric was deposed he was not, nor could he be, deprived of the sacred orders which he had received in ordination, for these were inherent in the indelible character impressed on his soul by the sacrament of orders. Hence, an act of orders performed by a deposed cleric as long as it did not involve jurisdiction, as, for example, sacramental absolution, was valid.[25] However, the Church, as already noted, could forever forbid a cleric to exercise his power of orders. Such a prohibition was contained in deposition. The deposed cleric could no longer continue to exercise lawfully his power of orders. If a deposed bishop, priest or deacon presumed to violate this prohibition and exercised the ministry he formerly enjoyed, he incurred an irregularity.[26] Moreover, contempt for this prohibition exposed the

---

[20] Cf. Rainer, *Suspension of Clerics,* p. 17 ff.

[21] C. 1, *de homicidio,* V, 4, in VI°.

[22] C. 8, X, *de dolo et contumacia,* II, 14.

[23] Cf. c. 2, X, *de raptoribus, incendiariis et violatoribus ecclesiarum,* V, 17: "ordinis sui damnum irrecuperabiliter patiantur et ecclesiastico beneficio careant."

[24] Fagnanus, *Commentaria,* lib. II, tit. 1, cap. 10, n. 23.

[25] Cf. Gonzalez-Tellez, *Commentaria,* lib. V, tit. 27, cap. 2, nn. 7, 8.

[26] ". . . suspensione durante damnabiliter ingesserit se divinis, irregularitas

deposed cleric to excommunication. Decretal legislation provided that if any bishop, priest or deacon, justly deposed for established crimes, dared to fulfill the ministry formerly committed to him he was to be completely separated from the Church.[27]

Thus it is evident that deposition deprived the cleric of the lawful use of his powers of orders. It also deprived him of his office and jurisdiction. The powers of jurisdiction, however, he lost completely, for these, unlike the powers of orders, depended exclusively on the will of the legislative authority in the Church. All the acts of jurisdiction which he ventured to accomplish after deposition were null and void.[28] While suspension deprived a cleric of his use of jurisdiction, deposition went further and deprived him of the jurisdiction itself as well as of the office he enjoyed in the Church.[29]

Deposition also brought with it the loss of benefice. The one who had the right to confer the benefice was then free to bestow it on another.[30] Deposition deprived the cleric of the exercise of his orders, of his office and in consequence also of his benefice, for the law then obtained that a benefice was conferred because of the office, *"beneficium datur propter officium."* [31] Moreover, as deposition was by its nature perpetual the deposed cleric was disqualified for obtaining any benefice in the Church.[32] Thus the penalty of privation dif-

---

laqueo se involvit secundum canonicas sanctiones . . . "—C. 1, *de sententia et re iudicata,* II, 14, in VI°.

[27] Cc. 1, 2, X, *de clerico excommunicato, deposito vel interdicto ministrante,* V, 27.

[28] "Cum sententia statim arctet etiam ignorantem si contra praelatum aliquem absentem depositionis sententia proferetur, contractus, quos iniit ignoranter postea ut praelatus, nullum robur obtinent firmitatis . . ."—C. 1, *de concessione praebendae et ecclesiae non vacantis,* III, 7, in VI°.

[29] Cf. Gonzalez-Tellez, *Commentaria,* lib. V, tit. 27, cap. 1, n. 7.

[30] C. 15, X, *de excessibus praelatorum et subditorum,* V, 31: ". . . ipsum tamquam membrum putridum, ne sua contaminat alios corruptela, ab . . . ecclesia perpetuo abscindatis et removeatis omnino beneficia sua facientes personis idoneis per illos, ad quos donatio eorum pertinet, assignari." Cf. also c. 1, *de homicidio,* V, 4, in VI°.

[31] C. 15, *de rescriptis,* I, 3, in VI°.

[32] Cf. Reiffenstuel, *Ius Canonicum Universum* (Romae, 1833), lib. V, tit. 37, n. 26.

fered from the penalty of deposition. While the two agreed in this that they deprived the cleric of his benefice, privation took away only the benefice, but it did not, as deposition, disqualify him from obtaining another benefice.[83]

So also the penalty of deposition differed from a suspension from benefice. Both indeed removed a cleric from his benefice, but deposition represented a perpetual removal whereas suspension, as a medicinal penalty, meant only a temporary removal. The suspended cleric upon contrition and absolution could regain his benefice. Even if suspension was inflicted as a vindictive penalty, it did not deprive the cleric of his office and benefice, as was the case with deposition, but it only deprived him of the fruits of the benefice, the administration of his office and the use of jurisdiction.[34]

Although excommunication could follow upon deposition in the event of subsequently committed crimes, as was noted above, yet excommunication was not inherent in the penalty of deposition. Although a deposed cleric lost the rights and honors of the clerical state, he still continued to participate in the life of the Church even as a cleric, for the vestiges of his former state were not all effaced. He was still granted the clerical privileges, especially the privileges of the *forum* and the *canon*.[85] Whereas in the earlier practice of the Church deposition brought with it a reduction of the delinquent cleric to the lay state, after the twelfth century this effect was attached exclusively to the now distinct penalty of degradation.

[83] Cf. Reiffenstuel, *Ius Canonicum Universum*, lib. V, tit. 37, n. 27; Schmalzgrueber, *Ius Ecclesiasticum Universum* (Romae, 1845), lib. V, tit. 37, n. 133.

[84] Schmalzgrueber, *Ius Ecclesiasticum*, lib. V, tit. 37, n. 134. Cf. Gonzalez-Tellez, *Commentaria*, lib. V, tit. 27, cap. 2, n. 7.

[85] The privilege of the canon is that of personal inviolability, guaranteed for clerics and religious alike by the famous decree: "Si quis suadente diabolo huius sacrilegii vitium incurrerit, quod in clericum vel monachum violentas manus iniecerit, anathematis vinculo subiaceat, et nullus episcoporum illum praesumat absolvere, nisi mortis urgente periculo, donec apostolico conspectui praesententur, et eius mandatum suscipiat."—C. 29, C. XVII, q. 4. Cf. II General Council of the Lateran (1139), c. 15—Mansi, XXI, 530; Schroeder, *Disciplinary Decrees*, p. 204. In its substantial import this canon may already be recognized in the Council of Rheims (1131), c. 13—Mansi, XXI, 461.

The decretal letter of Pope Celestine III, already quoted, reflects these facts.[36]   In this letter, as Fagnanus observes, the Pope set forth a fourfold gradation of penalties.[37]   First: If it was proved that a cleric had committed a crime liable to deposition he was to be deposed.   Secondly: If he was contumacious and continued in his crimes he was to be excommunicated.   Should he, however, have corrected himself, observed his sentence and fulfilled his penance he received no further penalties.   Thirdly: Were he still obdurate he was to be anathematized.[38]   Fourthly and finally: Should all the former penalties be of no avail in curbing the delinquent, then, because of the actual harm to others caused by his crimes and bad example, he was to be abandoned by the ecclesiastical court to the secular power.[39]

Thus it is evident that even a deposed cleric did not become subject to the civil courts as were ordinary laymen.   With deposition the cleric still retained the *privilegium fori* of clerics.   The letter of Pope Alexander III in the *Corpus Iuris Canonici* clearly states this when it forbids deposed clerics to be judged by secular courts.[40]   The decretal of Pope Innocent III, which, as already noted, distinguished between deposition and degradation, deprived degraded clerics of the *privilegium fori*, but did not take it from those who were deposed.[41]   Very often the canons prescribed seclusion in a monastery after deposition, as in the case of priests deposed for revealing a sacramental confession.[42]   This provision clearly indicates that the deposed cleric remained exclusively subject to ecclesiastical tribunals.[43]

As always, deposition, though it was by its nature a perpetual

---

[36] C. 10, X, *de iudiciis*, II, 1.   Cf. *supra,* pp. 69-70.

[37] *Commentaria,* lib. II, tit. 1, cap. 10, n. 34.

[38] An *anathema* was a solemn excommunication with all the prescribed rites and ceremonies. Cf. Fagnanus, *Commentaria,* lib. II, tit. 1, cap. 10, n. 23; Hyland, *Excommunication,* p. 24; Canon 2257, § 2.

[39] Cf. Fagnanus, *Commentaria,* lib. II, tit. 1, cap. 10, n. 34.

[40] C. 4, X, *de iudiciis,* II, 1.

[41] C. 7, X, *de crimine falsi,* V, 20.

[42] C. 12, X, *de poenitentia et remissionibus,* V, 38.

[43] Cf. Benedictus XIV, *De synodo dioecesana,* lib. IX, cap. 6, n. 3.

penalty, depended for its later possible remission as well as for its continued application on the authority which established it. Hence, when circumstances warranted it a dispensation from this penalty could be obtained. In all cases the Roman Pontiff could grant this dispensation and he alone could do so when the deposition was reserved to him. The law of this period, moreover, allowed bishops to dispense clerics whom they had deposed for adultery or lesser crimes.[44] Since infamy followed deposition [45] and could be directly removed only by the Roman Pontiff,[46] canonists commonly taught that a bishop could dispense a deposed cleric and restore him to his former dignity only when the law expressly authorized him to do so.[47] Equity, of course, demanded that bishops restore those whom they had unjustly deposed, but such a restitution cannot properly be termed a dispensation.

ARTICLE 3. PARTIAL DEPOSITION

Along with the penalty of complete deposition there also existed during this period, as in earlier legislation, partial depositions. Like deposition, this penalty also received clarification in the *Corpus Iuris Canonici.* The earlier rule of the Church, namely, to ordain a cleric only in view of a determined office changed with the enactment which permitted absolute ordinations.[48] At the same time the distinction between the powers of orders and the powers of jurisdiction was given clearer recognition.[49] These principles were basic in the

---

[44] C. 4, X, *de iudiciis,* II, 1. Cf. also c. 4, X, *de clericis coniugatis,* III, 3; c. 1, X, *qui clerici vel voventes matrimonium contrahere possunt,* IV, 6.

[45] C. 17, C. VI, q. 1.

[46] C. 23, X, *de sententia et re iudicata,* II, 27.

[47] Cf. Gonzalez-Tellez, *Commentaria,* lib. II, tit. 1, cap. 4, § 2, n. 2; Reiffenstuel, *Ius Canonicum Universum,* lib. V, tit. 37, nn. 28, 29; Schmalzgrueber, *Ius Ecclesiasticum Universum,* lib. V, tit. 37, n. 137.

[48] C. 16, X, *de praebendis et dignitatibus,* III, 5: "Licet autem praedecessores nostri ordinationes eorum, qui sine certo titulo promoventur, in iniuriam ordinantium irritas esse voluerint et inanes, nos tamen benignius agere cupientes, tam diu per ordinatores vel successores eorum provideri volumus ordinatis, donec per eos ecclesiastica beneficia consequantur . . ."

[49] Cf. C. 15, X, *de electione et electi potestate,* I, 6; c. 9, X, *de consecratione ecclesiae vel altaris,* III, 40.

qualifications which at times modified deposition and by way of
consequence constituted in the law a partial deposition. One finds
a deposition *"ab altaris ministerio,"* [50] *"ab officio sacerdotali,"* [51]
"ab officio ecclesiastico," [52] *"a beneficio."* [53]

These qualifications of deposition were interpreted by canonists
as constituting only a partial deposition in virtue of the principle
"odia restringi et favores convenit ampliari." [54] When there was no
qualification added to a penalty of deposition, it was understood to
mean complete deposition. When the penalty was expressed in reference to certain rights or offices, the deposition was interpreted to
include only those which were expressly stated. Thus, a law which
provided for a deposition from benefice did not include a deposition
from orders and office.[55] The converse, however, was not true. If
the law pointed to merely a deposition from office it simultaneously
involved a deposition from benefices, for, as has been noted previously, the benefice was conferred because of the office. With perpetual loss of office, the right to a benefice was forever lost.[56]

With the development of decretal legislation on suspension and
privation, the use of partial deposition began to wane. Wernz testifies that according to the discipline prevailing in the nineteenth century the division of deposition into total and partial was no longer
of much importance.[57] Partial deposition had served its rôle in the
evolution of ecclesiastical penalties. The Code of Canon Law, in
1918, continued to provide for the possibility of partial suspensions,
but made no mention of a partial deposition.[58]

[50] C. 4, X, *de iudiciis*, II, 1.

[51] C. 4, X, *de clerico excommunicato, deposito vel interdicto ministrante*,
V, 27; c. 12, X, *de poenitentiis et remissionibus*, V, 38.

[52] C. 8, X, *de vita et honestate clericorum*, III, 1.

[53] C. 6, X, *de clerico excommunicato, deposito vel interdicto ministrante*,
V, 27; c. 13, X, *de simonia, et ne aliquid pro spiritualibus exigatur vel promittatur*, V, 3.

[54] Reg. 15, R. J., in VI°.

[55] Cf. Reiffenstuel, *Ius Canonicum Universum*, lib. V, tit. 37, n. 24.

[56] Cf. Reiffenstuel, *loc cit.*, n. 26.

[57] *Ius Decretalium*, VI, n. 120, not. 163.

[58] Cf. Canon 2278 ff. and canon 2303.

ARTICLE 4. INFLICTION OF THE PENALTY

A. The Deposition of Bishops

The discipline which prevailed after the ninth century, whereby criminal causes of bishops were reserved exclusively to the Holy See, continued in the laws of this period. The right of passing a definitive sentence of deposition against a bishop pertained solely to the Roman Pontiff. The universal legislation of this period stated that whereas bishops are consecrated by their metropolitans, nevertheless, in charges leading to deposition or degradation they are judged only by the Roman Pontiff.[59]

Pope Innocent III restated this law when he required the authority of the Holy See for breaking the spiritual bond which united a bishop with his church. Whether this dissolution was effected by transfer, deposition or resignation remained immaterial, for all three procedures were reserved to the Holy See and indeed not only by canonical legislation but also by divine institution.[60] In a letter to the Patriarch of Antioch, Pope Innocent III explained more precisely what he meant by the divine institution of this reservation. He stated that this originated in the divinely instituted power of the keys which his predecessors employed in enumerating the deposition of bishops among the major causes properly reserved to the jurisdiction of the Holy See.[61]

Thus, throughout the Middle Ages no bishop could be deposed and, *a fortiori*, no bishop could be degraded except by the Holy See.

---

[59] Cf. c. 2, X, *de translatione episcopi*, I, 7: "Episcopi quoque a metropolitanis suis munus consecrationis accipiunt, qui tamen non possunt nisi per Romanum Pontificem condemnari."

[60] C. 2, X, *de translatione episcopi*, I, 7: ". . . non tam constitutione canonica, quam institutione divina soli sunt Romano Pontifici reservata."

[61] *Regestorum Lib. I, ep. L:* "Cum ex illo generali principio, quod beato Petro et per eum Ecclesiae Romanae Dominus noster indulsit, canonica postmodum manaverint institua continentia maiores causas esse ad sedem apostolicam perferendas, ac per hoc translationes episcoporum sicut depositiones eorum et sedium mutationes ad summum apostolicae sedis antistitem de iure pertineant, nec super his praeter eius assensum aliquid debeat attentari."—*MPL*, CCXIV, 45. Cf. also *Lib. I, ep. XVI, Capitulo S. Anastasiae—MPL,* CCXIV, 14; Barbosa, *De Officio et Potestate Episcopi,* pars. III, alleg. CXII, n. 8. Cf. *supra,* p. 57, n. 89.

B. *The Deposition of Priests, Deacons and Inferior Clerics*

The traditionally recognized right of the bishop to depose the clerics of his diocese if they had committed crimes warranting this penalty was restated in the laws of this period.[62] However, it seems that the prescriptions of the earlier laws which required a bishop to be assisted by six other bishops in the deposition of a priest, and by at least three others in the deposition of a deacon [63] were no longer observed. Rather, they were interpreted now as applying to the requirements for the infliction of the penalty of degradation.[64] Apart from the requirements of the natural law, positive legislation demanded only that the bishop consult his chapter in applying such penalties as deposition.[65]

Durantis (+ 1296) testifies to the practice of this period. According to this authority the bishop alone could depose clerics in minor orders. With his chapter, but without the presence of other bishops, he could hear the causes of clerics in major orders and proceed when it was warranted to the sentence of deposition.[66] However, there also existed a custom whereby bishops proceeded to depose their clerics *"per se vel per officiales suos,"* even without the participation of the chapter. This custom was generally recognized as having the force of law.[67] Later Pope Boniface VIII (1294-1303)

---

[62] C. 2, X, *de translatione episcopi*, I, 7: ". . . [episcopus] tam cleri quam populi sibi commissi, studeat gubernare, ut praeveniente divina gratia et sequente plus prodesse velit et valeat, quam praeesse." C. 12, X, *de haereticis*, V, 7: "Quodsi forte necessitas postularet, ut sacerdos tamquam inutilis et indignus a cura gregis debeat removeri: agendum est ordinate apud episcopum ad cuius officium *tam institutio quam destitutio* sacerdotum noscitur pertinere." C. 1, X, *de capellis monachorum et aliorum religiosorum*, III, 36: "Capellanus . . . ex solius episcopi arbitrio tam ordinatio eius quam depositio, et totius vitae pendeat conversatio." Cf. also c. 7, *de officio Ordinarii*, I, 16, in VI°.

[63] Cf. cc. 1, 7, C. XV, q. 7; c. 65, C. V, q. 3.

[64] C. 1, *de hereticis*, V, 2, in VI°; c. 2, *de poenis*, V, 9, in VI°. Cf. *Speculum Iuris Gulielmi Durandi cum Ioanne Andreae, Baldi de Ubaldis aliorumque aliquot praestantissimorum Iurisconsultorum Theorematibus* (Venetiis, 1577), lib. III, partic. I, *de accusatione*, n. 4.

[65] C. 1, X, *de excessibus praelatorum et subditorum*, V, 31.

[66] *Speculum Iuris*, lib. III, partic. I, *de accusatione*, n. 4.

[67] *Speculum Iuris*, lib. III, partic. I, *de accusatione*, n. 4.

ratified the custom whereby a bishop was exempted from requiring the counsel of the chapter in taking action against the excesses of his clerics.[68]

ARTICLE 5. CRIMES WARRANTING DEPOSITION

Since the distinction between deposition and degradation originated in the legislation of this period, it will be helpful in clarifying the law on these two penalties to mention some of the crimes for which a cleric could then be deposed according to the provisions of the common law. In a subsequent section the crimes warranting degradation will be considered.

Deposition is stated as the penalty for clerics who committed homicide, theft, or perjury,[69] who forged the royal seal or falsified papal documents,[70] who committed simony,[71] incest [72] or sodomy.[73] Clerics who lived in concubinage were to be suspended upon their failure to comply with the administered warnings. If they still continued to live in this state they were to be deposed.[74]

A bishop who was negligent in expelling heresy from his diocese was liable to deposition.[75] The same penalty was incurred for violation of the seal of sacramental confession.[76] Absolution and burial of an impenitent sacrilegious thief warranted deposition.[77]

Clerics were subject to deposition if they received lay investiture

---

[68] C. 3, *de consuetudine*, III, 4 in VI°: "Non est, dum tamen alias sit praescripta canonice, consuetudo, quam allegat episcopus, reprobanda, quod in inquirendis, puniendis et corrigendis subditorum excessibus consilium sui capituli requirere minime teneatur."

[69] C. 10, X, *de iudiciis*, II, 1; c. 6, X, *de poenis*, V, 37; c. 7, X, *de homicidio voluntario vel casuali*, V, 12.

[70] Cc., 3, 7, X, *de crimine falsi*, V, 20.

[71] C. 11, X, *de simonia, et ne aliquid pro spiritualibus exigatur vel promittatur*, V, 3.

[72] C. 15, X, *de purgatione canonica*, V, 34.

[73] C. 4, X, *de excessibus praelatorum et subditorum*, V, 31.

[74] Cc. 4, 6, X, *de cohabitatione clericorum et mulierum*, III, 2.

[75] C. 13, X, *de hereticis*, V, 7.

[76] IV Council of the Lateran (1215), c. 21—Schroeder, *Disciplinary Decrees*, p. 260; c. 12, X, *de poenitentiis et remissionibus*, V, 38.

[77] C. 2, X, *de raptoribus, incendiariis et violatoribus ecclesiarum*, V, 17.

without episcopal authorization,[78] gave sureties or bailments,[79] or took an active part in military service.[80] Clerics who fought a duel—it mattered not whether they offered or accepted the duel— were to be deposed. However, the law authorized the bishop to dispense with this penalty if loss of limb or homicide did not result from the duel.[81] A cleric who habitually committed acts of physical violence and did not amend upon correction was subject to deposition.[82] A cleric who participated with others in the passing of a death sentence was likewise to be deposed.[83] One who repeatedly refused obedience to his bishop could be punished with deposition.[84] Clerics under interdict or excommunication who, even after correction, continued to celebrate divine offices were to be deposed.[85] So also a cleric who, even though he was suspended for his incontinent life, presumed to celebrate the sacred mysteries was to be deposed.[86] There was also a law which singled out deposition as the penalty for a cleric who repeatedly and without good reason continued, even after a prohibition from his bishop, to visit the cloisters of nuns.[87]

As a general rule these penalties were incurred only when a condemnatory sentence had been delivered by a competent tribunal. However, a law passed by Pope Innocent IV (1243-1254) and published by the First General Council of Lyons (1245) offered an exception to this rule. The decree concerned the employment or hiring of assassins for the murder of one's enemies: "With horrible cruelty and inhuman savagery some men so thirst for the death of others that they cause them to be slain by assassins and thus bring about the death not only of the body but also of the soul, unless they

[78] Cc. 4, 21, X, *de iure patronatus*, III, 38.
[79] C. 1, X, *de fideiussoribus*, III, 22.
[80] C. 5, X, *de poenis*, V, 37.
[81] C. 1, X, *de clericis pugnantibus in duello*, V, 14.
[82] C. 1, X, *de clerico percussore*, V, 25.
[83] C. 5, X, *ne clerici vel monachi saecularibus negotiis se immisceant*, III, 50.
[84] C. 15, X, *de excessibus praelatorum et subditorum*, V, 31.
[85] C. 3, X, *de clerico excommunicato, deposito vel interdicto ministrante*, V, 27.
[86] C. 13, X, *de vita et honestate clericorum*, III, 1.
[87] C. 8, X, *de vita et honestate clericorum*, III, 1.

happen to be fortified with divine grace. Therefore, wishing to avert such danger to souls and to chastise such execrable presumptions with the sword of ecclesiastical censure, so that the fear of punishment may put an end to such conduct . . . with the approval of the holy council we decree that any prince or prelate, or for that matter any ecclesiastical or secular person, who shall cause or command any Christian to be slain by the aforesaid assassins, though death may perchance not follow the attack, as well as anyone who shall receive, defend or conceal them, incurs *ipso facto* the sentence of excommunication and *deposition* from dignity, honor, order, office, and benefice, which may then be freely conferred on others by those to whom such collation pertains." [88]

In regard to the *latae sententiae* deposition it was the common opinion of canonists that even this penalty was not incurred without the declaratory sentence of a competent tribunal to establish the deed as fully committed in contravention of the law.[89] The principle was generally admitted in law that a person was not bound to apply to himself the rigor of the law, that is, to be himself the accuser, and, as it were, the judge and executor of such a grave sentence against himself.[90]

The law passed by Pope Boniface VIII (1294-1303) against heretics illustrates this fact. The property of heretics was *ipso iure* confiscated, but the state could not seize it before judgment on the crime had been passed by a competent ecclesiastical tribunal.[91] Thus, canonists made the same requirement apply to the great losses

[88] C. 17—Schroeder, *Disciplinary Decrees*, p. 312; c. 1, X, *de homicidio*, V, 4, in VI°: ". . . excommunicationis et depositionis a dignitate, honore, ordine, officio, et beneficio incurrat sententias ipso facto, et illas libere aliis per illos, ad quos eorum collatio pertinet, conferantur."

[89] Cf. Barbosa, *Collectanea Doctorum tam Veterum quam Recentiorum in Ius Pontificium Universum* (Lugduni, 1656), lib. V, tit. IV, c. 1, n. 22; Pirhing, *Ius Canonicum in Quinque Libros Decretalium Distributum Nova Methodo Explicatum* (Dilingae, 1674), lib. I, tit. IX, sec. 3, n. 26 sq.; Reiffenstuel, *Ius Canonicum Universum*, lib. I, tit. IX, n. 52.

[90] Cf. Reiffenstuel, *Ius Canonicum Universum*, lib. I, tit. II, n. 227.

[91] C. 19, *de haereticis*, V, 2, in VI°: ". . . confiscationis tamen huiusmodi exsecutio vel bonorum ipsorum occupatio fieri non debet . . . antequam per episcopum loci, vel aliam personam ecclesiasticam, quae super hoc habeat potestatem, sententia super eodem crimine fuerit promulgata."

involved in deposition. They stated that a *latae sententiae* penalty of deposition was effective only after a declaratory sentence. The very law passed against the hiring of assassins stated that "should it in the future *be established* that anyone has committed so execrable a crime, no new declaration of excommunication or deposition is required." [92]

ARTICLE 6. DEGRADATION

"Though ecclesiastical discipline contents itself with spiritual judgment and does not inflict bloody punishments, it is, however, aided by the ordinances of Catholic princes, for men often seek a salutary remedy for their souls only when they fear that some severe corporal punishment will be imposed upon them." [93]

These thoughts, expressed by the Fathers of the III General Lateran Council (1179), undoubtedly reflect the desire for the salvation of souls which motivated Pope Lucius III in 1184 to decree, in an avowed effort to abolish the depravities of heresy, that clerics who were found guilty of this crime should be deprived of their prerogatives of orders, ecclesiastical offices and benefices, and be abandoned to the judgment of the secular power to be punished with due penalties unless they abjured their errors.[94]

Pope Celestine III (1191-1198) took similar action against deposed clerics who, while they were shielded by the clerical privileges from the secular court and its punishments,[95] failed to respond to ecclesiastical censures and penalties. The Pontiff decreed that such incorrigible clerics, after being deprived of their clerical privileges, should be restrained by the legitimate and salutary remedies of the secular power.[96]

In 1202 Pope Innocent III, as has been noted previously, de-

---

[92] C. 1, X, *de homicidio*, V, 4, in VI°; cf. also c. 5, *de poenis*, V, 9, in VI°.

[93] This text offers the introductory sentence to canon 27 of the III General Lateran Council (1179)—Schroeder, *Disciplinary Decrees*, p. 234; in c. 8, X, *de hereticis*, V, 7.

[94] C. 9, X, *de hereticis*, V, 7.

[95] Cc. 4, 8, 17, X, *de iudiciis*, II, 1; cc. 2, 12, X, *de foro competenti*, II, 2.

[96] C. 10, X, *de iudiciis*, II, 1; cf. Kober, *Die Deposition und Degradation*, p. 147; Wernz, *Ius Decretalium*, VI, n. 149.

veloped and clarified this penal measure. In order to crush the malicious continuance of forgery Innocent III expressly ordained that clerics who forged papal letters were to be degraded and delivered to the secular courts for punishment.[97] Thence arose the penalty of degradation as distinct from the ancient penalty of deposition.[98] Pope Innocent III gave to this special penalty the proper name of degradation,[99] which he defined as *depriving the cleric of all his privileges and rendering him subject to the secular court* in the presence of whose representative the ceremony of degradation was to proceed and to whom at its completion the degraded cleric was to be committed with the urgent entreaty that death be not inflicted on him.[100]

Degradation, then, involved the penalty of deposition but proceeded further, depriving the cleric of all clerical privileges and subjecting him to the penalties of the secular court.[101] Thus in the IV General Lateran Council, celebrated under Pope Innocent III in 1215, the essential elements of this penalty were expressed when it was enacted as the punishment for the crime of heresy: "Clerics convicted of this crime, having been degraded from their orders are to be committed to the secular power or its bailiffs who are present, to be punished with due justice."[102]

The character of this penalty is further revealed in an analysis of the procedure which accompanied it. This shows that there existed a twofold penalty of degradation, one called verbal, the other actual. A consideration of this distinction follows.

[97] C. 7, X, *de crimine falsi*, V, 20.

[98] Cf. Wernz, *Ius Decretalium*, VI, n. 119; Devoti, *Institutiones*, lib. I, tit. IV, 19; Fagnanus, *Commentaria*, lib. V, tit. 20, cap. 7, n. 40; Lega, *De Delictis et Poenis*, n. 208.

[99] C. 27, X, *de verborum significatione*, V, 40; cf. Chelodi, *Ius Poenale*, n. 52.

[100] C. 27, X, *de verborum significatione*, V, 40. Wernz stated that the presence of the civil authorities was never required for the validity of degradation.—*Ius Decretalium*, VI, n. 134.

[101] Cf. Fagnanus, *Commentaria*, lib. II, tit. I, cap. 10, n. 16.

[102] C. 13—Schroeder, *Disciplinary Decrees*, p. 242; in the Decretals of Gregory IX: c. 13, X, *de hereticis*, V, 7: "Damnati vero praesentibus saecularibus potestatibus aut eorum ballivis relinquantur animadversione debita puniendi, clericis prius a suis ordinibus degradatis."

Article 7. Infliction of the Penalty: Verbal and Real Degradation

Durantis, citing the decrees of Pope Innocent III,[103] testified that the assistance of other bishops was required when the *sentence* of degradation was to be pronounced. This was verbal degradation. The ancient canons requiring six bishops in the deposition of a priest, and three in the deposition of a deacon or subdeacon, were now applied as requirements for the sentence of degradation. Since bishops, however, could be condemned only by the Roman Pontiff, the delegates could only hear the case.[104]

These assisting bishops were not required, however, for the execution of the sentence of degradation, that is, for the solemn ceremony in which the bishop took from the cleric all the insignia which he received in his ordination. This was called solemn degradation and Durantis describes it in this way: The bishop in the presence of the secular judge to whom the one to be degraded was to be committed, publicly scraped those parts of the deposed cleric's head and hands which were anointed in his ordination; then he withdrew individually all the insignia which the cleric received in ordination, and finally divested him of the clerical habit and clothed him in lay garb directing the civil judge to receive the deposed and despoiled cleric into his courts.[105]

While the decrees of Pope Innocent III definitely established the penalty of degradation and eliminated any question as to its character,[106] the legal procedure to be followed still caused some doubts even in the time of Pope Boniface VIII (1294-1303). The Bishop of Beziers accordingly asked Pope Boniface to explain how this penalty was to be inflicted. In replying to this query Pope Boniface VIII distinguished between verbal degradation and actual or solemn degradation. *Verbal degradation*, the pronouncement of judicial sentence, in the case of a cleric in major orders was per-

---

[103] C. 7, X, *de crimine falsi*, V, 20; c. 27, X, *de verborum significatione*, V, 40.

[104] *Speculum Iuris*, lib. III, partic. 1, *de accusatione*, § 2, n. 4.

[105] *Ibidem.*

[106] C. 7, X, *de crimine falsi*, V, 20; c. 27, X, *de verborum significatione*, V, 40.

formed by the ordinary assisted by the number of bishops required by the canons. In the case of clerics who had received only minor orders the sentence of the bishop alone was sufficient.[107] *Actual* or *solemn degradation* was the ceremonial stripping of all clerical insignia. By this act the cleric was deprived of his membership in the clergy, his clerical rank and his clerical privileges.[108]

While the penalty of deposition in earlier times was often accompanied by a ceremony wherein the ignominy of this penalty was visibly expressed,[109] it was, nevertheless, juridically completed merely with the pronouncing of sentence, or as Durantis expressed it, *"deponitur quis solo verbo."* [110] In real degradation, however, the solemn ceremony had now become an essential element.[111] It was to proceed like the degradation of a soldier in the army for, as Pope Boniface VIII stated, the cleric was a member of the heavenly militia.[112] This idea was traditional in the Church. The figure was employed already by St. Paul, who encouraged Timothy, Bishop of Ephesus, to "labor as a good soldier of Jesus Christ." [113]

---

[107] C. 2, *de poenis*, V, 9, in VI°: "Degradatio qualiter fieri debeat, a nobis tua fraternitas requisivit. Super quo tibi taliter respondemus, quod verbalis degradatio seu depositio ab ordinibus vel gradibus ecclesiasticis est a proprio episcopo, sibi assistente in degradatione clericorum in sacris constitutorum ordinibus certo episcoporum numero definito canonibus, facienda, quamquam proprii episcopi sententia sine aliorum episcoporum praesentia sufficiat in degradatione eorum, qui minores dumtaxat ordines receperunt."

[108] C. 2, *de poenis*, V, 9, in VI°: "Actualis vero sive sollemnis coelestis militiae militis, id est clerici, degradatio, quum ad eam fuerit procedendum, fiet ut exauctorizatio eius, qui militiae deservit armatae, cui militaria detrahuntur insignia, sicque a militia remotus castris reiicitur, privatus consortio et privilegio militari."

[109] Cf. Martène, *De Antiquis Ecclesiae Ritibus*, lib. III, cap. 2.

[110] *Speculum Iuris*, lib. III, partic. I, *de accusatione*, § 2, n. 4.

[111] C. 27, X, *de verborum significatione*, V, 40; c. 2; *de poenis*, V, 9, in VI°.

[112] C. 2, *de poenis*, V, 9, in VI°; quoted above, note 108.

[113] II Tim., II: 3; cf. also I Cor., I: 9; II Cor., X: 3, 4. So also Pope Gelasius I (492-496) referred to clerics as constituting a "militia clericalis."—cf. *Ep. V, ad episcopos Lucaniae.*—Hardouin, II, 892, 898; Pope Felix III (526-530) spoke of the clergy as forming the "militia ecclesiastica."—cf. *Ep. IX, ad universos episcopos*, c. 5.—Hardouin, II, 834; Pope Gregory the Great (590-604) frequently employed the figure by designating clerics as the "milites

The military ceremony of degradation which Pope Boniface VIII established as the pattern for the rite of degradation of clerics had its origin in early Roman times. Justinian referred to it in his Digest when he treated of those who were marked with infamy: "Dishonorable discharge occurs whenever he who orders it adds expressly that it was done on account of disgraceful conduct. The cause for the soldier's dismissal should always be added. But when a man is *degraded,* that is to say, *deprived of his insignia of rank,* he becomes infamous, even though the words 'degraded on account of disgraceful conduct' were not added." [114]

Thus two traditional concepts were merged in the penalty of a real degradation: a cleric, a member of the celestial militia, because of certain crimes was to be cast forth from this army in a ceremony modelled upon the degradation of soldiers in the army of the state.

Pope Boniface VIII described this procedure more in detail. The cleric to be degraded, carrying a book, vessel, or other instrument symbolizing his order, and clothed in his sacred vestments as if he were about to celebrate the divine offices, was brought before the bishop who publicly took away from him each article with which he was endowed on the day of his ordination, beginning with the last and continuing to the first which he received in tonsure. Then his hair was shorn lest any vestige of clerical tonsure should remain. At each step in the ceremony the bishop, in order to inspire an effective fear, could pronounce a formula directly opposed to the one employed in ordination, as, for example, in taking away the chasuble from a priest: "We take from you the sacerdotal vestment and we deprive you of the honors of the priesthood." At the conclusion of this ceremony the bishop was to make the following pronouncement: *"Auctoritate Dei omnipotentis Patris et Filii et Spiritus Sancti ac nostra, tibi auferimus habitum clericalem et deponimus, degradamus, spoliamus et exuimus te omni ordine, beneficio et privilegio clericali."* [115]

Ecclesiae."—cf. *Ep. LX,* Epist. lib. I—*MPL,* LXXVII, 519; *Ep. VIII,* Epist. lib. II—*ibid.,* 545; *Ep. XXXI,* Epist. lib. III—*ibid.,* 628.

[114] D. (3, 2), 2, 2.

[115] C. 2, *de poenis,* V, 9, in VI°.

This lengthy response of Pope Boniface VIII clarified the earlier law and practice, described by Durantis,[116] following the decrees of Pope Celestine III [117] and of Pope Innocent III.[118] The pronouncing of the sentence of degradation was termed *non-solemn degradation* by Durantis. Pope Boniface VIII officially designated it as *verbal degradation.* The execution of this sentence, called *solemn deposition* or *degradation* by Durantis, Pope Boniface designated as *solemn* or *actual degradation.*[119]

While the bishop could proceed unassisted to the execution of the sentence in solemn or actual degradation, he could not pronounce the sentence of verbal degradation on a cleric in major orders unless he was assisted by other bishops as required by the canons.[120] This general law, however, had already been limited by Pope Gregory IX (1227-1241). Since the number of bishops required by the canons for the degradation of clerics could not be easily assembled, this Pontiff, in a rescript to the Archbishop of Rheims and his suffragans, permitted a more convenient procedure in the case of degradation for heresy of a priest or other cleric in major orders. In this case the rescript, later incorporated in the *Liber Sextus,* permitted a bishop to summon abbots, prelates, or learned and religious persons of his diocese in place of the bishops required by the canons.[121]

These assistants of the bishop who aided him in passing a sentence of degradation, whether they were themselves bishops or simply lawful substitutes, acted as true judges who enjoyed a decisive vote.[122]

[116] *Speculum Iuris,* lib. III, partic. I, *de accusatione,* § 2, n. 4.

[117] C. 10, X, *de iudiciis,* II, 1.

[118] C. 7, X, *de crimine falsi,* V, 20; c. 27, X, *de verborum significatione,* V, 40.

[119] Cf. *Speculum Iuris,* lib. III, partic. I, *de accusatione,* § 2, nn. 4, 5; c. 2, *de poenis,* V, 9, in VI°.

[120] C. 2, *de poenis,* V, 9, in VI°.

[121] C. 1, *de hereticis,* V, 2, in VI°.

[122] This was the common teaching of canonists based on c. 3, X, *de sententia et re iudicata,* II, 27; cf. Schmalzgrueber, *Ius Ecclesiasticum Universum,* lib. V, tit. 37, n. 145; Leurenius, *Ius Canonicum Universum* (Venetiis, 1729), lib. V, tit. 37, q. 528.

Like deposition, degradation was a vindictive penalty and by its nature was perpetual in duration. Only the pope could dispense a cleric who was justly and solemnly degraded. The bishop could dispense a cleric who was only verbally degraded and could restore him to his former dignity by simple decree. Restoration after solemn degradation, however, required a solemn ceremony.[123]

ARTICLE 8. CRIMES WARRANTING DEGRADATION

The severe nature of degradation was recognized by the Church from the first institution of this penalty. It was invoked only for a limited number of clerical excesses and these had to be of a very grave character to justify the application of this dire penalty.

The earliest use of the penalty in ecclesiastical legislation is found in the decree of Innocent III against the crime of falsification of apostolic letters.[124] Previous to this enactment, however, the Decree of Gratian contained three laws of Pseudo-Isidore which expressed a penal sanction, interpreted by many as degradation, against clerics who manifested grave contumely or insult towards their bishop or who plotted and conspired against him.[125] Authorities state that these decrees enjoyed the force of law throughout the period of the Decretals, evidently by custom, for the Decree as such never established a law.[126]

The most frequent use of the penalty of degradation in the legislation of the Church during this period was reflected in the laws

---

[123] Durantis, *Speculum Iuris,* lib. III, partic. I, *de accusatione,* § 2; cf. *Pontificale Romanum,* pars III, *Degradationis forma;* Schmalzgrueber, *op. cit.,* lib. V, tit. 37, n. 140, 150.

[124] C. 7, X, *de crimine falsi,* V, 20; c. 27, X, *de verborum significatione,* V, 40.

[125] Cc. 18, 31, C. XI, q. 1; c. 8, C. III, q. 4. The fabrication of these canons by Pseudo-Isidore and their subsequent connection with the development of the penalty of degradation has already been noted. Cf. *supra,* pp. 49, 68, 71-72.

[126] Cf. Barbosa, *Collectanea,* lib. V, tit. 9, in VI°, cap. 2, n. 6; Schmalzgrueber, *Ius Ecclesiasticum Universum,* lib. V, tit. 37, nn. 143, 157; Reiffenstuel, *Ius Canonicum Universum,* lib. V, tit. 37, n. 38; Fagnanus, *Commentaria,* lib. II, tit. 1, cap. 10, n. 7.

issued against heresy.[127] Degradation was also enacted in the law against schismatics.[128]

Finally, there was a broader field for this penalty in the enactment of Pope Celestine III (1191-1198), which sanctioned the penalty of degradation in the case of those clerics who, when they had been deposed because of theft, homicide, perjury or other grave crimes, failed to respond to further ecclesiastical censures and penalties and thereby proved themselves incorrigible.[129]

According to the law of this period, then, the penalty of degradation was expressly stated for certain specified crimes. For other grave crimes it was sanctioned only when the delinquent cleric proved himself incorrigible.[130]

---

[127] Cf. cc. 9, 13, 15, X, *de haereticis*, V, 7; cc. 1, 2, *de hereticis*, V, 2, in VI°; cf. Fagnanus, *Commentaria*, lib. II, tit. I, cap. 10, n. 69; Reiffenstuel, *op. cit.*, lib. V, tit. 37, n. 143.

[128] C. 26, X, *de verborum significatione*, V, 40; c. un., *de schismaticis*, V, 3, in VI°.

[129] C. 10, X, *de iudiciis*, II, 1.

[130] Cf. Schmalzgrueber, *Ius Ecclesiasticum Universum*, lib. V, tit. 37, n. 153; Benedictus XIV, *De synodo dioecesana*, lib. IX, cap. 6, n. 3.

CHAPTER IV

DEPOSITION AND DEGRADATION FROM THE COUNCIL OF TRENT TO THE CODE OF CANON LAW

ARTICLE 1. NATURE AND EFFECTS OF THE PENALTIES

IT has already been observed how the penalty of degradation, a severe development of the penalty of deposition, grew from the legislation of the Church which was designed on the one hand to eliminate the abuses of which certain and especially the deposed clerics were guilty relative to their clerical privileges, and on the other hand to apply to gravely delinquent or incorrigible clerics an effective remedy. At the same time there was involved, in particular applications of the penalty, a concession to the state to punish the former cleric.

The fathers of the Council of Trent (1545-1563), in order to put an end to the contemporary complaints about certain abuses in connection with the maintenance of the privileged forum, introduced a twofold reform.[1] They issued a decree whereby clerics in minor orders who abused the privileged forum were more easily than theretofore subjected to the lay courts: "No one after being initiated by the first tonsure, or even after being constituted in minor orders can obtain a benefice before his fourteenth year. Further, he shall not enjoy the privilege of the ecclesiastical court, *unless* he has an ecclesiastical benefice, or, wearing the ecclesiastical garb and tonsure, he serves in some church by the bishop's order, or lives with the bishop's permission in an ecclesiastical seminary or in some school or university on the way as it were to receive major orders."[2] Secondly, the council facilitated the verbal degradation of clerics in major orders by authorizing the substitution of other prelates for the bishops formerly required by the canons for this process.[3]

Properly considered, however, in neither case did the council ef-

---

[1] Cf. Wernz, *Ius Decretalium*, VI, n. 123.

[2] Sess. XXIII, *de ref.* c. 6.

[3] Sess. XIII, *de ref.* c. 4.

92

fect a change in the legal constitution of the penalties, or of their nature and effects, which are the aspects of the question considered in this section. The first decree only determined more precisely who were clerics in reference to the penalty of degradation, inasmuch as only clerics who enjoyed the privileged forum could be deprived of it through this penalty. The latter decree regulated the procedure governing the infliction of the penalty upon major clerics.

Thus it may be said with all authors on this subject that the constitutive elements of the penalties of deposition and degradation as contained in the law of the Decretals remained unchanged as to their essential determinants during this period from the Council of Trent to the Code. Changes which were introduced in regard to the crimes warranting these penalties as well as the reformation governing the procedure for their infliction will be treated under their proper titles in subsequent sections.

As previously noted, the only difference between the penalty of deposition and actual degradation consisted in this that deposition, while it deprived a delinquent cleric of the use of his orders and took away completely his offices, honors, dignities and benefices, left him with the clerical privileges. A deposed cleric remained nonetheless a cleric. Actual degradation included all the effects of deposition but went further by depriving the cleric of all his clerical rights and privileges, reducing him juridically to the status of a layman, and delivering him to the secular court for further punishment. After degradation the former cleric was juridically considered a layman.

The distinction made by Pope Boniface VIII [4] between verbal and real degradation did not receive a unanimous interpretation from the canonists of this period. The crux of the question is to be found in the explanations of verbal degradation and deposition. Some canonists [5] assimilated verbal degradation entirely to deposi-

---

[4] C. 2, *de poenis*, V, 9, in VI°.

[5] Cf. Ferraris, *Prompta Bibliotheca*, s.v. "*Degradatio*," n. 1; Fagnanus, *Commentaria*, lib. V, tit. 1, cap. 6, n. 76; Reiffenstuel, *Ius Canonicum Universum*, lib. V, tit. 37, nn. 22, 32; Gennari, *Sulla Privazione del beneficio ec-*

tion. Others, however, in following the early decretalists preserved a complete distinction between verbal degradation and deposition.[6]

According to this second doctrine, which has justly been termed the prevalent one,[7] verbal degradation consisted in the sentence in which the delinquent cleric was declared worthy of real degradation; real degradation was the execution of this sentence in the solemn ceremony already considered. Only *real* degradation deprived the delinquent of the clerical privileges.[8] Like deposition, verbal degradation did not take away the clerical privileges. The difference between deposition and verbal degradation consisted in this that verbal degradation was directly ordained as intermediate to real degradation: it was the sentence preceding the real degradation which it decreed. Deposition, on the other hand, was a penalty constituted in its own right as unrelated to real degradation. A deposed cleric could not be subjected to real degradation without a sentence of verbal degradation. One verbally degraded, however, could, without further legal action, be subjected to real degradation. Finally, verbal degradation could only be inflicted in a procedure distinct from that of deposition and only for crimes warranting real degradation.[9]

According to the common teaching of canonists, clerics in major orders who were punished with either deposition or degradation, whether verbal or real, were not liberated thereby from their clerical

clesiastico (2. ed., Romae, 1905), p. 58; Barbosa, *Collectanea*, lib. V, tit. IX, in VI°, cap. 2, n. 4.

[6] Schmalzgrueber, *Ius Ecclesiasticum Universum*, lib. V, tit. 37, n. 138; Benedictus XIV, *De synodo dioecesana*, lib. IX, cap. 6, n. 3; Leurenius, *Ius Canonicum Universum*, lib. V, tit. 37, q. 527; Kober, *Die Deposition und Degradation*, p. 184; Lega, *De Delictis et Poenis*, n. 207; Wernz, *Ius Decretalium*, VI, n. 127; Santi, *Praelectiones Iuris Canonici* (2. ed., Ratisbonae, 1892), V, 116; Aichner, *Compendium Iuris Ecclesiastici*, p. 748.

[7] Chelodi, *Ius Poenale*, n. 53.

[8] Cf. Benedictus XIV, ep. encycl., *Quam grave*, 2 Aug. 1757—*Fontes*, n. 443.

[9] Cf. Benedictus XIV, *loc cit.; Pontificale Rom.*, III, tit. *Degradationis forma;* Schmalzgrueber, *Ius Ecclesiasticum Universum*, lib. V, tit. 37, n. 138; Wernz, *Ius Decretalium*, VI, n. 127.

obligations.[10] They maintained that these penalties were not imposed to relieve obligations but to impose punishment and take away honors. Hence, the obligations remained "lest the one deposed or degraded obtain an advantage from his penalty." [11]

Moreover, in conformity with the traditional practice of the Church, canonists sanctioned a charitable aid to deposed clerics, if they were in need, to preserve at lease the dignity of the clerical state.[12]

Such was the discipline of the Church regarding the nature and effects of the penalties of deposition and degradation which prevailed until the appearance of the Code of Canon Law.

ARTICLE 2. INFLICTION OF THE PENALTY OF DEPOSITION

A. The Deposition of Bishops

The discipline inaugurated in the ninth century and thereafter maintained in the law of the Decretals, in virtue of which the deposition of bishops was reserved exclusively to the Roman Pontiff, received in the Council of Trent complete confirmation: "The graver criminal causes against bishops, even that of heresy (*quod absit*), which warrant deposition or deprivation shall be taken cognizance of and decided only by the sovereign Roman Pontiff himself." [13] The lesser criminal causes of bishops could be taken cognizance of and decided in the provincial council or by persons deputed thereunto by the provincial council.[14]

The law reserving exclusively to the Roman Pontiff the deposition or degradation of bishops, thus confirmed and renewed by the Council of Trent, was frequently restated thereafter in legal enact-

---

[10] Schmalzgrueber, *op cit.*, nn. 135, 164; Wernz, *Ius Decretalium*, VI, nn. 125, 138; Lega, *De Delictis et Poenis*, n. 207; Chelodi, *Ius Poenale*, n. 52.

[11] Arguing from the general principle "ne quis ex sua malitia commodum reportet"; cf. c. 7, X, *de iudiciis*, II, 1; c. 9, X, *de dolo et contumacia*, II, 14.

[12] Cf. Wernz, *Ius Decretalium*, VI, n. 125.

[13] Sess. XXIV, *de ref.*, c. 5: "Causae criminales graviores contra episcopos, etiam haeresis, quod absit, quae depositione aut privatione dignae sunt, ab ipso tantum summo Romano Pontifice cognoscantur et terminentur."

[14] Conc. Trident., sess. XXIV, *de ref.*, c. 5.

ments issuing from the Holy See.[15] Today the same law obtains in virtue of the provision of the Code of Canon Law which reserves exclusively to the Roman Pontiff the judgment of bishops in criminal causes.[16]

B. *The Deposition of Priests and Inferior Clerics*

The law of the Decretals allowing a bishop to proceed alone to the deposition of his clerics was left unchanged by the Council of Trent. Indeed, the council established several canons to insure greater freedom for the bishop in the exercise of his jurisdiction in these matters. It emphasized that bishops were to reprove the vices of all their subjects, but particularly the vices of their clerics.[17] So personally was this obligation imposed on bishops by the council that no other ecclesiastics, such as visitators or legates, could proceed against any cleric until his bishop had first been notified and had shown himself negligent.[18]

In prescribing the manner of proceeding against clerics who lived in concubinage and who, in incorrigible cases, could be punished with deposition, the council stated "the cognizance of all these matters shall not belong to archdeacons or deans or other inferiors, but to the bishops themselves, who may proceed without the formalities of justice, and by the sole investigation of the truth of the fact." [19]

Even canons of the cathedral church were not exempt from this power of the bishop of inflicting the penalty of deposition.[20] In regard to exempt chapters, however, a special form of procedure was

---

[15] Cf. Pius IV, const. *De salute gregis,* 4 sept. 1560—*Fontes,* n. 98; S. C. Ep. et Reg., *Larinen.,* 30 maii 1586—*Fontes,* n. 1407; S. C. Ep. et Reg., *Monopolitana,* 16 oct. 1627—*Fontes,* n. 1730; S. C. C., *Oxomen.,* 7 ian. 1623—*Fontes,* n. 2435; S. C. C., *Viennen,* 16 mart. 1647—*Fontes,* n. 2673; Benedictus XIV, ep. *In postremo,* 20 oct. 1756, § 18—*Fontes,* n. 442; Leo XIII, litt. encycl. *Sapientia,* 10 ian. 1890, § 19—*Fontes,* n. 605.

[16] C. 1557, § 1: Ipsius Romani Pontificis dumtaxat ius est iudicandi: . . . 3° . . . in criminalibus Episcopos, etiam titulares.

[17] Sess. XIV, *de ref.,* proem.

[18] Sess. XXIV, *de ref.,* c. 20; cf. also sess. XIV, *de ref.,* c. 8.

[19] Sess. XXV, *de ref.,* c. 14.

[20] Conc. Trident., sess. VI, *de ref.,* c. 4; sess. XIV, *de ref.,* c. 4.

prescribed. It required the bishop to proceed against a member of the chapter assisted by the two delegates of the chapter who were annually elected.[21]

In virtue of a special mandate from the bishop, a vicar general could depose a cleric of the diocese.[22] When the see became vacant this prerogative passed to the chapter and through the chapter could be vested in the vicar capitular.[23] Deposition involved an exercise of jurisdiction and not of orders. Hence, the ordinary could delegate his power in this matter. So also this jurisdiction could be exercised by a bishop whose election was confirmed but whose consecration had not yet taken place.[24]

This discipline, according to which the bishop alone constituted a competent tribunal to pass a sentence of deposition on a criminal cleric of his diocese, continued in force until the promulgation of the Code of Canon Law.[25]

ARTICLE 3. CRIMES WARRANTING DEPOSITION

The crimes stated in the law of the Decretals as warranting deposition continued unchanged as the law of this period. As already noted, the penal sanction of deposition ordinarily was attached to these laws in such a way that the penalty was incurred by a delinquent cleric only when a competent judge had delivered a condemnatory sentence against him. Occasionally the law provided for the infliction of deposition *ipso facto* upon commission of the crime. Yet even in this case canonists maintained that at least a declaratory sentence was necessary in order to incur the penalty, unless the necessity of this sentence had been excluded by a special sanction.[26]

Moreover, while many laws containing the penalty of deposition continued in force, custom and practice came to impose this penalty only for atrocious crimes. A norm for this development was supplied

[21] Sess. XXV, *de ref.*, c. 6.
[22] C. 2, *de officio vicarii*, I, 13, in VI°.
[23] Conc. Trident., sess. XXIV, *de ref.*, c. 16.
[24] Cf. Reiffenstuel, *Ius Canonicum Universum*, lib. V, tit. 37, n. 39.
[25] Cf. Reiffenstuel, *loc. cit.*; Wernz, *Ius Decretalium*, VI, n. 121.
[26] Cf. Wernz, *Ius Decretalium*, VI, n. 123.

by the Council of Trent. The council had decreed that "ordinaries should not allow anyone who is publicly and notoriously stained with crime either to minister at the holy altar or to assist at the sacred services." [27] Likewise, in establishing the procedure to be followed against clerics living in concubinage, the Council ordered the penalty of deposition only after *repeated admonitions* and *milder penalties had proved ineffective*.[28]

In the following centuries, then, the practice developed whereby deposition ordinarily was imposed only for crimes which by their nature, object and circumstances were very grave and publicly scandalous, such as voluntary and premeditated homicide, violent rape or adultery, sacrilegious theft of precious articles, notorious fornication, repeated after admonitions, public simony, and other crimes committed under aggravating circumstances.[29] Moreover, towards the end of the nineteenth century the principle generally obtained in the courts of the Church that there should be no penalty unless it were expressly stated in the law: *"nulla poena sine lege."* [30] In view of this principle an official codification of the delicts involving deposition was greatly to be desired.[31] Such a collection, enumerating all the crimes for which deposition could be incurred, came into being only with the Code of Canon Law.

ARTICLE 4. INFLICTION OF THE PENALTY OF DEGRADATION

A. *Verbal Degradation*

Decretal legislation requiring the local ordinary to proceed to a sentence of degradation only when assisted by six other bishops in the case of a priest, and by three other bishops in the case of a deacon or a subdeacon [32] had been the target for calumniators who,

---

[27] Sess. XXII, *Decretum de observandis et evitandis in celebratione Missae.*

[28] Sess. XXV, *de ref.*, c. 14.

[29] Schmalzgrueber, *Ius Ecclesiasticum Universum*, lib. V, tit. 37, n. 136; Reiffenstuel, *Ius Canonicum Universum*, lib. V, tit. 37, n. 30.

[30] Cf. Wernz, *Ius Decretalium*, VI, n. 123.

[31] Cf. Wernz, *loc. cit.*

[32] C. 2, *de poenis*, V, 9, in VI° and c. 2, C. III, q. 8; cc. 1, 4, 5, 7, C. XV, q. 7.

according to Benedict XIV, charged the Church with exaggerating the requirements for the lawful infliction of this penalty, so that clerics regardless of their crimes would be left unpunished.[33]   Moreover, the princes of Germany, in a list of a hundred grievances delivered to Pope Hadrian VI (1522-1523), complained of this procedure.[34]   Accordingly, the Council of Trent in its thirteenth session introduced a change in this legislation, stating:

"Whereas crimes so grievous are sometimes committed by ecclesiastics, that, on account of the atrocity thereof, they have to be deposed from sacred orders, and delivered over to the secular court, in which case a certain number of bishops, according to the sacred canons, is required, and whereas, should there be a difficulty in assembling them all, the due execution of the law would be retarded, whilst, should they on any occasion be able to be present their residence would be interrupted, therefore hath the Council resolved and decreed that it shall be lawful for a bishop by himself or by his vicar general in spirituals to proceed against a cleric, even against one who is raised to the sacred order of the priesthood, even to his condemnation, as also to his verbal deposition, and he shall be able to proceed by himself even to actual and solemn degradation from orders and ecclesiastical degrees and he may proceed without the other bishops in those cases wherein the presence of other bishops in a specific number is required by the canons, employing, however, and being assisted therein by a like number of abbots who have the right of using the miter and crosier by apostolic privilege, if it so be that they can be found in the city or diocese and can conveniently be present, or in their default, being assisted by a like number of other persons constituted in ecclesiastical dignity, who are judicious, mature in years and recommended by their knowledge of law." [35]

By this decree the council changed the former general law governing the procedure of verbal degradation which had required the assistance of a definite number of bishops [36] and at the same time

---

[33] Cf. *De synodo dioecesana,* lib. IX, cap. 6, n. 4.
[34] *Ibidem.*
[35] Sess. XIII, *de ref.,* c. 4.
[36] C. 2, *de poenis,* V, 9, in VI°.

amplified the scope of the extraordinary procedure as permitted by Pope Gregory IX (1227-1241) in the degradation of heretical clerics by allowing the substitution of other prelates for the bishops.[37] The council, moreover, left unchanged the law authorizing bishops to proceed alone to the verbal and real degradation of those clerics who had only tonsure or minor orders.[38]

According to the more common opinion of canonists these prelates were employed to assist the bishop in the verbal degradation of a cleric in major orders not merely for solemnity but as true judges enjoying a decisive vote in passing sentence on the delinquent cleric.[39] Pope Benedict XIV stated that the abbots or other prelates who were substituted for the bishops in conformity with the law of the Council of Trent assisted not as mere councillors but as judges with a decisive vote.[40] The Council of Trent corrected the former law only in regard to the dignity of the assistants; it did not change the old law which accorded the assistants a decisive vote, and hence they continued to enjoy it.[41]

It was disputed among canonists whether a unanimous vote of these judges was required for the validity of the sentence of verbal degradation. Those who maintained that a unanimous vote was necessary based their opinion on the text of a law in the Decretals: "*Non potest quemquam a sacerdotali gradu, nisi iustis ex causis, concors sacerdotum sententia submovere.*" [42] Others, however, main-

---

[37] C. 1, *de haereticis*, V, 2, in VI°; cf. Fagnanus, *Commentaria*, lib. III, tit. 40, cap. 9, n. 29.

[38] Cf. c. 2, *de poenis*, V, 9, in VI°; Benedictus XIV, ep. encycl. *Quam grave*, 2 aug. 1757, § 4—*Fontes*, n. 443.

[39] Cf. Reiffenstuel, *Ius Canonicum Universum*, lib. V, tit. 37, n. 42; Schmalzgrueber, *Ius Ecclesiasticum Universum*, lib. V, tit. 37, n. 145; Kober, *Die Deposition und Degradation*, p. 223.

[40] *De synodo dioecesana*, lib. IX, cap. 6, n. 4.

[41] Benedictus XIV, ep. encycl. *Quam grave*, § 8: "in hos derivatum fuisse ius ferendi suffragii in degradationibus verbalibus, ad quas uti assessores invitantur."—*Fontes*, n. 443.

[42] C. 3, X, *de sententia et re iudicata*, II, 27; cf. Schmalzgrueber, *Ius Ecclesiasticum Universum*, lib. V, tit. 37, n. 146; Reiffenstuel, *Ius Canonicum Universum*, lib. V, tit. 37, n. 44.

tained that a majority vote sufficed for the validity of the sentence.[43] They argued that the law on which the first opinion was founded did not offer conclusive reasons for requiring unanimity. The law was taken from an epistle of St. Gregory the Great [44] which did not consider the question of unanimity but rather implicitly excluded it, for the letter spoke of conciliar action which was determined by majority vote. Nor is the law as incorporated in the Decretals pertinent, for the text refers to deposition which required only the presence of the clergy.[45] Thus the second opinion followed the *Glossa* [46] and maintained that a majority of votes sufficed for the sentence. Benedict XIV indeed referred to the first opinion which required the unanimous consent of the judges for the degradation of a priest, a deacon or a subdeacon, but it is not clearly certain whether he approved or rejected it.[47]

According to the law of the Council of Trent a bishop who was assisted by the required prelates could by himself or through his vicar general proceed to verbal degradation. This penalty as a judicial sentence involved an act of jurisdiction and not an act of orders. Hence, as was true before the Council of Trent, in order to pronounce this sentence it was not necessary for the competent bishop to be consecrated.[48] Moreover, the bishop could delegate a cleric by a special mandate to act in his place in passing this sentence,[49] and when the see was vacant the chapter could do likewise.[50]

The procedure governing the application of this penalty was changed again with the promulgation of the Code of Canon Law.

[43] Kober, *Die Deposition und Degradation*, p. 226; Wernz, *Ius Decretalium*, VI, n. 128.

[44] *Ep. VIII*, Epist. lib. III—*MPL*, LXXVII, 612.

[45] Cf. Wernz, *Ius Decretalium*, VI, n. 128.

[46] In c. 3, X, *de sententia et re iudicata*, II, 27 s. v. "Sacerdotum."

[47] *De synodo dioecesana*, lib. IX, cap. 6, n. 4.

[48] Cf. Reiffenstuel, *Ius Canonicum Universum*, lib. V, tit. 37, n. 39; Schmalzgrueber, *Ius Ecclesiasticum Universum*, lib. V, tit. 37, n. 139.

[49] Conc. Trident., sess. XIII, *de ref.*, c. 4; cf. Wernz, *Ius Decretalium*, VI, n. 128.

[50] Schmalzgrueber, *Ius Ecclesiasticum Universum*, lib. V, tit. 37, n. 142.

No longer are bishops or prelates required as assistant judges with the proper ordinary. According to the new law cases of degradation are to be tried before a tribunal of five judges.[51]

B. Real Degradation

With the Council of Trent, as before, *real degradation*, or the execution of the sentence of verbal degradation in a solemn ceremony, could be performed only by a bishop who was consecrated and canonically enthroned.[52] In regulating the procedure for verbal degradation the Council of Trent declared that " . . . the bishop by himself or through his vicar general may proceed," whereas in describing the procedure for real degradation, it stated that " . . . the bishop by himself may proceed," excluding thereby the vicar general. The reason for this exclusion is the fact that real degradation is an act of episcopal orders.[53] However, the bishop could delegate his rôle in real degradation, but only to another consecrated bishop.[54]

It was only for greater solemnity that the bishops or prelates who participated in the sentence of degradation took part in the solemn ceremony of real or actual degradation.[55] As noted previously, Durantis had already observed that the presence of these bishops at the actual degradation was not required by law for the validity of the act.[56] The Roman Pontifical repeated this observation.[57]

---

[51] Canon 1576, § 1, n. 2.

[52] Cf. Wernz, *Ius Decretalium*, VI, n. 134.

[53] Cf. Fagnanus, *Commentaria*, lib. III, tit. 40, cap. 9, n. 21 sq.

[54] Cf. Fagnanus, *loc. cit.;* Reiffenstuel, *Ius Canonicum Universum*, lib. V, tit. 37, n. 40; Schmalzgrueber, *Ius Ecclesiasticum Universum*, lib. V, tit. 37, nn. 139, 142, 147. It may be noted here that regular prelates, unless they were bishops, did not by common law have the faculty of degrading their subjects who were clerics; any rights enjoyed in this respect had to be derived from privileges granted by the Apostolic See. Cf. Schmalzgrueber, *op. cit.*, lib. V, tit. 37, nn. 139, 142, 147; Wernz, *Ius Decretalium*, VI, n. 134, not. 257.

[55] Cf. Benedictus XIV, *De synodo dioecesana*, lib. IX, cap. 6, n. 5; Schmalzgrueber, *Ius Ecclesiasticum Universum*, lib. V, tit. 37, n. 148.

[56] *Speculum Iuris*, lib. III, part. I, de accusatione, II, n. 5.

[57] Pars III tit., *Degradationis forma*: "Et est notandum quod in hac executione sententiae non est necessaria coepiscoporum praesentia."

After actual degradation had been accomplished according to the form outlined in the Roman Pontifical, only the Roman Pontiff could restore the degraded cleric. The bishop, however, could dispense a cleric who was only verbally degraded. Moreover, if after real degradation it was discovered that the process was unjust or null, then the bishop was to restore the degraded cleric in a solemn ceremony before the altar by returning to him all the insignia which he had received in his ordination, but which he had lost in the unjust degradation.[58]

The Roman Pontifical specified the ceremony according to which real degradation was accomplished. With its completion the cleric was deprived of the clerical privileges and delivered over to the secular court, whose representative was to be present to apprehend him. The sorrowful ceremony which effected the complete destitution of the delinquent's former rights as a cleric closed with an earnest entreaty that the life of the victim be spared.[59] It was controverted among canonists whether this intercession for the one degraded was necessary for the ecclesiastical judge to avoid an irregularity. Outstanding canonists maintained that it was not necessary, since such an irregularity was not expressed in the law.[60] Above all this entreaty reflected the solicitude of the Church who tried to the last to save the cleric from himself.

The Pontifical described a ceremony for each rank of the clerical order, descending from the procedure in the case of a bishop to that in the case of a cleric who had received only tonsure. Pope Benedict XIV remarked, however, that in many places the ceremony was no longer employed for those who were only in minor orders.[61] For a long time minor clerics in Spain, France and Belgium, who committed grave crimes were punished as laymen by the secular judges, even to the point of capital punishment, without a previous process of degradation. The Church at least tacitly tolerated this practice.[62] In modern times the real degradation of minor clerics

---

[58] *Pontificale Romanum*, pars III, tit., *Degradationis forma.*

[59] *Pontificale Romanum, loc. cit.*

[60] Cf. Schmalzgrueber, *Ius Ecclesiasticum Universum*, lib. V, tit. 37, n. 149.

[61] *De synodo dioecesana*, lib. IX, cap. 6, n. 4.

[62] Wernz, *Ius Decretalium*, VI, n. 135.

became even less important, for, as Wernz has pointed out, clerics in minor orders remained for the most part in seminaries, where there was little likelihood of the commission of a crime that warranted degradation. If they were expelled from the seminary, or freely departed and set aside the clerical garb, they were, so to speak, degraded *ipso facto* and likened to the laity even in criminal causes.[63]

The ceremonial surrounding the real degradation of major clerics likewise became difficult of achievement because of adverse civil laws and the unwillingness of clerics to submit freely to this procedure. The Code of Canon Law surmounted these legal difficulties. While it retained the traditional distinction of verbal and real degradation, the same juridical effects have been ascribed to each.[64] No longer is the execution of verbal degradation in a solemn ceremony necessary to obtain all the juridical effects of this penalty.

ARTICLE 5. CRIMES WARRANTING DEGRADATION

Mention has already been made of the crimes stated in the law of the Decretals as warranting degradation. These laws continued to have force during this period, threatening with degradation those clerics who were guilty of heresy, schism, apostasy; [65] the falsification of apostolic letters; [66] grave contumely, calumny or conspiracy against their bishop; [67] and, finally, incorrigibility in other grave crimes after milder penalties had proved ineffective in the correction of the delinquent.

[63] *Ius Decretalium*, VI, n. 135, citing decree of Pius IX, 20 sept. 1860, in *ASS*, III (1860), 433.

[64] Canon 2305.

[65] Renewed by Pope Paul IV (const. *Cum ex apostolatus*, 15 febr. 1559, § 2—*Fontes*, n. 94) and later by Pope S. Pius V (const. *Cum ex apostolatus*, 27 ian. 1567—*Fontes*, n. 117).

[66] In 1563 Pope Innocent X renewed this law and applied the penalty of degradation not only to the forgers themselves but also to their accomplices.— Const. *In supremo iustitiae*, 8 apr. 1563—*Fontes*, n. 234.

[67] These delicts warranted degradation only when accompanied with incorrigibility. Cf. Fagnanus, *Commentaria*, lib. II, tit. 1, cap. 10, n. 71; Benedictus XIV, *De synodo dioecesana*, lib. IX, cap. 6, n. 7.

During this period after the Council of Trent the penalty of degradation was stated for other crimes in universal laws issuing from the Holy See. Thus, in 1566, Pope St. Pius V published a law punishing with degradation clerics who practiced sodomy.[68] This crime had earlier been punished with deposition.[69]

The procuration of abortion by clerics was punished in the Decretals with deposition.[70] For this crime, however, Pope Sixtus V, in 1588, established degradation as the penalty.[71] Later Pope Gregory XIV in a renewed statement of this penal sanction restricted it to the abortion of an animated fetus and granted to local ordinaries the faculty of absolving from the excommunication which Pope Sixtus V in his law had reserved to the Holy See.[72]

Pope Pius IV, in 1561, in a letter addressed to the archbishop of Seville, sanctioned the penalty of degradation for priests who committed the crime of solicitation in confession.[73] This decree concerned only the Church in Spain. In 1622 Pope Gregory XV issued for the universal Church a law which sanctioned degradation for priests guilty of this crime. In the same decree this pontiff defined precisely the various elements constituting this crime.[74] Pope Benedict XIV, in 1741, renewed this law of Pope Gregory XV and further clarified its prescriptions.[75] It is interesting to note that the author of this second law, Pope Benedict XIV, remarked elsewhere that he could find no instance of the application of this penalty since the issuance of Pope Gregory's law. Hence he concluded that the constitution was primarily published to inspire fear for this crime.[76]

A law in the Decretals stated that a cleric who presumed to exer-

---

[68] Const. *Cum primum*, 1 apr. 1566, § 11—*Fontes*, n. 111; restated by the same pontiff in the const. *Horrendum*, 30 aug. 1568—*Fontes*, n. 128.

[69] Cf. c. 11, III General Lateran Council (1179)—Schroeder, *Disciplinary Decrees*, p. 224; c. 4, X, *de excessibus praelatorum et subditorum*, V, 31.

[70] C. 20, X, *de homicidio voluntario vel casuali*, V, 12.

[71] Const. *Effraenatam*, 29 oct. 1588, § 4—*Fontes*, n. 165.

[72] Const. *Sedes Apostolica*, 31 maii 1591—*Fontes*, n. 173.

[73] Ep. *Cum sicut nuper*, 16 apr. 1561—*Fontes*, n. 102.

[74] Const. *Universi*, 30 aug. 1622—*Fontes*, n. 201.

[75] Const. *Sacramentum Poenitentiae*, 1 iun. 1741—*CIC*, Documentum V.

[76] *De synodo dioecesana*, lib. IX, cap. 6, n. 7.

cise an order higher than he had received was to be suspended [77] or even deposed.[78] Pope Clement VIII, in 1601, decreed that any cleric not ordained to the priesthood who presumed to celebrate Mass or hear sacramental confessions was to be degraded.[79] Not long afterwards Pope Urban VIII renewed this penal law and declared subject to it all who had completed their twentieth year of age.[80] In 1744 Pope Benedict XIV confirmed and renewed this law and at the same time defined more clearly the various circumstances and conditions surrounding the crime for which the penalty was incurred.[81]

Pope Innocent XI, in 1677, decreed that sacrilegious theft of the Blessed Sacrament was to be condignly punished not only by the ecclesiastical authorities but also by the secular courts, even in the case of a first offender, unless it were evident that the theft was not committed for an evil purpose.[82] Although this constitution did not expressly mention clerics, a later decree of Pope Alexander VIII explicitly named all clerics who profaned the Blessed Sacrament as subject to the civil penalties after they had first been degraded.[83] This law which punished with degradation all clerics who desecrated the Blessed Sacrament was confirmed and renewed by Pope Benedict XIV in 1744.[84]

In the First General Council of Lyons (1245) Pope Innocent IV published a decree which punished with deposition clerics who hired assassins to commit murder.[85] This decree was inserted in the *Liber Sextus.*[86] Later canonists extended the scope of this penalty. According to their doctrine clerics who were themselves assassins incurred *ipso facto* the penalty of degradation.[87]

---

[77] C. 2, X, *de clerico non ordinato ministrante,* V, 28.

[78] C. 1, X, *de clerico non ordinato ministrante,* V, 28.

[79] Const. *Etsi alias,* 1 dec. 1601—*Fontes,* n. 188.

[80] Const. *Apostolatus officium,* 23 mart. 1628—*Fontes,* n. 207.

[81] Const. *Sacerdos in aeternum,* 20 apr. 1744—*Fontes,* n. 314.

[82] Const. *Ad Nostri Apostolatus,* 12 mart. 1677—*Fontes,* n. 250.

[83] Const. *Cum alias,* 22 dec. 1690—*Fontes,* n. 255.

[84] Const. *Ab augustissimo,* 5 mart. 1744—*Fontes,* n. 340.

[85] C. 17—Schroeder, *Disciplinary Decrees,* p. 312.

[86] C. 1, *de homicidio,* V, 4, in VI°; cf. *supra,* pp. 82-83.

[87] Cf. Fagnanus, *Commentaria,* lib. II, tit. 1, cap. 10, n. 72; lib. V, tit., 39, cap. 45, n. 19; Barbosa, *Collectanea,* lib. V, tit. 4, in VI°, cap. 1, n. 13; Benedictus XIV, *De synodo dioecesana,* lib. IX, cap. 6, n. 7.

Pope Urban VIII, in 1627, in issuing against counterfeiters of money a renewed statement of the law enacted by Pope Pius V in 1570,[88] extended it to all ecclesiastical persons and further added the sanction of degradation for clerics who committed this delict. This law, however, applied only to the clergy of Italy.[89]

Apart from the crimes expressly stated in the laws of the Church as warranting degradation there continued in force the law of Pope Celestine III (1191-1198), which, as already noted, provided for the degradation of a cleric who, after being deposed for theft, perjury, homicide or other grave crimes, continued to be incorrigible even after he had been subjected to other penalties.[90]

Some canonists maintained that it was not necessary to observe the series of penalties provided by this canon to determine incorrigibility. They held that if a cleric committed a grave crime, the bishop should proceed at once to this penalty without determining whether or not the cleric was incorrigible.[91] Others on the contrary maintained that degradation could be inflicted only on clerics who were incorrigible in crime according to the norm of this canon, or who had committed a crime expressly stated in the law as punishable with degradation.[92] Fagnanus, after refuting the reasons alleged for the first opinion, indicated that the second doctrine alone was in conformity with the teaching of the decretalists and alone was consonant with ecclesiastical liberty and the exemption of clerics from the secular power.[93] The first opinion adopted civil legislation as a norm in this matter: crimes which the civil law punished with death, ecclesiastical authority should punish with degradation. The majority of canonists, however, rightfully insisted that the norm

---

[88] Const. *Cum nihil magis—Bullarum Diplomatum et Privilegiorum Sanctorum Romanorum Pontificum Taurinensis Editio* (25 vols., Augustae Taurinorum, 1857-1872), VII, 861.

[89] Const. *In suprema pastorali—Bull. Rom. Taur.*, XIII, 615.

[90] C. 10, X, *de iudiciis*, II, 1.

[91] See Sebastian Berardi, quoted by Lega, *De Delictis et Poenis*, n. 209, and others listed by Schmalzgrueber, *Ius Ecclesiasticum Universum*, lib. V, tit. 37, n. 152; cf. Reiffenstuel, *Ius Canonicum Universum*, lib. V, tit. 37, nn. 35, 36.

[92] Cf. Schmalzgrueber, *loc. cit.*, n. 153.

[93] Cf. *Commentaria*, lib. II, tit. 1, cap. 10, nn. 26-68.

for an action of degradation must be found in ecclesiastical legislation.

Benedict XIV asserted that it was the common opinion of the doctors that, apart from the cases expressly designated in the law as warranting degradation, this penalty could not be inflicted on a cleric unless, after deposition for grave crimes, he remained incorrigible according to the norm supplied by the aforementioned decree of Pope Celestine III. It would have been superfluous for the law to state expressly certain grave crimes as warranting degradation if the penalty could have been inflicted for any serious crime.[94] Moreover, this doctrine was commonly accepted in the courts of the Church. Custom is the best interpreter of law. Benedict XIV accordingly served notice on bishops that this practice was to be observed.[95] Thus the law and practice continued to the eve of the appearance of the Code of Canon Law.[96]

[94] Cf. Benedictus XIV, *De synodo dioecesana*, lib. IX, cap. 6, n. 10.

[95] *Loc. cit.*, n. 11: "Ab hac regula communi usu recepta, non recedat Episcopus."

[96] Cf. Wernz, *Ius Decretalium*, VI, n. 136.

CONCLUSIONS

1. During the first twelve centuries deposition and degradation were synonymous terms for one and the same penalty.

2. This penalty, clearly established in ecclesiastical law after the third century, completely deprived a delinquent clergyman of all his clerical rights and privileges and juridically reduced him to the lay state.

3. With the sixth and subsequent centuries there was a mitigation of the use and rigor of this penalty. The deposed cleric, as a general rule, was compelled to live in a monastery.

4. From the sixth century it was customary to accompany the infliction of the penalty with some ceremony to manifest the debasement involved in the punishment.

5. Originally bishops could be deposed by a provincial council, but they had the right of appealing to the Holy See. Pope Nicholas I and the Pseudo-Isidorian Decretals reserved the deposition of bishops exclusively to the Roman Pontiff.

6. In many countries, especially in Africa, and subsequently in Gaul, Spain and Germany, six bishops were required for the deposition of a priest by his bishop, three in the case of a deacon. This law came to be neglected by custom; later this custom was ratified by Pope Boniface VIII.

7. Pope Innocent III, following the vague precedents established by Popes Lucius III and Celestine III, introduced a distinction between deposition and degradation.

8. Thereafter degradation alone involved loss of the clerical privileges and reduction to the lay state.

9. Pope Boniface VIII clearly established the distinction between verbal and real degradation. A solemn ceremony was now a necessary juridical element of degradation.

10. Thereafter, up to and through the time of the Council of Trent, six bishops were required for the verbal degradation of priests, three for that of deacons and subdeacons, with the mitigation established by the Council of Trent of substituting an equal number of minor prelates or clerics skilled in canon law.

PART II

CANONICAL COMMENTARY

INTRODUCTION

The Catholic Church, always the provident Mother, more than adequately answered the pleas voiced by countless prelates both before as well as after the Vatican Council [1] when, on the feast of Pentecost, May 27, 1917, she promulgated the Code of Canon Law and decreed that it would enjoy the force of universal law from the feast of Pentecost of the ensuing year, May 19, 1918.[2] The truth of this statement becomes immediately obvious after a consideration of the status of the earlier legislation. Before the appearance of the Code disciplinary laws had increased and multiplied to an overwhelming extent. Canonists described the situation in the words of Livy regarding Roman Law as "an immense fabric of laws heaped one upon another." [3] The difficulties arising from this multiplicity of laws were increased by the prolixity of the legislation and sometimes even by the contrariety which characterized it. Repetitions, omissions, obscurities and contrarieties abounded. Innumerable laws had long been obsolete, others had been abrogated, many had become useless with the changing times and conditions; yet all appeared in collections along with the existing laws. Needless to say, this situation led to many causes for doubts, anxieties and difficulties, even for those skilled in the law, especially when it became necessary to discover the pertinent law and to apply it to practical cases.[4] Hence it can readily be seen how truly great a

---

[1] Cf. Cicognani, *Canon Law*, p. 419.

[2] Benedictus XV, const. *Providentissima Mater Ecclesiae*, 27 maii 1917—*AAS*, IX (1917), 557.

[3] Livius, *Historia*, lib. III, c. 4: "immensum aliarum super alias coacervatarum legum cumulum."—Quoted by Gasparri in the *Preface* of his edition of the Code.

[4] Cf. Gasparri, *loc. cit.;* Van Hove, *Prolegomena*, nn. 357-361, pp. 335-339; Beste, *Introductio in Codicem*, pp. 30-31; Neuberger, *Canon 6 or The Relation of the Codex Iuris Canonici to Preceding Legislation* (Catholic University of America, Canon Law Studies, No. 44, Washington, D. C., 1927), 17.

blessing it was for the Church to obtain the Code of Canon Law which has admirably attained its objectives of eliminating useless or obsolete laws, of accommodating others to the needs of the times and of establishing new laws to meet the necessary demands.[5]

The uncertainty and confusion which prevailed before the appearance of the Code rendered particularly urgent the need of reform and codification in the realm of penal law. This need, it is true, had been partially satisfied by Pope Pius IX, in 1869, through the publication of a complete official list of the *latae sententiae* censures which were to be thereafter in force.[6] The greater part of ecclesiastical penal legislation, however, still awaited clarification. It was only with the promulgation of the Code of Canon Law that this arduous task was accomplished. In the Fifth Book of the Code, "Of Delicts and Penalties" (*De Delictis et Poenis*), the Church has stated the general principles of penal law and has collected and set forth the current penal legislation, reformed and accommodated to present times.[7]

Since a new codification essentially implies a transition from an old to a new order in legislation, the Code established a general principle governing the resultant relation between the old and the new: As a rule, the Code retains the discipline hitherto in force, though it makes some opportune changes.[8] In relation to penal legislation, however, the established principle is much more specific: Penalties not mentioned in the Code—whether they be spiritual or temporal, be they corrective *(medicinales)* or be they the so-called punitive penalties *(vindicativae)* and be they incurred *ipso facto (latae sententiae)* or only after judicial sentence *(ferendae sententiae)*—shall be regarded as abrogated.[9] In a word, all general penal legislation not contained in the Code itself lost its binding force. Thus it can truly be said that the Code occupies the first

[5] Cf. Pius X, motu propio *Arduum sane,* 19 mart. 1904—*ASS,* XXXVI (1903-1904), 549.

[6] Cf. Pius IX, const. *Apostolicae Sedis,* 12 oct. 1869—*Fontes,* n. 552.

[7] Cf. Roberti, *De Delictis et Poenis,* I, n. 9, p. 15; n. 6, p. 18; Ayrinhac-Lydon, *Penal Legislation,* xx.

[8] Canon 6.

[9] Canon 6, n. 5.

place, after the divine law, in the current penal legislation of the Church.[10]

Among the vindictive penalties enumerated by the Code as applied exclusively to clerics are deposition and degradation.[11] These two ancient ecclesiastical penalties are thereby retained in the present discipline of the Church. The application of these penalties to particular delicts is to be found in the Code in Book V, Part III, entitled "Penalties for the Individual Delicts."[12] Here in particular the aforementioned law governing the abrogation of earlier enactments must be applied.

The history of the penalties of deposition and degradation warrants the statement that these penalties have received in the Code their first clear and complete definition in universal legislation. Moreover, the law now expressly states the crimes for which these penalties may be inflicted. In similar fashion it carefully describes the procedure to be followed in the infliction of these penalties. Thus it may be said by way of transition to a consideration of the modern discipline governing deposition and degradation that the Code aptly summarized the former legislation and wisely adopted the best of the jurisprudential developments of the past while introducing several innovations adapted to the needs and conditions of the times.

As the penalty of degradation includes deposition even in the present law, the close affinity in the character of these two penalties as witnessed throughout their long history is still preserved. Hence the order of treatment established in the historical part of this work, namely, to explain first the law on deposition and then to set forth a comparative analysis and exposition of the penalty of degradation, will be maintained in the following commentary on the present canonical norms governing these penalties.

[10] Cf. Cicognani, *Canon Law*, 499.

[11] Canon 2298: "Poenae vindicativae quae clericis tantum applicantur, sunt: . . . n. 10: Depositio; . . . n. 12: Degradatio."

[12] *De Poenis in Singula Delicta*, canons 2314-2414.

CHAPTER V

DEPOSITION

ARTICLE 1. THE TERM *Deposition* IN THE CODE

IN the course of history many legal expressions have been derived from the Latin verb *deponere,* to depose. Several of these derivatives appear in the Code. The verb seems to have been early employed to signify the delivery of some object to another person for its faithful preservation. This transaction has always been termed, both in civil and canon law, *deposition,* while the object delivered has been named the *deposit.*[1] Thus the Code of Canon Law employs this usage, as did St. Paul,[2] when it refers to the divine truths committed by Christ to the Catholic Church as "the deposit of faith."[3]

Perhaps it was from this usage that the term came to be employed in law to signify also the giving of testimony in court, for one who testifies commits a known truth to the care either of a collegiate judiciary or of an individual judge. Thus the Code speaks of the act of testifying as "deposing" and the testimony itself as the "deposition" of the witness.[4] A similar use of the word *deposition,* employed as early as Apostolic times, is retained in the Code when it declares that the deposition, or interment, of the bodies of the

---

[1] Suarez, *Opera Omnia* (ed. nova, a Carolo Berton: Parisiis, Apud Ludovicum Vives, 1856-1866), Tom. XXIII bis, *De censuris in communi, excommunicatione, suspensione et interdicto, itemque de irregularitate,* Disp. XXX, *proem.* Hereafter this work will be referred to simply as *De Censuris.*

[2] I Tim., VI: 20; II Tim., I: 13, 14.

[3] Canon 1322: "Christus Dominus fidei *depositum* Ecclesiae concredidit, ut ipsa, Spiritu Sancto iugiter assistente, doctrinam revelatam sancte custodiret et fideliter exponeret." Cf. also canon 1909, § 2: "Potest autem iudex pro suo prudenti arbitrio exigere ut pecunia pro iudicialibus expensis . . . antea *deponatur* penes tribunalis cancellariam."

[4] Canon 1791, § 1: "Unius testis *depositio* plenam fidem non facit, nisi sit testis qualificatus qui *deponat* de rebus ex officio gestis."

faithful departed constitutes an integral part of ecclesiastical burial.[5]

Finally, the term *deposition* is employed in the Code, and most frequently, to signify a vindictive penalty proper to the clergy, by which a delinquent cleric, while retaining the clerical privileges and obligations, is deprived permanently of all offices, benefices, dignities, pensions and functions in the Church and becomes unable to acquire them in the future.[6] In this usage the term has been cleared of its former equivocation by the precise definition of the Code which will be considered in the following article. Before the Code appeared it was quite common to employ "deposition" as a generic term which embraced not only deposition properly so designated but verbal and real degradation as well. This equivocation led to much confusion among canonists in their expositions of these three penalties.[7] In the present legislation of the Church the term *deposition*, when employed in reference to the canonical penalty, has a specific signification clearly distinguishing it from every other penalty.[8] Degradation likewise is clearly and authoritatively defined.[9] Hence there is no longer any canonical basis for confusing these two distinct penalties.

ARTICLE 2. THE NATURE OF DEPOSITION

Canon 2303, § 1: Depositio, firmis obligationibus e suscepto ordine exortis et privilegiis clericalibus, secumfert tum suspensionem ab officio, et inhabilitatem ad quaelibet officia, dignitates, beneficia, pensiones, munera in Ecclesia, tum etiam privationem illorum quae reus habeat, licet eorum titulo fuerit ordinatus.

[5] Canon 1204: "Sepultura ecclesiastica consistit in cadaveris translatione ad ecclesiam, exsequiis super illud in eadem celebratis, illius *depositione* in loco legitime deputato fidelibus defunctis condendis."

[6] Cf. canon 2303, § 1.

[7] Cf. above p. 93; also Suarez, *De Censuris*, Disp. XXX, *proem.*; Wernz, *Ius Decretalium*, VI, n. 120, p. 124, not. 163.

[8] Canon 2303, § 1.

[9] Canon 2305.

In its definition of deposition as it exists in the Church today the Code of Canon Law presents the first comprehensive and authoritative explanation of a penalty long employed in the Church. According to this definition deposition, while leaving intact the clerical privileges and the obligations derived from ordination brings with it a suspension from office, and a disqualification for any offices, dignities, benefices, pensions or positions in the Church, as well as a privation of these, should the delinquent already possess them, indeed, even a privation of such of these as constituted his title of ordination. Viewing this penalty in the light of its history one notes at once that it does not differ in its conception from the punishment as established under the old law.[10] The Code, however, does bring precision and clarity as well as authority to the best canonical expositions of the penalty which flourished in conformity with earlier legislation.

A. General Character

Prior to any consideration of the constitutive elements of deposition which make this penalty, next to degradation, the most severe punishment employed by the Church against delinquent clerics, a few considerations concerning the general character of this penalty will be helpful. Like every penalty deposition involves by its nature the privation of some good. This is a common effect of all penalties, for, as St. Thomas says,[11] it is essential to a penalty that it be an affliction against one's own will for some guilt or crime. According to the Code every ecclesiastical penalty is the privation of some good, inflicted by legitimate authority for the correction of the delinquent and the punishment of his crime.[12] Ecclesiastical penalties, then, are concerned with privation rather than with the positive infliction of pain. However, the idea of penalty, or pain, is preserved in the suffering of the loss which is involved in privation.

[10] Cf. A Coronata, *Institutiones Iuris Canonici* (Taurini: Marietti, 1928-1936), IV, n. 1834, p. 261. Hereafter this work will be referred to simply as *Institutiones*.

[11] *Summa*, I, II, q. 46, art. 6 ad 2.

[12] Canon 2215.

Since penalties are the privation of some good, there can be as many specifically different penalties as there are specifically different goods of which man can be deprived. From the canonical viewpoint these goods are either temporal or natural, such as life, liberty, honor, material possessions, or they are spiritual or supernatural, such as the rights proper to the lay, clerical or religious states in the Church. Penalties affecting these goods will in consequence be either temporal or spiritual.[13] Deposition is a spiritual vindictive penalty, for it immediately deprives a delinquent cleric of rights intimately connected with the clerical state. While deposition is formally a spiritual penalty, it also produces, as will be seen, grave temporal effects.[14]

Deposition is always a vindictive penalty [15] and never a censure. Vindictive penalties tend directly towards the expiation of an offense so that their remission does not depend on the cessation of the contumacy of the offender.[16] On the other hand, medicinal penalties, or censures,[17] are primarily designed to effect the amendment of the delinquent.[18] Unlike vindictive penalties censures must be pardoned by the competent authority when the offender with proper dispositions seeks absolution, for these penalties have then attained their purpose.[19] Vindictive penalties are imposed independently of the offender's continued obstinacy or relinquished bad will. As their very name suggests, they are designed primarily for the expiation and reparation of the violation of law and order.

In the penal law of the Church, however, the restoration of the social order which was disturbed by a delict is not excluded from the purpose of censures, neither is the correction and amendment of the delinquent excluded from the aim of her vindictive penalties. In all her punishments the Church has always a twofold objective:

[13] Roberti, *De Delictis et Poenis,* I, n. 230, p. 255.

[14] Cf. Roberti, *op. cit.,* I, n. 230, pp. 263-264.

[15] Canon 2298: "Poenae vindicativae quae clericis tantum applicantur, sunt . . . n. 10: Depositio."

[16] Canon 2286.

[17] *CIC,* lib. V, sect. II, tit. VIII, *De poenis medicinalibus seu de censuris.*

[18] Cf. canon 2241, § 1.

[19] Canons 2248, §§ 1, 2; 2242, § 3.

(1) the correction and reformation of the individual delinquent, and (2) the reparation and restoration of the social order violated by the delict. In medicinal penalties, or censures, the emphasis rests on the first-mentioned objective, in vindictive penalties on the second.[20] The penal philosophy of the Church concerning vindictive penalties such as deposition is well expressed in the Code[21] when it repeats the admonition of the Council of Trent:[22]

"If on account of the grievousness of the transgression there be need of the *rod,* then is rigor to be tempered with compassion, judgment with mercy, severity with mildness, in order that the discipline which is so salutary and necessary for the people may be safeguarded without harshness and they who have been chastened may be amended in their ways, or, if they have repudiated all repentance, that through the salutary example of the administered punishment others may be deterred from vices."[28]

Deposition, then, is a spiritual vindictive penalty which is applied only to clerics[24] since it deprives them of rights enjoyed exclusively by members of the clerical state. This fact will become obvious in considering more specifically the nature of deposition. While reviewing the enormous privations consequent upon this penalty one must bear in mind that deposition does not deprive the delinquent of the clerical privileges or free him from the obligations arising from his orders.[25]

B. *Special Character*

An analysis of the penalty of deposition as defined by the Code shows that it involves three constitutive elements: (a) suspension from office; (b) disqualification for any office, dignity, benefice,

---

[20] Cf. Roberti, *De Delictis et Poenis,* I, n. 223, pp. 247-250; n. 231, p. 264; n. 232, p. 265; Woywod, *A Practical Commentary,* II, 424-425; 454; Sole, *De Delictis et Poenis,* n. 263, pp. 187-188.

[21] Canon 2214, § 2.

[22] Sess. XIII, *de ref.,* c. 1.

[28] The translation is the writer's. Cf. also Waterworth, *The Canons and Decrees of the Sacred and Oecumenical Council of Trent* (London, 1848), 85.

[24] Canon 2298, n. 10.

[25] Canon 2303, § 1: "Depositio, firmis obligationibus e suscepto ordine exortis et privilegiis clericalibus . . ."

pension or position in the Church; (c) privation of any office, dignity, benefice, pension, or position which the delinquent may have had even though it constituted his title of ordination. Any one of these elements may constitute a vindictive penalty in its own right and of itself.[26] By the will of the legislator, however, all three penalties are so combined, united and interwoven as to complement each other and form thereby one distinct and indivisible penalty called deposition. To appreciate the nature and scope of deposition it is therefore imperative to analyze the nature and effects of its constitutive penalties, which must be viewed not so much as individual penalties but as united with each other, for it is only through their legal combination that the penalty of deposition with its proper effects is produced.

(1) Suspension from Office

In the first place deposition involves a suspension from office.[27] In the penal system of the Church *suspension* signifies a punishment forbidding a delinquent cleric to exercise the rights or powers belonging to him either by reason of his office, or by reason of his benefice, or by reason of both.[28] It does not take away the rights but only prohibits their exercise. As Suarez has stated it, suspension does not represent a total loss or destruction, but only, as it were, a detention.[29] When a suspension is removed a cleric again lawfully exercises his office or enjoys his benefice without any new appointment. This is a sure sign that the office or benefice itself was never lost, but only restricted in its use.

Suspension affects only clerics and has a twofold purpose, for it may be employed either as a censure or as a vindictive penalty.[30]

---

[26] Canon 2298: "Poenae vindicativae quae clericis tantum applicantur, sunt: . . . n. 2: Suspensio in perpetuum . . . ; n. 4: Privatio alicuius iuris cum beneficio vel officio coniuncti; n. 5: Inhabilitas ad omnes vel ad aliquot dignitates, officia, beneficia aliave munera propria clericorum; n. 6: Privatio poenalis beneficii vel officii cum vel sine pensione."

[27] Canon 2303, § 1: "Depositio . . . secumfert tum suspensionem ab officio . . ."

[28] Canon 2278, § 1: "Suspensio . . . qua clericus officio vel beneficio vel utroque prohibetur."

[29] *De Censuris*, Disp. XXVI, sec. I, n. 1.

[30] Canon 2252, § 2.

If it is inflicted for the amendment of the cleric the suspension is a censure.[31]   If, on the other hand, the superior inflicts a suspension primarily for the reparation of the delict it is a vindictive penalty.[32] As a constitutive element of deposition suspension from office must be considered a vindictive penalty.   Indeed the fact that this suspension is an intrinsic and inseparable part of deposition precludes any possibility of its being treated as a separate legal entity.   Hence there can be no question of releasing the delinquent cleric from the suspension, no matter how repentant he may be, except by means of a dispensation from the indivisible vindictive penalty of deposition.   Should he be favored with such a dispensation he will also be dispensed in that same act from the suspension.

In order to describe the rôle played by suspension in the penalty of deposition it is necessary to recall that the effects of suspension, considered in themselves, are separable and follow the various kinds of suspension in varying degrees.[33]   Suspension may be general—from office and from benefice, or special—either from office or from benefice.   This special suspension may be either total or partial inasmuch as all the rights or only certain rights attached to the office or benefice are prohibited in their use.[34]   A general suspension prohibits a cleric from exercising all the rights pertaining to his orders, office and benefice.   A suspension is presumed to be general unless it is otherwise determined by the competent superior.[35] A special suspension, on the other hand, whether from office or from benefice, has only the effects specifically ascribed to it by law.[36]

It is the special suspension from office which is expressly in-

---

[31] Cf. canons 2241, § 1; 2278, § 1; Cappello, *De Censuris*, n. 497, p. 429; Aichner, *Compendium Iuris Ecclesiastici*, § 219, p. 740.

[32] Canons 2286; 2298, n. 2; Cappello, *loc. cit.;* Lega, *De Delictis et Poenis*, n. 199, p. 270.

[33] Cf. canon 2278, § 2: "Etiam suspensionis effectus separari queunt . . ."; Augustine, *A Commentary on Canon Law*, VIII, 217.

[34] Cf. canons 2281; 2278; 2279; Reiffenstuel, *Ius Canonicum Universum*, lib. V, tit. XXXIX, n. 162.

[35] Canon 2278, § 2: ". . . nisi aliud constat, in suspensione generaliter lata comprehenduntur omnes effectus . . ."

[36] Canon 2278, § 2: ". . . contra, in suspensione ab officio vel a beneficio omnes tantum effectus alterutrius speciei."

cluded by the legislator in the penalty of deposition.[37]   According to the Code a suspension from office without the additional specification of any limitation forbids every act of the power of orders and of jurisdiction and even of the mere administration attached to the office itself, but not the administration of the goods of one's benefice.[38]   Primarily the suspension from office is opposed to suspension from benefice.   In consequence it does not concern the rights affected by the latter.   The reason why the legislator did not include in deposition the suspension from benefice is quite obvious. Deposition brings with it not merely a suspension from benefice but a deprivation of benefices as well as a disability barring the delinquent cleric from ever acquiring any benefice in the future.[39]   In view of this fact it would be superfluous to include in deposition a suspension from benefice, a penalty which merely deprives the holder of the benefice of its accompanying fruits or income, but not of the benefice itself.[40]

On the other hand, the suspension from office makes a definite contribution to the effects of deposition despite the fact that this penalty also includes a privation of office.   The truth of this statement becomes apparent in the light of the fullness of meaning of the suspension *ab officio*.   In this suspension the term *office* cannot be limited to its strict sense as a permanent function created either by the divine or ecclesiastical law, conferred according to the rules of the sacred canons, and entailing at least some participation in ecclesiastical power, whether of orders or of jurisdiction.[41]   There is a ruling in the law that the term *office* is used in this strict sense unless the contrary is evident.[42]   Canon 2279, § 1, however, indicates that the term *officium* must be taken in a broad sense, for it defines the suspension *ab officio* as prohibiting *all* acts not only of

[37] Canon 2303, § 1.

[38] Canon 2279, § 1: "Suspensio ab officio simpliciter, nulla adiecta limitatione, vetat omnem actum tum potestatis ordinis et iurisdictionis, tum etiam merae administrationis ex officio competentis, excepta administratione bonorum proprii beneficii."

[39] Canon 2303, § 1.

[40] Canon 2280, § 1.

[41] Canon 145, § 1.

[42] Canon 145, § 2.

the power of orders and of jurisdiction, but also of mere administration.[48]

To demonstrate the significance of the suspension involved in deposition it should suffice to enumerate its essential prohibitions. In the first place the suspension *ab officio* forbids all use or exercise of the power of orders.[44] This power, whether it be ordinary—as when it is received in ordination,[45] or delegated—as when it is attached to an office by the legitimate ecclesiastical superior or committed by him to a particular person,[46] is directed towards divine public worship and the sanctification of souls,[47] especially through the composition and administration of the sacraments and sacramentals. In a word, this suspension prohibits the exercise of all those functions of the power of orders which by the institution of Christ or of His Church are ordained for divine worship and can be performed only by clerics.[48] The suspension, moreover, concerns all orders, the episcopacy as well as major and minor orders, but not the tonsure, for this rite confers no powers but only a disposition for the reception of orders.[49]

Secondly, the total suspension *ab officio* forbids every act of the power of jurisdiction,[50] that is, the exercise of that power which is

---

[48] Cf. Blat, *Commentarium Textus Codicis Iuris Canonici* (Romae: Collegio Angelico, 1921-1927), Lib. V *De Delictis et Poenis* (Romae: Collegio Angelico, 1924). Hereafter this work will be cited simply as *Commentarium*. Roberti, *De Delictis et Poenis*, I, n. 379, p. 479; A Coronata, *Institutiones*, IV, n. 1799, p. 233; Rainer, *Suspension of Clerics*, 68.

[44] Canon 2279, § 1: "Suspensio ab officio simpliciter . . . vetat omnem actum tum potestatis ordinis . . ."

[45] Cf. canon 109: "Qui in ecclesiasticam hierarchiam cooptantur . . . in gradibus potestatis ordinis constituuntur sacra ordinatione . . ."

[46] Cf. canon 210: "Potestas ordinis a legitimo Superiore ecclesiastico sive adnexa officio sive commissa personae . . . "

[47] Canon 948: "Ordo ex Christi institutione clericos a laicis in Ecclesia distinguit ad fidelium regimen et cultus divini ministerium."

[48] Cf. canon 2256, § 1.

[49] Canons 950, 949; cf. Roberti, *De Delictis et Poenis*, I, n. 379, pp. 479-480.

[50] Canon 2279, § 1: "Suspensio ab officio simpliciter . . . vetat omnem actum tum potestatis . . . iurisdictionis . . ."

conferred by divine institution upon the Church[51] and granted to clerics by canonical mission[52] for the governing of the faithful and the administering to them of the necessary means for eternal salvation. It prohibits the use or exercise of all jurisdiction, ordinary or delegated, judicial or extrajudicial, for the internal as well as for the external forum.[53]

Thirdly, the total suspension *ab officio* forbids all acts of administration proper to the office.[54] Through this prohibition it is forbidden to exercise any faculties founded on any office and ordained for a spiritual end, even though they involve no exercise of the power of orders or jurisdiction, as, for example, the faculty of electing, presenting, or nominating for ecclesiastical offices, the administration of ecclesiastical goods,[55] the making of investments and the alienation of church property.[56] Canonists since the Code also enumerate among the acts of administration rather than among the acts of jurisdiction such acts as the solemn administration of baptism, extreme unction, Viaticum, the granting of dimissorial letters, and the juridical assistance at marriage as a qualified witness.[57]

It is evident that the suspension *ab officio* which is decreed absolutely and without any restriction implies not only the prohibition to exercise the rights proper to the office which the delinquent cleric possesses but also the probihibition to exercise *any* acts of orders and jurisdiction of any kind. It is precisely this extensive prohibition of the suspension *ab officio* which enables it to bring a distinct contribution to the constitution of the penalty of deposition. In other words, this suspension is not rendered nugatory or super-

---

[51] Canon 196: "Potestas iurisdictionis seu regiminis quae ex divina institutione est in Ecclesia . . ."

[52] Canon 109.

[53] Canons 196; 197; 201; cf. Blat, *Commentarium*, V, n. 108, p. 160; Roberti, *op. cit.*, I, n. 379, p. 480.

[54] Canon 2279, § 1: "Suspensio ab officio simpliciter . . . vetat omnem actum . . . tum etiam merae administrationis ex officio competentis, excepta administratione bonorum proprii beneficii."

[55] Cf. Roberti, *De Delictis et Poenis*, I, n. 379, p. 480.

[56] Cf. Rainer, *Suspension of Clerics*, 70.

[57] Chelodi, *Ius Poenale*, n. 43, p. 48, not. 6; Cappello, *De Censuris*, n. 499, p. 434; Vermeersch-Creusen, *Epitome*, III, n. 483, p. 287.

fluous by its combination in the penalty of deposition with privation of offices, benefices and dignities.   As will be seen in a subsequent section, the penalty of privation deprives a cleric of his office
and in consequence radically takes from him his ordinary jurisdiction inasmuch as this power is attached by law to ecclesiastical
offices.[58]   In this particular point the penalty of privation included
in deposition exceeds the effects of the inherent suspension *ab officio,*
for the latter in itself does not deprive a cleric of his office, but
only prohibits its lawful use and in certain circumstances specifically determined in the Code even its valid use.[59]   On the other
hand, privation of office does not involve a loss of the power of
orders, or a loss of the strictly personal delegated jurisdiction, or
even a loss of the ordinary or delegated jurisdiction which is enjoyed in virtue of another office not included in the penalty.   The
privation involved in deposition, however, extends to all offices,
hence it revokes all ordinary jurisdiction as well as all delegated
jurisdiction granted by reason of the dignity or office.   In this regard suspension *ab officio* exceeds privation, for it not only prohibits every exercise of jurisdiction of any kind, but forbids as well
any act of orders, minor, major and even episcopal.   United in the
penalty of deposition both penalties play an essential rôle while at
the same time they fortify each other's effects.   Both in turn are
further strengthened or aggravated by the supervening disability
which is also involved in deposition.

A cleric who is suspended from office is not thereby disqualified
(inhabilis) for other offices or benefices.   This doctrine was not the
common teaching of canonists before the Code, but it was ably defended by Suarez[60] and Wernz.[61]   Even the Code has not put an
end to all discussion on this point.   In canon 2283 it is ordained
that the effects of excommunication as listed in canon 2265, which
includes mention of the offender's disqualification, should be applied

---

[58] Cf. canon 197: "Potestas iurisdictionis ordinaria ea est quae ipso iure
adnexa est officio . . ."; canon 183, § 1: "Amittitur officium ecclesiasticum . . .
privatione . . ."

[59] Canon 2284.

[60] *De Censuris,* Disp. XXVII, sec. I, n. 26.

[61] *Ius Decretalium,* VI, n. 209, p. 217.

also to suspension. Whether this application is to be limited to a general suspension or whether it is to be extended to every suspension is a subject open for discussion. Canonists for the greater part are inclined to recognize the application only for the general suspension,[62] and rightly so, for the Code properly defines the effects of its partial suspensions [63] and does not state that any other effects are contemplated. Indeed, the Code expressly declares that the general suspension shall have all the effects mentioned in Book V, Chapter II, Article III,[64] whereas the special suspension, either from office or from benefice, total or partial, shall have only the effects ascribed to the specific suspension.[65] At least it must be conceded that the law is sufficiently doubtful to call for a strict interpretation, which implies that the effect of disqualification is not to be attributed to suspensions which are not of a general character.[66]

As regards deposition there can be no question. The legislator in defining this penalty expressly adds to the suspension from office a disqualification for any future office, dignity or benefice in the Church.[67] Indeed, this disability includes also the offices and benefices which the delinquent formerly enjoyed, for in deposition the disqualification is combined with total privation. Hence, a deposed cleric not only loses the lawful use of orders but also the valid exercise of any jurisdiction.

The suspension *ab officio* is further qualified when combined in the penalty of deposition with privation. A cleric suspended from office is allowed to receive the fruits of his benefice and, although

---

[62] Augustine, *A Commentary on Canon Law*, VIII, 230; Ayrinhac-Lydon, *Penal Legislation*, n. 152, p. 112; Chelodi, *Ius Poenale*, n. 45, p. 61; A Coronata, *Institutiones*, IV, n. 1815, p. 245; Roberti, *De Delictis et Poenis*, I, n. 378, pp. 476-477; n. 379, p. 482; Rainer, *Suspension of Clerics*, 59-60; Woywod, *A Practical Commentary*, II, n. 2124, p. 452; Van Hove, *Commentarium Lovaniense in Codicem Iuris Canonici*, Vol. I, Tom. IV, *De Rescriptis* (Mechliniae: H. Dessain, 1936), n. 96, pp. 87-88. Hereafter this work will be referred to simply as *De Rescriptis*.

[63] Cf. canons 2279, 2280, 2281.

[64] Canons 2278-2285.

[65] Canon 2278, § 2.

[66] Cf. canons 19 and 2219, §§ 1, 3.

[67] Canon 2303, § 1.

he must make provision for a substitute in his office, he is permitted to administer personally the goods of his benefice.[68] In the penalty of deposition, however, the suspension from office is so united with privation of benefice [69] that not only is the beneficial income lost but the benefice itself with all its inherent rights and duties. This is a unique and characteristic feature of deposition. A suspension from office, even though it be perpetual, does not of itself deprive the affected cleric of his benefice or of his title to it. Even the special suspension from benefice does not produce this effect.[70] Suspension by its nature prohibits the exercise or enjoyment of specified rights but does not absolutely revoke them. However, canonists have always rightly maintained that it would be contrary to reason to allow a cleric to hold a benefice while he is perpetually suspended from its correspondent office. *Beneficium datur propter officium.*[71] Nevertheless, in virtue of a suspension, even a perpetual one, the benefice itself is not lost. To deprive the cleric of the benefice itself the penalty of privation must be invoked. Thus it is that in deposition the perpetual suspension from office is expressly combined with a perpetual privation of benefice. It should be noted that the Church unites these two penalties along with a perpetual disqualification for any office or benefice in the one penalty of deposition, making it distinct from all other penalties employed in the Church. Since the Church allows this penalty of deposition to be employed only as a punishment for crimes expressly mentioned in the law, one may readily find at least a negative norm for the use of the perpetual suspension of canon 2298.

The great similarity of the effects of suspension and deposition caused many canonists in the past to confuse the two penalties. They referred to deposition as a species of suspension or vice versa.[72]

---

[68] Cf. canons 2278, § 1; 2279, § 1; 2280; Schmalzgrueber, *Ius Ecclesiasticum Universum,* lib. V, tit. XXXIX, n. 297.

[69] Canon 2303, § 1.

[70] Canon 2280, § 1: "Suspensio a beneficio privat fructibus beneficii . . ."

[71] Cf. Suarez, *De Censuris,* Disp. XXX, sec. I, nn. 4, 16; Reiffenstuel, *Ius Canonicum Universum,* lib. V, tit. XXXIX, n. 170; Schmalzgrueber, *Ius Ecclesiasticum Universum,* lib. V, tit. XXXVII, n. 134.

[72] Cf. Suarez, *De Censuris,* Disp. XXX, sec. I, n. 10; Schmalzgrueber, *Ius*

It may be well, therefore, to insist on the distinction between these two penalties before one proceeds to an explicit consideration of the other penalties involved in deposition. Beyond all question the Code clearly establishes deposition as a very severe penalty, distinct from all others in her penal system and applied only in the cases expressly designated in the common law of the Church.[73]

It is true, however, in a general way that the two penalties share in common several points of similarity. Deposition certainly is a vindictive penalty. This characteristic is also proper to suspension when it is inflicted for a definite period of time or for always.[74] Again, suspension and deposition deprive the delinquent of the functions of order and of jurisdiction. One is never said to be suspended or deposed if he is barred from the reception of the sacraments or deprived of the common goods of the faithful. These privations pertain rather to excommunication and interdict.[75] Moreover, both penalties are proper only to clerics, for to them alone pertain the functions of orders and of jurisdiction, and also the incumbency in ecclesiastical offices and benefices.[76]

It is in regard to holy orders that suspension and deposition are especially similar. The power of holy orders conferred through a sacrament can neither be lost nor taken away. Only its lawful use can be governed by the Church. Suspension and deposition have this in common, then, that both prohibit only the lawful use of this power. Indeed, deposition has this effect precisely because it involves suspension. Neither privation nor disqualification, which are the other penalties inherent in deposition, can affect the continued existence of the power of orders already received in ordination. On the other hand, while suspension does not deprive the cleric of his orders, it is invoked for the purpose of prohibiting him from exercising them. In the penalty of deposition it performs the same function. Hence in this particular regard no distinction can be made

Ecclesiasticum Universum, lib. V, tit. XXVII, n. 134; Reiffenstuel, *Ius Canonicum Universum,* lib. V, tit. XXXIX, n. 160.

[73] Cf. canon 2303, §§ 1, 3.

[74] Suarez, *De Censuris,* Disp. XXX, sec. I, n. 1.

[75] Cf. canons 2257; 2268; Suarez, *op. cit.,* Disp. XXX, sec. I, n. 2.

[76] Cf. canon 118.

between perpetual suspension and deposition, for the effects are the same.[77]

Suspension and deposition, however, differ in this that suspension from office and benefice does not take away the title to them, but only deprives the cleric of the use of the rights of the office and the reception of the fruits of the benefice. Deposition, on the other hand, deprives the cleric of the very title to the office and benefice, so that if he is later rehabilitated by a dispensation it becomes necessary for him to obtain the forfeited office or benefice through a new canonical appointment.[78] Deposition, moreover, is distinct from suspension because it adds to this prohibition of exercising an office and of enjoying a benefice the disqualification in regard to future clerical rights as well as the privation of acquired clerical rights.[79] Suspension, moreover, can be employed as a temporary or as a perpetual punishment; deposition, on the other hand, by its very nature is perpetual. Even perpetual suspension does not exclude the hope of pardon and restoration, and in this it is far different from deposition.[80] Finally, the very notion of the penalty of deposition as given by the Code should make it obvious that this penalty is more severe than even a perpetual suspension, since it includes this punishment and aggravates it by combining with it disability and privation, whereby the delinquent becomes dispossessed even of the benefice or pension with the title to which he had been ordained.[81]

[77] Cf. Suarez, *De Censuris*, Disp. XXX, sec. I, nn. 10, 11; Wernz, *Ius Decretalium*, VI, n. 120, p. 125.

[78] Cf. Suarez, *De Censuris*, Disp. XXX, sec. I, n. 4; Wernz, *Ius Decretalium*, VI, n. 120, p. 125; Cocchi, *Commentarium in Codicem Iuris Canonici* (Taurinorum Augustae: Marietti, 1931-1938), Lib. V. *De Delictis et Poenis* (4. ed., Taurinorum Augustae: Marietti, 1938). Hereafter this work will be quoted as *Commentarium*. Konings, *Theologia Moralis* (Boston, 1874), n. 1691, p. 781; Ballerini-Palmieri, *Opus Theologicum Morale* (Prati, 1889-1893), VII, n. 544, p. 303; n. 545, p. 304; De Meester, *Juris Canonici et Juris Canonico-Civilis Compendium* (nova editio, Brugis: Desclée, 1921-1928), III, pars 2a, n. 1797, p. 225. Hereafter this work will be referred to simply as *Compendium*.

[79] Cf. Vermeersch-Creusen, *Epitome*, III, n. 498, p. 300.

[80] Cf. Aichner, *Compendium Iuris Ecclesiastici*, § 219, p. 744.

[81] Cf. canon 2303, § 1; A Coronata, *Institutiones*, IV, n. 1834, p. 261; Wernz, *Ius Decretalium*, VI, n. 201, p. 208.

(2) Disability

Deposition, according to the express declaration of the Code, brings with it a canonical disability for any office, dignity, benefice, pension or position *(munus)* in the Church.[82] As a constituent element of deposition this disability is manifestly a vindictive penalty. It is far different from the disabilities for ecclesiastical offices and dignities which flow from the natural law, such as the lack of age, of sanity, or of knowledge, or which derive from the positive divine law, such as the lack of baptism or the feminine sex of the person.[83] Certainly these latter disabilities are not penalties, nor are they even disqualifications in the strict sense, for a disqualification by its very nature supposes that the person was previously qualified by the constitutive law of the Church as well as by the natural and positive divine law, but is now by the will of the legislator disqualified for placing certain juridical acts.[84]

Properly considered a disqualifying law is one that renders a person juridically incapable of performing certain legal acts. While an invalidating law directly governs the act itself in such a way that the act will stand as invalid if it is performed by anyone contrary to the dispositions of the law,[85] a disqualifying law directly affects the agent by making him incapable of placing certain juridical acts or by rendering his will so legally ineffective in regard to them that should he perform any of these acts they are nonetheless null and void.[86] Such laws which render a person disqualified to act validly are manifestly odious because of the severe demand inherent in them. In consequence the Code states that no law should be con-

---

[82] Canon 2303, § 1: "Depositio . . . secumfert . . . et inhabilitatem ad quaelibet officia, dignitates, beneficia, pensiones, munera in Ecclesia . . ."

[83] Cf. Lega, *De Delictis et Poenis*, n. 202, p. 273.

[84] Cf. Van Hove, *Commentarium Lovaniense in Codicem Iuris Canonici*, Vol. I, Tom. II, *De Legibus Ecclesiasticis* (Mechliniae: H. Dessain, 1930), n. 157, p. 164. Hereafter this work will be referred to as *De Legibus*.

[85] Cf., *e. g.*, canon 1094, which precludes the validity of a matrimonial contract when it is exchanged by Catholics without their observance of the prescribed canonical form.

[86] Cf., *e. g.*, canon 1067, declaring a person disqualified who lacks the required age for marriage.

sidered as being disqualifying in its character unless the wording of
the law explicitly gives it this effect.[87]

Like all true laws, a disqualifying law has for its objective the
common good. However, since disqualification proves a detriment
to the individual, it may also be employed as a penalty for delinquency.[88] In this usage disqualification may be defined as an impediment which, when it is inflicted as a punishment for a delict,
prevents the lawful and valid acquisition of a right.[89] The Code
employs disqualification for certain rights and favors as a penalty
by itself,[90] or as a concomitant part of other penalties, as in juridical infamy [91] and deposition.[92] Indeed, it has been well termed the
characteristic element of deposition.[93]

With deposition a cleric is not only suspended from office and
deprived of all his benefices, offices, and dignities, but he is also rendered incapable of validly acquiring thereafter any ecclesiastical
office or benefice whatever. The disqualifying effect of deposition
has always been recognized as essential to this penalty as its long
history amply demonstrates.[94] The Code, however, in conformity
with its fundamental principle that there are no disqualifications
except those which are clearly stated in the law [95] includes in its
definition of deposition express mention of the disqualifications involved in this penalty. Accordingly, deposition disqualifies the
cleric for obtaining:

(a.) *Any ecclesiastical office.* An ecclesiastical office is a permanent function created by either the divine or the ecclesiastical

---

[87] Canon 11: " . . . inhabilitantes eae tantum leges habendae sint quibus
. . . inhabilem esse personam expresse vel aequivalenter statuitur."

[88] Cf. Michiels, *Normae Generales Iuris Canonici* (Lublin: Universitas Catholica, 1929), I, 271; Van Hove, *De Legibus*, n. 165, p. 172.

[89] Cf. Cocchi, *Commentarium*, VIII, n. 113, p. 195.

[90] Cf. canons 2291, n. 9; 2298, n. 5.

[91] Canon 2294, § 1.

[92] Canon 2303, § 1.

[93] Sipos, *Enchiridion Iuris Canonici* (Pécs: Ex Typographia Haladas R. T.,
1926), § 240, p. 947, not. 8.

[94] Cf. Part I of this dissertation; also Reiffenstuel, *Ius Canonicum Universum*, lib. V, tit. XXXVII, nn. 20, 26; S. Smith, *Elements of Ecclesiastical
Law* (3. ed., New York, 1888), III, n. 1924, p. 125.

[95] Cf. canon 11.

law, conferred according to the rules of the sacred canons and involving some participation in ecclesiastical power, whether of orders or of jurisdiction.[96] The term must be taken in its strict sense, for in the definition of deposition the disqualification is also expressly extended to include offices in the broad sense *(quaelibet munera)*. Deposition, therefore, renders the delinquent cleric juridically incapable of acquiring not only an office which implies a participation in the power of orders or of jurisdiction but also any assignment or authorized duty in the Church.

(b.) *Any dignities.* A dignity is a benefice enjoying besides jurisdiction the prerogatives of honor and precedence. The primary ecclesiastical dignities are these: 1. the supreme pontificate; 2. the cardinalate; 3. the patriarchate; 4. the archiepiscopate; 5. the episcopate; and 6. an abbacy or prelacy, especially when it is endowed with exemption.[97] Minor dignities exist in cathedral and collegiate churches.[98] According to Sipos, in some chapters there is one, in others there are two or more dignities, such as the archdeacon, the archpriest, the dean, the prior, the *primicerius* or chanter and the *scholasticus* who presides over the schools.[99] Cocchi declares that these dignities are today likened to minor prelacies, inasmuch as they establish the right of precedence but do not confer any jurisdiction.[100]

(c.) *Any benefices.* A benefice is a juridical entity, perpetually constituted or erected by competent ecclesiastical authority, consisting of a sacred office and the right of receiving the revenue from the endowment of the office.[101] The Code distinguishes various kinds of benefices.[102] They are called (a.) consistorial if they are usually conferred in consistory; all others are known as non-consistorial; (b.) secular or religious, according as they concern exclu-

---

[96] Canon 145, § 1.

[97] Ferraris, *Prompta Bibliotheca*, s.v. *"Beneficium,"* I, 549.

[98] Cf. Vermeersch-Creusen, *Epitome*, I, n. 491 [449], p. 364; III, n. 467, p. 279; Augustine, *A Commentary on Canon Law*, II, 426; Cappello, *De Censuris*, n. 154, p. 152; Cerato, *Censurae Vigentes*, 65.

[99] *Enchiridion Iuris Canonici*, § 54, p. 268.

[100] *Commentarium*, II, n. 297, p. 287.

[101] Canon 1409.

[102] Canon 1411.

sively the secular or the religious clergy; (c.) double (or residential) or simple (or non-residential) according as the duty of residence is or is not attached to the benefice besides the other duties incumbent on the holder of the benefice; (d.) manual (temporary) or perpetual (permanent) according as they are conferred either revocably or permanently; (e.) pastoral *(curata)* or non-pastoral *(non-curata)* according as the care of souls is or is not attached to the benefice. The disqualification contained in deposition extends to any and all of these benefices without distinction.

(d.) *Any pensions.* An ecclesiastical pension designates a cleric's lawfully approved right to a portion of the fruits of another's benefice.[103] Pensions are either perpetual or temporal. A perpetual pension is one that has been separated forever from the benefice and must be delivered by all successors in the benefice. In this type the pension constitutes a real obligation on the benefice itself. A temporal pension is one that has been imposed for the duration of the life of either the beneficiary or the pensionary. If imposed for the life of the pensionary it is a real, though only temporary, obligation imposed on the benefice. If imposed for the life of the beneficiary the obligation is personal, for it is imposed on the person of the beneficiary and not on the benefice itself. Such are the personal pensions which do not come under the name of benefices.[104] They are, nevertheless, part of the fruits of the benefice. In consequence, they can only be conferred on clerics.[105] In the penalty of deposition a cleric is disqualified for obtaining any ecclesiastical pension whatsover.

(e.) *Any positions (munera).* As has already been observed previously, the disqualification extends to all offices even in the broad sense of that term. The Code only emphasizes by its use of the term *munera* the complete disqualification of the deposed

---

[103] Cf. Reiffenstuel, *Ius Canonicum Universum*, lib. III, tit. V, n. 84; Cappello, *De Censuris*, n. 154, p. 152; Vermeersch-Creusen, *Epitome*, I, n. 240 [207], p. 210.

[104] Cf. canon 1412, n. 4; S.R.R., *Pensionis*, 18 dec. 1928, coram R.P.D. Francisco Parrillo, dec. LVI—*Decisiones*, XX (1928) 492-498.

[105] Cf. canon 118.

cleric for any office, commission or duty constituted or exercised for a spiritual purpose within the Church.[106]

Since legal capacity for obtaining these offices, benefices, dignities and pensions is established by the common law of the Church,[107] only the supreme authority, namely, the Holy See, can institute disqualifications in regard to them.[108] The Code itself expressly states that if there is question of acquiring things for which the common law ordains certain qualifications, then the penalty of disqualification can be inflicted by the Apostolic See alone.[109] While this prescript is contained among the canons governing the common vindictive penalties, this is no reason why it should not apply, and especially so, to vindictive penalties proper to clerics. It is true that in applying penalties it is not lawful to employ analogy,[110] but it is not unlawful to use it in defining the competence of superiors or in making a more benign interpretation of a penalty.[111] Moreover, the whole Code bespeaks the fundamental juridic principle that, as the status of a person in the Church is governed by the common law, so also any incapacity for exercising rights which are attached to the status, whether lay, clerical or religious, can only be established by the supreme legislator.[112]

In the past canonists found in the perpetual character of deposition the source of its consequent disqualification of clerics for ecclesiastical offices and benefices. Since deposition was a perpetual penalty in its nature and effects, it was by this very fact that it disqualified the cleric for any future office or benefice.[113] According to the present definition of the Code, however, deposition de-

---

[106] Cf. canon 145; Cappello, *De Censuris,* n. 154, p. 152.

[107] Cf. canon 118.

[108] Cf. Wernz, *Ius Decretalium,* VI, n. 109, p. 115; Chelodi, *Ius Poenale,* n. 51, p. 67; Hinschius, *Kirchenrecht,* IV, 731.

[109] Canon 2296, § 1.

[110] Canon 20.

[111] Hollweck, *Die kirchlichen Strafgesetze,* p. 116; Sipos, *Enchiridion Iuris Canonici,* § 240, p. 944; Vermeersch-Creusen, *Epitome,* III, n. 497, p. 298.

[112] Cf. Lega, *De Delictis et Poenis,* n. 191, p. 258, not. 1; Sole, *De Delictis et Poenis,* n. 280, p. 198.

[113] Cf. Reiffenstuel, *Ius Canonicum Universum,* lib. V, tit. 37, n. 26; Suarez, *De Censuris,* Disp. XXX, sec. I, nn. 5, 13.

rives its perpetual character precisely from its inherent disqualifications. As Cardinal Lega has observed, these disqualifications are by their very nature a perpetual penalty.[114] It is these disqualifications that impart to deposition the perpetual penal consequence in which they stand united with the suspension from and the privation of office. These latter penalties affect the acquired rights of a cleric and do not of themselves affect rights to be acquired. It is the supervening disqualification which forever guarantees the effects of the suspension and privation by rendering the cleric incapable of acquiring rights to any office, benefice, dignity or pension in the future.

It is, therefore, the incapacity which is involved in deposition that disqualifies the deposed cleric radically and absolutely for acquiring any office, benefice, dignity, or pension in the Church. This incapacity, when considered in itself, affects only those rights which a cleric has not yet acquired. As a penalty it is subject to strict interpretation. In consequence, it must be said that it only impedes the lawful and valid acquisition of an office, benefice or pension, but does not deprive a cleric of those rights he has already acquired.[115] Thus a cleric who incurs simply this penalty of incapacity cannot validly acquire any office or benefice in the future, but he does not thereby lose those which he already possesses. Acquired rights are completely lost by way of punishment only through privation.[116] Hence the Code states that rights already acquired are not lost by a supervening disqualification *unless* there is added to it the penalty of privation.[117] This, however, is accomplished in the penalty of deposition. Besides the suspension from office and the disqualification for obtaining any offices, benefices, dignities and pensions,

---

[114] Cf. *De Delictis et Poenis*, n. 202, p. 273.

[115] Suarez, *De Censuris*, Disp. XXX, sec. I, n. 14; Wernz, *Ius Decretalium*, VI, n. 112, pp. 116-117; Ayrinhac-Lydon, *Penal Legislation*, n. 162, pp. 122-123; Sipos, *Enchiridion Iuris Canonici*, § 240, p. 944; S. Smith *Elements of Ecclesiastical Law*, III, n. 1924, p. 125.

[116] Cf. Chelodi, *Ius Poenale*, n. 51, p. 67; Lega, *De Delictis et Poenis*, n. 203, p. 273.

[117] Canon 2296, § 2: "Iura iam quaesita non amittuntur ob supervenientem inhabilitatem, nisi huic addatur poena privationis."

deposition includes the privation of any and all these offices, etc., which the cleric possessed. The deposed cleric, therefore, is not only disqualified for validly acquiring any future benefice, office, dignity or pension, but he is also disqualified for regaining those which he formerly possessed.

(3) Privation

Deposition also brings with it a privation of all the delinquent cleric's offices, dignities, benefices, pensions, positions, and indeed, even such of these as constituted his title of ordination.[118] While the acquired rights of a cleric to an office, benefice, dignity or pension are not lost by a supervening disqualification, yet these rights are lost through deposition, for in this penalty disqualification is expressly combined with privation. The severity of deposition is clearly manifested: not only does it render the delinquent cleric juridically incapable of ever acquiring those rights which are proper to the clergy,[119] but it also deprives him of those which he has acquired up to this time. The nature of deposition is truly revealed, therefore, in considering the penalty of privation as a punishment in itself and as combined with the other penalties inherent in deposition.

Privation, as it is employed in the Code, may be defined in general as an act of lawful authority whereby a person is despoiled of some right or benefit. Not every privation, however, is a penalty. Only that privation which is accomplished in punishment of a delict constitutes in reality a canonical penalty.[120] Moreover, while the common element of ecclesiastical penalties is the privation of some good,[121] not all the penalties are designated by the generic term privation. For the greater part they have received specific names as well as determination as to the quantity and quality of the goods lost in the penalty.[122]

[118] Canon 2303, § 1: "Depositio . . . secumfert . . . tum etiam privationem illorum quae reus habeat, licet eorum titulo fuerit ordinatus."

[119] Cf. canon 118.

[120] Vermeersch-Creusen, *Epitome,* III, n. 403, p. 236: "Quare poenae non sunt: coactio ad actum ponendum, reparatio damni illati, poena mere conventionalis, impensae iudicii, solutio cautionis."

[121] Cf. canon 2215.

[122] Cf. *CIC,* lib. V, sec. II, *De poenis in specie,* esp. canons 2257; 2268; 2278; 2291, n. 9; 2293; 2294; 2297; 2298, n. 5; 2303; 2305.

On the other hand, some penalties are still designated by the term privation and are specified by the express mention of the goods or rights threatened with loss. Among the vindictive penalties common to all the members of the Church, for example, the Code mentions privation of the sacramentals.[123] The Code lists also the privation of ecclesiastical pensions and of other rights or privileges,[124] the privation of the right of precedence, of the active and passive vote, of the right of using honorary titles, of wearing robes and insignia granted by the Church.[125] Among the vindictive penalties for clerics the Code lists the privation of one or the other rights connected with a benefice,[126] for instance, the right of preaching or of hearing confessions, or, in the case of residential bishops, the right of granting faculties or of freely appointing to offices.[127] Still more severe than this penalty is the privation of the benefice or office itself, with or without a pension.[128]

The penalty of deposition brings with it a privation of any office, dignity, benefice or pension which the delinquent cleric possessed. The severity of the penalty of privation of benefice alone is amply demonstrated by the rigid provisions of law governing its use. In regard to the penal privation of a benefice the Code expressly states that an irremovable beneficiary can be deprived of his benefice only in those cases which are expressly mentioned in the law.[129] A removable beneficiary, however, can be deprived of his benefice also for other reasonable causes.[130] Even in this case the privation is a vindictive penalty and in consequence the reasonable causes of

[123] Canon 2291, n. 6.

[124] Canon 2291, n. 7.

[125] Canon 2291, n. 11.

[126] Canon 2298, n. 4.

[127] Cf. Augustine, *A Commentary on Canon Law*, VIII, 256.

[128] Canon 2298, n. 6.

[129] Canon 2299, § 1. Cases stated in the law are either *latae sententiae*: canons 2396; 2397; 2398; 2266; or *ferendae sententiae*: (a.) in preceptive terms: canons 2314, § 1, n. 2; 2331, § 2; 2340, § 2; 2343, § 2, n. 3; 2354, § 2; 2359, §§ 2, 3; 2368, § 1; 2345; 2346; 2350, § 2; 2381, n. 2; 2177, n. 3 and 2180, 2181; (b) in optional terms: canons 2324; 2336, § 1; 2355; 2359, § 3; 2360, § 2; 2394, n. 2; 2403; 2405.

[130] Canon 2299, § 1.

which the Code speaks must be interpreted in reference to delicts and indeed proportionately to the gravity of the punishment.

The vindictive penalty of privation is based solely on the commission of delicts. Hence it must be kept clearly distinct from the administrative privation of a pastor of his parish.[131] This is properly termed by the Code removal [132] rather than privation, for while the pastor is indeed deprived of his parish this is not the result of a penalty for delicts but simply a case in which private rights conflicting with the common welfare must be sacrificed. In other words, this administrative removal is accomplished not as a punishment for the pastor but as a provision for the spiritual welfare of his subjects.[133]

On the other hand, deprivation as a punishment, in whatever manner executed, whether judicially or administratively, is always a vindictive penalty. As such it is involved by the express will of the legislator in the penalty of deposition. It is immaterial to this penalty whether the benefice has annexed to it the care of souls or not, whether it connotes a removable or an irremovable incumbency, whether in its nature it is consistorial or non-consistorial, secular or religious. Universally and without distinction deposition totally deprives the cleric of any and all the offices, benefices or dignities which he possessed in the Church. In other words, whenever a sentence of deposition has been duly pronounced against a cleric no matter what rank or dignity he formerly enjoyed, he is forthwith deprived of all offices, dignities and benefices throughout the entire Church, for this is a penalty of the common law whose effects obtain universally.[134]

---

[131] Cf. canons 2147-2161.

[132] Lib. IV, pars III, tit. XXVII, *De modo procedendi in remotione parochorum inamovibilium*, canons 2147-2156; tit. XXVIII, *De modo procedendi in remotione parochorum amovibilium*, canons 2156-2161.

[133] Cf. Connor, *The Administrative Removal of Pastors* (Catholic University of America, Canon Law Studies, No. 104, Washington, D. C., 1937), pp. 1-6; Raus, *Institutiones Canonicae* (2. ed., Lugduni: Typis Emmanuelis Vitte, 1931), n. 75, p. 129; Prümmer, *Manuale Iuris Canonici* (5. ed., Friburgi Brisgoviae: Herder, 1927), q. 84, pp. 116-118; Maroto, *Institutiones Iuris Canonici ad Normam Novi Codicis* (3. ed., Romae: Apud Commentarium pro Religiosis, 1921), I, n. 685.

[134] Canon 2303, § 1.

It is readily seen, therefore, how the ordinary effects of privation are increased in this penalty of deposition. Privation as a canonical punishment consists in this that the cleric is deprived of his ecclesiastical office or benefice without at the same time being appointed to another, but without being disqualified to hold the same or other ecclesiastical offices or benefices in the future.[185] By privation the title or possession of an office or of a benefice is lost, and the office or benefice is then juridically vacant.[186] The privation, however, does not effect a disqualification for being validly appointed again to this office or benefice or to another.[187] In the penalty of deposition, however, a disqualification is expressly united with privation, so that a deposed cleric is not only deprived of his offices, benefices, dignities and pensions, but is also disqualified for obtaining these or any others again.[188]

While simple privation does not disqualify the cleric for acquiring anew the same or another benefice, neither does it necessarily extend to all the offices or benefices which a cleric may possess. As a cleric may lawfully hold several compatible offices,[189] so also he may be deprived of one of them without suffering the loss of others. Thus, a priest may be deprived of his office as vicar general and not be deprived of his office as pastor. Deposition on the contrary brings with it not only a disqualification for obtaining any office, benefice, dignity, or pension, but also a total privation of *all* the offices, benefices or dignities which the cleric possessed anywhere in the Church.

Privation of a benefice or office takes from the cleric, besides the right of receiving its income, the office itself and in consequence the rank, dignity and powers annexed to the office,[140] but it does not

---

[185] Cf. Reiffenstuel, *Ius Canonicum Universum*, lib. V, tit. 37, n. 21; Smith, *Elements of Ecclesiastical Law*, n. 1806, p. 77.

[186] Canon 183, § 1: "Amittitur officium ecclesiasticum . . . privatione . . ."

[187] Cf. Sipos, *Enchiridion Iuris Canonici*, § 240, p. 945.

[188] Cf. canon 2303, § 1; Suarez, *De Censuris*, Disp. XXX, sec. I, n. 6; Cocchi, *Commentarium*, VIII, n. 118, p. 200.

[189] Cf. canon 156, § 1.

[140] Cf. canons 197, § 1: "Potestas iurisdictionis ordinaria ea est quae ipso iure adnexa est officio"; 208: ". . . cessat amisso officio"; 183, § 1: "Amittitur officium ecclesiasticum . . . privatione . . ."

bring with it suspension.[141]   In deposition, however, privation is united with a suspension *ab officio* so that a cleric is not only deprived of his offices, benefices and dignities, but is also forever forbidden to perform any act of the ecclesiastical ministry.   Thus a priest who has been *deprived* of his office as pastor, though he loses thereby the rights and privileges inherent in that office,[142] can, nevertheless, continue to exercise the functions of the priesthood as much as any priest who has never been appointed to the care of souls.   A pastor, however, who has been *deposed* can exercise no act of orders or jurisdiction.

The sacred canons, moreover, strictly forbid a cleric to be deprived of a benefice or pension which constituted his title of ordination, unless his decent support is otherwise provided.[148]   This prohibition emerges from the very heart of the Church's legislation which governs the title of ordination.   The knowledge of the high dignity of the priesthood and the reverence due to it influenced the Church, early in her history, to demand that everyone approaching the sacred ministry be possessed of a title or the means of subsistence.   It has already been observed [144] how the Council of Chalcedon (451) entirely prohibited absolute ordinations and demanded that clerics be ordained not for the universal Church but for some particular church, martyry or monastery.[145]   When in the fifth century churches came to be called titles a cleric who was ordained for such a church was said to be ordained for this title and he himself was said to be *intitulatus*.[146]   In the twelfth century, however, it had become customary to confer not only tonsure and minor orders but also major orders without a title.   In order to put an end to this

[141] Cf. Lega, *De Delictis et Poenis,* n. 207, pp. 279-280; De Meester, *Compendium,* III, pars 2, n. 1797, p. 225.

[142] Cf., *e. g.,* canons 462; 738, § 1; 848; 850; 873, § 1.

[148] Canon 2299, § 3: "Nequit clericus privari beneficio aut pensione cuius titulo ordinatus fuit, nisi aliunde eius honeste sustentationi provideatur, salvo praescripto can. 2303, 2304."

[144] Cf. *supra,* p. 6, note 25.

[145] C. 6—Fulton, *Index Canonum,* p. 179.   A martyry was a church, or more properly a chapel, built over a martyr's grave.   In the West such chapels were called *memoriae martyrum.*—Schroeder, *Disciplinary Decrees,* 96.

[146] Cf. Many, *Praelectiones de Sacra Ordinatione,* n. 132, p. 336.

practice, Pope Alexander III (1159-1181) compelled bishops who
so ordained priests and deacons to provide from their own episcopal
funds a suitable maintenance for them, should they ever be in want,
until they had received a title that would assure them a respectable
subsistence.[147]   Pope Innocent III (1198-1216) extended this discipline to include the provision of a title for subdeacons.[148]   Since
then the common law of the Church has required a title only for the
major orders.[149]

The Code of Canon Law voices anew the perennial legislation
of the Church when it requires for lawful ordination to major orders
a canonical title.[150]   The canonical title for the secular clergy is
the title of a benefice or, in default of this, the title of a patrimony
or a pension.[151]   If none of these are available the deficiency may
be supplied by the title of "service of the diocese" and in place's
subject to the Sacred Congregation of the Propagation of the Faith
by the "title of the mission."   The ordinary, however, must give a
priest whom he has promoted under either of these titles a benefice
or an office with a salary sufficient for his proper support.[152]   The
canonical title for regulars is the solemn religious profession which
is called, by a marvelous association of concepts, the "title of poverty."   For religious with perpetual simple vows the title is *mensa
communis,* or *congregationis,* or a similar provision, according to
their constitutions.   All other religious are governed by the law for
seculars.[153]

Though these canonical titles differ in many respects they are
united in a common purpose.   In every case the title of ordination
is designed to assure the one ordained of a sufficient and perpetual
support.[154]   Behind each specific title lies the reverence and respect

---

[147] Cf. III General Lateran Council (1179), c. 5—Mansi, XXII, 220;
Schroeder, *Disciplinary Decrees,* 220.

[148] C. 16, X, *de praebendis,* III, 5.

[149] Cf. Conc. Trident., sess. XXI, *de ref.,* c. 2.

[150] Cf. canon 974, § 1, n. 7.

[151] Canon 979, § 1.

[152] Cf. canon 981, § 2.

[153] Cf. canon 982.

[154] Cf. canon 979.

of the Church for the dignity and honor of the ministers of God. Never should they be compelled to beg or engage in secular employments, to their own dishonor, to the disgrace of their sacred character, and to the scandal of the faithful.[155]

In conformity with its rigid provisions of law which govern the title of ordination the sacred canons strictly forbid a cleric to be deprived of a benefice or pension which constituted his title of ordination unless his decent support is otherwise secured.[156] If an ordinary should deprive a cleric of the benefice or pension to which he has been ordained, this ordinary is bound in justice to provide in some other way for the decent support of the cleric.[157] The law, however, does allow one exception. A cleric can be deprived of a benefice or pension which constituted his title of ordination if he has committed a delict which is punishable with deposition.[158] After the infliction of this penalty the ordinary is no longer obliged in justice to provide for the decent maintenance of the cleric. This singular property of deposition, even when it alone is considered, reveals the great severity of this penalty.

Whenever the penalty of deposition is fully warranted the Church continues to manifest a benevolent attitude. Just as the basic purposes of the title of ordination are not contingent upon the worthiness of individual clerics, so too the obligations of the ordinary toward the deposed cleric are not completely extinguished. The sacred canons ordain that if a cleric is truly in need after his deposition the ordinary shall charitably provide for him in the best possible manner lest he be forced to go begging and bring dishonor on the clerical state.[159] As will be seen in the discussion about the effects of deposition, this precept of the Code ceases when the de-

---

[155] Cf. Conc. Trident., sess. XXI, *de ref.*, c. 2; Pius V, const. *Romanus Pontifex*, 14 oct. 1568, §§ 1, 2, 3—*Fontes*, n. 129; S. C. de Prop. Fide, instr. 27 apr. 1871—*Fontes*, n. 4878.

[156] Canon 2299, § 3.

[157] Cf. Augustine, *A Commentary on Canon Law*, VIII, 257; Cocchi, *Commentarium*, VIII, n. 115, p. 197; Ayrinhac-Lydon, *Penal Legislation*, n. 165, p. 126; Sipos, *Enchiridion Iuris Canonici*, § 240, p. 946.

[158] Canon 2299, § 3.

[159] Canon 2303, § 2.

posed cleric persists in giving scandal and does not heed the warnings to amend his ways.[160] *"Caritas numquam excidit!"* [161]

ARTICLE 3. THE EFFECTS OF DEPOSITION

In the discussion about the nature of deposition its principal effects were necessarily indicated. In this article consideration will be given to these effects in themselves.

It has well been said that as natural death deprives a person of all advantages in the natural or physical order, so deposition deprives a cleric of all that he values in the social order of the Church.[162] In one blow it obliterates all the titles a clergyman may possess. Only the clerical state itself and its essential privileges remain for the deposed cleric.

A. Deposition Does Not Include Excommunication, Interdict or Infamy

Before considering more minutely the effects produced by deposition one must note that the penalty of itself does not deprive the cleric of the common goods of the faithful, such as the use or reception of the sacraments and sacramentals, the suffrages, indulgences and public prayers of the Church, passive assistance at divine offices, the reception of Christian burial. Deposition affects only the rights which are proper to clerics. In practice, however, even the enjoyment of such rights and privileges as are conceded to all members of the Church will usually be restricted in the case of a deposed clergyman, not as a consequence of the deposition itself but as a result of other penalties, such as excommunication,[163] interdict [164] or infamy,[165] which either precede or accompany the deposition according to the norms of the Code governing particular delicts.

---

[160] Canon 2304, § 1.
[161] I Cor., XIII: 8.
[162] Smith, *Elements of Ecclesiastical Law*, III, n. 1817, p. 81.
[163] Cf. canons 2257-2267.
[164] Cf. canons 2268-2277.
[165] Cf. canons 2293-2295.

This point is well illustrated by canon 2314, § 1, in its gradual accumulation of penalties. It rules that all formal apostates, heretics and schismatics incur *ipso facto* an excommunication. Furthermore, if these same offenders do not repent after an admonition they shall be deprived of any benefice, dignity, pension, office or other function they may have in the Church and they shall also be declared *infames*. After these penalties and a second admonition prove ineffective a cleric shall be deposed. Canon 2320 serves to reveal a simultaneous accumulation of deposition with other penalties. It decrees that all persons who throw away the Sacred Species or carry them off or keep them for an evil purpose become suspected of heresy, incur an excommunication *latae sententiae* reserved in a most special manner to the Apostolic See, incur infamy *ipso facto* and, if they are clerics, are to be deposed. Indeed, in six of the ten canons in which deposition is sanctioned it is preceded or accompanied either with excommunication,[166] infamy,[167] or personal interdict.[168] Clearly, then, these penalties with their proper effects are distinct from the penalty of deposition.

B. *Deposition Affects Clerical Rights*

Under the law of the Code it remains true that deposition, as always, formally deprives a cleric only of those rights which he has acquired or could acquire as a member of the clerical state. These rights are summarily indicated in the Code when it states that only clerics can obtain the power either of orders or ecclesiastical jurisdiction and that likewise only clerics can obtain ecclesiastical benefices and pensions.[169] Through the penalty of deposition a cleric is not only suspended from office and permanently deprived of all offices, benefices, dignities, pensions and functions in the Church but he also becomes unable to acquire them in the future.[170] Although this penalty is one and indivisible, it is immediately obvious that its effects will be greater or lesser in proportion to the rights actu-

---

[166] Cf. canons 2314, § 1, nn. 1, 2; 2320; 2322; 2350.
[167] Cf. canons 2314, § 1, n. 2; 2320; 2328; 2359, § 2.
[168] Cf. canon 2328.
[169] Canon 118.
[170] Canon 2303, § 1.

ally obtained by the individual cleric. All clerics are not of the same grade or rank. On the contrary, they form a sacred hierarchy in which some are subordinate to others.[171] As there is a twofold sacred power in the Church, namely, the power of orders and the power of jurisdiction, there is a twofold basis for inequality and subordination among the clergy according to the various degrees of participation in either power by the individual clerics. Consequently the effects of deposition will not be equally extensive in all cases.

(1) *Effects of Deposition in Regard to the Power of Orders*

Persons who are received into the ecclesiastical hierarchy are constituted in the degrees of the power of orders by sacred ordination,[172] which can be received validly only by baptized men.[173] The degrees of sacred ordination ascend from the minor orders of porter, lector, exorcist, and acolyte [174] through the major orders of subdiaconate and diaconate to that of the priesthood in its twofold manifestation of the exclusively sacerdotal and concomitantly episcopal character.[175]

It matters not, however, how far one has advanced in the hierarchy of orders, deposition will strip him of the lawful exercise of all the powers of orders which he has received and, so to speak, place him on a par with the simple tonsured cleric who enjoys no power of orders.[176] This is, of course, only a legal or extrinsic reduction, for the intrinsic power of orders is not taken away by deposition, as the Code itself professes when it states that sacred ordination once validly received is never invalidated.[177] No human authority can invalidate the power of orders which is of divine institution.[178] According to the common doctrine all orders other than the epis-

---

[171] Canon 108, § 2.

[172] Canon 109.

[173] Canon 968, § 1.

[174] Cf. canon 949.

[175] Cf. canons 949, 950.

[176] *Sententia communis*—Cf. Augustine, *A Commentary on Canon Law*, II, 44, note 4.

[177] Cf. canon 211, § 1.

[178] Cf. Conc. Trident, sess. XXIII, *de sacramento ordinis*, cc. 4, 6.—Denzinger, Bannwart, Umberg, *Enchiridion Symbolorum*, nn. 964, 966.

copacy, priesthood and diaconate, are of ecclesiastical origin.[179] Yet, even the orders of ecclesiastical origin, once they have been validly conferred, are never repeated.[180]

Although the Church cannot take away the power of orders acquired by sacred ordination which imprints an indelible character on the soul of the recipient, she is competent to decree what pertains to the lawful use of any order. This competency is exercised in the penalty of deposition when the Church deprives a cleric of the sacred ministry [181] by perpetually forbidding him the exercise of his power of orders.[182]

In regard to the power of orders, then, deposition does not take away the power itself but, like the suspension which it includes, renders its use unlawful. A deposed cleric would sin gravely by exercising his orders, nevertheless he would act validly. It is only when a power of jurisdiction would be simultaneously required with the power of orders that the act would stand invalid. Such a case would be had in the administration of the sacrament of penance. Thus a deposed bishop can truly ordain and a deposed priest can validly offer the holy sacrifice of the Mass, for they still retain the same power of orders from which these acts by divine institution have their value and efficacy. As the history of deposition has shown, this has been the common and constant doctrine of the Church.[183]

Moreover, deposition renders unlawful the use of any order, minor, major and episcopal. This is indicated by the Code when it states that deposition involves a suspension *ab officio*.[184] Before the Code Lega referred to the suspension inherent in deposition as a suspension *a divinis*.[185] This doctrine can no longer be upheld.

---

[179] Cf. Gasparri, *De Sacra Ordinatione*, I, n. 33.

[180] Cf. canon 212.

[181] Cf. Suarez, *De Censuris*, Disp. XXX, sec. I, n. 10.

[182] Cf. canon 2303, § 1; Suarez, *loc. cit.*, n. 12.

[183] Cf. Barbosa, *De Officio et Potestate Episcopi*, pars III, alleg. CX, n. 2; Suarez, *De Censuris*, Disp. XXX, sec. I, n. 7; Wernz, *Ius Decretalium*, VI, n. 125, p. 132.

[184] Cf. canon 2303, § 1; Blat, *Commentarium*, V, n. 108, p. 160; n. 136, p. 185.

[185] *De Delictis et Poenis*, n. 207, p. 279.

According to the Code a suspension *a divinis* forbids the exercise of
every act of the power of orders which one obtained either by sacred
orders or by privilege.[186]   Although the significance of this suspension is still controverted,[187] Cocchi,[188] Beste [189] and Vermeersch-
Creusen [190] declare that the exercise of the powers of major orders
alone is involved in this suspension.   Roberti [191] interprets the term
sacred ordination which is employed in this penalty as referring to
both major and minor orders.   The Code by identifying the suspension which is inherent in deposition with the suspension *ab officio*
leaves no doubt that deposition affects all the powers of orders received by the delinquent cleric.   Chelodi [192] consequently is not
correct in stating that deposition adds merely a suspension *ab ordine*
to the elements of privation and disqualification, for while this suspension indeed forbids every act of the power of orders received
through ordination,[193] it does not prohibit the exercise of those
powers which have been received in virtue of a privilege.[194]   Such
a prohibition is included in the suspension *a divinis*, and *a fortiori*
in the suspension *ab officio* which is expressly stated by the Code as
produced in deposition.

The deposed cleric, therefore, cannot exercise lawfully any power
of orders.   Since, however, the practice of the Church permits laymen to exercise certain functions of minor orders, these functions
must evidently be considered as not exclusively proper to the clerical state.   Canonists in consequence state that a suspended cleric
may also lawfully perform them as laymen.[195]   The same reasoning

---

[186] Cf. canon 2279, § 2, n. 2.

[187] Cf. Sipos, *Enchiridion Iuris Canonici*, § 237, p. 936, not. 8.

[188] *Commentarium*, VIII, n. 103, p. 175.

[189] *Introductio in Codicem*, 924.

[190] *Epitome*, III, n. 483, p. 287.

[191] *De Delictis et Poenis*, I, n. 381, pp. 486-487.

[192] *Ius Poenale*, n. 52, p. 69.

[193] Cf. canon 2279, § 2, n. 3.

[194] Cf. Cocchi, *Commentarium*, VIII, n. 103, p. 175; Vermeersch-Creusen,
Epitome, III, n. 483, pp. 287-288.

[195] Cf. Vermeersch-Creusen, *Epitome*, III, n. 482, p. 287; Cappello, *De
Censuris*, n. 499, p. 435; Cocchi, *Commentarium*, VIII, n. 103, p. 175; Roberti,
De Delictis et Poenis, n. 381, p. 487; n. 382, p. 491; A Coronata, *Institutiones*,
I, n. 181, p. 196.

remains true in the case of a deposed cleric even though deposition is a distinct penalty and much more severe than suspension. There can be no question that a deposed cleric, as any layman, can privately administer baptism to one in danger of death,[196] but he may lawfully perform only those rites which are necessary for the validity of baptism. He may not perform the ceremonies which are reserved to priests and deacons.[197] In like fashion deposition of itself does not prevent the deposed cleric from being employed in other functions now performed by laymen. The deposed cleric may act as a server at Mass, as a chanter in the choir, as an organist or as a sexton, for while deposition includes the privation of any function in the Church, this restriction of liberty must be limited to any and to all the offices exclusively proper to the clerical state. *In poenis benignior est interpretatio facienda.*[198] This is a penalty proper to clerics and in consequence should be interpreted in reference to rights of the clerical state as such.[199]

The severity of the prohibition inherent in deposition which proscribes the exercise of major orders is unquestionable. Before the Code Hinschius [200] rightly rejected the idea held by some canonists that the exercise of orders usurped by a deposed or degraded cleric brought with it an irregularity, for the law never made such a provision. The law, however, did state that a deposed cleric who presumed to exercise his sacred orders should be punished with excommunication.[201] If the deposed cleric after incurring excommunication presumed to exercise his former ministry he then incurred an irregularity.[202] The Code eliminates all the former dis-

---

[196] Cf. canon 742, § 1.

[197] Cf. canon 759, § 1; Roberti, *De Delictis et Poenis*, n. 382, p. 491.

[198] Canon 2219, § 1.

[199] Cf. Suarez, *De Censuris*, Disp. XXX, sec. I, n. 2; Schmalzgrueber, *Ius Ecclesiasticum Universum*, lib. V, tit. XXXVII, n. 132.

[200] *Kirchenrecht*, I, 53.

[201] Cf. cc. 1, 2, X, *de clerico excommunicato, deposito vel interdicto ministrante*, V, 27; Wernz, *Ius Decretalium*, VI, n. 125, p. 132.

[202] Cf. C. 10, X, *de clerico excommunicato, deposito vel interdicto ministrante*, V, 27; cc. 1, 18, 20, *de sententia excommunicationis*, V, 11 in VI°; Hinschius, *Kirchenrecht*, I, 53, not. 6; Hyland, *Excommunication*, 166.

putes in this matter[203] when it declares that all clerics in major orders who have been forbidden to exercise these orders by a canonical penalty incur an irregularity *ex delicto* should they perform any proscribed act of orders.[204] The irregularity is incurred, however, only when the act has been solemnly placed[205] and is at the same time a grave sin and an external act.[206]

A deposed cleric, moreover, may lawfully as well as validly exercise his power of orders, if he is a priest, in one instance. He can validly and licitly absolve from any sins and censures, no matter what be the character of their reservation or notoriety, any and every penitent who is constituted in danger of death. This he can do even if an approved priest is present.[207] In this canon the Church, whose supreme law is the salvation of souls, not only grants the jurisdiction necessary to absolve a dying penitent but permits even the deposed priest to perform lawfully an act of the ministry of which he has been deprived.[208]

(2) Effects of Deposition in Regard to the Power of Jurisdiction

In the hierarchy clerics are also unequal in rank and mutually subordinated on the basis of their divers degrees of participation in the power of jurisdiction.[209] They are established in these various ranks of jurisdiction by canonical commission except for the Roman Pontiff, who when he is legitimately elected and has freely accepted the election receives jurisdiction by the divine law itself.[210] Among the degrees of jurisdiction the supreme pontificate and the episco-

---

[203] Cf. Noval, *De Processibus* (Augustae Taurinorum—Romae: Marietti, 1932), II, n. 700, p. 610.

[204] Canon 985, n. 7: "Sunt irregulares ex delicto: . . . n. 7: Qui actum ordinis, clericis in ordine sacro constitutis reservatum, ponunt, vel eo ordine carentes, vel ab eius exercitio poena canonica sive personali, medicinali aut vindicativa, sive locali prohibiti."

[205] Cf. Vermeersch-Creusen, *Epitome*, II, n. 257, p. 176.

[206] Cf. canon 986.

[207] Canon 882.

[208] Cf. Kelly, *Jurisdiction of the Confessor According to the Code of Canon Law* (New York, Benziger Brothers, 1929), 93.

[209] Cf. canon 108, § 3.

[210] Cf. canon 109.

pate are of divine origin, the others are of human origin,[211] having been introduced by the Church in the course of the centuries, such as the rank of patriarchs, primates, metropolitans, prefects and vicars apostolic, ruling abbots and other superiors endowed with jurisdiction in the external forum as well as pastors who enjoy jurisdiction but only for the internal forum.

All who are inferior to the pope need the *missio canonica* to acquire and possess jurisdiction. As the Lord sent His apostles [212] so in turn they sent others to exercise their spiritual power with authority. Up to the twelfth century, as previously noted,[213] the canonical commission was included in the ordination or consecration. Since that time, when absolute ordination was legally recognized, ordination and canonical commission have constituted two distinct acts.[214] Today it is only through the canonical mission that inferiors of the Roman Pontiff derive from the Vicar of Christ a share in the power committed to the Church by her divine Founder.[215]

Since this share in the power of jurisdiction is granted by the Church,[216] it is governed completely by her laws. Though the power of orders is perpetual and may be validly exercised despite any authoritative ecclesiastical prohibition, the power of jurisdiction is possessed only in accordance with the lawful authority of the Church. It may be curtailed, or restrained, or even revoked.

Through the penalty of deposition the power of jurisdiction enjoyed by the delinquent cleric is completely revoked. Deposition deprives the cleric of his office, benefice or dignity,[217] and consequently also of his ordinary power of jurisdiction, for this is so attached by law to an ecclesiastical office that the cleric who acquires

---

[211] Cf. canon 108, § 3.

[212] Matt., XXVIII: 18; Rom., X: 15.

[213] III General Lateran Council (1179), c. 5—Hardouin, VII, 1676.

[214] Cf. Sägmüller, *Lehrbuch des katholischen Kirchenrechts* (Freiburg im Breisgau: Herder, 1930), 147; A Coronata, *Institutiones*, I, n. 171, p. 187; Augustine, *A Commentary on Canon Law*, II, 48.

[215] Cf. Chelodi, *Ius de Personis*, 201; Cocchi, *Commentarium*, II, n. 255, pp. 194-195.

[216] Cf. Kearney, *The Principles of Delegation* (Catholic University of America, Canon Law Studies, No. 55, Washington, D. C., 1929), 45-46.

[217] Cf. canon 2303, § 1.

the office automatically obtains the jurisdiction connected with it,[218] and in similar fashion loses this power [219] when he is deprived of the office.[220] Deposition also strips the cleric of any delegated jurisdictional power possessed by him. Delegated jurisdiction may be called real delegation when it is granted by reason of a dignity or office and strictly personal delegation when it is granted simply by reason of the person,[221] but in every case it is committed to a person [222] to act with authority in the Church. In deposition such a commission is also lost, for this penalty deprives a cleric not only of offices in the strict canonical sense,[223] but also of any office, function or charge (*munera*) committed only to clerics under the ordinary law of the Church. To this privation, moreover, deposition adds a disqualification for validly acquiring or fulfilling these positions in the future.[224]

Under the present discipline, then, as always in the past, deposition not only prohibits the lawful use of jurisdiction but takes away its very title, so that any act of jurisdiction attempted thereafter by the deposed cleric is *ipso facto* invalid.[225] As already noted, the Church has always allowed one exception to this rule, and it still obtains, namely, when she supplies jurisdiction even to a deposed priest or bishop to assist a person in danger of death with the sacrament of penance.[226]

---

[218] Cf. canon 197, § 1.

[219] Cf. canons 208; 873, § 3.

[220] Cf. canon 183, § 1.

[221] Cf. Kearney, *The Principles of Delegation*, 59; Miaskiewicz, *Supplied Jurisdiction According to Canon 209*, 17.

[222] Cf. canon 197, § 1: "Potestas iurisdictionis . . . delegata quae commissa est personae."

[223] Cf. canon 145, § 1.

[224] Cf. canon 2303, § 1; A Coronata, *Institutiones*, I, n. 290, p. 339.

[225] Cf. Barbosa, *De Officio et Potestate Episcopi*, pars III, alleg. CX, n. 2; Suarez, *De Censuris*, Disp. XXX, sec. I, n. 7; Chelodi, *Ius Poenale*, n. 52, p. 69; Wernz, *Ius Decretalium*, VI, n. 125, p. 132; Hollweck, *Die kirchlichen Strafgesetze*, § 91, p. 159, note 2; A Coronata, *Institutiones*, IV, n. 1834, p. 261; Sipos, *Enchiridion Iuris Canonici*, § 240, p. 947.

[226] Cf. canon 882; Cappello, *Tractatus Canonico-Moralis de Sacramentis*, Vol. II, *De Poenitentia* (3. ed., Taurinorum Augustae: Marietti, 1938), n. 408, pp. 321-322; Kelly, *The Jurisdiction of the Confessor*, 92-93.

Before the advent of absolute ordination in the Church[227] deposition always involved loss of office as well as the exercise of orders just as ordination always included acquisition of office besides the power of orders. With the actual separation of the two powers deposition could be visited upon a cleric who held no office in the Church. In this case it effected, as it does today, a perpetual suspension from the power of orders in union with a perpetual disqualification for any ecclesiastical office.[228] On the other hand, any offices actually enjoyed by the cleric were formerly, and are today, lost through deposition. Hence, despite the separate acts of ordination and canonical deputation, deposition continued as a single act to nullify the effects of both insofar as it was possible. However, it may be observed here that parallel with the development of the two-fold act of conferring power on a cleric the penalty of deposition came to be stated no longer merely by the simple term *deposition* but with the added explicit reference to any office, benefice, or dignity acquired by the cleric,[229] privations indeed always implied if not actually expressed in this penalty. So the Code in defining the penalty of deposition makes explicit enumeration of all offices, benefices, dignities and positions as constituting the object of the privation effected by deposition.

(3) Effects of Deposition Upon the Offices of a Cleric

In the treatment concerning the loss of jurisdiction consequent upon deposition the loss of office effected by this penalty was necessarily considered. It should suffice, then, to state here in the language of the Code that an office is lost, among other ways, by privation[230] and that privation is included in deposition.[231] With deposition comes the loss not only of the office and its inherent jurisdiction, but also of every other right or privilege attached to the office. As a result of this an enumeration of all the effects conse-

---

[227] III General Lateran Council (1179), c. 5—Hardouin VII, 1676; cf. *supra*, pp. 139, 149.

[228] Cf. Aichner, *Compendium Iuris Ecclesiastici*, § 220, p. 747, not. 8.

[229] Cf., *e. g.*, c. 1, *de homicidio*, V, 4, in VI°.

[230] Cf. canon 183, § 1.

[231] Cf. canon 2303, § 1.

quent upon deposition will depend on the rank of the individual who is deposed. Obviously the higher one has been elevated in the hierarchy of jurisdiction the greater will be his fall through deposition, for this penalty destroys all that the canonical commission has built up for the afflicted cleric. It is a canonical demotion. In every case deposition deprives a cleric of all his offices and leaves him in a condition juridically inferior to one who has only received tonsure, for the latter, at least, is capable of acquiring ecclesiastical offices.[232]

Upon deposition the office formerly held by the delinquent cleric becomes juridically vacant [233] and another cleric may then be appointed to it by whomsoever this right is legitimately enjoyed.[234] Should this office, though vacant by law, be held in illegal possession by the deposed cleric, it may nevertheless be conferred on another provided that a declaration of the illegal possession has been issued according to the sacred canons and mention is made of this declaration in the letter of appointment.[235]

(4) Effects of Deposition Upon the Benefices of a Cleric

A sentence of deposition brings with it a loss of any and all benefices possessed by the cleric. A benefice is a species of ecclesiastical office, namely, one in which there inheres the right to receive the revenue accruing from the endowment annexed to the sacred office.[236] Every ecclesiastical benefice connotes the presence of two essential elements: (1) the existence of a sacred office as a basic requirement, and (2) the co-existence of the right to the revenues from that office as the characteristic requirement. The general rule still obtains, now as before, that the benefice is given on account of the office.[237] With the total privation of office which is inherent in the

---

[232] Cf. A Coronata, *Institutiones*, I, n. 181, p. 196: "Per se clericus simplex seu vir prima tonsura initiatus nec ordinis nec jurisdictionis potestatem habet, sed solum ad utrumque capacitatem."

[233] Cf. canon 183, § 1.

[234] Cf. canons 148; 150.

[235] Cf. canon 151.

[236] Cf. canon 1409; *supra*, p. 131.

[237] Cf. A Coronata, *Institutiones*, I, n. 205, p. 226.

penalty of deposition there is reasonably included also the total privation of benefice.[238]

In the United States the office of a diocesan bishop is a benefice; so also is that of a pastor.[239] Benefices which have the care of souls attached to them can be obtained only by clerics who are priests.[240] The office of a cathedral canon in Europe is a benefice but it does not have attached to it the care of souls. Indeed, the Code, as already noted, enumerates various kinds of benefices.[241] The penalty of deposition, however, makes no distinction. Any and all (*quaelibet*) of the benefices enjoyed by a cleric are irrevocably lost in his deposition. And if he was ordained under the title of benefice even this benefice is lost.[242] Moreover, the deposed cleric not only loses the benefices which he had acquired but he is also disqualified for obtaining any others in the future. He is deprived of the fundamental capacity which clerics have for acquiring them.[243]

(5) Effects of Deposition Upon the Dignities of a Cleric

The losses involved in deposition include also any dignity already acquired by the cleric. Here there is reference to another type of office. As has been previously intimated, a dignity formerly meant an ecclesiastical benefice which had attached to it precedence with some jurisdiction. According to a study of the present law it usually signifies a capitular benefice which enjoys preëminence in rank in virtue of jurisdiction, institution, custom and denomination.[244] The conferring of dignities is reserved to the Holy See.[245]

---

[238] "Ablato fundamento ruunt reliqua"—Suarez, *De Censuris*, Disp. XXX, sec. I, n. 13.

[239] Cf. *A Letter of the Most Rev. Apostolic Delegate to the Bishops of the United States*, Nov. 10, 1922—Bouscaren, *Canon Law Digest*, I, 149; Augustine, *A Commentary on Canon Law*, VIII, 224.

[240] Cf. canon 154.

[241] Cf. canon 1411; *supra*, pp. 131-132.

[242] Canon 2303, § 1.

[243] Cf. canons 118 and 2303, § 1.

[244] Cf. A. Bondini, "Dignitas capitularis ex quibus constat"—*Jus Pontificium*, XIII (1933), 249-253. Hereafter reference to the *Jus Pontificium* will be made by the use of the abbreviation *Jus Pont.*

[245] Cf. canon 396.

Deposition extends to all dignities, major as well as minor, with the sole exception of the supreme pontificate, for it alone is endowed with a jurisdiction which in its continued maintenance is altogether independent of the norms of ecclesiastical law since it derives its origin solely from the divine law.[246] No other dignity is excluded or exempted from the deprivative character of deposition. In the loss of the dignity all rights pertaining to it are likewise lost. In illustration of this point mention may be made of the loss suffered by a deposed cardinal of the right to vote in the election of the Roman Pontiff.[247]

(6) Effects of Deposition Upon the Pensions of a Cleric

Deposition also deprives the cleric of any ecclesiastical pension he may have acquired and disqualifies him for obtaining any pension in the future. This privation includes even the pension which constituted his title of ordination if he was so ordained. It extends to all ecclesiastical pensions, whether real, namely, those imposed on the benefice itself, or personal, that is to say, those imposed on a beneficiary which do not in law come under the name of benefices.[248]

The penalty of deposition, however, does not deprive a cleric of any state pensions or pensions paid by private persons or companies, even though they may have an ecclesiastical name or be under ecclesiastical administration.[249] Deposition is concerned only with pensions which the Church has authorized to be paid from ecclesiastical property. If, for example, the local ordinary has imposed a pension on a parish in favor of a resigning pastor [250] then in the event of his deposition this former pastor will lose his pension in consequence of the inflicted penalty.

---

[246] Cf. canon 219.

[247] Cf. Pius X, const. *Vacante Sede Apostolica*, 25 dec. 1904, n. 31—*CIC*, Documentum I; canon 233, § 1.

[248] Cf. canon 1412, n. 4; Noval, *De Processibus*, II, n. 589, pp. 515-518.

[249] Cf. Augustine, *A Commentary on Canon Law*, VIII, 249.

[250] Cf. canon 2150.

(7) *Effects of Deposition Upon the Assignments (Munera)*
of a Cleric

After indicating the extension of deposition to the loss of any
office, benefice or dignity possessed by a cleric, the definition of the
Code rejects the possibility of the cleric's retaining any official position in the Church by adding the term *munera*—assignments or
charges—to the list of privations involved in this penalty. *Munera*
signify ecclesiastical offices in the broad sense of the word.[251] The
word *munera* therefore refers to any employment which is legitimately practiced for a spiritual purpose, as the position of confessor,[252] of curate,[253] or of chancellor,[254] and any other assignment
of spiritual import lawfully committed by ecclesiastical authority to
a cleric.[255]

The deposed cleric is not only deprived of all ecclesiastical
offices but he is also disqualified for acquiring any in the future.
This disability prevents him from validly receiving any office, dignity, benefice, pension or position even through a papal rescript
of favor.[256] Certainly the deposed cleric may ask for a papal rescript, for this is not forbidden to him.[257] Indeed, if he ever seeks
to be dispensed from the penalty of deposition he must petition
the Holy See for this favor, for no other authority is competent
to grant it.[258] Before such a dispensation has been obtained,
however, the disability inherent in deposition prevents his valid acquisition of benefices, offices, dignities, assignments or pensions. In
regard to these matters, then, a rescript, even though it be granted
motu proprio, is of no effect since the beneficiary is incapable by
common law of receiving these favors. Even when a favor has been
unwittingly granted in these matters the grant remains invalid, for

---

[251] Cf. canon 145, § 1.

[252] Cf. canons 871; 872.

[253] Cf. canon 476.

[254] Cf. canon 372.

[255] Cf. canon 128.

[256] Cf. canon 46; O'Neill, *Papal Rescripts of Favor* (Catholic University
of America, Canon Law Studies, No. 57, Washington, D. C., 1930), 79.

[257] Cf. canon 36.

[258] Cf. canon 2237, § 1, n. 3.

as long as a cleric remains in the same juridical state of disqualification he is simply barred from acquiring any valid title to any ecclesiastical benefice whatsoever. There is but a single exception to this comprehensive rule. It obtains when an explicit derogatory clause in the papal rescript counteracts the otherwise universal effect of the cleric's disqualification.[259] In this case the disqualified cleric may of course validly acquire whatever favor has been accorded him by the Holy See. In this manner a deposed cleric could, for instance, acquire a pension or some other similar concession which it is beyond the powers of the ordinary to grant in view of the cleric's juridically effected disability.

With the extensive spoliation of clerical rights and powers effected in deposition it may be asked if the cleric who is punished with this penalty can any longer be considered a cleric. The whole history of this penalty, in its differentiation from degradation after the twelfth century as well as in its present constitution in the Code, supplies a definite answer to this question. Despite its effect of the total deprivation of the use of orders and the effect of the complete revocation of all offices, benefices, dignities, pensions and positions as well as of the rights, obligations and privileges connected with these, the penalty of deposition does not deprive the cleric of the common clerical privileges nor of the obligations which he undertook in ordination. The Code states these reservations in unmistakable language:

> Canon 2303, § 1: Depositio, firmis obligationibus e suscepto ordine exortis et privilegiis clericalibus. . . .

C. Obligations

Through deposition the cleric is not only deprived of the rights and privileges but he is also freed of the duties and obligations connected with his former office, benefice, dignity, pension or position in the Church. These rights and obligations depend for their existence upon his canonical commission. With its total revocation in

---

[259] Cf. canon 46; O'Neill, *Papal Rescripts of Favor*, 147-149; Van Hove, *Commentarium Lovaniense in Codicem Iuris Canonici*, vol. I, tom. IV, *De Rescriptis* (H. Dessain, 1936), nn. 183-184, pp. 170-171.

deposition they too follow the same course.[260]   On the other hand the obligations undertaken by the cleric in ordination remain intact as does the power of orders from which they emanate.

As a cleric obtains special rights and privileges in ordination so also does he acquire special obligations.   They are intimately associated with the clerical state.   Deposition, however, does not destroy membership in the clerical state, neither does it in consequence liberate the delinquent cleric from its obligations.[261]

All these obligations arise from ordination and from the cleric's incorporation into the clerical state.   Some of them, however, are actually contracted by individual clerics only with the reception of major orders, others only with the priesthood.   The obligations, then, which the deposed cleric will retain must be determined, as the Code states,[262] from the order which he has received.   The more obligations he has assumed by his advance in orders, the more he will retain in deposition.

While there was no positive legislation before the Code to define the extent of the obligations which remained after deposition, it was the unanimous teaching of canonists that a deposed cleric was still bound to comply with the obligations imposed by ordination, especially the daily recitation of the divine office and the perpetual observance of celibacy.   Consequently, a cleric in minor orders who was obliged to the recitation of the divine office solely in virtue of a benefice which he had received was liberated from this obligation with the loss of his benefice in deposition.[263]   On the other hand, while deposition juridically deprived clerics forever of the active ministry, it did not bring about a legal separation from the obligations consequent upon ordination, which in the case of clerics in major orders included the daily recitation of the office and the lifelong observance of celibacy.

[260] "Accessorium naturam sequi congruit principalis."—Reg. 42, R. J., in VI°.

[261] These obligations are defined by the Code particularly in its third title of the second book (canons 124-144).

[262] Cf. canon 2303, § 1.

[263] Cf. Wernz, *Ius Decretalium*, VI, n. 125, p. 132; Hinschius, *Kirchenrecht*, I, 144.

Three reasons were alleged by canonists to support this teaching. First, it was held that the clerical obligations follow sacred orders and as the orders remain after deposition so also do the obligations arising from them. Secondly, the principle of law was applied to deposition that no one should derive a benefit from his crime.[264] Thirdly, deposition by the positive provision of law did not deprive the cleric of the clerical privileges, neither did it in consequence deprive him of the clerical state and its obligations.[265]

With a practical point of view, since deposition will rarely be inflicted on a cleric in minor orders when a cause for such action will certainly justify the simpler process of reducing him to the lay state,[266] canonists since the Code, as those who preceded its appearance, stress only the obligations of a deposed cleric who has received major orders, and in particular the obligations of observing celibacy and of reciting the divine office.[267] The emphasis is evidently well placed, for even the Code mentions only these two obligations of celibacy and of the canonical hours when it declares that no clerical obligations are established by an invalid ordination to sacred orders.[268] The Sacred Roman Rota has likewise been exclusively

---

[264] D (50, 17), 134: "Nemo ex suo delicto meliorem suam conditionem facere potest"; c. 7, X, *de iudiciis*, II, 1: "ne ex sua malitia commodum reportet"; also in c. 9, X, *de dolo et contumacia*, II, 14.

[265] Cf. Barbosa, *De Officio et Potestate Episcopi*, pars III, alleg. CX, nn. 2, 3; Suarez, *De Censuris*, Disp. XXX, sec. I, n. 9; Schmalzgrueber, *Ius Ecclesiasticum Universum*, lib. V, tit. XXXVII, n. 135; Wernz, *Ius Decretalium*, VI, n. 125, p. 132; Lega, *De Delictis et Poenis*, n. 207, p. 280; Hinschius, *Kirchenrecht*, I, 144; Hollweck, *Die kirchlichen Strafgesetze*, § 91, p. 158.

[266] Cf. canon 211, § 2.

[267] Cf. Vermeersch-Creusen, *Epitome*, III, n. 498, p. 300; Cocchi, *Commentarium*, VIII, n. 118, p. 200; Blat, *Commentarium*, V, n. 136, p. 185; Prümmer, *Manuale Iuris Canonici*, q. 579, p. 669; Ferreres, *Institutiones Canonicae* (2. ed., Barcinona: Eugenius Subirana, 1920), II, n. 1070, p. 442; Augustine, *A Commentary on Canon Law*, VIII, 260; Ayrinhac-Lydon, *Penal Legislation*, n. 168, p. 128; Sipos, *Enchiridion Iuris Canonici*, § 240, p. 947; Chelodi, *Ius Poenale*, n. 52, p. 69; Sole, *De Delictis et Poenis*, n. 290, p. 205; Eichmann, *Strafrecht*, 119-120.

[268] Cf. canon 214, § 1: "Clericus qui metu gravi coactus ordinem sacrum recipit nec postea remoto metu, eandem ordinationem ratam habuit saltem tacite per ordinis exercitium, volens tamen per talem actum *obligationibus clericalibus* se subiicere, ad statum laicalem, legitime probata coactione et

concerned with the obligations of reciting the divine office and of observing chastity in reviewing the cases in which the obligations contracted by sacred ordination were attacked.[269]

The principal obligations of the clerical state will remain, therefore, only in the case of the deposition of a cleric who has already received major orders. One of these will be the obligation of reciting the breviary as is demanded by canon 135: Clerics in major orders, namely, subdeacons, deacons, priests and bishops,[270] are obliged to recite daily all the canonical hours according to their proper and approved liturgical books unless they have been lawfully reduced to the lay state.[271] Hence, while this obligation arises with orders by positive ecclesiastical law, it is also juridically extinguished by the same power, but only upon reduction to the lay state, an effect not attributed by law to deposition or to any other penalty except degradation.[272]

The deposed cleric who has received major orders will also be bound to the obligation of observing celibacy and chastity. This obligation is expressed by the Code in canon 132: Clerics in major orders are forbidden to marry and are so bound by the obligation of observing chastity that sins against this virtue are also a sacrilege. It may be noted here, moreover, that unlike the obligation of reciting the breviary the obligation of celibacy is so annexed to major orders that it is not extinguished by any penalty, not even by degradation.[273] According to the discipline of the Church a cleric who has received only minor orders may enter marriage, but by the very

ratihabitionis defectu, sententia iudicis redigatur, *sine ullis coelibatus ac horarum canonicarum obligationibus."* Cf. also canon 1993.

[269] Cf. S. R. R., *Sacrae Ordinationis,* 13 Ianuarii 1928, *coram R. P. D. Andrea Jullien,* dec. I: "Iamvero si sacra ordinatio est invalida non tenent obligationes ei adnexae, nam ubi principale deficit, deficit accessorium (Reg. J., 42, in VI°) sed obligatio ad castitatem et obligatio ad officium divinum sunt Ordini accessoriae, ergo, hoc non subsistente, nec illae subsistunt"—*Decisiones,* XX (1928), 3; cf. S. R. R., *Onerum sacrae Ordinationis,* 16 Aprilis 1928, *coram R. P. D. Iosepho Florczak,* dec. XIII—*Decisiones* XX (1928), 128-129; 136.

[270] Cf. canons 949, 950.

[271] Cf. canons 211-214.

[272] Cf. canon 211, § 1; *infra,* p. 208.

[273] Cf. canons 132, 213, 214.

fact of a valid marriage he ceases to be a cleric.[274]   A cleric in major orders, however, is not only forbidden to marry [275] but he is canonically unable to do so.   Should such a cleric, even after deposition, attempt marriage it is null and void.[276]   Moreover, in consequence of the commission of this delict the cleric becomes irregular [277] and incurs *ipso facto* an excommunication reserved to the Holy See in a simple manner.[278]   Yet, even though a cleric in major orders had been deposed before this attempted marriage he is still liable to further punishment.   If he does not show signs of repentance, after due warning and within the time fixed according to circumstances by the ordinary, he is to be degraded.[279]   With this penalty alone is he deprived of his status as a cleric, of the right to wear the ecclesiastical garb and of all claim to enjoy the clerical privileges.

D. Privileges

In declaring that deposition leaves intact the clerical privileges the Code succinctly expresses the point of law on which the distinction between deposition and degradation has always been founded.   A study of the history of these penalties reveals that despite the diminution of status effected by it, deposition did not deprive the cleric of the clerical state with its proper privileges, especially the privileges of the forum and canon.   The deposed cleric remained subject exclusively to the ecclesiastical court.   According to canon law he was entirely exempt from lay jurisdiction.   Anyone who laid violent hands upon him incurred an excommunication.   Through degradation, however, the cleric was deprived not only of all the rights and privileges which he lost through deposition, but he was also despoiled of the privilege of the forum and in consequence became subjected to the lay power by whom after real degradation he could be imprisoned, judged, condemned and

---

[274] Cf. canon 132, § 2.

[275] Cf. canon 132, § 1.

[276] Canon 1072: "Invalide matrimonium attentant clerici in sacris ordinibus constituti."

[277] Cf. canon 985, n. 3.

[278] Cf. canon 2388, § 1.

[279] Cf. canon 2388, § 1.

punished according to the civil laws as any layman. But before his real degradation he retained the privilege of the canon, so that anyone who laid violent hands upon a cleric who had been only verbally and not actually degraded incurred the excommunication.[280] Real degradation alone, then, so completely deprived the cleric of his clerical status that he was not only despoiled of its privileges but by positive action was reduced to the lay state.

In the law of the Code a similar progression may be noted today. First there is the canonical penalty of deposition, which leaves intact the clerical privileges. Then there is an aggravated form of deposition, a distinct penalty, which deprives the cleric of the right of wearing the ecclesiastical garb and implies also the forfeiture of all the clerical privileges otherwise inherent in his clerical status.[281] Finally, there is degradation which includes besides the loss of the ecclesiastical garb and of the clerical privileges a positive reduction to the lay state.[282] In the present law of the Church, then, as in the past, deposition leaves intact the right of wearing the ecclesiastical garb and of enjoying the clerical privileges. This fact especially indicates that the cleric, though deposed, is still legally a member of the clerical state.

The privileges retained by the deposed cleric are those which are proper to the clerical state, and not those which are enjoyed in virtue of a title to an office, benefice, dignity or pension.[283] As already observed, these latter are lost along with their title through deposition. Only the common clerical privileges as set forth in the second title of the second book of the Code remain with the deposed cleric.

This title of the Code (*De iuribus et privilegiis clericorum*) contains canons 118-123. The eminent canonist Augustine without any limitation or qualification states that the deposed cleric retains the prerogatives mentioned in canons 118-123.[284] It has already been demonstrated, however, that deposition deprives the cleric of the

---

[280] Cf. Benedictus XIV, *De synodo diocesana*, lib. IX, c. 6, n. 4; Hinschius, *Kirchenrecht*, I, 119; Schmalzgrueber, *Ius Ecclesiasticum Universum*, lib. V, tit. XXXVII, n. 138.

[281] Cf. canon 2304; *infra*, p. 171.

[282] Cf. canon 2305.

[283] Cf. Lega, *De Delictis et Poenis*, n. 207, p. 280.

[284] *A Commentary on Canon Law*, VIII, 260.

prerogatives mentioned in canon 118,[285] except for the power of orders which he has already acquired through ordination and which is incapable of being lost. Canon 123, on the other hand, does not set forth any prerogatives, but presents the law governing the renunciation, loss and recuperation of the clerical rights and privileges. Properly conceived, then, the privileges retained by the deposed cleric are those which are defined in canons 119-122, as Blat,[286] Sole [287] and Beste [288] have taken the care to specify. They are the following:

(1) *Privilegium Canonis*

According to canon 119 all the faithful owe the clergy reverence *according to their various degrees and offices,* and they become guilty of sacrilege if they inflict a real injury on clerics. The qualifying clause in the first part of this canon has been italicized to emphasize the fact that the special signs of reverence are no longer due to a cleric who has been deposed and thereby deprived of his rank and office with its allied prerogatives of a special place in the Church or in processions, a distinctive garb and appropriate titles of honor. Nevertheless, the deposed cleric remains a person consecrated to God by public authority and as he retains the right of wearing the ordinary ecclesiastical garb so also is he entitled to a proportionate degree of reverence. Consequently the Code declares that anyone who inflicts a real injury upon a deposed cleric commits a sacrilege and incurs *ipso facto* an excommunication.[289] This is the *Privilegium Canonis* which a deposed cleric enjoyed even under the discipline preceding the Code.[290]

Formerly the excommunication for the violation of this privilege was reserved to the Holy See, regardless of the dignity of the person against whom the injury was committed.[291] Hence one who laid violent hands upon any deposed cleric incurred this excommunica-

---

[285] "Soli clerici possunt potestatem sive ordinis sive iurisdictionis ecclesiasticae et beneficia ac pensiones ecclesiasticas obtinere."

[286] *Commentarium,* V, n. 136, p. 185.

[287] *De Delictis et Poenis,* n. 289, p. 205.

[288] *Introductio in Codicem,* 930.

[289] Cf. canons 2303, § 1; 2343.

[290] Cf. *supra,* p. 75, note 35.

[291] II General Council of the Lateran (1139), c. 15—Schroeder, *Disciplinary*

tion reserved to the Holy See. The present law sanctions this clerical privilege in accordance with the general principle that a delict is increased in proportion to the greater dignity of the person offended.[292] When the offense is committed against the person of a cardinal, legate, patriarch, archbishop or bishop the excommunication is reserved *speciali modo* to the Holy See.[293] In regard to other clerics, since their dignity is less than that of the prelates, the penalty for the violation of their right is less severe, not in its nature, for in every case it is excommunication, but in the degree of its reservation, for in these cases it is reserved only to the ordinary of the offender.[294] With this distinction introduced by the Code it must be held that one who does violence to a deposed cleric commits a sacrilege and incurs indeed an excommunication, but one which is reserved only to his own ordinary and not as formerly to the Holy See. The reason for this assertion is based on the law itself which increases the penalty of excommunication with reservation to the Holy See only when violence is brought to bear upon prelates of the Church [295] "for he who lays violent hands upon such persons commits more than a sacrilege, since he despises the divine constitution of the Church and thereby so augments the sacrilege as to render it a public crime in the society of the Church." [296] These aggravating circumstances, however, are not verified in the case of a deposed cleric. In this case it is immaterial whatever office, rank or dignity the deposed cleric formerly enjoyed in the Church, for he has canonically lost it forever through the penalty of deposition.

(2) *Privilegium Fori*

The deposed cleric also retains the *Privilegium Fori*. This privilege demands that clerics in all causes, contentious as well as crim

---

Decrees, 204; Pius I, const. *Apostolicae Sedis*, 12 Octobris 1869, § II, n. 2—*Fontes*, n. 552.

[292] Cf. canon 2207: "Praeter alia adiuncta aggravantia, delictum augetur: n. 1: Pro maiore dignitate personae quae delictum committit, aut quae delicto offenditur . . . "

[293] Cf. canon 2343, §§ 2, 3.

[294] Cf. canon 2343, § 4.

[295] Cf. canon 2343.

[296] Leech, *A Comparative Study of the Constitution "Apostolicae Sedis"*

inal, be tried only by ecclesiastical judges, unless other provisions have been lawfully established for a particular territory.[297] It has already been observed how in the early history of Christian nations this privilege was recognized in civil law. It was deemed repugnant to a Catholic sense of values to have bishops and priests, the fathers and teachers of the faithful, brought before a lay tribunal to be judged and sentenced.[298] In decretal legislation the exclusive competence of ecclesiastical judges over clerics in all causes was firmly established.[299] The Church even vindicated this privilege for clerics who had been deposed, and deprived delinquent clerics of this exemption only when they were degraded for crimes expressly stated in canon law. This is also the law of the Church today, except that a deposed cleric who continues to persist in his evil ways may be deprived forever of the right to wear the ecclesiastical garb. In consequence he is despoiled of all the clerical privileges.[300]

Although modern civil codes ignore the privilege of the forum,[301] the Code of Canon Law insists on its principle with due allowance for the lawful provisions of particular regions.[302] Cardinals, legates of the Apostolic See, bishops, the supreme heads of religious organizations approved by the Holy See, and the major officials of the Roman Curia may not be sued in the secular courts in matters pertaining to their offices without permission of the Apostolic See. All others who enjoy the privilege of the forum may not be sued in the

---

and the "Codex Iuris Canonici" (Catholic University of America, Canon Law Studies, No. 15, Washington, D. C., 1922), 23.

[297] Canon 120, § 1.

[298] Cf. Ayrinhac-Lydon, *Penal Legislation*, n. 272, p. 211.

[299] Cf. cc. 4, 8, 10, 17, X, *de iudiciis*, II, 1; cc. 1, 2, 9, 12, 13, X, *de foro competente*, II, 2.

[300] Cf. canon 2304.

[301] Cf. Chelodi, *Ius Poenale*, n. 74, p. 101.

[302] In many countries the privilege has been abrogated by concordats and agreements with the Holy See, as in Austria, Costa Rica, Colombia; in other places it has been derogated with at least the tacit toleration of the Holy See or by a contrary custom, as in Germany, Belgium, Holland and France; in the United States the civil government does not recognize a special forum for clerics.—Cf. A. Coronata, *Institutiones*, I, n. 183, p. 199, not. 5; Beste, *Introductio in Codicem*, 177; Vermeersch-Creusen, *Epitome*, I, n. 242 [240], p. 212; Wernz, *Ius Decretalium*, VI, n. 135, p. 140.

secular courts without the permission of the ordinary of the place in which the case is to be tried. The ordinary, however, should not refuse such permission without a just and serious reason, especially when the plaintiff is a lay person—all the more so, when the bishop has vainly endeavored to effect a friendly settlement between the parties.[303] Since deposition leaves a cleric without any rank or dignity in the Church, but merely with a participation in the clerical privileges, it suffices to obtain the permission of the ordinary of the place in which the case is to be tried in order to avoid violating the privilege of the forum which he still enjoys.

This conclusion is warranted especially in view of the penalties decreed against violations of the privilege of the forum. The general principle of proportion between the penalty and the dignity of the person offended has been applied by the Code also in this matter. One who without the required authorization sues a cardinal, a legate of the Holy See, or a major official of the Roman Curia in matters pertaining to their office, or even one's own ordinary, incurs an excommunication reserved *speciali modo* to the Holy See; in the case of any other bishop, abbot or prelate *nullius,* or of the highest superior of a pontifical religion the excommunication is reserved only *simpliciter* to the Holy See. Finally the suing, without due permission, of any lesser cleric brings upon an offending cleric suspension from office reserved to the ordinary, but laymen now incur no *latae sententiae* penalty, their punishment being left to the judgment of their respective ordinaries.[304] *Odiosa sunt restringenda.* One who summons a deposed cleric to court is certainly not violating the privilege of a prelate. Regardless of his former rank or dignity the deposed cleric can now assert only the right of the lesser clerics, for canonically he is the least among the clergy.

(3) *Privilegium Immunitatis*

Another privilege enjoyed by the deposed cleric is that of personal immunity whereby he is exempt from military service and from all civil duties and offices which are alien to the clerical state.[305]

---

[303] Canon 120, § 2.
[304] Cf. canon 2341.
[305] Cf. canons 2303, § 1; 121.

Considering the military life repugnant to the clerical state, the Church on the one hand vindicates for all her clerics, even for those who have been deposed, the privilege of exemption from military service, and on the other hand forbids clerics to volunteer for this service unless they do so with the permission of their ordinary for the purpose of liberating themselves the sooner from the service in those countries where it is compulsory for all able-bodied men.[306] In the United States all clerics as well as all students preparing for the ministry are exempt. A legislative enactment of the Seventy-sixth Congress approved on September 16, 1940, and known as the *Selective Training and Service Act of 1940*, provides as follows: "Regular or duly ordained ministers of religion, and students who are preparing for the ministry in theological or divinity schools recognized as such for more than one year prior to the date of enactment of this Act, shall be exempt from training and service (but not from registration) under this Act." [307]

Besides military service the canonical privilege of exemption extends to other public duties and offices which are unbecoming to the clerical state. Public duties of a servile character are now performed by workmen paid from the public treasury. Clerics, however, are not exempt from personal taxation, an exemption long since fallen into disuse and no longer stated in the Code.[308] While the sacred canons insist on the exemption of clerics from all public offices of a civil character which are incompatible with the clerical state, such as those of a judge, a juryman, an advocate, a senator, a governor, a mayor, a notary public, etc., the laws of most Christian countries, and particularly of the United States, do not oblige a clergyman to take up these offices.

(4) Privilegium Competentiae

Finally, the deposed cleric enjoys the privilege of all clerics which is known as the *Beneficium* or *Privilegium Competentiae*. It provides that clerics who are compelled to pay their creditors may

[306] Cf. canons 141, 188, n. 6, 2379.

[307] Sec. 5 (d)—*Selective Service Regulations* (Washington, D. C.: U. S. Government Printing Office, 1940), I, 22.

[308] Cf. Augustine, *A Commentary on Canon Law*, II, 67; Beste, *Introductio in Codicem*, 178; A Coronata, *Institutiones*, I, n. 184, p. 199, not. 9.

not be deprived of what is necessary for their decent maintenance, according to the prudent judgment of the ecclesiastical judge; but they remain under the obligation to satisfy their creditors as soon as possible.[309] In virtue of this privilege a sufficient support must be left to an indebted cleryman, so that he may not be forced to beg or engage in secular work to the disgrace of his clerical state. According to the civil law of many countries today all debtors are allowed to retain a sufficient amount of their goods to supply their actual needs.[310]

The *Privilegium Competentiae* may be invoked by any cleric to assist him in a contentious case regarding his debts in order to secure what is necessary for his decent maintenance.[311] Among the goods necessary for the honorable maintenance of a cleric certainly must be computed the income of his title of ordination, whether it is derived from a benefice, a pension or a patrimony, and *a fortiori* the patrimony itself which constitutes this title.[312] There is a difference, however, in the case of a deposed cleric. Through deposition he has lost his title of ordination and every right to a *congrua sustentatio* from the Church. Nevertheless, he still retains the clerical privileges. The *beneficium competentiae*, therefore, must at least retain for him a sufficiency of goods to preserve him from beggary. This norm is based on a special concession of the law to deposed clerics which is now to be considered.

E. Charitable Support

Canon 2303, § 2: Sed hoc ultimo in casu, si clericus vere indigeat, Ordinarius pro sua caritate, quo meliore modo fieri potest, ei providere curet, ne cum dedecore status clericalis mendicare cogatur.

Deposition deprives a cleric of all his ecclesiastical sources of income, even the benefice or pension which constituted his title of ordination. But in this case, the Code ordains, if the cleric is truly

---

[309] Canon 122.

[310] Cf. Beste, *Introductio in Codicem*, 178; Vermeersch-Creusen, *Epitome*, I, n. 244 [211], p. 214.

[311] Cf. Lega, *De Delictis et Poenis*, n. 207, p. 280, not. 1; Vecchiotti, *Institutiones Canonicae* (19. ed., Augustae Taurinorum, 1886), I, 408.

[312] Cf. A Coronata, *Institutiones*, I, n. 185, p. 200.

in need the ordinary should in his charity provide for him lest he be forced to beg and thus disgrace the clerical state. It has already been observed how the penalty of deposition is more severe than any other privation, since it *alone* takes away even the benefice or pension which constituted the delinquent cleric's title of ordination without at the same time obliging the ordinary in justice to compensate for this privation.[313] The legislator, however, foreseeing that so complete a financial deprivation might redound to the disgrace of the whole clerical state in that the deposed cleric through lack of any other income may be forced to gain his livelihood by engaging in secular employment or even by begging, imposes on the ordinary an obligation in charity to come to the aid of a deposed cleric who is truly in need.

The reason for imposing this precept upon the ordinary to provide charitable assistance is clearly indicated. With deposition the cleric still retains membership in the clerical state and enjoys the right of wearing the ecclesiastical garb and shares in the clerical privileges. Even though he has been convicted of a crime, the deposed cleric remains a cleric and should therefore not be left in such a position as to be obliged to go begging or engage in secular pursuits to the disgrace of the clerical state. It is not so much the concern for the individual delinquent, but the respect for the clerical state, which induces the Church to command ordinaries to provide a charitable subsidy for their deposed clergymen. Constantly recurring through the legislation of the Church is the conviction that "it beseems not those who are enrolled in the divine ministry to beg or to exercise any sordid trade to the disgrace of their order." [314]

---

[313] Cf. canon 2299, § 3: "Nequit clericus privari beneficio aut pensione cuius titulo ordinatus fuit, nisi aliunde eius honestae sustentationi provideatur, salvo praescripto can. 2303-2304." Cf. Prümmer, *Manuale Iuris Canonici*, q. 578, p. 669; Vermeersch-Creusen, *Epitome*, III, n. 498, p. 300; A Coronata, *Institutiones*, IV, n. 1830, p. 259; Augustine, *A Commentary on Canon Law*, VIII, 257-258.

[314] Conc. Trident., sess. XXI, *de ref.*, c. 2. Cf. S. C. de Prop. Fide, instr. 27 apr. 1871: "Cum indecorum omnino sit atque a clericorum, qui in sacris Ordinibus constituuntur dignitate prorsus alienum, ut ipsi aut emendicatis subsidiis, aut ex sordido quaestu ea quae ad victum necessaria sunt, sibi comparare cogantur, nemo ignorat."—*Fontes*, n. 4878.

Hence the Church has not only constantly forbidden these activities to her clergy but has also efficaciously rendered them needless, on the one hand, by requiring for clerics in major orders a title which will guarantee their honorable support and, on the other, by admonishing ordinaries to provide a charitable subsidy to those clerics who have lost their right to support from this source.

It is obvious that only those clerics are entitled in justice to a comfortable living [315] who are engaged in the ministry in conformity with the discipline of the Church. Those who by their criminal conduct have rendered themselves unfit for this service are justly deprived of their right to a decent support according to the provisions of the sacred canons. For the deposed cleric the Code prescribes only a charitable assistance sufficient to supply him with the necessities of life, a sufficiency that will eliminate his need of begging. Before the Code embodied this precept in its legislation it was advanced as a general principle by canonists and was carried into practice by the Church.[316]

The support rendered by the ordinary in conformity with this law of the Code is governed by the rules of charity and not of justice. The deposed cleric has no strict right on which to base a demand for this assistance.[317] As Sole has stated,[318] no one can

---

[315] Cf. canon 979, § 2. "By *congrua sustentatio* is meant not a *scanty*, but a *comfortable* and honorable support; that is, a living which supplies, not merely the necessaries, but also the *comforts* of life in keeping with the ecclesiastical state."—Smith, *Elements of Ecclesiastical Law*, III, p. 95, note 2.

[316] Cf. Wernz, *Ius Decretalium*, VI, n. 125, p. 133: "Ut consulatur dignitati status clericalis, Ecclesia curare solet, ut clericus depositus etiam nunc percipiat necessariam alimentationem." Cf. c. 6, X, *de clerico non ordinato ministrante*, V, 28: "misericorditer agatur cum eo ne sustentatione privatus ad saeculi negotia revertatur"; *Glossa* ad c. 25, X, *de electione et electi potestate*, I, 6 s. v. *"admiserunt"*: "Tamen modicam sustentationem debent tunc habere ne ex toto egeant"; Schmalzgrueber, *Ius Ecclesiasticum Universum*, lib. V, tit. XXXIX, n. 305; Smith, *Elements of Ecclesiastical Law*, III, n. 1862, p. 96.

[317] Cf. Sipos, *Enchiridion Iuris Canonici*, § 240, p. 947; Eichmann, *Strafrecht*, 119-120; Ferreres, *Institutiones Canonicae*, II, n. 1071, p. 442; Prümmer, *Manuale Iuris Canonici*, q. 579, p. 669; Ayrinhac-Lydon, *Penal Legislation*, n. 171, pp. 129, 130.

[318] *De Delictis et Poenis*, n. 289, p. 205.

fail to see the difference between the certain and absolute law of canon 2299, § 3, which demands a just compensation for a cleric who is deprived of the benefice or pension which constituted his title of ordination and the exhortation of canon 2303, § 2, which provides for a charitable subsidy for a deposed cleric who is indigent. This prescript obliges the ordinary only when the cleric is truly in need. Hence if he has saved sufficient funds or enjoys sources of income other than ecclesiastical, or even a patrimony which may have constituted his title of ordination, since these are not lost through deposition, the ordinary is not obliged to assist him. The same may be said of financial support derived from membership in a clerical aid society. This is not lost through deposition unless the constitution or by-laws so provide.[319] But if the cleric did not have any other means of living or, if indeed he draw upon other sources of revenue, but these fail to provide him with a sufficient sustenance to keep him from begging, the prescript of the Code obliges his ordinary to furnish him with a charitable subsistence.

The manner of making this provision for the deposed cleric is left to the conscience of the ordinary to determine in the light of all the particular circumstances surrounding individual cases both in regard to his own ability to provide and in regard to the cleric's unquestioned need of assistance. In the past the Church usually provided for deposed clerics by supporting them in monasteries, religious houses, or other ecclesiastical institutions. In the present law the manner of making provision for the indigent deposed cleric is left entirely to the discretion of the ordinary. It should be noted, however, that through deposition the cleric is disqualified by the common law for an ecclesiastical pension. On the other hand the charitable support should not be tantamount to a pension, for deposition would then be rendered illusory inasmuch as the delinquent would obtain a benefit rather than suffer a privation. This has been the common teaching of canonists, both before as well as after the Code,[320] and is implied in the law itself which prescribes only a sufficiency to keep the cleric from begging.

[319] Cf. Augustine, *A Commentary on Canon Law*, VIII, 260, 261.
[320] Cf. *Wernz, Ius Decretalium*, VI, n. 117, p. 119; n. 125, p. 133, not. 231;

While the Code prescribes such a support as will enable the deposed cleric to meet his actual wants, it does so not as a matter of justice but as a consideration of charity and for the common good of the clerical state. Nevertheless, it is a positive prescript occupying a significant position in the penal system of the Church. Deposition is not a censure to be withdrawn in justice as soon as the offender amends and seeks pardon. Rather it is a vindictive penalty inflicted for past crimes and normally is to endure forever. Repentance or sorrow for his delinquency can no longer of itself effectuate the restoration of the deposed cleric. As he can no longer be employed in ecclesiastical functions, then the deposed cleric, if he enjoys no other source of income, has no alternative but to beg or to engage himself in secular employment in order to acquire his livelihood. But this extremity is averted and the honor and dignity of the clerical state is upheld by the prescript of the Code which directs the delinquent's ordinary to provide a charitable subsistence for him. However, should the deposed cleric persist in his delinquency and continue to give scandal, then the ordinary may deprive him forever of the right to wear the ecclesiastical garb, which privation simultaneously brings with it the loss of all claim to even this charitable support, as the following canon of the Code clearly indicates.

ARTICLE 4. AGGRAVATED DEPOSITION

Canon 2304, § 1: Si clericus depositus non det emendationis signa et praesertim si scandalum dare pergat monitusque non resipiscat, Ordinarius potest eum perpetuo privare iure deferendi habitum ecclesiasticum.

§ 2: Haec privatio secumfert privationem privilegiorum clericalium et cessationem praescripti can. 2303, § 2.

A. *Nature and Effects of This Penalty*

If a deposed cleric does not show any signs of amendment, and especially if he persists in giving scandal and does not heed warn-

Wernz-Vidal, *Ius Canonicum*, VII, n. 357, p. 383; Cocchi, *Commentarium*, VIII, n. 118, p. 200; Blat, *Commentarium*, V, n. 136, p. 185; Sipos, *Enchiridion Iuris Canonici*, § 240, p. 947.

ings, the ordinary may deprive him forever of the right to wear the ecclesiastical garb. This deprivation entails the privation of the clerical privileges and the cessation of the prescript of canon 2303, § 2, which provides for a charitable support for the deposed cleric. As already observed, the Code here introduces an aggravated form of deposition. It is a penalty which by its very nature and positive declaration of the law can only be inflicted on a cleric who has already been deposed. It aggravates the penalty of deposition by adding to its effects the perpetual privation of the right to wear the ecclesiastical garb, the deprivation of the clerical privileges and the loss of any and every claim to the charitable sustenance accorded to a deposed cleric.

Some canonists since the Code have referred to this penalty of canon 2304 as the perpetual privation of the ecclesiastical garb.[321] While it is true that this is the specific element of the penalty—and indeed it is listed in canon 2298 as if it were a penalty by itself[322]—nevertheless its definition in canon 2304 clearly indicates that it cannot legally exist apart from a previous deposition to which it brings added privations. Hence it is far more appropriate to designate this penalty of canon 2304 as aggravated deposition.

Before the Code clerics who had been ordained to major orders and in consequence had been perpetually ascribed to the clerical state[323] could not be deprived of the privileges of the clerical state except through the penalty of degradation, nor could they in any other manner be despoiled of the right of wearing the ecclesiastical garb or be reduced to the lay state. With the changed relations between Church and State in modern times the common law penalty of real degradation could not always be inflicted on an unwilling cleric. The scandal given by a criminal cleric publicly wearing the ecclesiastical garb had to be eliminated by other means. Wherefore the practice was introduced in many dioceses of adding to the sentence of deposition a prohibition forbidding the delinquent cleric to

---

[321] Cf. Augustine, *A Commentary on Canon Law*, VIII, 261; Blat, *Commentarium*, V, n. 137, p. 186; Sipos, *Enchiridion Iuris Canonici*, § 240, p. 948.

[322] Canon 2298: "Poenae vindicativae quae clericis tantum applicantur, sunt: . . . n. 11: Privatio perpetua habitus ecclesiastici."

[323] Cf. Benedictus XIV, *De synodo dioecesana*, lib. XII, cap. 3, n. 5.

wear the ecclesiastical garb.[324] This procedure, however, did not involve loss of the clerical privileges, for these were conceded by the common law and were lost only according to its provisions, namely, by real degradation.[325] Clerics in minor orders, however, could be reduced to the lay state and deprived of the clerical privileges with greater facility, namely, by a decree of the ordinary issued according to the law.[326]

The Code has followed up earlier practices and put them into law. Degradation is still a penalty of the common law which effects the perpetual privation of the clerical garb and the reduction to the lay state. As before the Code so also now this penalty can be inflicted only for the crimes expressly stated in the law.[327] Besides this penalty, however, the Code has authorized other punishments to deprive a delinquent cleric in major orders of the right of wearing the ecclesiastical garb when he persists in giving scandal. As penalties the Code sanctions a twofold privation of this right, one temporary, the other perpetual. If a cleric gives grave scandal, and after being warned does not amend, and if the scandal cannot otherwise be removed, he may meanwhile be deprived of the right to wear the ecclesiastical garb. This deprivation entails *for the time of its duration* the prohibition to exercise any ecclesiastical ministry and the deprivation of the clerical privileges.[328] Although the Code here speaks of the temporary deprivation of the clerical privileges it evidently signifies no more than their penal suspension.[329] On the other hand, the Code establishes a perpetual privation of the ecclesiastical garb in which the clerical privileges are truly lost forever.[330] This penalty, as already noted, is constituted in the Code only as an

[324] Cf. Wernz, *Ius Decretalium*, VI, n. 140, pp. 145-146.

[325] Cf. Lega, *De Delictis et Poenis*, n. 207, p. 280, not. 1.

[326] Cf. c. un., *de bigamis*, I, 12, in VI°; Conc. Trident., sess. XXIII, *de ref.*, c. 6; Benedictus XIV, *De synodo dioecesana*, lib. V, cap. 12, nn. 1, 2, 3; lib. XII, cap. 3, nn. 3, 4; Pius IX, *Epistola Declaratoria Circa Privilegia Clericorum*, 20 Septembris 1860—*ASS*, III (1867), 433.

[327] Cf. canon 2305.

[328] Canon 2300.

[329] Cf. canon 123; Blat, *Commentarium*, V, n. 133, pp. 183-184; De Meester, *Compendium*, III, pars 2, n. 1795, p. 224, not. 6; *Diarium Romanae Curiae, Communicato—AAS*, XIX (1927), 290.

[330] Cf. canons 2304, § 2, and 123.

aggravated form of deposition. In other words, while the law empowers ordinaries to punish a cleric in minor orders with reduction to the lay state and, in consequence, with perpetual privation of all clerical rights and privileges simply by a decree issued after the prudent judgment that, all things considered, the cleric could not with due respect for the clerical state be promoted to sacred orders,[881] no cleric in major orders can be punished with perpetual privation of the ecclesiastical garb and clerical privileges except in aggravated deposition [882] nor can he be penalized with reduction to the lay state except in degradation.[883]

Finally, it should be emphasized that the canon under consideration adds to the penalty of deposition a perpetual *penal privation of the right* to wear the ecclesiastical garb, and not merely a perpetual prohibition against wearing it, as A Coronata erroneously asserts.[884] As Vermeersch-Creusen have pointed out,[885] the Code does not always employ the prohibition of wearing the ecclesiastical garb as a penalty.[886] The prohibition to exercise a right and the deprivation of this right are two distinct legal entities. Canon 123 declares that the clerical privileges are lost through reduction to the lay state or by perpetual deprivation of the ecclesiastical garb. While reduction to the lay state may or may not be a penalty,[887] perpetual deprivation of the ecclesiastical garb is always a vindictive penalty applicable solely to the clergy.[888] As a penalty it must be interpreted strictly. The effects of the perpetual privation of the right to wear the ecclesiastical garb should not be attributed to a temporary privation of this right [889] nor, *a fortiori*, to a perpetual prohibition of exercising this right.

A perpetual prohibition of this kind is visited by the law itself

---

[881] Cf. canons 211, 213.

[882] Cf. canon 2304.

[883] Cf. canon 2305.

[884] *Institutiones*, IV, n. 1835, p. 262.

[885] *Epitome*, III, n. 497, p. 300.

[886] Cf. canon 213 which prohibits the wearing of the ecclesiastical garb by those who have lawfully returned from the clerical to the lay state.

[887] Cf. canons 211, 2305.

[888] Cf. canon 2298, n. 11.

[889] Cf. canons 2300 and 123.

upon perpetually professed religious in major orders on the occasion of their dismissal from religion for the crimes stated in canon 646 (*ipso facto* effective dismissal) or for offenses punished by the common law with juridical infamy, deposition or degradation.[340] The Code considers here the dismissal of these religious only when it results upon the commission of grave specific crimes. When the dismissal has been effected, whether by the operation of the law itself in virtue of canon 646 or as the result of a legitimate process, the legislator imposes upon the dismissed religious a prohibition of ever wearing the ecclesiastical garb. It is an administrative measure rather than a penal sanction, a necessary precautionary measure to prevent scandals. This is evident from the fact that the prohibition is extended to include those who are dismissed for delicts punished by the common law with degradation. If besides the decree of dismissal a sentence of degradation had been passed against this religious, then the prohibition of the canon would no longer serve any positive purpose. In aggravated deposition as well as in degradation there is involved not merely a perpetual *prohibition* which forbids the wearing of the ecclesiastical garb but a perpetual *privation* of the right to wear it. Accordingly, if and when these penalties are inflicted upon the aforementioned religious in conformity with the sacred canons, he will not only be forbidden to wear the ecclesiastical garb but will be deprived of the right to do so. Only then is he forever deprived of the clerical privileges, an effect nowhere attributed in law to a prohibition, even perpetual, of wearing the ecclesiastical garb.[341]

[340] Canon 670: "Clericus in sacris qui aliquod delictum commisit de quo in can. 646, aut dimissus est ob delictum quod iure communi punitur infamia iuris vel depositione vel degradatione, perpetuo prohibetur deferre habitum ecclesiasticum."

[341] The distinction here set forth and based on internal evidences of the Code as well as on the general principles of penal law provides the only reasonable approach to an interpretation of canon 670. Without making this distinction A Coronata (*Institutiones*, I, n. 660, p. 868) points to the difficulty of this canon but fails to solve it: "Item difficultas est in explicando modo quo prohibitio deferendi habitum ecclesiasticum applicari possit: talis enim poenae inflictio depositionem praeviam supponere videtur (can. 2304). At forte difficultas solvitur dicendo in casu tribunal qui dimissionem decernit, debere simul ex connexione causarum primo depositionem et deinde etiam habitus priva-

B. *Infliction of the Penalty*

The penalty of the perpetual privation of the right to wear the ecclesiastical garb can be inflicted solely on a cleric:

1. who has been previously deposed;

2. who shows no signs of repentance but rather continues to give scandal;

3. who does not heed the admonitions addressed to him.[342] All these circumstances must be verified before the penalty can be employed.[343] They may be reduced to two fundamental requirements on the part of the delinquent, namely deposition united with incorrigibility.

In this penalty the law of the Church seeks vindication only against the deposed cleric. This fact in itself reveals that ecclesiastical vindictive penalties do not exclude from their scope the amendment and reformation of the delinquent. If a delinquent cleric does not show signs of repentance after deposition, which is indeed a severe penalty inflicted only for grave crimes expressly stated in the law,[344] he is to be warned, and if he still does not amend he is to be punished with perpetual privation of the ecclesiastical garb,[345] and if notwithstanding these penalties he continues in his delinquency for another year he is to be degraded.[346] Recognition of the reformative aspect of these penalties leads to a better appreciation of the law governing their infliction.

After deposition, then, if the delinquent cleric manifests signs of repentance by accepting the penalty and submitting to ecclesiastical

tionem decernere" Schäfer [*Compendium De Religiosis ad Norman Codicis Iuris Canonici* (2 ed., Münster: Ex Officina Libraria Aschendorff, 1931), n. 597, p. 780] is no less gratuitous in his assertion: "Talis clericus in sacris amittit iura et privilegia clericalia (cf. can. 123 et 2304, § 2), at tenetur ad obligationes Status Clerialis, idest ad caelibatum et recitationem Officii divini. Pro religione cessat praescriptum can. 2303, § 2, subsidii caritativi (cf. can. 2304, § 2)."

[342] Canon 2304.

[343] Cf. Augustine, *A Commentary on Canon Law*, VIII, 261, 262; Sipos, *Enchiridion Iuris Canonici*, § 240, p. 948.

[344] Cf. canon 2303, § 3.

[345] Cf. canon 2304.

[346] Cf. canon 2305, § 2.

discipline, the Church allows him to retain the clerical privileges and urges support for his needs.[347]   If, on the other hand, he does not evince signs of amendment and especially if he continues to give scandal, even after due warning, the Church no longer co-operates with him but, on the contrary, authorizes the perpetual privation of his right to wear the ecclesiastical garb and abandons him to his own devices.[348]   The delict punishable with this penalty is precisely incorrigibility.

Since deposition is inflicted on a cleric only in punishment of a crime expressly stated in the law, the added penalty of perpetual privation of the ecclesiastical garb is inflicted only in punishment of consequent incorrigibility.   The material element of this delict may be an act of omission, namely, the failure to amend for the original delict which was punished with deposition (*non det signa emendationis*), or an act of commission, namely, the perseverance in this delict or the commission of others of an equally grave character (*scandalum dare pergat*).   The formal element of this delict is the deliberate repetition of these acts by the delinquent contrary to the lawful corrections employed against him (*monitusque non resipiscat*), for by such a repetition he excludes all hope of his amendment.[349] For the establishment of this delict, therefore, the Code absolutely requires a canonical warning.[350]   If the delinquent cleric heeds the warning he cannot be punished with this penalty for the delict is not consummated.   It is only upon failure to conform to this warning that the delict becomes punishable.[351]

The penalty, namely, the perpetual privation of the right to wear the ecclesiastical garb, which implies a further intensification of the penalty of deposition and unquestionably stands as one of the most severe penalties employed on delinquent clerics by the Church, can be inflicted only by a tribunal of five judges.[352]   It rests

---

[347] Cf. canon 2303, § 2.

[348] Cf. canon 2304, § 2.

[349] Cf. Gonzalez-Tellez, *Commentaria*, lib. II, tit. 1, cap. 10, n. 12; Barbosa, *De Officio et Potestate Episcopi*, pars III, alleg. CX, nn. 14-19.

[350] Cf. canon 2143; A Coronata, *Institutiones*, IV, n. 1832, p. 260.

[351] Cf. Augustine, *A Commentary on Canon Law*, VIII, 261-262.

[352] Cf. canon 1576, § 1: "Reprobata contraria consuetudine et revocato quolibet contrario privilegio . . . n. 2: Causae vero quibus agitur de delictis

with them to determine whether the canonical warning has been duly given to the deposed cleric, and with what results, and to inflict the penalty when the delinquent has evinced no signs of amendment and especially when he continues to give scandal.[353]

The only difference between deposition aggravated by the addition of the perpetual privation of the right to wear the ecclesiastical garb and degradation is that the latter includes also the reduction to the lay state.[354] Perpetual deprivation of the right to wear the ecclesiastical garb does not of itself reduce the cleric to the lay state, as Leitner considered probable.[355] The deposed cleric, though he be perpetually deprived of the right of wearing the ecclesiastical garb, remains, nevertheless, a cleric.[356] His juridical condition is similar to that of a deposed cleric who was punished under the old law in conformity with the legal order of penalties established in the decretal *Cum non ab homine.*[357] According to this law, as already observed,[358] a deposed cleric was finally abandoned to the secular power if he persistently continued in his delinquency by despising the warnings contained in the penalties gradually inflicted upon him.[359] In the present law a deposed cleric who remains incorrigible after warning is directly deprived of the right to wear the ecclesiastical garb and, in consequence, is also deprived of the clerical privileges. In the past as well as in the present law the penal

quae . . . privationis perpetuae habitus ecclesiastici . . . poenam important, reservantur tribunali quinque iudicum." Manifestly erroneous, therefore, is the assertion of A Coronata (*Institutiones*, IV, n. 1835, p. 262): "Specialis modus procedendi aut speciale tribunal ad hanc poenam infligendam non requiritur." Cf. Vermeersch-Creusen, *Epitome*, III, n. 497, p. 300; Sipos, *Enchiridion Iuris Canonici*, § 240, p. 948; Beste, *Introductio in Codicem*, 930.

[353] Cf. Blat, *Commentarium*, V, n. 137, p. 186.

[354] Cf. canon 2305; Vermeersch-Creusen, *Epitome*, III, n. 498, p. 301; A Coronata, *Institutiones*, IV, n. 1835, p. 262; De Meester, *Compendium*, III, pars 2, n. 1798, p. 226.

[355] *Lehrbuch des katholischen Eherechts* (Paderborn, 1902), p. 256; cf. Hilling, *Das Personenrecht des Codex Iuris Canonici* (Paderborn: Ferdinand Schöningh, 1924), p. 84, note 1.

[356] Cf. Chelodi, *Ius Poenale*, n. 52, p. 69.

[357] C. 10, X, *de iudiciis*, II, 1.

[358] Cf. *supra*, p. 76.

[359] Cf. Benedictus XIV, *De synodo dioecesana*, lib. IX, cap. 6, nn. 9, 10.

system is based on the principle that penalties should be so commensurate with delicts that only the graver crimes are to be punished with the graver penalties.[360] This systematic progression of penalties commences with deposition and is followed by more severe penalties accordingly as the original delict is aggravated with the incorrigibility of the delinquent. It is imperative, therefore, to consider the delicts punishable by law with deposition.

ARTICLE 5. CAUSES FOR DEPOSITION

Canon 2303, § 3: **Poena depositionis infligi nequit, nisi in casibus iure expressis.**

It has already been observed in the preceding chapter how in the period antecedent to the promulgation of the Code it was the common doctrine of canonists that deposition could be inflicted only for the crimes expressly stated in the law. The former legislation, however, embodied a multiplicity of laws, many of which had in the course of time fallen into desuetude, taking along with them, at least in some cases, their penal sanction of deposition. Consequently in the practice of the Church the usage developed of inflicting the penalty of deposition only for stated crimes which by their nature and object as well as by the circumstances of their commission were deemed especially grave, atrocious and scandalous in the prudent estimation of the ecclesiastical judge.[361] In keeping with this development an authoritative codification of the delicts punishable by law with deposition and accommodated to the conditions of the times was greatly to be desired.[362] In this way all occasion for arbitrariness would be ruled out by a complete definition of the delicts warranting so severe a penalty. *Ecclesia abhorret ab arbitrio.*[363]

[360] Cf. Schmalzgrueber, *Ius Ecclesiasticum Universum*, lib. V, tit. XXXVII, nn. 152-154.

[361] Cf. *supra*, p. 98; Schmalzgruber, *Ius Ecclesiasticum Universum*, lib. V, tit. XXXVII, n. 136; Reiffenstuel, *Ius Canonicum Universum*, lib. V, tit. XXXVII, n. 30; Hollweck, *Die kirchlichen Strafgesetze*, § 91, p. 158.

[362] Cf. Wernz, *Ius Decretalium*, VI, n. 123, p. 131.

[363] S. R. R., *Remotionis*, 8 Augustii 1925, *coram R. P. D. Parillo*, dec. XLIII—*Decisiones*, XVII (1925), pp. 336-337.

The Code has brought to completion the developments in the practice of the Church as regards the causes for deposition by introducing into positive legislation the provision that this penalty can be inflicted only for the delicts expressed in the law. Without question the reference is to the common law of the Church. The terminology *in iure* without further qualification is never employed by the Code in any other signification. It designates the law of the Church and not the particular law of some restricted territory of the universal Church. Moreover, the Code has not only enacted the legislation that deposition cannot be inflicted except in the cases expressly stated in the law, but has also in its third title of the fifth book set forth the delicts which warrant this penalty. It would have been a useless task to codify these delicts if the penalty could be inflicted for other crimes stated in the law of inferior legislators in the Church. Until the Roman Pontiff [364] or an eumenical council [365] employ this penalty as a sanction against the violation of other laws, the causes for deposition will be only those which are defined by the Code. Under the present discipline of the Church, then, it must be held that deposition cannot validly or lawfully be inflicted except in those cases which are expressly designated in the law of the Code.[366]

The delicts punishable with deposition under the discipline of the Code are most serious offenses and are recognized as especially unbecoming to clerics. Indeed it is worthy of note that besides deposition, other penalties, more expeditious in their execution, are sanctioned against these delicts. For an appreciation of the relative

[364] Canon 218, § 1: "Romanus Pontifex, Beati Petri in primatu successor, habet non solum primatum honoris, sed supremam et plenam potestatem iurisdictionis in universam ecclesiam. . . . "

[365] Canon 228, § 1: "Concilium Oecumenicum suprema pollet in universam Ecclesiam potestate."

[366] Cf. Blat, *Commentarium*, V, n. 136, p. 185; Augustine, *A Commentary on Canon Law*, VIII, 261; Vermeersch-Creusen, *Epitome*, III, n. 498, p. 301; Cocchi, *Commentarium*, VIII, n. 118, p. 201; Sipos, *Enchiridion Iuris Canonici*, § 240, p. 947; Ayrinhac-Lydon, *Penal Legislation*, n. 170, p. 129; De Meester, *Compendium*, III, pars 2, n. 1797, p. 225; Sole, *De Delictis et Poenis*, n. 294, p. 209; Eichmann, *Strafrecht*, pp. 119-120; Chelodi, *Ius Poenale*, n. 52, p. 69; Beste, *Introductio in Codicem*, 930; A Coronata, *Institutiones*, IV, n. 1834, p. 262.

position of deposition in the penal system of the Church it will be helpful to mention the other penalties incurred by one who commits a delict warranting deposition. The law of the Code expressly provides for deposition in the following cases.

A. Apostasy, Heresy, Schism

All apostates from the Christian faith and all heretics and schismatics *ipso facto* incur excommunication, and if they have been admonished and do not repent they shall be deprived of any benefice, dignity, pension, office or other assignment which they may hold in the Church; they shall be declared infamous; and if they are clerics they shall after another fruitless admonition be deposed.[367] It should be noted that it is only after a second warning has been left unheeded that the delict of apostasy, heresy or schism is punishable with deposition.

While suspected heresy is not a delict which is immediately punished with deposition, it may become such as to warrant this penalty. The law itself attaches the suspicion of heresy to certain delicts. A cleric, for example, who appeals from the pope to a general council,[368] or remains under sentence of excommunication for more than a year,[369] or commits simony in the administration or reception of the sacraments [370] is thereby suspect of heresy. He must be warned to remove the cause of suspicion. If the warning proves fruitless the suspect cleric must be forbidden to perform any legitimate acts in the Church.[371] If a second warning proves in vain he must be suspended *a divinis*. If he has not amended after the lapse of six months, computed from the contraction of the first

---

[367] Canon 2314, § 1: "Omnes a christiana fide apostatae et omnes et singuli haeretici aut schismatici: n. 1. Incurrunt ipso facto excommunicationem; n. 2. Nisi moniti resipuerint, priventur beneficio, dignitate, pensione, officio aliove munere, si quod in Ecclesia habeant, infames declarentur, et clerici, iterata monitione, deponantur."

[368] Cf. canon 2332.

[369] Cf. canon 2340.

[370] Cf. canon 2371.

[371] Cf. canon 2256, n. 2.

penalty,[372] he must be regarded as a heretic and punished accordingly.[373] Hence in this last instance the Code expressly provides for deposition though the penalty itself is stated only indirectly.

B. Profanation of the Sacred Species

A cleric who throws away the Sacred Species, or carries them away or retains them for an evil purpose is a suspect of heresy; incurs a *latae sententiae* excommunication reserved in a most special manner to the Holy See; is *ipso facto* infamous and must be deposed.[374] Before the Code a cleric was degraded for this delict.[375]

C. Simulation of Priestly Powers

A cleric who is not ordained to the priesthood and pretends to say Mass or to hear sacramental confession incurs *ipso facto* an excommunication reserved in a special manner to the Holy See, and must be deposed.[376] It may be emphasized that this penalty applies only to those clerics who have never been ordained to the priesthood; hence it applies to all clerics from first tonsure to deaconship inclusively, but not to a priest who perchance is forbidden to exercise these sacerdotal functions. In the old law the penalty for this delict was degradation.[377]

[372] Cf. Ayrinhac-Lydon, *Penal Legislation*, n. 205, p. 160.

[373] Canon 2315: "Suspectus de haeresi, qui monitus causam suspicionis non removeat, actibus legitimis prohibeatur, et clericus praeterea, repetita inutiliter monitione, suspendatur a divinis; quod si intra sex menses a contracta poena completos suspectus de haeresi sese non emendaverit, habeatur tamquam haereticus, haereticorum poenis obnoxius."

[374] Canon 2320: "Qui species consecratas abiecerit vel ad malum finem abduxerit aut retinuerit, est suspectus de heresi; incurrit in excommunicationem latae sententiae specialissimo modo Sedi Apostolicae reservatam; est ipso facto infamis, et clericus praeterea est deponendus."

[375] Cf. *supra*, p. 106; Benedictus XIV, const. *Ab augustissimo*, 5 mart. 1744—*Fontes*, n. 340.

[376] Canon 2322: "Ad ordinem sacerdotalem non promotus: n. 1. Si Missae celebrationem simulaverit aut sacramentalem confessionem exceperit, excommunicationem ipso facto contrahit, speciali modo Sedi Apostolicae reservatam; et insuper laicus quidem privetur pensione aut munere, si quod habeat in Ecclesia, aliisque poenis pro gravitate culpae puniatur; clericus vero deponatur." He is also irregular *ex delicto*.—Cf. canon 985, n. 7.

[377] Cf. *supra*, pp. 105-106.

D. *Violation of Corpses or Graves*

Any cleric who violates the bodies or graves of the dead with a view to theft or any other evil purpose is to be punished with personal interdict, is *ipso facto* infamous and must be deposed.[378] It matters not whether the bodies are the bodies of the faithful or of infidels, whether the place of sepulture is blessed or unblessed. The delict is completed in the theft or other evil act which violates the natural sanctity of the bodies and graves of the deceased.[379] Before the Code deposition was not sanctioned for this delict in the common law. A chapter of the Decree of Gratian declared clerics infamous who committed such crimes.[380]

E. *Abortion*

Clerics who procure abortion incur a *latae sententiae* excommunication reserved to the ordinary at the moment the crime takes effect and they are also to be deposed.[381] Abortion here means the direct and intentional expulsion of a nonviable human fetus from the maternal womb.[382] The abortion must really take place, willed as an end or as a means to an end, in order to complete this delict. It should also be noted that besides the principal perpetrators those who insist on the performance of the crime as well as those who counsel it or make it possible in such manner that without their positive co-operation the crime would not have been committed are all equally guilty of this delict.[383] Before the promulgation of the

---

[378] Canon 2328: "Qui cadavera vel sepulcra mortuorum ad furtum vel alium malum finem violaverit, interdicto personali puniatur, sit ipso facto infamis, et clericus praeterea deponatur."

[379] Cf. Chelodi, *Ius Poenale*, n. 67, p. 87; Cocchi, *Commentarium*, VIII, n. 162, p. 250; Woywod, *A Practical Commentary*, II, 749.

[380] C. 17, C. VI, q. 1.

[381] Cf. canon 2350, § 1: "Procurantes abortum, matre non excepta, incurrunt, effectu secuto, in excommunicationem latae sententiae Ordinario reservatam; et si sint clerici praeterea deponantur." They also incur irregularity *ex delicto.*—Cf. canon 985, n. 4.

[382] Ayrinhac-Lydon, *Penal Legislation*, n. 304, p. 240.

[383] Cf. canon 2209, §§ 1-3; Chelodi, *Ius Poenale*, n. 80, p. 110; Augustine, *A Commentary on Canon Law*, VIII, 400; Cocchi, *Commentarium*, VIII, n. 200, p. 305.

Code clerics who were guilty of abortion were punished with degradation,[384] but prior to the sixteenth century they were penalized with deposition.[385]

F. *Violations of Personality, Liberty, Property*

In canon 2354 the Code sets forth certain crimes which may be punished with deposition if the circumstances warrant such a severe penalty. The delicts as defined in the first paragraph of this canon in relation to laymen are properly termed cases of the mixed forum since in these affairs the civil courts have concurrent jurisdiction with the ecclesiastical courts.[386] Thus the law decrees: Laymen are *ipso iure* excluded from legitimate ecclesiastical acts and any charge they may hold in the Church, save the obligation of indemnity, if they have been lawfully condemned for

(a) Homicide;

(b) The abduction of persons of either sex under the age of puberty;

(c) The selling of a human being as a slave or for any other evil purpose;

(d) Usury (as understood and condemned by civil legislation, *i. e.*, excessive interest); [387]

(e) Rapine or robbery accompanied with force;

(f) Theft, either qualified, *i. e.*, marked by aggravating circumstances such as theft of things sacred, or unqualified, but in a very grave matter;

---

[384] Cf. *supra,* p. 105; Sixtus V, const. *Effraenatam,* 29 oct. 1588, § 4—*Fontes,* n. 165; Gregory XIV, const. *Sedes Apostolica,* 31 maii 1591—*Fontes,* n. 173.

[385] C. 20, X, *de homicidio voluntario vel casuali,* V, 12.

[386] Cf. canon 2198: " . . . delictum quod laedit utriusque societatis legem, ab utraque potestate puniri potest." Canon 1553, § 2: "In causis in quibus tum Ecclesia tum civilis potestas aeque competentes sunt, quaeque dicuntur mixti fori, est locus praeventioni." Cf. c. 13, X, *de iudiciis,* II 1: "No sane person is ignorant of the fact that it pertains to our office to punish every Christian for any mortal sin."

[387] Cf. Augustine, *A Commentary on Canon Law,* VIII, 409; Chelodi, *Ius Poenale,* n. 82, p. 115; Ayrinhac-Lydon, *Penal Legislation,* n. 313, p. 250.

(g) Arson or other malicious and very grave destruction of property;

(h) Grave mutilation, the infliction of serious wounds or the perpetration of dire violence.

In view of the privileged forum of clerics the Code, after defining these delicts in relation to laymen, continues: If a clergyman has committed any of the aforementioned crimes, he must be punished by the *ecclesiastical court* in proportion to the gravity of his guilt with penances, censures, privation of office and benefice, and even with deposition if the circumstances demand it; if he has been guilty of culpable homicide, he must be degraded.[388]

In regard to the penalty of deposition for these delicts two points are to be noted. In the first place it is left to the prudence and discretion of the ecclesiastical judge to decide when this penalty is warranted. Secondly, while the delicts specified are grave by their nature and object, they do not warrant deposition unless they are aggravated by accompanying circumstances. According to the eminent canonists Schmalzgrueber,[389] Reiffenstuel[390] and Wernz[391] these circumstances must be such as to render the delict enormous, atrocious, and publicly scandalous, so that the additional severe penalty of deposition is not only strictly justifiable but also morally necessary. In this matter the decision is left not to the wish or caprice of the judge, but to his prudence and conscience. On the other hand, while the law here allows the judge to impose the severer penalty of deposition when the particular case warrants it, there may be concomitant circumstances justifying a diminution or even an omission of the canonical penalty. Reference is had to the *de facto* situation in many countries today where, either by concession of the Holy See or through an abuse of power on the part of civil authority, clerics are brought before lay tribunals and are punished as laymen. Equity demands that the ecclesiastical judge give due consideration to this fact. If he finds that the delinquent has been or will be sufficiently punished by the civil authority, he should

---

[388] Cf. canon 2354, § 2.
[389] *Ius Ecclesiasticum Universum*, lib. V, tit. XXXVII, n. 136.
[390] *Ius Canonicum Universum*, lib. V, tit. XXXVII, n. 30.
[391] *Ius Decretalium*, VI, n. 123, pp. 130-131.

abstain from inflicting the canonical penalty altogether or at least he should mitigate the punishment specified by law.[892]

G. *Violations contra sextum*

Deposition is also expressly stated in the Code for certain delicts against the sixth commandment when these are committed by clerics in major orders. Clerics in minor orders who are proved guilty of any offense against the sixth commandment are to be punished in proportion to the seriousness of the transgression, even with dismissal from the clerical state if the circumstances demand it.[893] Clerics in major orders who have committed a delict against the sixth commandment with minors under sixteen years of age, or who have committed adultery, rape, bestiality, sodomy, panderage, incest with blood relatives or relations by marriage in the first degree, are to be suspended, declared infamous, deprived of every office, benefice, dignity and position they may hold, and in the more grievous cases they are to be deposed.[894] It may be observed that deposition is specified solely for clerics who are in major orders when they are convicted of determined qualified delicts *contra sextum* and indeed only in the more serious cases. It rests with the prudence of the competent judge, informed of all the circumstances connected with individual cases, to determine when the evident gravity of these delicts is sufficiently aggravated to warrant the severer penalty of deposition. As a general rule this condition will be verified only when the delict has been continued after repeated warnings.[895]

[892] Cf. canon 2223, § 3, nn. 2, 3; Chelodi, *Ius Poenale*, n. 82, pp. 114-115; Ayrinhac-Lydon, *Penal Legislation*, n. 314, p. 250.

[893] Cf. canon 2358.

[894] Canon 2359, § 2: "Si delictum admiserint contra sextum decalogi praeceptum cum minoribus infra aetatem sexdecim annorum, vel adulterium, stuprum, bestialitatem, sodomiam, lenocinium, incestum cum consanguineis aut affinibus in primo gradu exercuerint, suspendantur, infames declarentur, quolibet officio, beneficio, dignitate, munere, si quod habeant, priventur, et in casibus gravioribus deponantur."

[895] Cf. Reiffenstuel, *Ius Canonicum Universum*, lib. V, tit. XXXVII, n. 30; Schmalzgrueber, *Ius Ecclesiasticum Universum*, lib. V, tit. XXXVII, n. 136; Wernz, *Ius Decretalium*, VI, n. 123, pp. 130-131.

H. *Violations of the Law Governing the Use of Ecclesiastical Garb*

The Code establishes deposition as the penalty for clerics in sacred orders who obstinately refuse for three months to wear the clerical garb or to give up a mode of life unbecoming to their state. The law, distinguishing between clerics in minor and major orders in regard to the penalties, is as follows: Clerics who do not wear the clerical garb or tonsure as prescribed by canon 136 should be given a severe warning. If this warning remains fruitless and there is no amendment within a month:

(a) Clerics in minor orders forfeit the ecclesiastical state *ipso facto* (canon 136 § 3).

(b) Clerics in major orders, besides forfeiting *ipso facto* and without the need of any declaration every office which they hold (canon 188, n. 7) shall be suspended from the orders which they have received; if they notoriously take up a mode of life not compatible with the clerical state, they must again be warned and if within three months the admonition has produced no effect they are to be deposed.[896] Augustine points out that since these penalties for clerics in major orders are *ferendae sententiae,* if a cleric has never been suspended or deposed, even though he may have been for several years a public teacher, unknown to the people as a priest, no absolution or dispensation is required.[897] To this it may be added that even were it publicly known that he was a priest the dispensation still would not be required *if* the cleric had never been deposed. The notoriety of his changed mode of life is a condition which calls for a canonical admonition and the eventual infliction of the penalty, but it does not change the manner of contracting the penalty.

[896] Canon 2379: "Clerici, contra praescriptum can. 136, habitum ecclesiasticum et tonsuram clericalem non gestantes, graviter moneantur; transacto inutiliter mense a monitione, quod ad clericos minores attinet, servetur praescriptum eiusdem can. 136, § 3; clerici autem maiores, salvo praescripto can. 188, n. 7, ab ordinibus receptis suspendantur, et si ad vitae genus a statu clericali alienum notorie transierint, nec, rursus moniti, resipuerint, post tres menses ab hac ultima monitione deponantur."

[897] *A Commentary on Canon Law,* VIII, 459-460.

I. *Unlawful Possession of Ecclesiastical Offices, Benefices, Dignities*

Deposition is also expressed in the Code as the penalty to be visited on those who are exceptionally guilty in regard to the unlawful possession of an ecclesiastical office, benefice, or dignity. The law of the Church requires that no one should, of his own authority, take possession of an ecclesiastical office, benefice, or dignity.[398] Those who have been elected, nominated, or presented to the same should not assume possession, government, or administration before they have received the necessary letters of confirmation or investiture and have shown them to such persons as the law indicates; otherwise,

(a) They become by that very fact incapable of acquiring the office, benefice, or dignity in question and they must besides, be punished by the ordinary according to the gravity of the fault.

(b) They are to be compelled to give up the possession, the government, or the administration of the office, benefice, or ecclesiastical dignity without any delay; if they stubbornly fail to do so, then upon previous warning they shall be suspended, deprived of any office, benefice, or dignity previously obtained, and they may even be deposed if the gravity of the delict calls for it.[399] Again, therefore, deposition is sanctioned by the common law of the Church only after warnings and other milder penalties have failed to correct the delinquent.

J. *Continuation in Office after Privation or Removal*

Finally, deposition is expressly stated in the law of the Church as the penalty to be visited upon those clerics who persistently continue in office after their lawful privation or removal. It may be observed that this severe penalty is sanctioned only in those cases in which milder penalties have failed to produce a correction of the delinquent. In establishing the penalty for this delict the Code decrees: If a cleric who has been canonically deprived of, or removed from, an office, benefice, or dignity, persists in holding it, or unreasonably multiplies delays in abandoning it, he should be compelled

[398] Cf. canon 1443.
[399] Cf. canon 2394, nn. 1, 2.

to withdraw therefrom, after due and proper warning, by means of suspension *a divinis* and of other penalties, and even by deposition itself if it be found necessary in the circumstances of the case.[400]

ARTICLE 6. INFLICTION OF THE PENALTY

In the preceding article consideration was given to the various delicts which warrant deposition according to the present discipline of the Church. In this connection it should further be observed that the Code in no case prescribes deposition as a *latae sententiae* penalty, that is to say, it never adds the determined penalty of deposition to the law in such a way that it is incurred *ipso facto* upon the commission of the delict.[401] On this point canonists cannot now but agree,[402] whereas formerly the ambiguity of the Decretals provided a basis for controversy. Some canonists found in that legislation instances of *latae sententiae* deposition,[403] while others stoutly denied that such a penalty could be read into the old law.[404] Undoubtedly the divergence of opinion in this matter may to a great extent be traced to the unfortunate but not unaccustomed usage among canonists of employing the term *deposition* to signify the penalty of simple privation.[405] This latter penalty was clearly em-

---

[400] Canon 2401: "Si quis in detinendo officio, beneficio, dignitate, non obstante legitima privatione aut remotione, persistat, aut ne ea dimittat, moras illegitime nectat, ea, praemissa monitione, deserere cogatur per suspensionem a divinis aliasve poenas, depositione, si res ferat, non exclusa."

[401] Cf. canon 2217, § 1: "Poena dicitur: . . . n. 2: *Latae sententiae*, si poena determinata ita sit addita legi vel praecepto ut incurratur ipso facto commissi delicti."

[402] Cf. Augustine, *A Commentary on Canon Law*, VIII, 261; Sipos, *Enchiridion Iuris Canonici*, § 240, p. 947; De Meester, *Compendium*, III, pars 2, n. 1797, p. 225; A Coronata, *Institutiones*, IV, n. 1834, p. 262; Vermeersch-Creusen, *Epitome*, III, n. 498, p. 301; Beste, *Introductio in Codicem*, 930; Eichmann, *Strafrecht*, 119-120.

[403] Cf. Sipos, *Enchiridion Iuris Canonici*, § 240, p. 947, not. 10; Thesaurus-Giraldi (P. I, c. 27) cited by Augustine, *op. cit.*, p. 261, note 1.

[404] Hollweck, *Die kirchlichen Strafgesetze*, § 91, p. 158; Blat, *Commentarium*, V, n. 136, p. 185.

[405] Cf. Lega, *De Delictis et Poenis*, n. 207, p. 280.

ployed by the law in some instances as a *latae sententiae* penalty, especially in the delict of heresy.[406]

The law of the Code is clear. In every case deposition is expressed as a *ferendae sententiae* penalty, which means that it is never incurred until it has actually been inflicted by a competent ecclesiastical judge.[407] In other words, no cleric is deposed except through a condemnatory sentence which convicts the delinquent and thereupon inflicts this penalty previously ordained by law.[408] If there are certain or at least probable and sufficient reasons for instituting a criminal trial which may lead to the pronouncement of this sentence, then the procedure established by the sacred canons must be observed.[409] As regards deposition this criminal action can be instituted only for public delicts [410] which are expressly sanctioned with this penalty in the common law of the Church.[411]

Deposition cannot be inflicted unless it is proved with certainty that the delict punishable with this penalty has been committed and that prosecution is not barred by legitimate prescription.[412] In the prosecution of offenses which are reserved to the judgment of the Sacred Congregation of the Holy Office (*e. g.*, heresy, solicitation in confession, absolution of one's accomplice in external sins of impurity), the ordinary time-limits for prosecution do not apply; the Holy Office follows its own rules.[413] In other offenses the delinquent

---

[406] Cf. Paulus IV, const. *Cum ex apostolatus*, 15 febr. 1559—*Fontes*, n. 94; Heiner, *De Processu Criminali Ecclesiastico* (Latine vertit ac denuo edidit A. Wynen, Romae: Fridericus Pustet, 1912), p. 151.

[407] Cf. canon 2217, § 1: "Poena dicitur: . . . n. 2 . . . *ferendae sententiae*, si a iudice vel Superiore infligi debeat." Cf. Cocchi, *Commentarium*, VIII, n. 118, p. 201; Raus, *Institutiones*, n. 461, p. 709; Sole, *De Delictis et Poenis*, n. 294, p. 209; Chelodi, *Ius Poenale*, n. 52, p. 69.

[408] Cf. Lemieux, *The Sentence in Ecclesiastical Procedure* (Catholic University of America, Canon Law Studies, No. 87, Washington, D. C., 1934), 5, 6; Vermeersch-Creusen, *Epitome*, III, n. 498, p. 301; De Meester, *Compendium*, III, pars 2, n. 1797, p. 25.

[409] Cf. canons 2225; 1946, § 2, n. 3; 1947-1959.

[410] Canon 1933, § 1.

[411] Canon 2303, § 3.

[412] Cf. canon 2233, § 1.

[413] Cf. canons 1703; 1555, § 1.

can be prosecuted only within three years from the commission of the offense, with the following exceptions:

1. Actions for injuries (*e. g.*, defamation, insult, striking, wounding) are extinguished by the lapse of one year;

2. Actions for qualified offenses against the sixth and seventh commandments are extinguished by a lapse of five years;

3. Actions for simony and for homicide are extinguished by a lapse of ten years.[414] If the prosecutor fails within the period of prescription to obtain the decree of execution [415] and to do what is in his power to execute the decree, the penalty becomes extinct with the lapse of the prescribed periods of limitation for the criminal action.[416]

The procedural law of the Code allows an ordinary to employ a judicial rebuke instead of the criminal procedure if the accused when questioned confesses his offense.[417] The judicial rebuke ordinarily contains not only salutary admonitions but also some appropriate remedies or prescriptions of penances or good works which serve to make public reparation for the violation of law or for scandal.[418] The Code, however, does not admit the use of the judicial rebuke in delicts which involve deposition or degradation.[419] In these cases there is no option. The ordinary must institute criminal proceedings. The Code having expressly defined all the delicts for which deposition or degradation may be inflicted has thereby predetermined the penalty adequate to restore the social order or repair scandal in the given cases. Consistently the Code here excludes the substitution of a judicial rebuke for the criminal trial, the very object of which is to inflict the established penalty for these grave delicts.[420]

[414] Canon 1703.

[415] Cf. canon 1918.

[416] Cf. canon 2240.

[417] Cf. canon 1747.

[418] Cf. canon 1952, § 1.

[419] Canon 1948: "Correptio iudicialis locum habere nequit: n. 1: In delictis quae poenam secumferunt excommunicationis specialissimo vel speciali modo Sedi Apostolicae reservatae, aut privationis beneficii, infamiae, depositionis aut degradationis."

[420] Cf. canon 1552, § 2, n. 2.

It should also be observed that in designating the *ferendae sententiae* penalty of deposition the Code invariably employs preceptive terms, that is to say, terms implying a precept to impose the penalty. This is an important consideration for the competent judge in trials on these delicts, since the Code itself ordains that if in enacting a *ferendae sententiae* penalty the law employs preceptive terms then this penalty ordinarily must be imposed. The judge must apply the law, not establish it; his office is not to judge the law but to judge according to the law.[421] However, while mandatory penalties ordinarily must be applied, the law itself, providing for certain exceptional conditions, has committed it to the conscience and prudence of the judge:

1. To delay the imposition of the penalty to a more opportune time if it is judged that greater evils may flow from the delinquent's punishment when it is accomplished with undue haste;

2. To refrain from inflicting the penalty if the delinquent has shown complete amendment and has repaired the scandal, or if he has been or will be sufficiently punished by the civil authorities;

3. To moderate the determined penalty or to employ instead some penal remedy or penance, if there is some circumstance which considerably diminishes his imputability or if the delinquent has amended or has been sufficiently punished by the civil authorities and the judge or superior moreover deems it advisable that some lighter punishment in place of the specified penalty be administered.[422] It may be rare indeed that these circumstances will be verified in a criminal process leading to deposition, and rarer still in a case of prospective degradation, for both penalties are established in the law for extreme cases only. Nevertheless, the Code has committed these equitable powers to the conscience and prudence of the judge or superior who is competent to apply a mandatory penalty. To exclude absolutely from this commission the penalties of deposition and degradation would be contrary to the Code.

When the competent tribunal has inflicted the penalty of deposition—or degradation—its power in the case is exhausted. It can no longer remit the penalty or dispense from it for its power con-

---

[421] Cf. c. 3, D. IV.
[422] Cf. canon 2223, § 3, nn. 1-3.

sists exclusively in the application of the penalty as determined by the law.[423] Indeed once the tribunal has applied the penal sanction of deposition it cannot even suspend the execution of this sentence. The Code has introduced, at least in legal terms, the suspended sentence employed in civil courts as a conditional pardon contingent upon future good behavior. When the necessity of repairing scandal is not urgent the Code leaves it to the prudence of the judge to suspend the execution of an ordinary penalty inflicted by a condemnatory sentence if the offender after a laudable life has become a delinquent for the first time. The judge, however, may suspend the execution of such a sentence only on the condition that if the guilty person within the next three years commits another offense either of the same or of a different kind he shall be liable to the penalty for each delict. The Code expressly excludes from this benefit of the law of a suspended execution the penalties of deposition and degradation.[424] As already observed, these penalties usually follow upon a protracted period of delinquency. In every case they are inflicted only for grave crimes in respect of which satisfaction can ordinarily be made only through the infliction of the penalties established by law.[425]

To recapitulate briefly: the penalty of deposition in the present discipline of the Church can only be inflicted for crimes expressly designated in the law; it is always a *ferendae sententiae* penalty, which means that it is never incurred except when the delict is public and the delinquent has been convicted through a condemnatory sentence issued by a competent tribunal. The ordinary cannot substitute a judicial rebuke for the required criminal process, even when the delinquent has confessed his crime. The tribunal, however, may exercise in the process conscientious discretion as regards the infliction of the penalty when the case is accompanied by very exceptional circumstances as they are delineated in the Code. Once it has inflicted the penalty the tribunal is incompetent to remit or even suspend deposition. Since the competent tribunal is desig-

---

[423] Cf. canon 2236, § 3.

[424] Cf. canon 2288.

[425] Cf. Sole, *De Delictis et Poenis*, n. 266, pp. 188-189; Vermeersch-Creusen, *Epitome*, III, n. 490, pp. 291-292.

nated in relation to the dignity of the status attaching to the clerical delinquent, this particular point is reviewed in reference to bishops and priests in the two separate sections which follow.

A. *The Deposition of Bishops*

As regards the Bishop of Rome, the Supreme Pontiff, there can be no question of deposition. To depose the pope a coercive authority would be required competent to pass judgment upon him and to execute a condemnatory sentence. The Roman Pontiff, however, in virtue of his divinely bestowed primacy is subject to no human authority but only to the power and judgment of God.[426] Not only the nature of the primacy but the whole tradition and practice of the Church have constantly declared that the Primatial See can be judged by no one, a perennial principle repeated in the law of the Code.[427]

As regards all other bishops the discipline governing their deposition which prevailed under the former legislation continues unchanged in the law of the Code. According to the provisions of the sacred canons only the Roman Pontiff can inflict the penalty of deposition on bishops, titular as well as residential.[428] This is a

[426] Cf. canon 218, §§ 1, 2; c. 13, *de iudiciis*, II, 1; c. 6, X, *de electione et electi potestate*, I, 6; Fagnanus, *Commentaria*, lib. I, tit. 6, cap. 6, n. 21; Wernz, *Ius Decretalium*, II, n. 617, p. 697.

[427] Canon 1556: "Prima Sedes a nemine iudicatur." Cf. Conc. Constantinopolitan. IV, actio X, can. 21—*Fontes*, n. 6; Conc. Vatican., sess. IV, c. III, *de vi et ratione primatus Romani Pontificis*—*Fontes*, n. 10; S. Zosimus, ep. *Quamvis Patrum traditio*, 21 mart. 418—*Fontes*, n. 21; S. Bonifacius I, ep. *Retro maioribus tuis*, 11 mart. 422—*Fontes*, n. 22; S. Leo IX, ep. *In terra pax hominibus*, 2 sept. 1053, c. 32—*Fontes*, n. 27; Ioannes XXII, const. *Licet*, 23 Oct. 1327, art. errorum Marsilii Patavini et Ioannis de Ianduno damn. —*Fontes*, n. 38; Clemens VI, ep. *Super quibusdam*, 29 sept. 1351—*Fontes*, n. 42; Paulus IV, const. *Cum ex Apostolatus*, 15 febr. 1559, § 1—*Fontes*, n. 94; Pius IX, Syllabus errorum, prop. 34, 41—*Fontes*, n. 543; Pius IX, const. *Apostolicae Sedis*, 12 oct. 1869, § 1, n. 4; § VI, n. 1—*Fontes*, n. 552; Leo XIII, const. *Romanos Pontifices*, 8 maii 1881—*Fontes*, n. 582; Leo XIII, allocut. *Mirandum sane*, 1 iun. 1888, § 5—*Fontes*, n. 599.

[428] Cf. canons 2227, § 1: "Poena nonnisi a Romano Pontifice infligi aut declarari potest in eos de quibus in can. 1557, § 1"; 1557, § 1: "Ipsius Romani Pontificis dumtaxat ius est iudicandi . . . n. 3: . . . in criminalibus Episcopos, etiam titulares."

major cause [429] reserved to the Roman Pontiff in such a manner that every other judge or tribunal in the Church is absolutely incompetent.[430] A metropolitan, for example, who would initiate or complete on his own authority criminal proceedings for the deposition of one of his suffragan bishops would act invalidly. Even a titular bishop [431] can be validly and lawfully deposed only by the Roman Pontiff. As Roberti has observed,[432] the reservation is apparently founded on the episcopal character.

The reservation to the pope of the right of deposing bishops was initiated, as previously observed, in the Middle Ages and was confirmed by the Council of Trent.[433] The right itself, however, is inherent in the primacy. The pope as the chief pastor is the *iudex ordinarius* of all bishops. While he alone is competent to pronounce the sentence of deposition upon any bishop, the Roman Pontiff need not take personal cognizance of the cause but may commission others to act for him. Usually he delegates the cause to one of the congregations or to a commission of cardinals.[434] Thus the Council of Trent ordained that if the cause be of such a nature that it must necessarily be committed out of the Roman Curia it should not be delegated to any others but metropolitans or bishops chosen by the pope with a special commission signed by the pontiff's own hand; nor should he ever grant more to these delegates than this, that in due procedural form they draw up an organized report which they must transmit immediately to the Roman Pontiff, the definitive sentence being reserved to him.[435] Notwithstanding this disposition of the Council, the pope, as Bouix has observed,[436] could by ordinary law and without resorting to the fullness of his power commit these major causes of bishops outside the Roman Curia to other judges than metropolitans and bishops; could delegate these judges

---

[429] Cf. canon 220; Hinschius, *Kirchenrecht*, I, 514; *supra*, pp. 56, 79.

[430] Cf. canon 1558.

[431] Cf. canon 349.

[432] *De Processibus* (2. ed., Romae: Apud Aedes Facultatis Iuridicae ad S. Apollinaris, 1938-1941), I, n. 63, p. 184.

[433] Sess. XXIV, *de ref.* c. 5; sess. XIII, *de ref.*, cc. 5-8; cf. *supra*, p. 95.

[434] Cf. Roberti, *De Processibus*, I, n. 63, p. 184.

[435] Sess. XXIV, *de ref.*, c. 5.

[436] *Tractatus de Episcopo* (2 ed., Parisiis, 1873), I, pp. 323-330.

even for the pronouncement of the sentence; could delegate them to take cognizance of the cause and terminate it even in the Roman Curia; could establish judges or tribunals with ordinary jurisdiction for the deposition of bishops. In so acting an express derogation of the Tridentine enactment would not be required, for the Council itself had declared its decrees were to be understood in conformity with the authority enjoyed by the Holy See.[437]

In the fullness of his power the Roman Pontiff can abrogate any disciplinary law of his predecessors or of ecumenical councils, not to mention the laws of inferior legislative authorities in the Church. As he can abrogate these laws so also is he free not to observe them. When the pope accommodates himself to the procedure established by ecclesiastical law he is said to proceed by ordinary law. However, this formal procedure is never necessary for the valid deposition of a bishop. In order to proceed lawfully, however, the claims of the natural law demand that the Roman Pontiff depose a bishop only for proportionately grave causes, such as the delicts which are expressed in the law as punishable with deposition or degradation.[438] In practice, according to Wernz,[439] when the cause for deposition has been sufficiently established, the bishop is invited to submit spontaneously the resignation of his office. If he refuses deposition follows.

B. The Deposition of Priests and Lesser Clerics

Canon 1576, § 1: Reprobata contraria consuetudine et revocato quolibet contrario privilegio: . . . n. 2: Causae vero quibus agitur de delicto quae depositionis, privationis perpetuae habitus ecclesiastici vel degradationis poenam important, reservantur tribunali quinque iudicum.

The Code has reprobated contrary custom and revoked every contrary privilege in establishing its law which reserves to a tribunal of five judges all criminal causes concerned with the delicts involving the penalty of deposition, perpetual privation of the ecclesias-

---

[437] Cf. Conc. Trident., sess. XXV, *de ref.*, c. 21.

[438] Cf. Smith, *Elements of Ecclesiastical Law*, I, n. 405, pp. 172-173; Cocchi, *Commentarium*, II, n. 269, pp. 223-224.

[439] *Ius Decretalium*, II, n. 764, p. 918.

tical garb or degradation. The discipline of the Code, therefore, not only limits the causes for deposition to those expressly stated in the law and not only establishes this penalty in every case as a *ferendae sententiae* penalty, but also reserves the pronouncement of this sentence to a collegiate tribunal of five judges. It may also be noted here that the same requirements obtain in regard to degradation.

There can be no question that the Code restricts the rights formerly enjoyed by ordinaries in the infliction of deposition upon delinquent clerics subject to them. It has been seen that in the early Church a bishop pronounced a sentence of deposition against a priest or deacon simply with the consent of his *presbyterium* or of some neighboring bishops. Later in Africa, and afterward in Spain, Germany and Gaul, the deliberative counsel of six bishops was required in the deposition of a priest, and of three in the case of a deacon. As regards the lower clergy the bishop could proceed alone. In decretal law, however, only the consent of the chapter was required for the deposition of a priest or deacon. Even this requirement fell into disuse. Pope Boniface VIII (1294-1303) ratified the contrary custom which allowed a bishop to proceed alone in every case of deposition whether it involved a priest, a deacon or merely a cleric in lower orders. Wherefore in the discipline preceding the Code an ordinary could on his own authority depose a cleric in major or minor orders if he had committed delicts punishable with this penalty.[440]

The law of the Code to some extent reverts to the discipline of the Church antecedent to the period of the Decretals when deposition and degradation were synonomous terms for the one penalty. According to the sacred canons an ordinary who has cause to depose or degrade a clergyman must proceed in the judiciary manner prescribed by the Code and commit the case to a collegiate tribunal of five judges. Otherwise the trial is null and void and the sentence of deposition is invalid.[441] Absolutely considered this law obtains

---

[440] Cf. *supra*, p. 96; Wernz, *Ius Decretalium*, VI, n. 121, pp. 126-128; Cocchi, *Commentarium*, VIII, n. 118, p. 201; Ojetti, *Synopsis Rerum Moralium*, n. 1754.

[441] Cf. canons 1576, § 1, n. 2; 1892, n. 1; Augustine, *A Commentary on*

whether the cause involves a cleric in major orders or only one in minor orders for the law does not distinguish. However, as the Code authorizes ordinaries on their own authority and for a just cause to reduce to the lay state clerics in minor orders, it may reasonably be concluded that the Code does not envision the use of the penalty of deposition in their case, since it can be employed only for very grave delicts expressed in the law and does not involve a complete dismissal from the clerical state.

The ordinary of the delinquent as well as the ordinary of the place in which the cleric committed his delict may set up the required tribunal of five judges to pass judgment and sentence upon the delinquent.[442] In law these ordinaries are, within their respective territories, the residential bishops; [443] the apostolic administrators; [444] the vicars and prefects apostolic; [445] the abbots and prelates who rule over autonomous independent territories; [446] the cathedral chapters—diocesan consultors in the United States—but only while the see is vacant after the death of the bishop and before the election of the vicar capitular [447] — the administrator in the United States; so also the vicars capitular, or administrators in the United States, appointed to govern the vacant see; [448] and the major superiors and general chapters in exempt clerical religions.[449] The following are major superiors: (a) the abbot primate, and (b) the

Canon Law, VIII, 261; Sipos, *Enchiridion Iuris Canonici*, § 240, p. 947; Blat, *Commentarium*, V, n. 136, p. 185; Eichmann, *Strafrecht*, 119-120; De Meester, *Compendium*, III, pars 2, n. 1797, p. 225; Cocchi, *Commentarium*, VIII, n. 118, p. 201; Vermeersch-Creusen, *Epitome*, III, n. 498, p. 301; Raus, *Institutiones*, n. 461, p. 709; A Coronata, *Institutiones*, IV, n. 1834, p 262; Sole, *De Delictis et Poenis*, n. 294, p. 209; Chelodi, *Ius Poenale*, n. 52, p. 69; Beste, *Introductio in Codicem*, 929.

[442] Cf. canons 1561, 1566.

[443] Cf. canon 329, § 1.

[444] Cf. canons 312, 315, § 2, n. 1.

[445] Cf. canon 294, § 1.

[446] Cf. canons 319, § 1; 323, § 1.

[447] Cf. canon 435, § 1.

[448] Cf. canon 435, § 1.

[449] Cf. canons 488, nn. 2, 4; 501, § 1.

abbot superior of a monastic congregation—these two do not enjoy this power of jurisdiction unless it is expressly granted to them by the constitutions or by a decree of the Holy See; (c) the abbot of an independent monastery; (d) the supreme moderator; (e) the provincial, and (f) the vicar and anyone who has power after the fashion of a provincial.[450] The powers of local superiors in this matter must be determined from the constitutions of the clerical religious institute.[451]

When the collegiate tribunal established by the competent superior has inflicted the penalty of deposition or degradation the offender enjoys today as much as in the past the right of an appeal which in the interim suspends the operative effect of the sentence.[452] This appeal holds the penalty in abeyance and leaves it to the higher court to conform to, to remit or to modify the earlier sentence in accordance with its judicial discretion. The appeal against the sentence of deposition or degradation issuing from the court of a suffragan bishop is carried to the metropolitan court. If the case was tried in the first instance by the metropolitan court, then the appeal is carried to the court of that local ordinary whom the metropolitan, with the approval of the Holy See, has chosen once for all as his court of appeal. Canon 285 insists that archbishops who have no suffragans, and ordinaries (including prelates or abbots *nullius*) who are immediately subject to the Holy See, must choose a neighboring metropolitan for conciliar or synodal purposes. The court of this same metropolitan serves as their court of appeals.[453] For exempt religious the appeal is carried to the superior general from a sentence delivered by the court of the provincial, to the abbot president of the congregation from the court of the local abbot.[454] In every case the court of appeal must be established in the same

---

[450] Cf. canon 488, n. 8.

[451] Cf. Roberti, *De Delictis et Poenis*, I, n. 56, p. 79; Cerato, *Censurae Vigentes*, 13; Cocchi, *Commentarium*, VIII, n. 29, p. 54; Chelodi, *Ius Poenale*, p. 23, not. 5; Cappello, *De Censuris*, n. 12, p. 13, not. 8.

[452] Cf. canon 2287.

[453] Cf. canon 1594, §§ 1-3.

[454] Cf. canon 1594, § 4.

fashion as the court of first instance; hence a collegiate board must be constituted with five judges who must try the case in the collegiate manner prescribed by the canons.[455]   It should also be observed here that the Code has completely vindicated the right of appeal to the Apostolic See, a principle acknowledged since time immemorial.   In view of the primacy of the Roman Pontiff any cleric may appeal his case to the Holy See at any stage whatsoever of the procedure (first instance or court of appeal, at the beginning of the trial or at any other stage) or may take it there in the first place.[456]

ARTICLE 7. CESSATION OF THE PENALTY

Since deposition and degradation are vindictive penalties there can be no question of their absolution.[457]   Their remission does not depend upon the cessation of contumacy on the part of the delinquent [458] as does the absolution of a censure.[459]   It need hardly be stated, therefore, that a confessor has no power at all in regard to these penalties.   While it is true that in the more urgent occult cases, when from the observance of a *latae sententiae* vindictive penalty the delinquent would expose himself to infamy and scandal, the law authorizes a confessor to suspend the obligation of observing the vindictive penalty, yet this benefit of the law does not extend to the penalties of deposition or degradation.[460]   Neither of these penalties is employed as a *latae sententiae* punishment nor is either ever inflicted in occult cases.

Deposition as well as degradation are perpetual penalties and as such they cease only with death.   Even in this sacred hour they cease by their legal nature and not through the intervention of the confessor.   Canon 882 ordains that any priest may absolve from all sins and censures no matter in what manner they may be reserved. No authorization is conceded, however, for the remission of vin-

---

[455] Cf. canon 1596.
[456] Cf. canon 1569.
[457] Cf. canon 2236, § 1.
[458] Cf. canon 2286.
[459] Cf. canon 2241, § 1.
[460] Cf. canon 2290.

dictive penalties. Only one who enjoys authority to act in and for the external forum can grant the remission of the public penalties of deposition and degradation. Since these penalties expire upon the death of the delinquent their remission is not necessitated at the approach of death, for they in no way interfere with the reconciliation of the soul before God.

The lawgiver in establishing deposition and degradation as perpetual penalties has predetermined the time necessary for the expiation of the crimes which warranted these punishments. These penalties are not inflicted to be subsequently dispensed from, but to be sustained and expiated, so that through their sufferance the delinquent's violation of the public order may be repaired. Nevertheless, both deposition and degradation can be remitted before their total expiation by a dispensation granted by the competent ecclesiastical authority,[461] to wit, the Roman Pontiff. This law is expressed in the general principle of the Code which declares that the remission of a penalty by dispensation may be granted, but only by him who has established the penalty or by his competent superior or successor, or by him to whom this faculty has been committed.[462] Only the universal legislator can dispense from the vindicative penalties established by his law. Therefore, although ordinaries and others delegated by them can dispense from the vindictive penalties established by themselves or by their predecessors, they cannot dispense from the vindictive penalties of the common law unless they have obtained from the Roman Pontiff a special faculty to do so. The Code does not grant to ordinaries a general commission to dispense from the penalties of deposition and degradation, as it does in some cases involving other common law penalties, namely, such as were incurred as *latae sententiae* penalties.[463] Thus the Code rejects the opinion of some canonists who attributed to ordinaries the right to dispense from the penalty of deposition when it was in-

---

[461] Cf. canon 2289: "Poena vindicativa finitur eius expiatione vel dispensatione ab eo concessa qui legitimam habeat dispensandi potestatem ad normam can. 2236."

[462] Cf. canon 2236, § 1.

[463] Cf. canon 2237.

flicted for delicts lesser than adultery.[464] The Code departs from such a difficult criterion—one that is scarcely juridical—and precisely defines the dispensing power of ordinaries inferior to the Roman Pontiff in reference to the penalties themselves. For deposition and degradation once lawfully and validly inflicted a dispensation can be obtained only from the Roman Pontiff or his delegate.

[464] Cf. *supra*, p. 77.

CHAPTER VI

DEGRADATION

ARTICLE 1. THE NATURE OF DEGRADATION

Canon 2305, § 1: Degradatio in se continet depositionem, perpetuam privationem habitus ecclesiastici et
reductionem clerici ad statum laicalem.

THE term degradation was early introduced into canonical usage
to signify a penalty proper to clerics, by which they were deprived
of their orders insofar as this could be done by the Church. As the
reception of orders represents so many advances in the degrees or
grades of the hierarchy [1] the penal privation and loss of these grades
was properly termed degradation.

Before the end of the twelfth century degradation was employed
synonymously with deposition to signify one and the same penalty.
After the decree of Pope Innocent III (1198-1216) [2] degradation
properly signified the total reduction of a cleric to the lay state,
whereas deposition represented a complete privation of clerical rights
and functions, but not a loss of the clerical state with its essential
privileges. The similarity between the two penalties, however, en-
gendered much confusion in terminology. Many canonists failed to
adhere to the distinction introduced by Pope Boniface VIII (1294-
1303) [3] between verbal and real degradation. They chose rather
to speak of verbal and real degradation as verbal and real deposition,
and in order to distinguish them from deposition itself referred to
the latter penalty as simple or absolute deposition.[4] The code cuts

---

[1] Cf. canon 108.

[2] C. 27, X, *de verborum significatione*, V, 40.

[3] C. 2, *de poenis*, V, 9, in VI°.

[4] Cf. Suarez, *De Censuris*, Disp. XXX, sec. II, n. 1: Fagnanus, *Commentaria*, lib. V, tit. 1, cap. 6, n. 76; Barbosa, *Collectanea*, lib. V, tit. IX, in
VI°, cap. 2, n. 4; Reiffenstuel, *Ius Canonicum Universum*, lib. V, tit. XXXVII,
nn. 22, 32; Ferraris, *Prompta Bibliotheca*, s. v. "*Degradatio*," n. 1.

away all foundations in support of any false or misleading terminology in regard to deposition and degradation. While the penalties, as always, retain much in common, they have specifically distinct properties clearly delineated in the law, distinguishing them not only in name but also in substance. With the precise definitions of the Code it is now wholly inexcusable to confuse the two penalties.[5]

In the penal system of the Church degradation is the most severe vindictive punishment visited upon delinquent clerics. It brings to an end the clerical life of the delinquent; it is the legal destruction of clerical personality. Degradation is a spiritual vindictive penalty applied only to clerics,[6] for they alone possess the rights affected by it. The severity and distinct character of this penalty is immediately obvious from its definition in the Code: Degradation contains within itself deposition, perpetual privation of the ecclesiastical garb and reduction of the cleric to the lay state. It is the combination of these three elements in the one penalty of degradation which gives it its distinct character and severity. A consideration of its integral parts reveals the nature of this penalty.

A. Deposition

While degradation involves more than deposition it nevertheless includes all the effects of this penalty and in consequence has much in common with it. This fact more than any other led canonists in the past to confuse the two penalties. A distinction was recognized, however, and it was based on this fact that degradation by its nature and of itself primarily affected orders and only by consequence involved a privation of benefices and other ecclesiastical offices and ministries. Deposition directly produced a privation of dignities, offices and benefices.[7]

The privations consequent upon the penalty of deposition have

---

[5] Cf. Wernz, *Ius Decretalium*, VI, n. 120, p. 124, not. 163; Vermeersch-Creusen, *Epitome*, III, n. 499, p. 301.

[6] Canon 2298: "Poenae vindicativae quae clericis tantum applicantur, sunt: . . . n. 12: Degradatio."

[7] Cf. Suarez, *De Censuris*, Disp. XXX, sec. II, n. 2; *Pontificale Romanum:* "proprie tamen loquendo, quis a dignitatibus et honoribus deponitur, sed ab Ordinibus degradatur."—Tit. VII *Degradationis forma*, § II.

already been considered. Degradation, inasmuch as it includes deposition, produces the same effects, namely, a suspension from all power of orders, a privation of all offices, dignities, benefices, pensions and positions enjoyed in the Church by the delinquent cleric and a disqualification for acquiring any of these in the future.[8] While deposition leaves intact the clerical privileges and the right of wearing the ecclesiastical garb, degradation by its very nature implies the forfeiture of these in their entirety.

B. Perpetual Privation of the Ecclesiastical Garb

Degradation includes within itself the aggravated form of deposition established in the Code as comprising, in addition to the usual effects of deposition, the perpetual privation of the ecclesiastical garb. Since the nature and effects of this penalty have been previously considered, it suffices to recall here that this privation brings with it the forfeiture of the charitable sustenance afforded the deposed cleric as well as the loss of the clerical privileges.

It has already been observed how in the former discipline this complete spoliation of the clerical privileges was effected only through the punishment of real degradation. At the end of the ceremony of real degradation the celebrant declared the delinquent to be deprived of these privileges: *"Auctoritate Dei omnipotentis, Patris et Filii et Spiritus Sancti, ac nostra, tibi auferimus habitum clericalem, et nudamus te religionis ornatu, ac deponimus, degradamus, spoliamus, et exuimus te omni ordine, beneficio, et privilegio Clericali, et, velut Clericalis professionis indignum, redigimus te in servitutem et ignominiam habitus saecularis ac status."* [9] It was only with real degradation, as this formula indicates and as canonists commonly taught,[10] that the delinquent cleric was: (a) deprived of the clerical garb, (b) despoiled of all the clerical privileges, and (c) reduced to the lay state.

Under the present discipline of the Church a deposed cleric

---

[8] Cf. canon 2303, § 1.

[9] *Pontificale Romanum*, tit. *Degradationis forma.*

[10] Cf. Catalanus, *Pontificale Romanum*, III, 229-230; Suarez, *De Censuris*, Disp. XXX, sec. II, nn. 7, 8; Benedictus XIV, *De synodo dioecesana*, lib. IX, cap. 6, n. 3.

who proves himself incorrigible may be further punished with perpetual privation of the ecclesiastical garb. In this case the deposed cleric is perpetually deprived of the ecclesiastical garb and all the clerical privileges, *but* he is not yet reduced to the lay state. Patently, this penalty of the Code could be termed mitigated degradation for it includes all the effects except reduction to the lay state. This effect is still reserved to the extreme penalty of degradation.

C. *Reduction to the Lay State*

Degradation is the only ecclesiastical penalty whereby a cleric in major orders is totally deprived of his status in punishment for delinquency. It is the characteristic and proper element of degradation which clearly distinguishes it from all other penalties, and in particular from deposition, even when the latter is aggravated with the perpetual privation of the right of wearing the ecclesiastical garb. Only when a cleric has been punished with degradation is he by penalty reduced to the lay state.

Reduction to the lay state, as the Code itself declares,[11] must be understood in its proper sense as an external, juridical or canonical reduction, one that leaves intact the power of orders while it renders their use or exercise unlawful. A theological or intrinsic reduction of clerics to the lay state such as would involve the loss of the sacramental character with its inherent power of orders and which would in consequence render the acts of orders invalid does not exist in the Church and never did, not even by means of the penalty of degradation. There is certainly no intrinsic reduction in regard to the orders which derive from the divine law, namely, the episcopate, the priesthood and the diaconate,[12] for their power is established by the divine law itself and is dependent upon the indelible character impressed on the soul of the cleric. This power in itself cannot be lost or taken away or limited by any authority for

[11] Cf. canon 211, § 1: "Etsi sacra ordinatio, semel valide recepta, numquam irrita fiat, clericus tamen maior ad statum laicalem redigitur rescripto Sanctae Sedis, decreto vel sententia ad normam can. 214, demum poena degradationis."

[12] Cf. Conc. Trident., sess. XXIII, *Doctrina de sacramento ordinis*, c. 1; *Canones de sacramento ordinis,* can. 3 et 6—Denzinger-Bannwart-Umberg, *Enchiridion Symbolorum,* n. 957; nn. 963, 966.

any cause. Hence a cleric who has received a hierarchical order cannot be truly and internally expelled from the clerical state and be reduced to the lay state.[13]

Since it is commonly taught that the other orders are of ecclesiastical origin, their power could in consequence be taken away by the Church. However, since there are some theologians and canonists who, following St. Thomas, maintain that the orders below the diaconate are not merely of ecclesiastical institution but of divine origin, the Roman Pontiffs *de facto* never employ the power of rescinding these orders because of the danger of violating the divine law.[14] Moreover, the constant practice of the Church has always been never to confer through an absolute reordination any order, tonsure included, once it has been validly received.[15] From this it is evident that whoever has been enrolled in the clerical state, even through his reception of a minor order, is never again reduced, by an absolute and internal withdrawal of the order, to that state of the laity in which he was before ordination.

The Church, however, though she declares that sacred ordination once validly received is never invalidated,[16] does recognize and employ a juridical or external reduction to the lay state, which leaves intact the power of orders but forbids its lawful exercise, deprives the cleric of the rights, privileges and juridical status of clerics and renders him equal to laymen.[17] The Church can authorize such an extrinsic reduction, since the lawful exercise of the power of orders, even of those which are of divine origin, as well as the active enjoyment of the rights and privileges of the clerical state is subject

---

[13] Cf. Gasparri, *De Sacra Ordinatione*, n. 1142; Maroto, *Institutiones*, § 732, p. 876; Wernz, *Ius Decretalium*, II, n. 229, p. 332; Sipos, *Enchiridion Iuris Canonici*, § 34, p. 160.

[14] Cf. Beste, *Introductio in Codicem*, 223; Sipos, *Enchiridion Iuris Canonici*, § 34, p. 160; Goyeneche, *Iuris Canonici Summa Principia* (Romae: Typis Polyglottis "Cuore di Maria," 1935), I, 221.

[15] Cf. Wernz, *Ius Decretalium*, II, n. 230, pp. 332-333. For particular exceptions of repeated ordinations in the history of the Church, cf. Many, *Praelectiones de Sacra Ordinatione*, nn. 18-26, pp. 57-76.

[16] Cf. canons 211, § 1; 950

[17] Cf. canons 211; 213; Vermeersch-Creusen, *Epitome*, I, n. 324, p. 271; Raus, *Institutiones Canonicae*, n. 64, p. 103; Maroto, *Institutiones*, I, n. 732, p. 877; Wernz, *Ius Decretalium*, II, n. 228, p. 331.

in its control to ecclesiastical jurisdiction.[18]   In the past as in the present the Church effects this reduction as a penalty for delicts through the punishment of degradation.

It should be observed, however, that reduction to the lay state is not always accomplished as a penalty. The Church allows other means, based on causes other than delicts, for producing this reduction. They differ in conformity with the greater degree of stability which in the clerical state is effected by major orders as distinguished from minor orders. A consideration of the various lawful measures employable in producing a reduction to the lay state serves to indicate the relative importance of degradation in the design of ecclesiastical descipline.

According to the sacred canons a cleric in major orders can be reduced to the state of the laity: (a) by a rescript of the Holy See; [19] (b) by an administrative decree or judicial sentence in the case of a cleric who has received a major order through grave fear and has not ratified his ordination at least tacitly by the exercise of orders after the removal of this compulsion; [20] (c) by the penalty of degradation.[21]   A cleric, therefore, who has received a major order can never return to the lay state of his own accord. In every case the intervention of the public authority of the Church is required. Apart from the provisions of law governing the case of a cleric who has major orders only through compulsion, reduction to the lay state of a major cleric is authorized for one of two reasons, either as a favor granted only for grave causes [22] or as a punishment inflicted only for the most serious delicts defined in the law.

A cleric in minor orders, however, may be reduced to the lay state: (a) of the cleric's own accord when he has previously notified the local ordinary of his intention; (b) by a decree of the local ordinary issued for a just cause, namely, when he prudently judges that, all things considered, the cleric cannot with due respect for the clerical state be promoted to sacred orders; (c) *ipso facto* for

---

[18] Cf. Wernz, *Ius Decretalium*, II, n. 229, p. 332.

[19] Canon 211, § 1.

[20] Cf. canons 211, § 1; 214; 1993-1998.

[21] Cf. canons 211, § 1; 2305.

[22] Cf. Vermeersch-Creusen, *Epitome*, I, n. 325, p. 271.

the causes described and enumerated in the law.[23] The causes stated in the law as implying an automatic reduction to the lay state for a cleric in minor orders are consonant with his freedom to return to the state of the laity. They are causes which create a presumption of his renunciation of the clerical state, namely, (1) the contracting of a marriage which is not invalid by reason of force or fear;[24] (2) the laying aside of his own accord and without a legitimate reason the ecclesiastical garb for a month after due warning;[25] (3) the voluntary entering of the military service without lawful permission.[26] Peculiar to the religious clergy is the automatic reduction to the lay state decreed by the law in the case of a minor cleric upon his lawful dismissal from a religious organization in which he had professed temporary or perpetual vows.[27]

In the past degradation was also included among the legal means by which a cleric in minor orders could be reduced to the lay state for especially grave delinquencies.[28] The Code, however, does not mention this penalty among the means for the reduction of a cleric who is in minor orders.[29] Absolutely considered the penalty can nevertheless be employed against minor clerics who commit the delicts specified in the law as warranting this penalty; but, given the greater facility which the Code supplies for the reduction of these clerics to the lay state, to have recourse to such an extreme measure will ordinarily be needless and will only delay the ultimate

[23] Canon 211, § 2.

[24] Cf. canon 132, § 2.

[25] Cf. canon 136, § 3.

[26] Cf. canon 141, § 2.

[27] Cf. canons 648, 669. The decree of the religious organization separates this cleric from the religious state; the supervening decree of the common law separates him from the clerical state; the resultant juridical condition of this twofold separation implies his complete reduction to the lay state.

[28] Cf. cc. 1, 3, 7, 8, X, *de clericis coniugatis*, III, 3; c. un *de bigamis*, I, 12, in VI°; c. un. *de vita et honestate clericorum*, III, 1, in VI°; c. 1, *de vita et honestate clericorum*, III, 1, in Clem.; S. C. Immunitatis, *Epistola*, 20 Septembris 1860—*AAS*, III (1867), 433; Benedictus XIV, *De synodo diocesana*, lib. XII, cc. 2, 6; *Pontificale Romanum*, tit., *Degradatio a Prima Tonsura; Degradatio ab Ordine Ostiariatus*, etc.

[29] Cf. canon 211, § 2.

effects.[30] A cleric in major orders, however, cannot be reduced to the lay state by way of punishment except through the penalty of degradation inflicted for the crimes stated in the law.

ARTICLE 2. THE EFFECTS OF DEGRADATION

The effects consequent upon degradation are succinctly declared in its very definition in the Code as a penalty which contains within itself deposition, perpetual privation of the ecclesiastical garb and reduction of the cleric to the lay state.[31] Accordingly degradation immediately produces:

1. A perpetual suspension *ab officio;*
2. The deprivation of all offices, benefices, dignities, pensions and positions in the Church;
3. A disqualification or disability for acquiring in the future any office, benefice, dignity, pension or position in the Church;
4. A perpetual privation of the right to wear the ecclesiastical garb;
5. The spoliation of all clerical privileges;
6. The loss of every title to ecclesiastical support;
7. Deprivation of the clerical state;
8. Reduction to the lay state.

The degraded cleric can no longer lawfully exercise the power of orders except in regard to the necessary sacraments in cases of extreme necessity.[32] He may then lawfully as well as validly absolve from all sins and censures any penitent who is in the danger of death,[33] and if no other priest is available he may even impart to the dying penitent, extreme unction and Viaticum.[34] Otherwise the degraded cleric acts unlawfully but nevertheless validly if he exercises those powers of orders which flow from the ordination

---

[30] Cf. Sägmüller, *Lehrbuch des katholischen Kirchenrechts,* § 81, p. 441; Maroto, *Institutiones,* I, n. 734, p. 880; Wernz-Vidal, *Ius Canonicum,* II, n. 392, p. 390.

[31] Canon 2305, § 1.

[32] Cf. Raus, *Institutiones Canonicae,* n. 64, p. 103; Maroto, *Institutiones,* I, n. 733, p. 878.

[33] Cf. canons 882; 2252.

[34] Cf. Cappello, *De Sacramentis,* I, n. 91, p. 77; canon 2261, § 3.

itself, whether by the divine or ecclesiastical law, as long as jurisdiction is not required for the same act. A degraded bishop, for example, would validly but unlawfully and indeed sacrilegiously, confer orders, confirm, consecrate churches, chalices, etc.; a degraded priest would validly but unlawfully offer Holy Mass.[35] On the other hand, except for absolution granted to a penitent in danger of death, the degraded cleric does not even validly exercise those rights which besides orders require jurisdiction. The same is true of the exercise of those powers of orders derived not from ordination itself but from a delegation either by law or indult. Thus a degraded abbot would invalidly confer tonsure and minor orders;[36] a degraded priest would invalidly confirm even though he formerly had the faculty of confirming.[37]

Although the sacramental character and inherent power of orders remains undiminished, the degraded cleric is considered before the law as a layman. Deprived of the right to wear the ecclesiastical garb the degraded cleric, like any layman,[38] is now positively forbidden to wear it.[39] So also like any layman he may freely enter the military service or take up any mode of life, activity or employment formerly forbidden to him as a cleric.[40] But, on the other hand, he is incapable of acquiring any office in the Church, even such positions which laymen in good standing are legally capable of fulfilling, such as that of an administrator of ecclesiastical property,[41] of a notary,[42] of a courier or constable,[43] of a procurator

---

[35] Cf. Suarez, *De Censuris*, Disp. XXX, sec. II, n. 2; Schmalzgrueber, *Ius Ecclesiasticum Universum*, lib. V, tit. XXXVII, n. 141; Ferraris, *Prompta Bibliotheca*, s. v. "Degradatio," III, p. 40; Barbosa, *De Officio et Potestate Episcopi*, pars III, alleg. CX, n. 5; Ferreres, *Institutiones Canonicae*, II, n. 1076, p. 443.

[36] Cf. canon 964, n. 1.

[37] Cf. canon 782, §§ 2, 3; Maroto, *Institutiones*, n. 733, p. 878; Wernz, *Ius Decretalium*, II, n. 231, p. 333.

[38] Cf. canon 683.

[39] Cf. canon 213, § 1.

[40] Cf. canons 137-144; Vermeersch-Creusen, *Epitome*, I, n. 327, p. 272.

[41] Cf. canon 1521.

[42] Cf. canon 373.

[43] Cf. canons 1591, 1592.

or advocate in ecclesiastical causes [44] or of a sponsor at baptism [45] or at confirmation.[46]

A. Obligations

In other respects also the degraded cleric is not completely in the same juridical condition of laymen to whose status he has been reduced. Canonists before the Code unanimously maintained that a cleric who had received major orders was, after degradation, still bound by the obligations consequent upon these orders, namely, the obligations of perpetually observing chastity and celibacy and of daily reciting the divine office.[47] The reasons asserted for this opinion were chiefly two: Degradation is not inflicted to take away obligations but to impose burdens and take away honors.[48] Degradation does not deprive the cleric in major orders of the sacramental character or of the power of orders and in consequence it does not take away the obligations consequent upon major orders.[49]

1. Celibacy

In regard to the obligations of chastity and celibacy the law of the Code is clear: Clerics in major orders are forbidden to marry and are so bound by the obligation of observing chastity that any sins committed against this virtue constitute also a sacrilege. Clerics in minor orders can indeed enter marriage but, unless the marriage is null from force or fear, they automatically cease to be clerics.[50] A cleric in major orders who has been degraded, that is, one who

---

[44] Cf. canon 1657.

[45] Cf. canon 765, n. 2.

[46] Cf. canon 795, n. 2; Kearney, *Sponsors at Baptism According to the Code of Canon Law* (Catholic University of America, Canon Law Studies, No. 30, Washington, D. C., 1925), 76; 92-94.

[47] Cf. Suarez, *De Censuris*, Disp. XXX. sec. II, n. 2; Schmalzgrueber, *Ius Ecclesiasticum Universum*, lib. V, tit. XXXVII, n. 164; Ferraris, *Prompta Bibliotheca*, s. v. "*Degradatio*," III, p. 40; Hinschius, *Kirchenrecht*, I, 144; Wernz, *Ius Decretalium*, VI, n. 138, p. 144.

[48] So Suarez, *loc. cit.*; Schmalzgrueber, *loc. cit.*; Ferraris, *loc. cit.*; Wernz, *loc. cit.*

[49] So Suarez, *loc. cit.*; Hinschius, *loc. cit.*

[50] Cf. canon 132, §§ 1, 2.

in punishment has been legitimately reduced to the lay state, is still bound by the obligation of celibacy.[51]

It is the better and more common opinion that the obligation of chastity which is connected with sacred orders results immediately from the vow which is implicit in the reception of orders. Hence, the obligation usually flows from the will of the party. However, should the candidate for major orders exclude this vow by a positive contrary act of the will made at the time of ordination, he would still be bound, not in this case by the vow, but by positive ecclesiastical law.[52] In like fashion at least positive ecclesiastical law binds a cleric in major orders to the obligation of celibacy even after he has been degraded.[53] Every sin committed against chastity by the degraded cleric is a sacrilege.[54] He cannot enter a valid marriage.[55]

2. *Divine Office*

The aforementioned common opinion of canonists before the Code also obliged degraded major clerics to the daily recitation of the divine office. Since the promulgation of the Code, however, the opinion of canonists has been divided. Vermeersch-Creusen maintain that the degraded cleric must recite the office at least privately: he is not held to the public recitation of the canonical hours by his office, since he has been deprived of it, nor by solemn profession, since he has been reduced to the lay state.[56] Raus holds that the degraded cleric is obliged to the office unless he is lawfully impeded.[57] Ferreres merely asserts that the degraded cleric in major

[51] Cf. canon 213, § 2: "Clericus tamen maior obligatione coelibatus tenetur salvo praescripto can. 214."

[52] Cf. S. R. R., *Sacrae Ordinationis*, 1 Augusti 1928, *coram R. P. D. Francisco Parillo*, dec. XXXVIII—*Decisiones*, XX (1928), 349, 355.

[53] Cf. canons 213, § 2; 211; 132, § 1.

[54] Cf. canons 132; 213, § 2.

[55] Canon 1072: "Invalide matrimonium attentant clerici in sacris ordinibus constituti." Cf. Raus, *Institutiones Canonicae*, n. 462, p. 710; Ferreres, *Institutiones Canonicae*, II, n. 1076, p. 443; De Meester, *Compendium*, III, pars 2, n. 1799, p. 226; Blat, *Commentarium*, V, nn. 138, p. 186; Eichmann, *Strafrecht*, p. 120.

[56] *Epitome*, III, n. 499, p. 301.

[57] *Institutiones Canonicae*, n. 462, p. 710.

orders is not liberated from the obligation of reciting the divine office.[58]   Looking more to the law of the Code, Sipos,[59] Cocchi,[60] De Meester[61] and Beste[62] doubt the existence of this obligation for the degraded cleric and incline to a negative opinion in view of the silence of canon 213, § 2.   Finally, Augustine[63] and Chelodi[64] without doubt or hesitation assert that the degraded cleric is freed from the obligation of reciting the breviary.   This opinion alone is in complete accord with the express provisions of the Code.

According to the sacred canons the obligation of a cleric to recite daily the divine office may arise from the possession of a benefice or from the reception of major orders.   Every cleric who is in possession of a benefice is obliged to fulfill faithfully the special duties attached to it and he is, morever, bound by the obligation of reciting daily the canonical hours.[65]   This law of the Code merely repeats the former legislation.[66]   It obliges even a cleric in minor orders: any cleric who holds a benefice must recite daily the canonical hours. It should be noted, however, that under the present law of the Code a benefice which has attached to it the care of souls can only be validly conferred on a cleric who has been ordained to the priesthood.[67]

Juridically distinct from the private recitation of the divine office is the public celebration of the office in choir.   Every cathedral or collegiate chapter is bound to perform daily and properly in choir

[58] *Institutiones Canonicae*, II, n. 1076, p. 443.

[59] *Enchiridion Iuris Canonici*, § 240, p. 948, not. 12; § 34, p. 161, not. 4.

[60] *Commentarium*, VIII, n. 119, p. 202.

[61] *Compendium*, III, pars 2, n. 1799, p. 226.

[62] *Introductio in Codicem*, 930.

[63] *A Commentary on Canon Law*, VIII, 262, note 19.

[64] *Ius Poenale*, n. 53, p. 71.

[65] Canon 1475, § 1: "Beneficiarius tenetur peculiaria onera beneficio adnexa fideliter implere et praeterea canonicas horas quotidie recitare."

[66] Cf. Leo X (in Conc. Lateranen. V) const. *Supernae dispositionis*, 5 maii 1514, § 38—*Fontes*, n. 65; S. Pius V, const. *Ex proximo*, 20 sept. 1571—*Fontes*, n. 140; S. C. S. Off., decr., 24 sept. 1665, prop. 21 damn.—*Fontes*, n. 734; S. C. S. Off., decr. 4 mart. 1679, prop. 54, damn.—*Fontes*, n. 754; S. R. C. *Cusentina*, 10 iul. 1677, ad 2—*Fontes*, n. 5621; S. R. C., *Marsorum*, 12 nov. 1831, ad 46—*Fontes*, n. 5858.

[67] Cf. canon 154.

the divine offices. A chapter of canons, either cathedral or collegiate, is a corporation of clerics, instituted for the very purpose of more solemnly celebrating the divine service.[68] The divine offices here comprise the chanting of the canonical hours and the celebration of a conventual High Mass, besides other Masses to be celebrated according to the rubrics of the missal or the laws of foundation.[69] The obligation does not rest solely on the chapter as such: All who hold a choir benefice are bound to perform the divine offices in choir every day, unless the Apostolic See or the law of foundation allows the service to be performed by turns (*per turnum*).[70] This same obligation existed in the law long before the promulgation of the Code.[71] Every beneficiary, therefore, is held at least to the private recitation of the divine office, whereas the holder of a choral benefice is obliged to celebrate the divine office publicly, in choir. In either case the obligation arises with possession of the benefice and ceases with its loss,[72] as is the case in the penalty of degradation.

Apart from the possession of a benefice a cleric may be bound to the recitation of the divine office by another title, namely, by major orders. This obligation imposed on all clerics in major orders is clearly stated for the first time in written law by the Code.[73] Heretofore immemorial custom alone had obliged all clerics to the recitation of the breviary simply from the title of sacred orders.[74]

[68] Cf. canon 391, § 1.

[69] Cf. canon 413, §§ 1, 2.

[70] Canon 414.

[71] Cf. Conc. Trident., sess. XXIV, *de ref.*, c. 12; Benedictus XIV, ep. encycl. *Cum semper oblatas*, 19 aug. 1744, §§ 23, 24—*Fontes*, n. 345; Benedictus XIV, ep. *Praeclara*, 19 ian. 1748, §§ 6-8—*Fontes*, n. 384; Benedictus XIV, ep. encycl. *Annus qui*, 19 febr. 1749; § 2—*Fontes*, n. 395; S. C. Ep. et Reg., *Anagnina*, 28 ian. 1603—*Fontes*, n. 1617; S. C. C., *Puteolana*, mense iulii 1589, ad 3—*Fontes*, n. 2210; S. C. C., *Acerrarum*, 5 iul., 2 et 23 aug. 1727, ad XV —*Fontes*, n. 3330; S. C. C., *Tergestina*, 23 nov. 1850, ad 2—*Fontes*, n. 4114.

[72] Cf. S. R. C., *Iuvenacen.*, 2 sept. 1597—*Fontes*, n. 5182.

[73] Cf. Sipos, *Enchiridion Iuris Canonici*, § 26, p. 117; Raus, *Institutiones Canonicae*, n. 68, p. 110; Vermeersch-Creusen, *Epitome*, I, n. 253 [220], p. 221.

[74] Cf. cc. 1, 9, X, *de celebratione missarum, et sacramento Eucharistiae, et divinis officiis*, III, 41; c. 1, *de celebratione missarum et aliis divinis officiis*, III, 14, in Clem; Benedictus XIV, const. *Etsi pastoralis*, 26 maii. 1742,

With the universal written law promulgated in the Code this obligation is exactly defined in all its essential details. It provides that clerics in major orders, *except* those considered in canons 213, 214, are held to the obligation of reciting the canonical hours daily and completely according to their proper and approved liturgical books.[75] The legislator clearly defines those who are bound by this obligation as well as those who are excepted from it. Held to the obligation are clerics in major orders. Not obliged to it are the clerics in major orders treated in canons 213, 214. These canons govern all clerics lawfully restored or reduced to the lay state. But a cleric in major orders who is degraded is thereby canonically reduced to the lay state.[76] Therefore, a cleric in major orders who has been degraded is not obliged to the daily recitation of the divine office.

It is necessary to emphasize the fact that the exception from the obligation is properly and directly stated in canon 135 where the obligation itself is defined. Hesitantly to seek exemption from the obligation for degraded clerics in the silence of canon 213, § 2, as some canonists have done,[77] is to miss the precise and explicit exemption of the Code as radically stated in canon 135.

It must be held, therefore, that no cleric in major or minor orders is obliged to recite the divine office, either publicly or privately, once he has been degraded. More apparent than real is an exception to this statement. A degraded cleric may still be bound to the obligations of the divine office as a result of religious profession. The obligation, however, in this case binds him as a religious and not as a cleric, for the clerical status has been lost through

§ VII, n. V—*Fontes*, n. 328; Benedictus XIV, instr. *Eo quamvis tempore*, 4 maii 1745, § 42 sq.—*Fontes*, n. 357; Pius X, const. *Divino afflatu*, 1 nov. 1911 —*Fontes*, n. 696; S. C. Ep. et Reg., instr. (ad Ep. Hungariae), 28 maii 1896, n. III—*Fontes*, n. 2030; S. R. C., *Adrien.*, 7 sept. 1850—*Fontes*, n. 5960; S. R. C., *Marianopolitana*, 27 ian. 1899, ad III—*Fontes*, n. 6289.

[75] Canon 135: "Clerici in maioribus ordinibus constituti, exceptis iis de quibus in can. 213, 214, tenentur obligatione quotidie horas canonicas integre recitandi secundum proprios et probatos liturgicos libros."

[76] Cf. canons 211, § 1; 2305.

[77] Cocchi, *Commentarium*, VIII, n. 119, p. 202, not. 3; Sipos, *Enchiridion Iuris Canonici*, § 240, p. 948, not. 12; De Meester, *Compendium*, III, pars 2, n. 1799, p. 226; Beste, *Introductio in Codicem*, 930.

degradation. According to canon 610 in those institutes, whether of men or women, in which the choral obligation exists the divine office conformably to the constitutions must be recited in common in every house in which there are at least four religious who are bound to choir and who are not lawfully impeded, and even in those houses where there are fewer, if the constitutions so prescribe. In such institutes the solemnly professed—except for the *conversi*—who are absent from choir must recite the canonical hours privately.[78] Should a cleric in major orders who is a solemnly professed member of such an institute be punished with the canonical penalty of degradation he will indeed be freed of his obligation to recite the divine office as arising from major orders, but he will still be bound to the same obligation as a result of his profession. This obligation attaches to his status as a religious and not to his condition as a cleric. The penalty of degradation affects only the rights, duties and privileges of the clerical state. It certainly does not dissolve the bonds consequent upon religious profession. These persevere after degradation unless or until other canonical means have brought about their dissolution.

B. Lay Communion

Although sacred ordination, once validly received, can never be annulled, a cleric in major orders may be reduced to the lay state by the penalty of degradation.[79] Only the inherent sacramental character and power of orders as well as the obligations of the law of celibacy remain as vestiges of his former state. He is forever deprived of all clerical offices, benefices, rights and privileges, even of the right to wear the ecclesiastical garb.[80] As already observed, these effects to a certain extent are consequent upon simple deposition and upon deposition when it is coupled with the perpetual privation of the ecclesiastical garb, both of which penalties are included in the still more severe penalty of degradation. Distinctly proper to degradation, however, is the reduction of the delinquent cleric to the lay state. This effect comprises the others and aggravates

---

[78] Canon 610, §§ 1, 2.

[79] Canon 211, § 1.

[80] Cf. canons 2305; 213.

them by its fundamental deprivation of the clerical state itself. No longer does the degraded cleric enjoy even the name of cleric. Before the law he stands as a layman, as one who has never received first tonsure.[81]   Just as the degraded cleric once was elevated into the hierarchy of the Church by sacred ordination and canonical commissions,[82] so now by the same authority of the Church he is juridically returned to the state from which he was previously elevated. He is forever rejected and permanently disqualified from the service of the altar.

In itself, however, degradation does not bar the delinquent from all communion with the Church. Degradation dissolves the juridical bonds of membership in the clerical state, but does not affect the fundamental union of the individual with the Church. The legal effects of ordination are effaced but the juridical effects of baptism are left untouched. The degraded cleric may still continue to participate in the goods of the Church, but only as a layman. This is the meaning of reduction to the lay state. In degradation it has the character of a penalty, for in consequence of his grave delinquency a cleric is even against his will deprived of the degree of participation proper to the clergy in the life of the Church, the Mystical Body of Christ, and is reduced to a lesser degree of communion.

In an earlier age, especially during the first twelve centuries, it was customary, as already observed, to speak of a degraded cleric as of one reduced to lay communion. It had the same significance as the present terminology of reduction to the lay state. The degraded cleric remained subject to ecclesiastical authority and discipline, but was reckoned as a layman, especially in relation to the manner of his participation through the Church in divine and ecclesiastical goods.[83] Yet even this degree of participation in the life of the Church could be lost by the degraded cleric, as in the present law, through the penalty of excommunication.[84] Until the degraded cleric, however, has been excommunicated he has the right to re-

---

[81] Cf. canon 108, § 1.

[82] Cf. canon 109.

[83] Cf. Lega, *De Delictis et Poenis*, n. 208, p. 281.

[84] Cf. canon 2257.

ceive from the clergy the spiritual goods and especially the necessary aids to salvation according to the rules of ecclesiastical discipline.[85]

From this it is evident that whereas degradation remains the most severe vindictive penalty with which a cleric as cleric can be punished, there is still the more severe medicinal penalty of excommunication with which even the degraded cleric as a member of the Church may be punished. This comparison is mentioned only to clarify the juridical condition of the degraded cleric, for from another viewpoint it could be maintained that degradation is even a more severe penalty than excommunication. The latter is always a censure, and never a vindictive penalty.[86] In consequence it must be absolved as soon as the delinquent with proper dispositions seeks absolution.[87] Degradation on the other hand is never a censure but always a vindictive penalty.[88] No matter how repentant the degraded cleric may become, he acquires thereby no right to have his penalty removed. Only a favor of the Holy See can restore him to his former rank once he has received major orders.[89] The distinction may be illustrated by means of a case related by Soglia [90] in regard to priests who had apostatized during the French Revolution. When they later sought pardon and absolution the Holy See issued instructions to their ordinaries to the effect that those delinquents who were truly repentant could be absolved and admitted to lay communion but were to remain forever despoiled of their clerical rights and privileges. They were allowed to communicate with the Church forever afterward only as laymen.

It is this element of lay communion which expresses the fullness of the penalty of degradation as employed in the Code. Whereas in an earlier age degradation was often followed by delivery of the delinquent to the lay court to undergo the civil punishments for his delict, this was never considered to be of the essence of the penalty. It was a necessary consequence of real degradation only insofar as

85 Cf. canon 682.
86 Cf. canon 2255, § 2.
87 Cf. canon 2241, § 1.
88 Cf. canon 2298, n. 12.
89 Cf. canons 212, § 2, 2236, § 3.
90 *Institutiones Iuris Privati*, § 248.

this penalty deprived a delinquent cleric of the privileges of the clerical state among which was the privileged forum. Since a cleric was exempt from the secular courts through the enjoyment of this privilege, it was as a consequence of its loss in degradation that the delinquent immediately became subject to the jurisdiction of the civil power. Directly and of itself degradation deprived the cleric of the privileges of his former state. The subjection of the delinquent to the secular power was at best an indirect or secondary effect.[91]

In view of its penal privation of the clerical privileges, however, degradation possessed the character of a necessary condition preceding the trial and punishment of a delinquent cleric by the civil authorities. This liability to civil punishment consequent upon degradation naturally added to its horrors, especially when the penalty was inflicted for crimes punishable by the state with death. Nevertheless—and it must be strongly emphasized—degradation remained a canonical penalty applied only in conformity with the dictates of canon law for delicts canonically punishable with this penalty. It would be a grave mistake to think that the law of the Church sanctioned the penalty merely as a means of abandoning clerics to the state for each and every delict punishable in the civil codes.[92]

In the present as in the past degradation is a canonical penalty with effects which terminate directly and completely within the

---

[91] Cf. c. 27, X, *de verborum significatione*, V, 40: "Qui fuerit degradatus tamquam exutus privilegio clericali, saeculari foro per consequentiam applicetur." Cf. Suarez, *De Censuris*, Disp. XXX, sec. II, n. 9: "Quod vero spectat ad effectus, iidem sunt effectus degradationis, qui depositionis, addita privatione clericalis privilegii . . . ex qua privatione tamquam ex causa per accidens removente prohibens, sequi solet saeculare iudicium circa talem personam, et poenae, quae per illud imponuntur; illi tamen non possunt dici effectus degradationis, nisi valde remote, et per accidens."

[92] Cf. *supra*, pp. 107-108. Von Schulte [*Lehrbuch des katholischen Kirchenrechts*, pp. 375-376] mentions the fact that a number of the civil laws of Germany made it possible for bishops to impose first the penalty of degradation when one of their priests had been condemned to death or dishonorable imprisonment by the secular authorities. This "liberality" certainly does not square with the canonical concept of degradation as expressed in the common law of the Church. Unless it was authorized by the Holy See for particular places, such an extension of the penalty of degradation was unwarranted.

sphere of ecclesiastical privations. The Code makes no mention of a commitment of the degraded cleric to the secular power. If actual delivery to the secular courts ever follows upon degradation this is entirely extraneous to the canonical completion of the penalty. When the Code refers to the Roman Pontifical for the form to be observed in real degradation it indirectly approves the prescript which is found there and which requires the ecclesiastical judge to direct the civil authorities, whose representatives should be present at the ceremony, to apprehend the degraded cleric.[93] However, inasmuch as this rubric of the Pontifical is based on the condition that the case is such as canonically to require this delivery, it clearly contains the insinuation that degradation need not necessarily or even generally involve the actual, physical transfer of the delinquent to the civil courts. Nowhere does the Code sanction the delivery of a delinquent to the civil courts. As will be seen, morever, the Code now attributes all the effects of degradation to the canonical sentence. As a result, any civil effects consequent upon the execution of the solemn ceremony of degradation must be considered as reflecting a purely accidental relationship to the juridical effects of the penalty consummated in the canonical sentence.[94]

The essential effect of the penalty of degradation must therefore be found directly and immediately in the penal reduction of the cleric to the lay state, his lifelong loss of the dignity of the sacred ministry, his perpetual rejection from the service of the altar, his everlasting restriction to a communion with the Church in the mere capacity of a layman. If one were to appreciate the clerical state with the depths of vision and Faith with which Holy Mother Church appraises it, then the horror as well as the enormity of this penalty would certainly be manifest. Eloquently bespeaking the mind of the Church on this subject is the form of real degradation contained in the Roman Pontifical. This ceremony strikingly reveals the punishment of degradation as a spiritual vindictive penalty formally directed to the termination of the clerical career of the delinquent. In view of its significance to the study of the penalty

---

[93] Cf. *Pontificale Romanum,* tit. *Degradationis forma, infra,* p. 247.

[94] Cf. canon 2305, § 3.

of degradation the ritual as copied from the Pontifical is appended to this work.

The Code itself indicates the enormity of this penalty in its definition of the delicts punishable with degradation. It is, as a rule, only when the love and the humility of the Church has been wasted in vain that the insolence and contempt of the delinquent cleric is punished with the rod of degradation. If the rough ways of the world ultimately lead him to penance, God's mercy will provide him with an asylum elsewhere than in the clerical state. The sacred canons which govern the degradation of clerics at the same time manifest the deep anguish of soul with which the Church writes this sentence. To her it is as a sentence of death, indeed, almost as a sentence of irremediable reprobation. Ever new and repeated admonitions as well as the accompanying and progressively intensified punishments are invoked to stave off the final word or at least to delay its inevitable sequel: nothing but dire urgency and extreme necessity, nothing but the Church's awesome fear and maternal solicitude for the salvation of the souls of others can prevail upon her reluctance to speak this verdict.

ARTICLE 3. CAUSES FOR DEGRADATION

Canon 2305, § 2: Haec poena ferri solummodo potest propter delictum in iure expressum, aut si clericus, iam depositus et habitu clericali privatus, grave adhuc scandalum per annum praebere pergat.

According to the explicit provisions of the Code degradation can be inflicted only:

1. for a delict expressed in the law, or

2. when a cleric, already deposed and deprived of the clerical garb, continues for a year to give grave scandal. In establishing in the written law of the Church these two principles which completely comprise all possible causes for degradation, the Code has adopted the traditional doctrine and practice of the Church. Although the second norm differs slightly in details, it is nevertheless in substantial agreement with the rule of law followed under the former discipline.

The fundamental law governing the causes for degradation restricts its infliction to delicts expressly stated in the common law of the Church. This law, although heretofore unwritten, has long been observed in the courts of the Church. Fagnanus (1598-1678) cited a decision (n. 241) of the Rota on a date as early as June 4, 1607, in which it was expressly declared that a bishop could not proceed to the degradation of a cleric except in the cases defined in the general law of the Church.[95] Before the promulgation of the Code it was the common opinion of canonists that no authority inferior to the Holy See could decree degradation against a delinquent cleric except for the crimes to which the common law of the Church attached this penalty.[96] The Code explicitly confirms this doctrine. Degradation can be inflicted on a cleric for only such delicts as are expressly designated in the law as punishable with this penalty. For other crimes, no matter how atrocious they may be, degradation cannot be employed, even though these delicts may be as serious as, if not more serious than, those expressed in the law as warranting degradation.[97]

The second norm adopted by the Code as indicative of the causes which justify degradation is restricted in its application to certain clerics. In conformity with this rule the penalty of degradation can be imposed upon a cleric who (1) besides being deposed (2) has been deprived of the clerical garb and (3) still continues to give grave scandal after the lapse of a year. All three elements must be verified in the same delinquent before the penalty becomes applicable

[95] *Commentaria*, lib. II, tit. 1, cap. 10, n. 79.

[96] Cf. Suarez, *De Censuris*, Disp. XXX, sec. II, n. 4; Fagnanus, *Commentaria*, lib. II, tit. 1, cap. 10, nn. 50, 65; Reiffenstuel, *Ius Canonicum Universum*, lib. V, tit. XXXVII, nn. 37, 38; Barbosa, *De Officio et Potestate Episcopi*, pars III, alleg. CX, n. 9; Schmalzgrueber, *Ius Ecclesiasticum Universum*, lib. V, tit. XXXVII, nn. 153, 157; Benedictus XIV, *De synodo dioecesana*, lib. IX, cap. 6, n. 7; Ferraris, *Prompta Bibliotheca*, s.v. "*Degradatio*," III, pp. 40-41; Zitelli, *Apparatus Iuris Ecclesiastici* (2. ed. Romae, 1888), p. 31; Lega, *De Delictis et Poenis*, n. 209, pp. 279-280; Wernz, *Ius Decretalium*, VI, n. 136, pp. 141-142.

[97] Cf. Fagnanus, *Commentaria*, lib. II, tit. 1, cap. 10, n. 89; Barbosa, *De Officio et Potestate Episcopi*, pars III, alleg. CX, n. 12; Benedictus XIV, *De synodo dioecesana*, lib. IX, cap. 6, n. 9; Schmalzgrueber, *Ius Ecclesiasticum Universum*, lib. V, tit. XXXVII, n. 154.

in conformity with this law. While this rule opens a wider avenue for the possible application of degradation than does the sum of the individual delicts which are expressly designated in the Code as punishable with this penalty, it opens this avenue only to a restricted class of clerics.

The penal system of the Church also provides that deposition can be inflicted only for the delicts expressly designated in the common law of the Church. As already observed, there are ten such cases. If the delinquent becomes subject to this punishment but thereupon desists from his criminal violation of law no further action is taken against him. If, on the contrary, he does not manifest signs of amendment after deposition, but rather continues to give scandal, his ordinary can, after another warning has proved futile, take action to deprive him of the clerical garb and, by way of consequence, to despoil him also of the clerical privileges. If for a year after the infliction of this penalty the delinquent still continues to give grave scandal he can then be degraded.[98]

A similar progression of penalties obtained under the former discipline, but instead of the perpetual privation of the clerical garb excommunication was visited upon the delinquent cleric who proved himself incorrigible after deposition.[99] If he did not amend his ways after excommunication he then became liable to degradation. The law of the Code substitutes the penalty of perpetual privation of the clerical garb for the penalty of excommunication and more precisely defines the period of one year after this privation as the limit within which the delinquent must correct himself or become liable to degradation.

The succession of penalties culminating in the degradation of the cleric who continues to give grave scandal indicates that this grave scandal of which the Code speaks arises not from any and every conceivable delict but from one which is of a character to warrant the penalty of deposition. Obstinately persisting in this delict, rejecting warnings and ignoring milder penalties, the delinquent con-

---

[98] Cf. canons 2303-2305.

[99] Cf. c. 10, **X**, *de iudiciis*, II, 1; *Pontificale Romanum*, tit. *Ordo suspensionis, reconciliationis, depositionis, dispensationis, degradationis, et restitutionis sacrorum ordinum.*

tinues to give grave scandal. By his grave delinquency in violating a law which sanctions deposition for its transgressor and by his subsequent contempt for the authority and discipline of the Church he not only gives bad example to others but the occasion for their spiritual ruin. In this case, then, the due order of penalties and warnings having been applied in vain, the Church, today as in the past, sanctions the penalty of degradation as the final step to check the scandal given by the delinquent.[100]

Apart from this case the law expressly sanctions degradation for six delicts. In the following enumeration of these cases the other penalties preceding or accompanying degradation are also mentioned. This procedure helps to indicate the relative position of degradation in the penal system of the Church. Moreover it will serve to exclude any false notion that the Church leaves these delicts unpunished prior to the infliction of the penalty of degradation.

A. *Adherence to a non-Catholic Sect*

It has already been observed that canon 2314, § 1, punishes all apostates from the Christian faith as well as each and every heretic or schismatic with an excommunication incurred *ipso facto*. Moreover, unless these delinquents repent after a warning they are to be deprived of every benefice, dignity, pension, office or other position in the Church and they are to be declared infamous. After a second warning has been given in vain clerics are to be deposed.[101] In this matter the law defines another delict which is expressly punishable with degradation. If clerics who are apostates, heretics or schismatics enroll in a non-Catholic sect or publicly adhere to it they incur infamy *ipso facto,* they are automatically deprived of every

---

[100] Cf. c. 10, X, *de iudiciis*, II, 1: "ne possit esse ultra perditio plurimorum." Cf. *Glossa* in c. 27, X, *de verborum significatione*, V, 40, s.v. *"tradatur"*; Fagnanus, *Commentaria*, lib. II, tit. 1, cap. 10, n. 34; Gonzalez Tellez, *Commentaria*, lib. II, tit. 1, cap. 10, n. 12; Reiffenstuel, *Ius Canonicum Universum*, lib. V, tit. XXXVII, n. 38; Barbosa, *De Officio et Potestate Episcopi*, pars III, alleg. CX, nn. 4, 13; Benedictus XIV, *De synodo dioecesana*, lib. IX, cap. 6, n. 10.

[101] Cf. canon 2314, § 1, nn. 1, 2; *supra,* p. 181, n. 367.

office and benefice and if they do not amend after a warning they are to be degraded.[102]

It may be noted that a cleric who persists in heresy, schism or apostasy upon ignoring two canonical warnings is to be deposed, not degraded. However, if he should obstinately persist in his delict for the duration of a year after he has been not only deposed but also deprived of his right to wear the clerical garb, he can be degraded according to the norms of canon 2305, § 2. Directly punishable with degradation, however, is the specific delict of apostate, heretical or schismatic clerics who have enrolled in a non-Catholic sect or who have publicly adhered to it and do not desist from their crime after receiving a canonical warning.

Enrollment in the membership of such a sect is accomplished by a cleric when he enscribes his name in the register of the sect or when he freely submits to any public rite or ceremony prescribed for admission according to the rules and usages of the sect. Such enrollment is equally perpetrated by a cleric when he publicly adheres to the sect, declares his affiliation with it, publicly approves it or gives it his support, or publicly and repeatedly participates in its services.[103]

Vermeersch-Creusen [104] and Salucci [105] advance the opinion that the term *non-Catholic sect* must be taken in a strict sense as a religious body which, although it retains the Christian name, denies the Catholic Faith by its doctrine or practice. In consequence, non-Christian religions, such as Judaism or Mohammedanism, would be excluded from its concept. Such an interpretation in the present consideration may perhaps not lack some degree of probability in favor of its correctness in view of the fact that canon 2314, § 1, n. 3,

---

[102] Cf. canon 2314, § 1: "Omnes a christiana fide apostatae et omnes et singuli haeretici aut schismatici: . . . n. 3: Si sectae acatholicae nomen dederint vel publice adhaeserint, ipso facto infames sunt et, firmo praescripto can. 188, n. 4, clerici, monitione incassum praemissa, degradentur."

[103] Cf. Sipos, *Enchiridion Iuris Canonici*, § 162, p. 686; Ayrinhac-Lydon, *Penal Legislation*, n. 201, p. 155; Blat, *Commentarium*, V, n. 151, p. 200; Vermeersch-Creusen, *Epitome*, III, n. 513, p. 311; Cocchi, *Commentarium*, VIII, n. 138, p. 229.

[104] *Epitome*, III, n. 513, p. 311.

[105] *Il Diritto Poenale*, II, n. 16.

employes the word "sect" and deals with penal matters which always call for a strict interpretation. However, since the canon expressly makes mention of apostates as well as of heretics and schismatics when it refers to affiliation with non-Catholic sects, it appears not only much more tenable but also practically necessary to interpret the term *non-Catholic sect* as referring to any religious body which in its doctrine or practice denies either the Catholic Faith or the Christian religion.[106] There can be no question that atheistic sects are included under the term *non-Catholic sects* and that correspondingly any enrollment in the former implies the presence of a delict equally as well as an enrollment in the latter. According to the Pontifical Commission for the Authentic Interpretation of the Code persons who belong or have belonged to an atheistic sect are to be considered as regards all legal effects in the same class with persons who belong to or who have belonged to a non-Catholic sect.[107]

B. *Violence Against the Roman Pontiff*

Clerics who lay violent hands on the person of the Roman Pontiff automatically incur excommunication reserved in a most special manner to the Holy See and *ipso facto* become *excommunicati vitandi;* in addition they are automatically branded with infamy and must be degraded.[108] To bring physical violence to bear upon the person of the Roman Pontiff, the Vicar of Christ on earth, is manifestly one of the worst crimes a Christian can commit. It offers the only instance in which a delinquent becomes *vitandus* without any sentence or proclamation.[109] If a cleric commits this delict he must be degraded.

[106] Cf. A Coronata, *Institutiones*, IV, n. 1865, p. 290; Sipos, *Enchiridion Iuris Canonici*, § 162, p. 686; Cocchi, *Commentarium*, VIII, n. 138, p. 229.

[107] *PCI*, 30 iul. 1934—*AAS*, XXVI (1934), 494.

[108] Canon 2343, § 1: "Qui violentas manus in personam Romani Pontificis iniecerit: 1.: Excommunicationem contrahit latae sententiae Sedi Apostolicae specialissimo modo reservatam; et est ipso facto vitandus; 2.: Est ipso iure infamis; 3.: Clericus est degradandus."

[109] Cf. canon 2258, § 2: "Nemo est vitandus, nisi fuerit nominatim a Sede Apostolica excommunicatus, excommunicatio fuerit publice denuntiata et in decreto vel sententia expresse dicatur ipsum vitari debere, salvo praescripto can. 2343, § 1, n. 1."

The phrase "lay violent hands upon" is derived from the law of the II General Lateran Council (1139),[110] which formally invoked the privilege of personal immunity for clerics with severe canonical sanctions. It has always been interpreted to signify violent injury to the person not by words but by deeds. It was never limited to the literal sense of violence merely by hand, but was extended to include any means for inflicting injury, whether by foot, missiles, firearms, etc. The injury is understood as a personal injury of the pope (1) in his body, by murder, by poisoning, by maiming, by assault and battery, by any violent physical attack; (2) in his liberty, by imprisonment or enforced confinement; (3) in his dignity, by spitting upon him, by tearing his garments, by casting slush, muck or mire at him. The Roman Pontiff must be known as such and the perpetrated injury must be deliberate. While violence implies a real injury, it is evident that even a slight blow delivered to the pope by a cleric will ordinary constitute a grave injury.[111]

In virtue of the decree of the Holy Office of July 21, 1934, the penal sanction of degradation obtains also for the clergy of the Oriental Church if they should attack the person of the Roman Pontiff.[112]

It should also be noted, in as far as clerics are liable to civil penalties after degradation, that a law of the Vatican State, according to the testimony of A Coronata,[113] has established capital punishment for delicts against the life, integrity or personal liberty of the Supreme Pontiff.

---

[110] Canon 15—Schroeder, *Disciplinary Decrees*, 204-205.

[111] Cf. Ayrinhac-Lydon, *Penal Legislation*, nn. 287-291, pp. 222-225; Cocchi, *Commentarium*, VIII, n. 187, pp. 284-286; Cappello, *De Censuris*, n. 271, p. 248; Sipos, *Enchiridion Iuris Canonici*, § 25, p. 100; Blat, *Commentarium*, V, n. 184, p. 236; Sole, *De Delictis et Poenis*, n. 377, pp. 295-297; Chelodi, *Ius Poenale*, n. 75, p. 101; Augustine, *A Commentary on Canon Law*, VIII, 376-378.

[112] *AAS*, XXVI (1934), 550.

[113] *Institutiones*, IV, n. 1986, p. 429, not. 11: "Praeterea vi legum Civitatis Vaticanae, 7 Iunii 1929, poena capitis statuta est 'contro chi nel territorio del Città del Vaticano commete un fatto contro la vita, integrità o la libertà personale del Sommo Pontefice.' "

C. Culpable Homicide

Under the title which in the fifth book of the Code deals with delicts against life, liberty, property, good name and good morals, the only delict which is directly and expressly punished with degradation is that of culpable homicide. The law provides that a cleric who is guilty of culpable homicide should be degraded.[114] Homicide in its broadest sense is the killing of a man or the taking of his life.[115] According to the usual distinctions proffered by canonists homicide is either voluntary or involuntary. It is voluntary when the killing is intended directly, in itself, or indirectly, in its cause. It is involuntary or casual when it results apart from the direct or indirect intention of the agent. Voluntary homicide is subdivided into just homicide which is forbidden by no law and unjust homicide which is prohibited by the divine or human law. Just homicide may be defensive, namely, when it is committed either by an individual to protect himself and his possessions or by the public authority in a just war to guard its rights, or it may be punitive, namely, when by public authority the penalty of death is inflicted in a criminal process on those who are guilty of capital offenses. Unjust homicide is distinguished either as simple homicide, that is, when it is perpetrated voluntarily but without previous deliberation, or as premeditated homicide, that is, when it is accomplished not only voluntarily but in consequence of a previous deliberately conceived resolve to kill. When some special malice is inherent in the act of homicide, as in the case of parricide, fratricide or assassination, the homicide is termed qualified. Casual or involuntary homicide is either purely involuntary, when all fault is lacking on the part of the killer, or culpable, when the homicide occurs without the direct or indirect intention of killing but not without grave fault due to the omission of the diligence requisite for avoiding the homicide which could prudently have been foreseen.[116]

---

[114] Canon 2354, § 2: "Clericus . . . reus vero homicidii culpabilis degradetur."

[115] Cf. Wernz, *Ius Decretalium*, VI, n. 362, p. 362; Vermeersch-Creusen, *Epitome*, III, n. 556, p. 344. Abortion is a distinct delict.—Cf. canon 2350.

[116] Cf. Wernz, *Ius Decretalium*, VI, n. 363, pp. 363-364; Noldin, *De Poenis Ecclesiasticis* (5 ed., Oeniponte, 1905), nn. 134, 135, pp. 114, 115;

Under the law of the Code the fundamental criterion for determining penal liability in the case of homicide committed by clerics [117] looks to the element of culpability. All other distinctions or qualifications occupy a secondary place. Not only the cleric who commits voluntary homicide but also the one who commits involuntary homicide, if he is found to be gravely culpable, must be degraded. Canon 2354, § 2, leaves open no other interpretation: If a cleric has committed any of the delicts enumerated in the first paragraph of this canon he shall be punished by the ecclesiastical court in proportion to his guilt with penances, censures, deprivation of office, benefice and dignity and even with deposition if the circumstances demand it; if he has been guilty of culpable homicide he shall be degraded. It rests with the ecclesiastical court, therefore, to determine in particular cases whether there is present that degree of culpability which amounts to a determinative or constitutive element in this delict. The foundation for culpability here rests on the juridical principle that one who is obliged to observe a law is indirectly obliged also to employ the necessary diligence lest the forbidden effects follow even apart from one's intention. The penal law which sanctions degradation for culpable homicide implicitly but nonetheless gravely prescribes that the necessary diligence be employed lest the death of a man follow even apart from one's volition.

To establish the degree of culpability requisite for effecting the delict of homicide as delineated in the Code, besides consideration for the extreme severity of its mandatory penalty, attention must be given to the sacred canons which specify how the nature and the degree of the imputability of a delict are to be determined,[118] for it is quite evident that the term *culpable* of canon 2354, § 2, is used

---

Vermeersch-Creusen, *Epitome*, III, n. 556, pp. 344-345; Sipos, *Enchiridion Iuris Ecclesiastici*, § 245, p. 956.

[117] In the case of laymen canon 2354, § 1, leaves the crimes there mentioned to the punishment of the state. Among these crimes homicide is included without any qualification. It should therefore be taken in its strict sense, well defined by Chelodi [*Ius Poenale*, n. 82, p. 115] as "violenta hominis occisio dolo malo facta."

[118] Cf. *CIC*, lib. V, pars I, tit. II, canons 2199-2211.

as a synonym for *imputable*.[119]   Since culpability is the formal element of the delict of homicide no matter whether the unjust killing of a man resulted from the evil will of his slayer (voluntary homicide) or from the slayer's omission of the proper diligence (involuntary homicide) it follows that all causes which increase, diminish, or destroy the evil will or culpability must automatically also increase, diminish or destroy the imputability of the delict and will therefore govern and regulate the application of the penalty of degradation accordingly.

Unquestionably the law of the Code which sanctions degradation for culpable homicide is more severe than the former discipline which employed the penalty of deposition.[120]   The times, however, have also changed and so have the relations between Church and State in the matter of punishing delinquencies harmful to both societies.

D. *Solicitation*

According to the norm of canon 904 a priest commits the delict of solicitation if in the act of confession, or on its occasion or under its pretext, he strives in any way to induce any person to a grave sin against the sixth commandment.   While this delict, so enormous and so injurious to God's Church,[121] does not involve any automatic penalties, it is, nevertheless, punishable with some of the most severe penalties in the Code, even with degradation.   The law explicitly mentions this penalty: The priest who commits the crime of solicitation as mentioned in canon 904 shall be suspended from the celebration of Mass and from the hearing of sacramental confessions, and, if the gravity of his offense demands it, he shall be declared disqualified for the hearing of confessions, he shall be deprived of all benefices and dignities and of the active and passive vote, he shall be declared disqualified for all these, and in the more serious cases he shall be punished with degradation.[122]

---

[119] Cf. Roberti, *De Delictis et Poenis*, n. 67, p. 93, not. 2.

[120] Cf. cc. 5, 6, D. L.; cc. 6, 7, 8, X, *de homicidio voluntario vel casuali*, V, 12.

[121] Cf. Benedictus XIV, const. *Sacramentum Poenitentiae*, 1 Iunii 1741, § 1, in fine—*CIC*, Documentum V.

[122] Canon 2368, § 1.   Cf. Cerato, *De Delicto Sollicitationis* (Patavii: Typis

It is to be noted that the penalty of degradation is sanctioned only for the more serious cases of solicitation. In this regard the law of the Code agrees with the earlier legislation. Pope Gregory XV (1621-1623), in extending to the universal Church [123] the penalties enacted by Pope Pius IV (1559-1565) against priests in Spain who were guilty of solicitation,[124] declared that degradation accompanied with the commitment of the delinquent to the secular courts was to be applied then only when the enormity of the delict warranted this graver penalty. Two and a half centuries later, in 1866, the changed conditions of the Christian world are reflected in an instruction of the Holy Office, which directed local ordinaries to abstain from imposing degradation and committing the delinquent to the secular power. The instruction added that these provisions were indeed established by Pope Gregory XV, but that this was done with the motive of inspiring fear rather than with any insistence that the threat be executed.[125]

While the commitment of delinquent clerics to the secular courts has been abandoned, the penalty of degradation has been introduced anew in the Code as one of the punishments for solicitation. As in the past, the penalty still serves to inspire a salutary fear and to emphasize the abhorrence of the Church for this delict but at the same time it must be admitted that the penalty can actually be inflicted when the enormity of the delict warrants it. Instructions of the Holy Office [126] describe in detail the manner of procedure in establishing the guilt of the priest. When such guilt has been ascertained, then the proportionate penalty according to the norms of canon 2368, § 1, must be applied.

Seminarii, 1922), 1-112; Murphy, *Delinquencies and Penalties in the Administration and Reception of the Sacraments* (Catholic University of America, Canon Law Studies, No. 17, Washington, D. C., 1923), 47-57; Cappello, *De Poenitentia*, nn. 640-723, pp. 498-566.

[123] Cf. const. *Universi*, 30 aug. 1622, § 4—*Fontes*, n. 201.

[124] Cf. ep. *Cum sicut nuper*, 16 apr. 1561—*Fontes*, n. 102.

[125] S. C. S. Off. instr., 20 febr. 1866, § 12—*Fontes*, n. 990.

[126] February 20, 1866—*Fontes*, n. 990; August 6, 1897—*ASS*, XXX (1897), 249-257.

E. Violations of the Seal of Confession

The technical term *"seal of confession"* describes the sacred obligation, which principally binds the confessor, to keep secret whatever has been revealed in sacramental confession. This obligation is directly violated when both the sin which was told in confession and the person who told it in confession are revealed; it is violated indirectly when through the words or deeds of the confessor a real danger is presented for the sin or the penitent to become known or for the sacrament to be rendered odious.[127] In both cases the Code makes the violation of the seal a delict punishable with grave penalties, in certain instances even with degradation.

It may here be recalled that under the former discipline a priest who was guilty of violating the seal was liable to deposition but not to degradation. For this delict the IV General Lateran Council (1215) [128] had decreed deposition and perpetual confinement in a monastery. This law was incorporated in the Decretals [129] and was repeated by local councils, although some of these employed the term degradation to signify deposition.[130] Later, other penalties replaced that of the cleric's seclusion in a monastery as prescribed by the Decretals. Indeed, with the unjust limitations placed by the state upon the right of the Church to inflict temporal punishment, a voluntary withdrawal to a house for delinquent clerics, to a monastery or to some other religious house was encouraged. But the penalty of deposition remained in force until the appearance of the Code.[131]

---

[127] Cf. Kurtscheid-Marks, *A History of the Seal of Confession* (St. Louis: Herder Book Company, 1927), 1-4; Murphy, *Delinquencies and Penalties in the Administration and Reception of the Sacraments,* 58-63, esp. 59.

[128] Canon 21—Schroeder, *Disciplinary Decrees,* 259, 260; Denzinger-Bannwart-Umberg, *Enchiridion Symbolorum,* nn. 437, 438.

[129] C. 12, X, *de poenitentiis et remissionibus,* V, 38.

[130] Council of Treves (1227), c. 4—Mansi, XXII, 29; Council of Cologne (1279), c. 17—Mansi, XXIV, 217; Council of Lambeth (1330), c. 3—Mansi, XXV, 893. Cf. Benedictus XIV, *De synodo dioecesana,* lib. IX, cap. 6, n. 3; Hinschius, *Kirchenrecht,* IV, 133.

[131] Cf. Schmalzgrueber, *Ius Ecclesiasticum Universum,* lib. V, tit. XXXVII, n. 79; Reiffenstuel, *Ius Canonicum Universum,* lib. V, tit. XXXVII, n. 4;

The law of the Code which clearly distinguishes between the delicts of direct and of indirect violation of the seal ordains that if a confessor presumes to violate directly the seal of confession he incurs an excommunication reserved in a most special manner to the Apostolic See, but that if he violates the seal only indirectly he becomes liable to the penalties of canon 2368, § 1,[132] as enacted against those who are guilty of the crime of solicitation, namely, he shall be suspended from celebrating Mass and from hearing sacramental confessions, and, if the gravity of the offense warrants it, he shall be declared disqualified for hearing confessions, he moreover shall be deprived of all benefices and dignities, and of both the active and passive vote in canonical elections, in addition he shall be declared disqualified for all of these, and in the more grievous cases he shall also be punished with degradation.

In specifically designating the penalties of canon 2368, § 1, without any limitation or restriction, as properly applicable to the delict of the indirect violation of the seal of confession the Code thereby expressly designates another delict as furnishing a possible cause for degradation. It may be noted that deposition is no longer explicitly sanctioned as a penalty for the delicts either of the direct or of the indirect violation of the seal. On the other hand degradation is nowhere explicitly mentioned as a punishment for the direct violation of the seal. It is specified, however, for the delict of the indirect violation, but only in extreme cases.[133]

Hollweck, *Die kirchlichen Strafgesetze*, p. 333, not. 12; Wernz, *Ius Decretalium*, VI, n. 466, p. 444.

[132] Canon 2369.

[133] Not a few of the commentators on the Code in treating of degradation have failed to include this particular case in their list of the delicts punishable with this penalty. Among others who missed this point are Vermeersch-Creusen, *Epitome*, III, n. 499, p. 302; Chelodi, *Ius Poenale*, n. 53, p. 70; Ayrinhac-Lydon, *Penal Legislation*, n. 175, p. 132; Cocchi, *Commentarium*, VIII, n. 119, p. 123; Augustine, *A Commentary on Canon Law*, VIII, 262; Sipos, *Enchiridion Iuris Canonici*, § 240, p. 949; Prummer, *Manuale Iuris Canonici*, q. 580, p. 670. The reason for this omission may be traceable to the fact that this delict is not enumerated in the list given under the word *Degradatio* in the analytical-alphabetical index of Gasparri's edition of the Code.

F. *Attempted Marriage*

The sixth and final delict punishable with degradation by the express provision of the Code is the crime which is committed by clerics in major orders when they presume to contract marriage and refuse to retrace their steps after a warning has been given them. The delict is defined in law with its established penalties in canon 2388, § 1: Clerics in major orders and regulars or nuns who have made the solemn vow of chastity automatically incur excommunication reserved simply to the Holy See when they presume to contract marriage, even by a mere civil ceremony; this excommunication is likewise incurred by all persons who similarly presume to contract marriage, even by a mere civil ceremony, with the aforesaid clerics, regulars and nuns. Clerics, moreover, who have been admonished by the ordinary and do not repent within the time specified by the ordinary according to the circumstances of the case, shall be degraded. By their attempted marriage clerics automatically forfeit every office which they hold [134] and incur an irregularity.[135]

A cleric in minor orders does not incur the excommunication. If he has contracted a valid marriage, then according to canon 132, § 2, he is automatically reduced to the lay state. The penalties apply only to clerics in major orders who have attempted marriage by the observance of some formality, civil or religious, in manifestation of their intention. Yet even the established fact of the attempted marriage does not constitute the delict which is punishable with degradation. This penalty can be inflicted only when after due warning the delinquent cleric still persists in his crime beyond the reasonable period of time for repentance as determined by the ordinary. It may be noted again that even if the delict is proved before the competent ecclesiastical tribunal and even when the condemnatory sentence of degradation has been passed, the delinquent is not thereby liberated from the obligations of celibacy.

ARTICLE 4. PROCEDURE

Before the Code the full effects of degradation were obtained only upon the completion of a twofold process. This involved in

[134] Canon 188, n. 5.
[135] Canon 985, n. 5.

the first place the condemnation of the delinquent in a sentence of degradation, described as verbal degradation, and secondly, the execution of this sentence in a solemn ceremony known as real or actual degradation.[186] According to the common doctrine verbal degradation had the same effects as deposition but differed from the latter penalty in that it directly tended towards real degradation and was inflicted only with certain formalities and for definite crimes punishable with degradation. Failure to consider these three essential points of distinction led some canonists in the past to confuse verbal degradation with deposition.[187] Deposition, however, was distinct and complete in itself, whereas verbal degradation was a necessary prerequisite for real degradation. A cleric who merely had been deposed could not be degraded without a new sentence, namely, a verbal degradation which had to be issued according to the norms of the law for delicts which warranted this penalty.[188]

On the other hand, verbal and real degradation were intimately associated. They respectively connoted the pronouncement of a sentence and its execution. Through verbal degradation there was effected the pronouncement of the sentence which then remained to be executed in real degradation.[189] It was only with real degradation that the delinquent cleric was finally and totally deprived of the clerical privileges and reduced to the lay state.[140] At the dawn of the twentieth century Hollweck, among others, objected to this doc-

---

[186] Cf. c. 2, *de poenis*, V, 9, in VI°; Conc. Trident., sess. XIII, *de ref.* c. 4; Benedictus XIV, ep. encycl. *Quam grave*, 2 aug. 1757, §§ 3-9, 16—*Fontes*, n. 443; *Pontificale Romanum*, tit. *Degradationis forma*.

[187] Cf. *supra*, p. 93; also Hinchius, *Kirchenrecht*, V, 565; Hollweck, *Die kirchlichen Strafgesetze*, §92, p. 159, not. 2.

[188] Cf. Suarez, *De Censuris*, Disp. XXX, sec. II, nn. 6, 12, 18, 21; Schmalzgrueber, *Ius Ecclesiasticum Universum*, lib. V, tit. XXXVII, n. 138; Wernz, *Ius Decretalium*, VI, n. 120, p. 124; Lega, *De Delictis et Poenis*, n. 208, pp. 280-281.

[189] Cf. c. 2, *de poenis*, V, 9, in VI°; Suarez, *De Censuris*, Disp. XXX, sec. II, nn. 2, 3, 9, 17; Disp. XL, sec. II, n. 24.

[140] Cf. *Glossa* in c. 2, *de poenis*, V, 9, in VI°, s.v. *"privilegio"*; Suarez, *De Censuris*, Disp. XXX, sec. II, nn. 2, 7, 8; Benedictus XIV, *De synodo dioecesana*, lib. IX, cap. 6, n. 3; Ferraris, *Prompta Bibliotheca*, s.v. *"Degradatio,"* III, 39-40; Reiffenstuel, *Ius Canonicum Universum*, lib. V, tit. XXXVII, nn. 22, 27, 32, 34; Wernz, *Ius Decretalium*, VI, n. 127, p. 134.

trine, which, he admitted, was the current as well as the traditional one on the grounds that verbal degradation necessarily defeated its own purpose whenever the sentence could not be executed in real degradation.[141]   However, as Chelodi has also noted,[142] while the arguments of this learned canonist presented a valid claim for seeking a change in the law, they could not of themselves alter the established law.

The Code of Canon Law, however, while it retains in name the former distinction between verbal and real degradation, has introduced a salutary change in the legal effects proper to each of these forms for the infliction of the penalty. Verbal degradation, as in the past, consists in the sentence, but it now has all the effects of the penalty without any additional execution in a solemn ceremony. Real degradation is still to be found in the solemn ceremony, but if and when it is performed it adds no new juridical effects to the penalty already completely inflicted through the judicial sentence.

> **Canon 2305, § 3:** Alia est *verbalis* seu *edictalis,* quae sola sententia irrogatur, ita tamen ut omnes suos effectus iuridicos statim habeat sine ulla executione; alia *realis,* si serventur sollemnia praescripta in Pontificali Romano.

A. *Verbal Degradation*

Under the law of the Code "verbal" and "real" are employed in reference to the penalty of degradation as technical terms which designate the manner in which the penalty is inflicted. Verbal or edictal degradation is inflicted by sentence alone, in such a manner, however, as to have all the juridical effects of the penalty even apart from its execution; it is real degradation if the solemnities prescribed by the Roman Pontifical are observed. The phrases "by sentence alone" and "without any execution" as employed in the definition of verbal degradation are used in apposition to the phrase "the solemnities prescribed by the Roman Pontifical" as used in the definition of real degradation. It is for this latter kind of degra-

---

[141] *Die kirchlichen Strafgesetze,* § 92, p. 159, note 2.
[142] *Ius Poenale,* n. 53, p. 71, not. 3.

dation alone that any ritual act of execution is required. This is not to say that the canonically required execution of every judicial sentence is here excluded. Indeed, it is very probable that the Code has employed the term "edictal" as a synonym for "verbal" inasmuch as the execution of this sentence now takes place immediately with the issuance of the executory *edict* by the tribunal which passes the sentence.[148] The synonym "edictal" thus expresses more precisely the idea of a sentence which historically was characterized by the use of the term "verbal." This interpretation conforms to the new rôle of verbal degradation and at the same time offers a reason for the use of the term "edictal," a term which is found neither in the old law, nor in the Roman Pontifical, nor yet in the writings of the commentators.

The significance of the definition of these terms by the Code is to be found in the authoritative revision of the effects proper to each. Contrary to the former legislation all the effects of the penalty are now obtained through a merely verbal degradation. The two terms "verbal" and "real," in consequence, designate two separate and distinct forms for the infliction of one and the same penalty. One is necessary, the other is optional. Verbal degradation is necessary and is in itself sufficient. Degradation is never incurred automatically upon the commission of a delict, but in every case there is required a condemnatory sentence, for without it there is no infliction of any penalty which the law has enacted as a *ferendae sententiae* penalty, as is the case with the penalty of degradation. When the condemnatory sentence has been passed there is present a verbal or edictal degradation. In consequence of its presence the delinquent suffers the full juridical effects of degradation without any need of the solemn ceremonies prescribed in the Roman Pontifical for the so-called real degradation. Since real degradation cannot, and for that matter never could precede verbal degradation, it is evident that the rôle of real degradation has been restricted by the Code to a ceremonial rite devoid of legal effects.

---

[148] Cf. canon 1918: "Non antea exsecutioni locus esse poterit, quam exsecutorium iudicis decretum habeatur, quo scilicet edicatur sententiam ipsam exsecutioni mandari debere; quod decretum pro diversa causarum natura vel in ipso sententiae tenore includatur vel separatim edatur."

The Code has not only broadened the scope of verbal degradation, but it has also reduced the requirements for the tribunal which is always demanded as a condition for the passing of this sentence. The legislator, in reprobating every contrary custom and revoking every contrary privilege, has reserved to a tribunal of five judges all criminal causes which involve the penalty of degradation.[144] Under the former discipline a bishop could proceed alone to the pronouncement of verbal degradation against a cleric in minor orders. In the case of clerics in major orders, however, Decretal law required that he be assisted by other bishops, six in the case of a priest, three in the case of a deacon or subdeacon.[145] The Council of Trent mitigated these requirements by allowing a substitution for the bishops of an equal number of abbots who had the right of using the miter and crosier by Apostolic privilege, or of other ecclesiastical dignitaries recommended by their maturity in years and their knowledge of the law.[146] Sole [147] and Sipos [148] erroneously interpret these requirements as applying with reference to real degradation. These assistants however, were required only in the process of verbal degradation in which they were employed as judges with a decisive vote.[149] The Council of Trent changed the requirement concerning the quality or dignity of the assisting prelates but left unaltered the rule of the law concerning their number or the manner of their assistance in the capacity of judges. Blat maintains that this law of the Council of Trent is implicitly retained in the Code. In corroboration of his statement he points to canon

[144] Canon 1576, § 1: "Reprobata contraria consuetudine et revocato quolibet contrario privilegio . . . n. 2: Causae vero quibus agitur de delictis quae depositionis, privationis perpetuae habitus ecclesiastici, vel degradationis poenam important, reservantur tribunali quinque iudicum."

[145] C. 2, *de poenis*, V, 9, in VI°; cf. *Glossa* in c. 2, *de poenis*, V, 9, in VI°, s.v. *"canonibus"*; *Pontificale Romanum*, tit. *Ordo suspensionis, reconsiliationis, depositionis, dispensationis, degradationis, et restitutionis sacrorum ordinum*.

[146] Conc. Trident. sess XIII, *de ref.*, c. 4.

[147] *De Delictis et Poenis*, n. 292, p. 297.

[148] *Enchiridion Iuris Canonici*, § 240, p. 948.

[149] Cf. c. 2, *de poenis*, V, 9, in VI°; *Pontificale Romanum*, tit. *Ordo suspensionis, reconciliationis, depositionis, dispensationis, degradationis, et restitutionis sacrorum ordinum*; Suarez, *De Censuris*, Disp. XXX, sec. II, n. 20; Benedictus XIV, *De synodo dioecesana*, lib. IX, cap. 6, n. 5.

2305, § 3.[150] This latter canon, however, offers a definition both
of the verbal and of the real degradation. So the reference of Blat
remains somewhat equivocal in that it does not single out the one
to the exclusion of the other. But, whichever form of degradation
is contemplated, the doctrine of this author on the present point
stands without any juridical support. Real degradation never did
require the presence of a body of bishops or prelates. And verbal
degradation no longer calls for the same requirement as in the past.
The Code has completely revised the provisions governing the constitution of the competent tribunal. Under the present law causes
involving the penalty of degradation are reserved to a tribunal of
five judges who need no special qualifications of rank or dignity
other than the common law requirements that they be priests of
approved morals and experts in canon law.[151]

In reserving the causes which involve degradation to a tribunal
of five judges the Code does not distinguish between delinquent
clerics in major or in minor orders. Absolutely considered the law
will oblige in either case. However, the Code authorizes local ordinaries to reduce to the lay state merely by decree but for a just
cause any cleric in minor orders [152] and in certain instances the law
itself automatically produces this effect.[153] Accordingly it will be
rare, indeed, if ever it happen, that there will be any need to have
recourse to this extreme penalty. However, it may be noted that
when a cleric in minor orders commits a delict punishable with
degradation the discretional power of the ordinary must be brought
into harmony with the precept of the Code to impose this penalty.

If delicts which involve degradation are committed by bishops,
such delicts do not come for trial under the absolute requirement of
the Code which demands a tribunal of five judges if sentence of
degradation is to be passed. The degradation of bishops is governed by the same law which governs their deposition: the Roman

---

[150] *Commentarium,* V, n. 138, pp. 186-187.

[151] Cf. canons 1573, § 3 and 1574, § 1.

[152] Cf. canon 211, § 2.

[153] Cf. canons 141, § 2; 132, § 2; 136, § 3; 2387; 2358; 648; 669.

Pontiff alone is competent to proceed against them in criminal causes.[154]

The ancient controversy as to whether or not a unanimous vote of the judges is required for the sentence of degradation in the case of a priest [155] is definitely settled by the Code. Canon 1577, § 1, declares that the collegiate tribunal must proceed as a body and voice its decision according to the majority vote of its members. A unanimous vote is not required. Dissenting judges, however, are obliged to accede to and to sign the majority decision.[156]

In all respects, then, verbal degradation or the infliction of the penalty of degradation is governed by the same procedural laws as deposition.[157] The ordinary cannot substitute a judicial rebuke for the criminal trial leading to this sentence [158] nor can the tribunal suspend execution of the sentence if the accused cleric has been found guilty.[159]

The Holy Office, however, judges crimes which according to its own proper law are reserved to it, with the power to judge these criminal cases not only in appeals from the court of the local ordinaries but also in the first instance if the case has been directly brought to it.[160] This tribunal proceeds according to its own laws and customs, and inferior tribunals must follow the norms given by it in matters pertaining to the tribunal of that congregation.[161] Since the appearance of the Code the Holy Office has published several of its sentences of degradation.[162]

B. Real Degradation

While a cleric today is truly and completely degraded solely in the execution of a valid sentence of degradation delivered against

[154] Cf. canons 2227, § 1; 1557, § 1; *supra*, p. 194.

[155] Cf. *supra*, pp. 100-101.

[156] Cf. canon 1868 sq.; Lemieux, *The Sentence in Ecclesiastical Procedure*, p. 86.

[157] Cf. *supra*, p. 189 ff.

[158] Cf. canon 1948, n. 1.

[159] Cf. canon 2288.

[160] Cf. canon 247.

[161] Cf. canon 1555.

[162] Cf. *AAS*, XV (1923), 152; 449; XXII (1930), 517; XXV (1933), 333.

him, the performance of the solemnities prescribed by the Roman
Pontifical continue, according to the provisions of the Code, to be
termed technically "real degradation." [163]   The propriety of this
term is immediately obvious upon a consideration of the ceremonies
which are signalized by it, ceremonies which involve acts designed
by their very nature to signify and manifest a penal debasement.
In as far as holy orders are conferred with the delivery to the candidate of the sacred vessels and vestments which are appropriate to
each order, there could be no more effectual or natural symbol of
the external deprivation of these orders as accomplished by degradation than the solemn ceremony wherein the delinquent is actually
despoiled of the sacred vessels and vestments which he received in
ordination.

While according to custom at an early time the pronouncement
of the sentence of degradation was accompanied with some ceremonial, it was only with the law of Pope Boniface VIII (1294-1303)
that an elaborate ceremony became a juridical necessity for the completion of the penalty.[164]   The Code, while endorsing the ritual contained in the Roman Pontifical, which substantially follows the ceremony prescribed by Pope Boniface VIII,[165] has stripped it of all
juridical effects.   These effects are now completely attained simply
by the verbal degradation.[166]   This salutary revision of the discipline governing degradation accommodates the penalty to the conditions of the times which, even as early as the days of Pope Benedict
XIV,[167] render the execution of real degradation impossible except
in the rare case when a cleric freely submits to it.

Under the law of the Code, then, if and when the solemn ceremony is performed, no new juridical effects are added to the penalty already inflicted by the sentence of verbal degradation.   The
execution of the solemnities prescribed in the Pontifical promulgates,

---

[163] Canon 2305, § 3 " . . . alia [degradatio] est *realis,* si serventur sollemnia
praescripta in Pontificali Romano."

[164] Cf. c. 2, *de poenis,* V, 9, in VI°.

[165] Cf. *Pontificale Romanum,* tit. *Degradationis forma,* contained also in
the appendix of this work, *infra,* p. 247.

[166] Cf. canon 2303, § 3.

[167] Cf. ep. encycl. *Quam grave,* 2 aug. 1757, § 16—*Fontes,* n. 443.

as it were, the accomplished effects and dramatically portrays them in order to increase the ignominy cast upon the delinquent and in order to inspire in others a salutary fear for this punishment. To appreciate this fact it is but necessary to read the prescribed form for real degradation which for this purpose has been appended to this study.

Before the Code it was the common opinion of canonists that the execution of real degradation could be performed only by bishops and indeed only by consecrated bishops.[168] This interpretation was based on the provisions of law which constantly referred to the bishop when real degradation was involved, but mentioned other ordinaries when verbal degradation was considered.[169] Real degradation was considered an act of episcopal orders. Since only a consecrated bishop could admit a candidate to orders or ordain him, so also only a consecrated bishop could cast forth the delinquent cleric from orders insofar as this was done by real degradation.

The law of the Code offers no reason for changing this opinion of the earlier canonists. Indeed, the Code confirms the traditional form for the infliction of real degradation as prescribed by the Roman Pontifical, and in the Pontifical only the bishop is specified for the performance of these solemnities. Hence it must be held that ordinaries who are not consecrated bishops cannot perform real degradation upon their subjects unless this faculty has been granted to them by privilege or by a custom tolerated by the Holy See.[170]

The ceremony of real degradation can for its performance be delegated to others, but only to consecrated bishops. The matter is of little practical importance, however, since the Code attributes all the effects of the penalty to the sentence of degradation for the legitimate pronouncement of which all ordinaries are competent in virtue of their power of jurisdiction when it is exercised in accord-

---

[168] Cf. Suarez, *De Censuris*, Disp. XXX, sec. II, n. 6; Disp. XL, sec. II, n. 25; Ferraris, *Prompta Bibliotheca*, s.v. "Degradatio," III, 41.

[169] Cf. c. 2, *de poenis*, V, 9, in VI°; Conc. Trident., sess. XIII, *de ref.*, c. 4; *Pontificale Romanum, tit. Degradationis forma.*

[170] Cf. Barbosa, *De Officio et Potestate Episcopi*, pars III, alleg. CX, n. 25; Schmalzgrueber, *Ius Ecclesiasticum Universum*, lib. V, tit. XXXVII, n. 147; De Meester, *Compendium*, III, pars 2, n. 1799, p. 226.

ance with the demands and the norms of the sacred canons. Should
the ceremony of real degradation have been employed and should
later the offender's penalty have been remitted by a specific grant
of the Holy See, then it is fitting that such a highly favored cleric
be restored to his former canonical status with the solemn ceremony
of restitution described in the Roman Pontifical.[171]

[171] Tit. *Ordo suspensionis, reconciliationis, depositionis, dispensationis, degradationis, et restitutionis sacrorum ordinum.*

CONCLUSIONS

1. Deposition and degradation are clearly distinct and separate penalties in the law of the Code.

2. Deposition is the complete penal demotion: the delinquent cleric is reduced to a juridical condition lower than that of the simple tonsured cleric inasmuch as he is disqualified for obtaining clerical rights.

3. Degradation is the canonical penal expulsion from the clerical state.

4. Occupying an intermediate position between deposition and degradation in the present discipline of the Church is the new penalty of perpetual privation of the right to wear the ecclesiastical garb.

5. The prescript of the Code which obliges ordinaries to provide a charitable sustenance for needy deposed clerics is extinguished only when the delinquent cleric has been perpetually deprived of the right to wear the ecclesiastical garb.

6. Degration is the only canonical penalty whereby a cleric in major orders is reduced to the lay state.

7. The Holy See alone can grant a dispensation from the continued observance of the penalties of deposition or degradation.

8. A degraded cleric is no longer obliged daily to recite the divine office. He is freed of this obligation whether it was the public or the private recitation to which he was previously bound.

9. While deposition and degradation are mandatory penalties, they are not absolutely beyond the pale of the equitable powers conceded by canon 2223, §3, nn. 1-3.

10. Verbal degradation today has all the effects of the penalty of degradation altogether apart from the execution which is manifested in real degradation.

11. Verbal degradation is also termed *edictal* by the Code, probably because the execution of the sentence of degradation achieves its intended effect immediately with the issuance of the executory edict of the tribunal which pronounces the sentence.

APPENDIX

Ex Pontificali Romano:

DEGRADATIONIS FORMA

Degradandus, indumentis sacerdotalibus, si Sacerdos sit, indutus, vel diaconalibus, si sit Diaconus, et sic de reliquis Ordinibus et indumentis offertur Pontifici. Pontifex vero quasi exsequendo sententiam depositionis in illum dudum prolatam, praesente iudice saeculari, cui degradandus debet relinqui, publice abradit cum vitro vel cultello vel alio huiusmodi, leviter sine sanguinis effusione, loca manuum illius quae in collatione Ordinum inuncta fuerunt, et etiam tonsuram, si velit. Et consequenter seriatim, et sigillatim detrahit illi omnia insignia, sive sacra ornamenta, quae in Ordinum susceptione recepit, et demum exuit illum habitu clericali, et induit laicali, dicens publice iudici saeculari praesenti, ut illum propter scelera sua sic depositum, degradatum, exspoliatum et exauctoratum in suum, si velit, forum recipiat.

Et est notandum, quod in hac exsecutione sententiae non est necessaria Coëpiscoporum praesentia, nec etiam refert, sive in Ecclesia fiat, sive extra in platea, sive Pontifex degradans indutus sit Pontificalibus ornamentis, sive non; et talis degradatio, solemnis depositio vocatur, proprie tamen loquendo, quis à dignitatibus, et honoribus deponitur, sed ab Ordinibus degradatur; et post talem degradationem, iuste et rite factam, solus Romanus Pontifex cum tali dispensat. Episcopus tamen ante ipsam insignium detractionem, et etiam post sententiae depositionis prolationem dispensare, et restituere solo verbo potest, sicut et verbaliter depositus fuit, ut praemissum est.

Sed si, priusquam saecularis iudex in illum animadverterit, talis depositio, et degradatio iniusta, vel nulla inveniatur, tunc non solum verbo, sed etiam facto secundum ea, quae praemissa sunt, dispensatio, et restitutio fiat, et insignia sibi detracta seriatim, sigillatim, et solemniter ei coram altari restituantur. Et, si sit Episcopus, recuperabit orarium, baculum, annulum, sandalia, mitram, et alia insignia Pontificalia; si Presbyter, orarium et planetam; si Diaconus, orarium et dalmaticam; si Subdiaconus, tunicellam, et manipulum. Et reliqui gradus in restitutiones sua recuperant ea, quae, cum ordinarentur, receperunt. Poterit tamen (quod convenientius videtur) ad aliorum terrorem actualis degradatio sic fieri:

In primis in publico extra Ecclesiam paratur aliquis eminens congruentis spatii locus, pro degradatione facienda; supra quem ordinatur una credentia simplici tobalea cooperta, supra quam ponuntur ampulla vini, ampulla aquae, calix cum patena, et hostia; unum vas vini, unum vas aquae, liber Evangeliorum, liber Epistolarum; bacile cum buccali, et mantili; unum candelabrum cum candela exstincta; liber Exorcismorum; liber Lectionum; claves; Antiphonarium; forcipes, cultellus, aut vitrum; paramenta pro degradando, videlicet,

247

si degradandus sit Archiepiscopus, ordinentur super dictam credentiam super-
pelliceum, sandalia, cum caligis, amictus, alba, cingulum, manipulus, tunicella,
stola, dalmatica, chirothecae, alia stola planeta, mitra, annulus pontificalis,
pallium baculus pastoralis, et aliqua vestis habitus saecularis. Si vero degra-
dandus non sit Archiepiscopus, sed Episcopus tantum, omisso pallio, ponuntur
super credentiam omnia alia praedicta. Si vero Presbyter tantum, omissis
pallio et aliis pontificalibus paramentis praedictis, ponuntur ibidem omnia alia
praedicta. Idem in aliis Ordinibus, etiam in ordinatione credentiae observatur.
Item paratur in dicto loco faldistorium pro Pontifice degradatore, sedilia pro
Officialibus. Vocantur, et ibidem adsint ministri Pontificis; iudex saecularis,
cui degradatus committatur; notarius, qui processum degradationis legit (si
opus erit, vel Pontifici placet) et barbitonsor.

Hora congruenti ducitur degradanus, sive sit Archiepiscopus, sive quicumque
alius, quotidiano suo habitu indutus, super dictum locum ad hoc praeparatum;
ubi cum fuerit, solvitur, et liber ibidem manet. Tum a Clericis induitur
omnibus paramentis sui Ordinis, ut praemittitur supra credentiam Ordine suo
positis, incipiendo a superpelliceo, et continuando usque ad ultimum paramen-
tum sui Ordinis. Quo sic induto, Pontifex degradator indutus amictu, alba,
cingulo, stola, et pluviali rubeis, ac mitra simplici baculum pastoralem in
sinistra tenens, ascendit ad locum praedictum, et ibidem sedet in faldistorio,
in convenienti loco sibi parato, versus ad populum, astante sibi iudice saeculari.
Tum degradandus, sive Archiepiscopus fuerit, sive alius, omnibus sui Ordinis
vestibus sacris indutus, et singulis ornamentis ornatus, habens in manibus
ornamentum ad Ordinem suum spectans, ac si deberet in suo officio ministrare,
adducitur ante Pontificem, coram quo genuflectit. Tum Pontifex, ut supra
sedens, populo in vulgari notificat degradationis huiusmodi causam; deinde
contra degradandum sententiam fert in haec verba, si sit Sacerdos, aut Diaconus,
aut Subdiaconus, vel Clericus, et prius huiusmodi sententia lata non sit.

In nomine Pa ✠ tris, et Fi ✠ lii, et Spiritus ✠ Sancti. Amen. Qui nos
N., Dei et Apostolicae Sedis gratia Episcopus *N.* per viam accustationis *vel*
denuntiationis, *aut* inquisitionis cognoscentes de crimine *N.* contra *N.* Presbyterum, *vel* Diaconum, *vel* Subdiaconum, seu Clericum propter ipsius confessionem, *vel* legitimas probationes, evidenter invenimus eum ipsum crimen
commisisse, quod cum non solum grande, sed etiam damnabile, et damnosum
sit, et adeo enorme quod exinde non tantum divina maiestas offensa, sed et
universa civitas commota est, et ob hoc indignus officio, et beneficio ecclesiastico sit redditus, idcirco nos auctoritate Dei omnipotentis, Patris, et Filii,
et Spiritus Sancti, et nostra, ipsum omni huiusmodi officio, et beneficio
ecclesiastico sententialiter perpetuo privamus in his scriptis, ipsumque ab illis
verbo deponimus, et pronuntiamus realiter et actualiter secundum traditionem
Canonum deponendum, et degradandum.

Qua sententia sic, ut praefertur, lata, Pontifex degradator aufert ab illo
singula ornamenta sibi iuxta Ordinem suum tradita, inchoando ab ultimo
ornamento, et descendendo gradatim, continuans usque ad primum, quod in
prima Tonsura sibi datum fuit, hoc Ordine:

DEGRADATIO AB ORDINE PONTIFICALI

Si degradandus sit Archiepiscopus, Pontifex degradator aufert ab eo pallium, sic dicendo:

Praerogativa pontificalis dignitatis, quae in pallio designatur, te exuimus, quia male usus es ea.

Deinde, vel si degradandus sit Episcopus tantum, Pontifex degradator amovet ei mitram, dicendo:

Mitra, pontificalis dignitatis videlicet ornatu, quia eam male praesidendo foedasti, tuum caput denudamus.

Deinde unus ex ministris tradit degradando librum Evangeliorum, quem Pontifex degradator aufert de manibus degradandi, dicens:

Redde Evangelium; quia praedicandi officio, quo spreta Dei gratia te indignum fecisti, te iuste privamus.

Deinde Pontifex degradator amovet annulum de digito degradandi, sic dicens:

Annulum, fidei scilicet signaculum, tibi digne subtrahimus, quia ipsam sponsam Dei Ecclesiam temere violasti.

Tum unus ex ministris tradit degradando in manus baculum Pastoralem, quem mox Pontifex degradator tollit de manibus degradandi, dicens:

Auferimus a te baculum pastoralem, ut inde correctionis officium, quod turbasti, non valeas exercere.

Deinde extractis sibi per ministros chirothecis, Pontifex degradator abradit degradando pollices et manus leviter cum cultello, aut vitro dicens:

Sic spiritualis benedictionis, et delibutionis mysticae gratia, quantum in nobis est, te privamus, ut sacrificandi et benedicendi perdas officium, et effectum.

Post haec Pontifex cum eodem cultello aut vitro abradit leviter caput degradandi, dicens:

Consecrationem, et benedictionem, atque unctionem tibi traditam radendo delemus, et te ab ordine pontificali, quo inhabilis es redditus, abdicamus.

Tum degradando per ministros extrahuntur sandalia.

DEGRADATIO AB ORDINE PRESBYTERATUS

Ministri tradunt in manus degradandi Calicem cum vino, et aqua, ac Patena, et Hostia, quem Pontifex degradator aufert de manibus degradandi, dicens:

Amovemus a te, quin potius amotam esse ostendimus, potestatem offerendi Deo sacrificium, Missamque celebrandi tam pro vivis, quam pro defunctis.

Deinde Pontifex degradator abradit leviter cum cultello vel vitro, pollices et indices utriusque manus degradandi, dicens:

Potestatem sacrificandi, consecrandi, et benedicendi, quam in unctiones manuum et pollicum recepisti, tibi tollimus hac rasura.

Quo dicto, Pontifex degradator accipit casulam sive planetam per posteriorem partem caputii, et degradandum exuit, dicens:

Veste sacerdotali caritatem signante te merito exspoliamus, quia ipsam, et omnem innocentiam exuisti.

Tum Pontifex degradator aufert a degradando stolam, dicens:

Signum Domini per hanc stolam turpiter abiecisti, ideoque ipsam a te amovemus, quem inhabilem reddimus ad omne sacerdotale officium exercendum.

DEGRADATIO AB ORDINE DIACONATUS

Ministri tradunt degradando in manus librum Evangeliorum, quem Pontifex degradator tollit de manibus eius, dicens:

Amovemus a te potestatem legendi Evangelium in Ecclesia Dei, quia id non competit, nisi dignis.

Tum Pontifex degradator exuit degradandum dalmatica, dicens:

Levitico ordine te privamus, quia tuum in eo ministerium non implevisti.

Deinde Pontifex degradator amovet degradando stolam de humeris, proiiciens eam post tergum, dicens:

Stolam candidam, quam acceperas immaculatam in conspectu Domini perferendam, quia non sic cognito mysterio, exemplum conversationis tuae fidelibus praebuisti, ut plebs dicata Christi nomine posset exinde imitationem acquirere, iuste a te amovemus, omne Diaconatus officium tibi prohibentes.

DEGRADATIO AB ORDINE SUBDIACONATUS

Ministri tradunt in manus degradandi librum Epistolarum, quem Pontifex degradator de manibus illius accipit, dicens:

Auferimus tibi potestatem legendi Epistolam in Ecclesia Dei, quia hoc ministerio indignus es redditus.

Tum Pontifex degradator exuit degradandum tunicella, dicens:

Tunica subdiaconali te exuimus, cuius cor et corpus, timor Domini castus et sanctus in aeternum permanens, non constringit.

Deinde Pontifex degradator accipit a degradando manipulum, dicens:

Depone manipulum; quia per fructus bonorum operum, quos designat, non expugnasti spirituales insidias inimici.

Tum Pontifex tangens amictum degradandi, dicit:

Quia vocem tuam non castigasti, ideo amictum a te auferimus.

Post haec unus ex ministris tradit in manus degradandi urceolos cum vino, et aqua, ac bacile cum manutergio, ac Calicem vacuum cum patena. Tum Archidiaconus tollit de manu degradandi urceolos cum vino, et aqua, ac bacile cum buccali, et manutergio. Pontifex vero Calicem vacuum, et patenam tollit, dicens:

Potestatem introeundi sacrarium, tangendi pallas, vasa, et alia indumenta sacra, omneque Subdiaconatus ministerium exercendi, a te amovemus.

Deinde ministri exuunt degradandum cingulum, albam, et amictum.

DEGRADATIO AB ORDINE ACOLYTHATUS

Unus ex ministris tradit in manus degradandi urceolum vacuum, quem Pontifex degradator tollit de manibus illius, dicens:
Immunde, vinum et aquam ad Eucharistiam de cetero non ministres.

Tum unus ministrorum tradit in manus degradandi candelabrum cum cereo exstincto, quod Pontifex degradator accipit de manibus illius, dicens:
Dimitte perferendi visibile lumen officium, quia praebere spirituale moribus neglexisti, atque universum Acolythatus officium hic depone.

DEGRADATIO AB ORDINE EXORCISTATUS

Unus ex ministris tradit degradando in manus librum Exorcismorum, quem Pontifex degradator tollit de manibus illius, dicens:
Privamus te potestate imponendi manum super energumenos, et daemones de obsessis corporibus expellendi, omni tibi Excorcistatus officio interdicto.

DEGRADATIO AB ORDINE LECTORATUS

Unus ministrorum tradit degradando in manus librum Lectionum, quem Pontifex degradator tollit de manibus illius, dicens:
In Ecclesia Dei non legas ulterius, aut cantes; nec panes aut fructus novos ullatenus benedicas, quia tuum officium non implevisti fideliter et devote.

DEGRADATIO AB ORDINE OSTIARIATUS

Unus ex ministris tradit degradando in manus claves Ecclesiae, quas Pontifex degradator tollit de manibus illius, dicens:
Quia in clavibus errasti, claves dimitte; et quia ostia cordis tui male daemonibus obserasti, amovemus a te officium Ostiarii; ut non percutias cymbalum; non aperias Ecclesiam, non sacrarium, non librum amplius praedicanti.

DEGRADATIO A PRIMA TONSURA

Pontifex degradator extrahit degradando superpelliceum, dicens:
Auctoritate Dei omnipotentis, Patris, et Filii, et Spiritus Sancti, ac nostra, tibi auferimus habitum clericalem, et nudamus te religionis ornatu, ac deponimus, degradamus, spoliamus, et exuimus te omni Ordine, beneficio, et

privilegio clericali; et velut clericalis professionis indignum, redigimus te in servitutem, et ignominiam habitus saecularis, ac status.

Tum Pontifex degradator cum forficibus tondere incipit, et per barbitonsorem ibidem praesentem totaliter tonderi facit caput degradandi, dicens:

Te velut ingratum filium a sorte Domini, ad quam vocatus fueras abiicimus, et coronam tui capitis, regale quidem signum Sacerdotii, de tuo capite amovemus, propter tui regiminis pravitatem.

Tum ministri Pontificis exuunt degradatum veste, et habitu clericali, et ipsum induunt habitum saecularem. Quo facto, si fuerit talis casus, quo degradatus tradi debeat Curiae saeculari, Pontifex degradator degradatum amplius non tangit, sed in hunc modum contra ipsum pronuntiat, dicens:

Pronuntiamus, ut hunc exutum omni Ordine ac privilegio clericali, Curia saecularis in suum forum recipiat degradatum.

Tum Pontifex degradator efficaciter, et ex corde, et omni instantia, pro miserrimo illo derelicto intercedit apud iudicem saecularem, ut citra mortis periculum, vel mutilationis, contra degradatum sententiam moderetur, dicens:

Domine iudex, rogamus vos cum omni affectu, quo possumus, ut amore Dei, pietatis et misericordiae intuitu, et nostrorum interventu precaminum, miserrimo huic nullum mortis vel mutilationis periculum inferatis.

Quo facto, ministri Curiae saecularis degradatum sub sua custodia recipiunt, et discedunt.

BIBLIOGRAPHY

SOURCES

Acta Apostolicae Sedis, Commentarium Officiale, Romae, 1909—

Acta et Decreta Sacrorum Conciliorum Recentiorum, Collectio Lacensis, 7 vols., Friburgi Brisgoviae, 1870-1890.

Acta Sanctae Sedis, 41 vols., Romae, 1865-1908.

Bullarium Diplomatum et Privilegiorum Sanctorum Romanorum Pontificum, Taurinensis Editio, 24 vols. et Appendix, Augustae Taurinorum-Neapoli, 1857-1872.

Bullarii Romani Continuatio Summorum Pontificum, 19 vols., Prato, 1756-1883.

Bullarium Sanctissimi Domini Nostri Benedicti Papae XIV, 4 vols. in 10, Venetiis, 1777-1784.

Canones et Decreta Sacrosancti Oecumenici Concilii Tridentini, Romae: Ex Typographia Polyglotta S. C. de Propaganda Fide, 1882.

Codex Iuris Canonici Pii X Pontificis Maximi issu digestus Benedicti Papae XV auctoritate promulgatus, Romae: Typis Polyglottis Vaticanis, 1917.

Codex Theodosianus cum perpetuis commentariis Iacobi Gothofredi, editio nova in VI tomos digesta, Lipsiae, 1743.

Codicis Iuris Canonici Fontes cura Emi. Petri Card. Gasparri editi, 9 vols., Romae [postea Civitate Vaticana]: Typis Polyglottis Vaticanis, 1923-1939. (Vols. VII, VIII, IX *ed. cura et studio Emi. Iustiniani Card. Serédi*.)

Corpus Iuris Canonici, ed. Lipsiensis 2., Aemilius Ludovicus Richter—Aemilius Friedberg, ed. anastatice repitita, 2 vols., Lipsiae: Tauchnitz, 1928.

Corpus Iuris Civilis, 3 vols., Berolini: Apud Weidmannos, 1928-1929. Vol. I, *Institutiones*—recognovit P. Krueger; *Digesta*—recognovit Theodorus Mommsen; vol. II, *Codex Iustinianus*—recognovit et retractavit P. Krueger; vol. III, *Novellae Constitutiones*—R. Schoell; opus Schoelli morte interceptum absolvit G. Kroll.

Corpus Scriptorum Ecclesiasticorum Latinorum, editum consilio et impensis Academiae Litterarum Caesareae Vindobonensis, Vindobonae, 1866—

Decretales D. Gregorii Papae IX, una cum Glossis Restitutae, Romae, 1582.

Denzinger, Henr., et Bannwart, Clem., et Umberg, Iohan., *Enchiridion Symbolorum, Definitionum et Declarationum de Rebus Fidei et Morum*, 21-23 ed., Friburgi Brisgoviae: Herder, 1937.

Fulton, J., *Index Canonum*, New York, 1892.

Hardouin, Jean, *Acta Conciliorum et Epistolae Decretales ac Constitutiones Summorum Pontificum*, 12 vols., Parisiis, 1715.

Mansi, Ioannes, *Sacrorum Conciliorum Nova et Amplissima Collectio*, 53 vols., Parisiis, 1901-1927.

Migne, Jacques Paul, *Patrologiae Cursus Completus, Series Graeca*, 161 vols., Parisiis, 1856-1866.

———, *Patrologiae Cursus Completus, Series Latina*, 221 vols., Parisiis, 1844-1864.

Monumenta Germaniae Historica, edidit Societas aperiendis fontibus rerum Germanicarum medii aevi. *Leges*, 5 vols.: I-IV ed. Pertz, V ed. Pertz-Waitz-Brunner, Hannoverae, 1835 (reprinted Hiersemann, Leipzig, 1925).

Pontificale Romanum, Summorum Pontificum iussu editum a Benedicto XIV et Leone XIII Pont. Max. recognitum et castigatum, 3 vols., Ratisbonae, Romae, Neo Eboraci et Cincinnati, 1908.

REFERENCE WORKS

Aertnys, I.—Damen, C., *Theologia Moralis*, 13 ed., 2 vols., Taurini: Marietti, 1939.

Aichner, Simon, *Compendium Iuris Ecclesiastici*, 6 ed., Brixinae, 1887.

Alteserra, Antonius, *Opera Omnia*, Tom. X *Commentarius Perpetuus in Singulas Decretales Innocentii III*, cura Michaelis Marotta, ed. prima Neapolitana, 1780.

Aquinas, Thomas, *Summa Theologica*, 6 vols., Taurini: Marietti, 1928.

Ayrinhac, H. A., *Penal Legislation in the New Code of Canon Law*, revised by P. J. Lydon, New York: Benziger Brothers, 1936.

[Bachofen], Charles Augustine, *A Commentary on the New Code of Canon Law*, 8 vols., St. Louis: Herder and Co., 1925-1938. Vol. I, 6 ed., 1931; vol. II, 6 ed., 1936; vol. III, 5 ed., 1938; vol. IV, 3 ed., 1925; vol. V, 5 ed., 1935; vol. VI, 3 ed., 1931; vol. VII, 3 ed., 1930; vol. VIII, 3 ed., 1931.

Ballerini-Palmieri, *Opus Theologicum Morale*, 7 vols., Prati, 1889-1893.

Barbosa, Augustinus, *Collectanea Doctorum tam Veterum quam Recentiorum in Ius Pontificium Universum*, 6 vols., Lugduni, 1656.

———, *De Officio et Potestate Episcopi*, 2 vols., Lugduni, 1665.

Bareille, Georges, *Code du Droit Canonique*, nouvelle edition, Arras: Librarie Brunet, 1929.

Baronius, Caesar, *Annales Ecclesiastici*, 37 vols., Barri-Ducis, 1864-1883.

Benedictus XIV, *De Synodo Dioecesana*, 2 ed., 2 vols., Parmae, 1764.

Bernhart, Joseph, *The Vatican as a World Power*, translated by Geo. U. Shuster, London, New York, Toronto: Longmans, Green & Co., 1939.

Beste, Udalricus, *Introductio in Codicem*, Collegeville, Minnesota: St. John's Abbey Press, 1938.

Beveregius, Gulielmus, *Synodicon sive Pandectae Canonum et Conciliorum*, 2 vols., Oxonii, 1672.

Bevilacqua, Americus, *De Episcopi seu Ordinarii ex Novo Codice Canonico Iuribus ac Obligationibus*, Romae: Fredericus Pustet, 1921.

Bingham, Joseph, *The Antiquities of the Christian Church*, 2 vols., London, 1865.

Blat, Albertus, *Commentarium Textus Codicis Iuris Canonici*, 5 vols. in 7, Romae: Collegio "Angelico," 1921-1938. Vol. I, 1921; vol. II, pars I, ed. altera, 1921; vol. II, partes II et III, 3 ed., 1938; vol. III, pars I, 2 ed., 1924; vol. III, partes II et III, 2 ed., 1934; vol. IV, 1927; vol. V, 1924.

Boak, Arthur, *A History of Rome to 565 A. D.*, 2 ed., New York: The Macmillan Co., 1938.

Bona, Cardinal, *Rerum Liturgicarum Libri Duo*, 6 vols. in 4, Augustae Taurinorum, 1753.

Bouix, Dominicus, *Tractatus de Episcopo ubi et de Synodo Dioecesana*, Parisiis, 1859.

Buckland, W. W., *A Text Book of Roman Law from Augustus to Justinian*, 2 ed., Cambridge: The University Press, 1932.

Cappello, Felix, *Tractatus Canonico-Moralis de Sacramentis*, 3 vols. in 6, Taurini: Marietti, 1932-1939. Vol. I, 3 ed., 1938; vol. II, pars I, 3 ed., 1938; vol. II, pars II, 1932; vol. II, pars III, 1935; vol. III, partes I et II, 4 ed., 1939.

————, *De Censuris iuxta Codicem Iuris Canonici*, 3 ed., Augustae Taurinorum: Marietti, 1933.

Catalanus, Iosephus, *Pontificale Romanum*, 3 vols., Parisiis, 1886-1892.

Catholic Encyclopedia, The, 15 vols. and 2 suppls., New York, 1907-1922.

Cerato, Prosdocimus, *Censurae Vigentes Ipso Facto a Codice Iuris Canonici Excerptae*, 2 ed., Patavii: Typis Seminarii, 1921.

————, *De Delicto Sollicitationis*, Patavii: Typis Semniarii, 1922.

Chelodi, Ioannes, *Ius Poenale et Ordo Procedendi in Iudiciis Criminalibus iuxta Codicem Iuris Canonici*, 4 ed., recognita et aucta a Vigilio Dalpiaz, Tridenti: Ardesi, 1935.

————, *Ius de Personis iuxta Codicem Iuris Canonici*, ed. altera, recognita et aucta ab Ernesto Bertagnolli, Tridenti: Ardesi, 1927.

Cicognani, Amleto, *Canon Law*, authorized English version by J. O'Hara and F. Brennan, Philadelphia: Dolphin Press, 1934.

Ciprotti, P., *De Consummatione Delictorum Attento Eorum Elemento Objectivo in Iure Canonico*, Romae, 1936.

Claeys Bouuaert, F. et Simenon, G., *Manuale Iuris Canonici*, 3 vols., Gandae et Leodii, vol. I and III, 4 ed., 1934, vol. II, 2 ed., 1935.

Cocchi, Guidus, *Commentarium in Codicem Iuris Canonici*, 8 vols., Taurinorum Augustae: Marietti, 1931-1940. Vol. I, 5 ed., 1938; vol. II, 4 ed., 1937; vol. III, 3 ed., 1931; vol. IV, 3 ed., 1932; vol. V, 3 ed., 1932; vol. VI, 3 ed., 1933; vol. VII, 3 ed., 1940; vol. VIII, 4 ed., 1938.

Connor, Maurice, *The Administrative Removal of Pastors*, The Catholic University of America, Canon Law Studies, No. 104, Washington, D. C.: The Catholic University of America, 1937.

Coronata, Matthaeus Conte a, *Institutiones Iuris Canonici*, 5 vols., Taurini: Marietti, 1928-1936.

Daremberg-Saglio, *Dictionnaire des Antiquités Grecques*, Paris, 1873.

De Meester, Alphonsus, *Juris Canonici et Juris Canonico-Civilis Compendium*, nova ed., 3 vols. in 4, Brugis: Desclée, 1921-1928.

Devoti, Ioannes, *Institutiones Canonicarum Libri IV*, ed. prima Romana post quintam, Romae, 1825.

Dictionnaire de Théologie Catholique, Vacant-Mangenot, 13 vols., Paris, 1903-1907.

Dionysius Halicarnassensis, *Opera Omnia*, 6 vols., ed. Henricus Stephanus, Lipsiae, 1774-1777.

Durandus, Gulielmus, *Speculum Iuris cum Ioanne Andreae, Baldi de Ubaldis aliorumque aliquot praestantissimorum Iurisconsultorum Theorematibus*, Venetiis, 1577.

Eichmann, Eduard, *Das Strafrecht des Codex Iuris Canonici*, Paderborn: Ferdinand Schöningh, 1920.

Enciclopedia Italiana, Milano-Roma: Instituto Treceani, 1929-1936.

Fagnanus, Prosper, *Commentaria in Quinque Libros Decretalium*, 4 vols., Venetiis, 1697.

Ferraris, F. Lucius, *Prompta Bibliotheca, Canonica, Iuridica, Moralis, Theologica, necnon Ascetica, Polemica, Rubricistica, Historica*, 9 vols., Romae, 1885-1899; vol. IX, ed. Bucceroni.

Ferreres, Ioannes, *Institutiones Canonicae*, 2 ed., Barcinone: Eugenius Subirana, 1920.

Gasparri, P., *Tractatus Canonicus de sacra ordinatione*, 2 vols, Parisiis, Delhomme et Briguet, 1893.

Gebhart, Harnack, Zahn, *Patrum Apostolicorum Opera*, 3 vols., Lipsiae, 1876-1877.

Gennari, C., *Sulla Privazione del Beneficio Ecclesiastico*, 2. ed., Romae, 1905.

Gonzalez-Tellez, Emmanuel, *Commentaria Perpetua in Singulos Textus Quinque Librorum Decretalium Gregorii IX*, 5 vols. in 4, Venetiis, 1699.

Goyeneche, S., *Iuris Canonici Summa Principia*, Romae: Typis Polyglottis "Cuore di Maria," 1935.

Hefele, Charles J., *A History of the Christian Councils*, translated by Clark., 2. ed., 5 vols., Edinburgh, 1883.

Heiner, Franciscus, *De Processu Criminali Ecclesiastico*, Latine vertit ac denuo edidit A. Wynen, Romae: Fridericus Pustet, 1912.

Hilling, Nicholaus, *Das Personenrecht des Codex Iuris Canonici*, Paderborn: Ferdinand Schöningh, 1924.

Hinschius, Paul, *Das Kirchenrecht der Katholiken und Protestanten in Deutschland*, 6 vols., Berlin, 1869-1897. Vols. I-IV, *System des katholischen Kirchenrechts*, Berlin, 1869-1888.

Hollweck, Joseph, *Die kirchlichen Strafgesetze*, Mainz, 1899.

Hyland, Francis, *Excommunication, Its Nature, Historical Development, and Effects*, The Catholic University of America, Canon Law Studies, No. 49, Washington, D. C.: The Catholic University of America, 1928.

Jolowicz, H., *Historical Introduction to the Study of Roman Law*, Cambridge: University Press, 1932.

Kearney, Raymond A., *The Principles of Delegation*, The Catholic University of America, Canon Law Studies, No. 55, Washington, D. C.: The Catholic University of America, 1929.

Kearney, Richard, *Sponsors at Baptism According to the Code of Canon Law*, The Catholic University of America, Canon Law Studies, No. 30, Washington, D. C.: The Catholic University of America, 1925.

Kelly, James P., *Jurisdiction of the Confessor According to the Code of Canon Law*, New York: Benziger Brothers, 1929.

Kober, F., *Die Deposition und Degradation nach den Grundsätzen des kirchlichen Rechts, historisch-dogmatisch dargestellt*, Tübingen, 1863.

Konings, A., *Theologia Moralis*, Boston, 1874.

Kurtscheid, Bertrand, *A History of the Seal of Confession*, authorized translation by F. A. Marks, St. Louis: Herder, 1927.

Leage, R. W.-Ziegler, C. H., *Roman Private Law*, 2 ed., London: Macmillan & Company, 1937.

Leech, George, *A Comparative Study of the Constitution "Apostolicae Sedis" and the "Codex Iuris Canonici,"* The Catholic University of America, Canon Law Studies, No. 15, Washington, D. C.: The Catholic University of America, 1922.

Lega, Michaelis, *De Delictis et Poenis*, 2 ed., Romae, 1910.

Leitner, *Lehrbuch des katholischen Eherechts*, Paderborn, 1902.

Lemieux, Deslisle, *The Sentence in Ecclesiastical Procedure*, The Catholic University of America, Canon Law Studies, No. 87, Washington, D. C.: The Catholic University of America, 1934.

Leurenius, P., *Ius Canonicum Universum*, 5 vols. in 3, Venetiis, 1729.

Lijdsman, Bernardus, *Introductio in Ius Canonicum*, 2 vols., Hilversum in Hollandia, 1924-1929.

Lupus, Christianus, *Synodorum Generalium ac Provincialium Decreta et Canones*, 5 vols., Venetiis, 1725.

Lydon, P. J., *Ready Answers in Canon Law*, New York: Benziger Brothers, 1937.

MacKenzie, Eric F., *The Delict of Heresy in Its Commission, Penalization, Absolution*, The Catholic University of America, Canon Law Studies, No. 77, Washington, D. C.: The Catholic University of America, 1932.

Maitland, Frederic, *Roman Canon Law in the Church of England, Six Essays*, London, 1898.

Many, S., *Praelectiones de sacra ordinatione*, Parisiis, 1905.

Maroto, Philippus, *Institutiones Iuris Canonici ad Normam Novi Codicis*, 2 vols., Vol. I, *Tractatus Fundamentales*, 3 ed., Romae: Apud Commentarium pro Religiosis, 1921.

Martène, Edmundus, *De Antiquis Ecclesiae Ritibus*, 3 vols., Rotomagi, 1702.

Maskell, *Monumenta Ritualia Ecclesiae Anglicanae*, London, 1846-1847.

McNeill, John T. and Gamer, Helena M., *Medieval Handbooks of Penance, Records of Civilization: Sources and Studies*, Columbia University, No. XXIX, New York: Columbia University Press, 1938.

Miaskiewicz, F., *Supplied Jurisdiction According to Canon 209*, The Catholic University of America, Canon Law Studies, No. 122, Washington, D. C.: The Catholic University of America, 1940.

Michiels, Gommarus, *Normae Generales Iuris Canonici*, Lublin: Universitas Catholica, 1929.

Moriarity, Francis, *The Extraordinary Absolution from Censures*, The Catholic University of America, Canon Law Studies, No. 113, Washington, D. C.: The Catholic University of America, 1938.

Murphy, George, *Delinquencies and Penalties in the Administration and Reception of the Sacraments*, The Catholic University of America, Canon Law Studies, No. 17, Washington, D. C.: The Catholic University of America, 1923.

Murphy, Edwin, *Suspension Ex Informata Conscientia*, The Catholic University of America, Canon Law Studies, No. 76, Washington, D. C.: The Catholic University of America, 1932.

Neuberger, N., *Canon 6 or The Relation of the Codex Iuris Canonici to Preceding Legislation*, The Catholic University of America, Canon Law Studies, No. 44, Washington, D. C.: The Catholic University of America, 1927.

Noldin, H., *De Poenis Ecclesiasticis*, 5 ed., Oeniponte, 1905.

Noval, Iosephus, *De Processibus*, Augustae Taurinorum-Romae: Marietti, 1932.

Ojetti B., *Synopsis Rerum Moralium et Iuris Pontificii*, 3 vols., Vol. II, 3 ed., Romae, 1911.

O'Neill, William, *Papal Rescripts of Favor*, The Catholic University of America, Canon Law Studies, No. 57, Washington, D. C.: The Catholic University of America, 1930.

Ottaviani, Alaphridus, *Institutiones Iuris Publici Ecclesiastici*, 2 ed., 2 vols., Romae: Typis Polyglottis Vaticanis, 1935.

Panormitanus, Abbas (Nicolaus de Tudeschis), *Commentaria in Quinque Libros Decretalium*, 5 vols. in 7, Venetiis, 1588.

Pichler, Vitus, *Ius Canonicum secundum Quinque Decretalium Titulos Explicatum*, 2 vols., Ravennae, 1741.

Pirhing, Ernricus, *Ius Canonicum in Quinque Libros Decretalium Distributum Nova Methodo Explicatum*, 5 vols. in 4, Dilingae, 1674-1678.

Pistocchi, Mario, *I Canoni Penali del Codice Ecclesiastico Eposti e Commentati*, Torino-Roma: Marietti, 1925.

Probst, Ferdinand, *Kirchliche Disciplin in den drei ersten christlichen Jahrhunderten*, Tübingen, 1873.

Prümmer, Dominicus M., *Manuale Iuris Canonici*, 4. et 5. ed., Friburgi Brisgoviae: Herder, 1927.

Rainer, Eligius G., *The Suspension of Clerics*, The Catholic University of America, Canon Law Studies, No. 111, Washington, D. C.: The Catholic University of America, 1937.

Raus, J. B., *Institutiones Canonicae*, 2 ed., Lugduni: Typis Emmanuelis Vitte, 1931.

Reiffenstuel, Anacletus, *Ius Canonicum Universum*, 5 vols., Romae, 1833.

Roberti, Franciscus, *De Delictis et Poenis*, 2nd printing, Romae: Apud Custodiam Librariam Pontificii Instituti Utriusque Iuris.

————, *De Processibus*, 2 ed., Romae; Apud Aedes Facultatis Iuridicae ad S. Apollinaris, 1938-1941.

Sägmüller, Johann Baptist, *Lehrbuch des katholischen Kirchenrechts*, 4 ed., Vol. I, 4 fascicles, Freiburg im Br., 1925-1935.

Salucci, R., *Il Diritto Penale secondo il Codice di Diritto Canonico*, 2 vols. in 1, Subiaco: Tipografia dei Monasteri, 1926-1930.

Santi, Franciscus, *Praelectiones Iuris Canonici*, 2 vols., Ratisbonae, Neo-Eboraci, Cincinnati, 1866.

Schaaf and Wace, *Nicene and Post-Nicene Fathers of the Christian Church*, Second Series, New York, 1890.

Schäfer, Timotheus, *Compendium De Religiosis ad Normam Codicis Iuris Canonici*, 2 ed., Münster: Ex Officina Libraria Aschendorff, 1931.

Schmalzgrueber, Franciscus, *Ius Ecclesiasticum Universum*, 5 vols. in 12, Romae, 1843-1845.

Schroeder, H. J., *Disciplinary Decrees of the General Councils*, St. Louis: Herder, 1937.

Selective Service Regulations, Washington, D. C.: U. S. Government Printing Office, 1940.

Sipos, Stephanus, *Enchiridion Iuris Canonici*, Pécs: Ex Typographis Haladás R. T., 1926.

Smith, Mariner T., *The Penal Law for Religious*, The Catholic University of America, Canon Law Studies, No. 98, Washington, D. C., The Catholic University of America, 1935.

Smith, S., *Elements of Ecclesiastical Law*, 3. ed., 3 vols., New York, 1888.

Smith, William-Cheetham, Samuel, *A Dictionary of Christian Antiquities*, 2 vols., Hartford, 1880.

Soglia, Ioannes, *Institutiones Iuris Publici et Privati Ecclesiastici*, 10. ed., 2 vols., Boscoduci, 1853.

Sohm, Rudolph, *Kirchenrecht*, 2. ed., 2 vols., München and Leipzig: Duncker and Humblot, 1923.

Stephenson, Carl, *Medieval History*, New York: Harper & Brothers, 1935.

Stewart, A. and Long, G., *Plutarch's Lives* (translated from the Greek), 4 vols., London and New York, 1889-1892.

Story of the Constitution, The, United States Constitution Sesquicentennial Commission, Washington, D. C.: House Office Building, 1937.

Suarez, Franciscus, *Opera Omnia*, ed. nova, a Carolo Berton, 26 vols., Parisiis, Apud Ludovicum Vives, 1856-1866.

Thomassinus, Ludovicus, *Vetus et Nova Ecclesiae Disciplina*, 3 vols., Venetiis, 1730.

Vacandard, E., *The Inquisition, A Critical and Historical Study of the Coercive Power of the Church*, 2. ed., New York: Longmans, Green & Co., 1908.

Van Espen, Zegerus, *Ius Ecclesiasticum Universum*, 5 vols., Lovanii, 1753.

Van Hove, A., *Commentarium Lovaniense in Codicem Iuris Canonici*, Mechliniae-Romae: H. Dessain, 1928; Vol. I, Tom. I, *Prolegomena ad Codicem Iuris Canonici*, Mechliniae-Romae: H. Dessain, 1928; Vol. I, Tom. II, *De Legibus Ecclesiasticis*, Mechliniae: H. Dessain, 1930; Vol. I, Tom. IV, *De Rescriptis*, Mechliniae: H. Dessain, 1936.

Vechiotti, *Institutiones Canonicae*, 19. ed., Augustae Taurinorum, 1886.

Vermeersch, Arturus and Creusen, Iosephus, *Epitome Iuris Canonici*, 3 vols., Vol. I, 6. ed., 1937; Vol. II, 5 ed., 1934; Vol. III, 5, ed., 1936, Mechliniae-Romae: Dessain, 1934-1937.

Waterworth, J., *The Canons and Decrees of the Sacred and Oecumenical Council of Trent*, New York and London, 1848.

Watkins, Oscar D., *A History of Penance*, 2 vols., London: Longmans, Green & Company, 1920.

Wenger, L. and Fisk, O., *Institutes of the Roman Law of Civil Procedure*, revised ed., New York; Veritas Press, 1940.

Wernz, Franciscus X., *Ius Decretalium*, 2. ed., 6 vols., Romae et Prati, 1906-1913.

Wernz, F. — Vidal, P., *Ius Canonicum*, 7 tom. in 8 vols., Romae: Apud Aedes Universitatis Gregorianiae, 1923-1938.

Woywood, Stanislaus, *A Practical Commentary on the Code of Canon Law*, 4. ed., 2 vols., New York: Wagner, 1932.

Zitelli, Z., *Apparatus Iuris Ecclesiastici*, 2 ed., Romae: 1888.

ABBREVIATIONS

AAS—Acta Apostolicae Sedis.
ASS—Acta Sanctae Sedis.
Bull. Rom. Taur.—Bullarium Romanum ed. Taurinensis.
C—Codex (Iustinianus).
CIC—Codex Iuris Canonici.
C. Th.—Codex Theodosianus.
D—Digesta (Iustiniana).
Fontes—Codicis Iuris Canonici Fontes.
Hardouin—*Acta Conciliorum,* etc.
I—Institutiones (Iustinianae).
Ius Pont.—Ius Pontificum.
Mansi—*Sacrorum Conciliorum Nova et Amplissima Collectio.*
MGH—Monumenta Germaniae Historica.
*MPG—*Migne, *Patrologia Graeca.*
*MPL—*Migne, *Patrologia Latina.*
N—Novellae (Iustinianae).
PCI—Pontificia Commissio Interpretationis.
S. C. C.—Sacra Congregatio Concilii.
S. C. Consist.—Sacra Congregatio Consistorialis.
S. C. de Rel.—Sacra Congregatio de Religiosis.
S. C. Ep. et Reg.—Sacra Congregatio Episcoporum et Regularium.
S. C. R.—Sacra Congregatio Rituum.
S. C. super Statu Reg.—Sacra Congregatio super Statu Regularium.
S. R. R. Dec.—Sacrae Romanae Rotae Decisiones seu Sententiae.

BIOGRAPHICAL NOTE

Stephen William Findlay was born on July 16, 1911, in Newark, N. J. After completing his elementary education in Columbian School, East Orange, N. J., he received his high school education at St. Benedict's Preparatory School in Newark. He matriculated at St. Anselm's College, Manchester, N. H., in the fall of 1929. After two years of college training, he entered the novitiate of the Order of St. Benedict, at Latrobe, Pa., where he made his religious profession as a member of St. Mary's Abbey, Newark, on July 2, 1932. In the fall of that year he entered St. Vincent's Seminary where he completed his philosophical studies, receiving the Bachelor of Arts degree in June, 1934. Thence he was sent to the Benedictine House of Studies at Morristown, N. J., to pursue the prescribed theological studies. He made his solemn profession on July 2, 1935, and on May 22, 1937, was ordained to the priesthood. After the completion of his seminary course in 1938 his superior sent him to the School of Canon Law at the Catholic University of America, where he received the degree of the Baccalaureate in Canon Law in June, 1939, and the degree of the Licentiate in Canon Law in June, 1940.

CANON LAW STUDIES

1. Freriks, Rev. Celestine A., C.PP.S., J.C.D., Religious Congregations in Their External Relations, 121 pp., 1916.
2. Galliher, Rev. Daniel M., O.P., J.C.D., Canonical Elections, 117 pp., 1917.
3. Borkowski, Rev. Aurelius L., O.F.M., J.C.D., De Confraternitatibus Ecclesiasticis, 136 pp., 1918.
4. Castillo, Rev. Cayo, J.C.D., Disertacion Historico-Canonica sobre la Potestad del Cabildo en Sede Vacante o Impedida del Vicario Capitular, 99 pp., 1919 (1918).
5. Kubelbeck, Rev. William J., S.T.B., J.C.D., The Sacred Penitentiaria and Its Relation to Faculties of Ordinaries and Priests, 129 pp., 1918.
6. Petrovits, Rev. Joseph, J.C., S.T.D., J.C.D., The New Church Law on Matrimony, X-461 pp., 1919.
7. Hickey, Rev. John J., S.T.B., J.C.D., Irregularities and Simple Impediments in the New Code of Canon Law, 100 pp., 1920.
8. Klekotka, Rev. Peter J., S.T.B., J.C.D., Diocesan Consultors, 179 pp., 1920.
9. Wanenmacher, Rev. Francis, J.C.D., The Evidence in Ecclesiastical Procedure Affecting the Marriage Bond, 1920 (Printed 1935).
10. Golden, Rev. Henry Francis, J.C.D., Parochial Benefices in the New Code, IV-119 pp., 1921 (Printed 1925).
11. Koudelka, Rev. Charles J., J.C.D., Pastors, Their Rights and Duties According to the New Code of Canon Law, 211 pp., 1921.
12. Melo, Rev. Antonius, O.F.M., J.C.D., De Exemptione Regularium, X-188 pp., 1921.
13. Schaaf, Rev. Valentine Theodore, O.F.M., S.T.B., J.C.D., The Cloister, X-180 pp., 1921.
14. Burke, Rev. Thomas Joseph, S.T.D., J.C.D., Competence in Ecclesiastical Tribunals, IV-117 pp., 1922.
15. Leech, Rev. George Leo, J.C.D., A Comparative Study of the Constitution "Apostolicae Sedis" and the "Codex Juris Canonici," 179 pp., 1922.
16. Motry, Rev. Hubert Louis, S.T.D., J.C.D., Diocesan Faculties According to the Code of Canon Law, II-167 pp., 1922.
17. Murphy, Rev. George Lawrence, J.C.D., Delinquencies and Penalties in the Administration and the Reception of the Sacraments, IV-121 pp., 1923.
18. O'Reilly, Rev. John Anthony, S.T.B., J.C.D., Ecclesiastical Sepulture in the New Code of Canon Law, II-129 pp., 1923.
19. Michalicka, Rev. Wenceslas Cyrill, O.S.B., J.C.D., Judicial Procedure in Dismissal of Clerical Exempt Religious, 107 pp., 1923.

20. DARGIN, REV. EDWARD VINCENT, S.T.B., J.C.D., Reserved Cases According to the Code of Canon Law, IV-103 pp., 1924.
21. GODFREY, REV. JOHN A., S.T.B., J.C.D., The Right of Patronage According to the Code of Canon Law, 153 pp., 1924.
22. HAGEDORN, REV. FRANCIS EDWARD, J.C.D., General Legislation on Indulgences, II-154 pp., 1924.
23. KING, REV. JAMES IGNATIUS, J.C.D., The Administration of the Sacraments to Dying Non-Catholics, V-141 pp., 1924.
24. WINSLOW, REV. FRANCIS JOSEPH, O.F.M., J.C.D., Vicars and Prefects Apostolic, IV-149 pp., 1924.
25. CORREA, REV. JOSE SERVELION, S.T.L., J.C.D., La Potestad Legislativa de la Iglesia Catolica, IV-127 pp., 1925.
26. DUGAN, REV. HENRY FRANCIS, A.M., J.C.D., The Judiciary Department of the Diocesan Curia, 87 pp., 1925.
27. KELLER, REV. CHARLES FREDERICK, S.T.B., J.C.D., Mass Stipends, 167 pp., 1925.
28. PASCHANG, REV. JOHN LINUS, J.C.D., The Sacramentals According to the Code of Canon Law, 129 pp., 1925.
29. PIONTEK, REV. CYRILLUS, O.F.M., S.T.B., J.C.D., De Indulto Exclaustrationis necnon Saecularizationis, XIII-289 pp., 1925.
30. KEARNEY, REV. RICHARD JOSEPH, S.T.B., J.C.D., Sponsors at Baptism According to the Code of Canon Law, IV-127 pp., 1925.
31. BARTLETT, REV. CHESTER JOSEPH, A.M., LL.B., J.C.D., The Tenure of Parochial Property in the United States of America, V-108 pp., 1926.
32. KILKER, REV. ADRIAN JEROME, J.C.D., Extreme Unction, V-425 pp., 1926.
33. McCORMICK, REV. ROBERT EMMETT, J.C.D., Confessors of Religious, VIII-266 pp., 1926.
34. MILLER, REV. NEWTON THOMAS, J.C.D., Founded Masses According to the Code of Canon Law, VII-93 pp., 1926.
35. ROELKER, REV. EDWARD G., S.T.D., J.C.D., Principles of Privilege According to the Code of Canon Law, XI-166 pp., 1926.
36. BAKALARCZYK, REV. RICHARDUS, M.I.C., J.U.D., De Novitiatu, VIII-208 pp., 1927.
37. PIZZUTI, REV. LAWRENCE, O.F.M., J.U.L., De Parochis Religiosis, 1927. (Not Printed.)
38. BLILEY, REV. NICHOLAS MARTIN, O.S.B., J.C.D., Altars According to the Code of Canon Law, XIX-132 pp., 1927.
39. BROWN, MR. BRENDAN FRANCIS, A.B., LL.M., J.U.D., The Canonical Juristic Personality with Special Reference to its Status in the United States of America, V-212 pp., 1927.
40. CAVANAUGH, REV. WILLIAM THOMAS, C.P., J.U.D., The Reservation of the Blessed Sacrament, VIII-101 pp., 1927.
41. DOHENY, REV. WILLIAM J., C.S.C., A.B., J.U.D., Church Property: Modes of Acquisition, X-118 pp., 1927.

42. FELDHAUS, REV. ALOYSIUS H., C.PP.S., J.C.D., Oratories, IX-141 pp., 1927.
43. KELLY, REV. JAMES PATRICK, A.B., J.C.D., The Jurisdiction of the Simple Confessor, X-208 pp., 1927.
44. NEUBERGER, REV. NICHOLAS J., J.C.D., Canon 6 or the Relation of the Codex Juris Canonici to the Preceding Legislation, V-95 pp., 1927.
45. O'KEEFE, REV. GERALD MICHAEL, J.C.D., Matrimonial Dispensations, Powers of Bishops, Priests, and Confessors, VIII-232 pp., 1927.
46. QUIGLEY, REV. JOSEPH A. M., A.B., J.C.D., Condemned Societies, 139 pp., 1927.
47. ZAPLOTNIK, REV. JOHANNES LEO, J.C.D., De Vicariis Foraneis, X-142 pp., 1927.
48. DUSKIE, REV. JOHN ALOYSIUS, A.B., J.C.D., The Canonical Status of the Orientals in the United States, VIII-196 pp., 1928.
49. HYLAND, REV. FRANCIS EDWARD, J.C.D., Excommuncation, Its Nature, Historical Development and Effects, VIII-181 pp., 1928.
50. REINMANN, REV. GERALD JOSEPH, O.M.C., J.C.D., The Third Order Secular of Saint Francis, 201 pp., 1928.
51. SCHENK, REV. FRANCIS J., J.C.D., The Matrimonial Impediments of Mixed Religion and Disparity of Cult, XVI-318 pp., 1929.
52. COADY, REV. JOHN JOSEPH, S.T.D., J.U.D., A.M., The Appointment of Pastors, VIII-150 pp., 1929.
53. KAY, REV. THOMAS HENRY, J.C.D., Competence in Matrimonial Procedure, VIII-164 pp., 1929.
54. TURNER, REV. SIDNEY JOSEPH, C.P., J.U.D., The Vow of Poverty, XLIX-217 pp., 1929.
55. KEARNEY, REV. RAYMOND A., A.B., S.T.D., J.C.D., The Principles of Delegation, VII-149 pp., 1929.
56. CONRAN, REV. EDWARD JAMES, A.B., J.C.D., The Interdict, V-163 pp., 1930.
57. O'NEILL, REV. WILLIAM H., J.C.D., Papal Rescripts of Favor, VII-218 pp., 1930.
58. BASTNAGEL, REV. CLEMENT VINCENT, J.U.D., The Appointment of Parochial Adjutants and Assistants, XV-257 pp., 1930.
59. FERRY, REV. WILLIAM A., A.B., J.C.D., Stole Fees, V-136 pp., 1930.
60. COSTELLO, REV. JOHN MICHAEL, A.B., J.C.D., Domicile and Quasi-Domicile, VII-201 pp., 1930.
61. KREMER, REV. MICHAEL NICHOLAS, A.B., S.T.B., J.C.D., Church Support in the United States, VI-136 pp., 1930.
62. ANGULO, REV. LUIS, C.M., J.C.D., Legislation de la Iglesia sobre la intencion en la application de la Santa Misa, VII-104 pp., 1931.
63. FREY, REV. WOLFGANG NORBERT, O.S.B., A.B., J.C.D., The Act of Religious Profession, VIII-174 pp., 1931.
64. ROBERTS, REV. JAMES BRENDAN, A.B., J.C.D., The Banns of Marriage, XIV-140 pp., 1931.
65. RYDER, REV. RAYMOND ALOYSIUS, A.B., J.C.D., Simony, IX-151 pp., 1931.

66. CAMPAGNA, REV. ANGELO, PH.D., J.U.D., Il Vicario Generale del Vescovo, VII-205 pp., 1931.
67. COX, REV. JOSEPH GODFREY, A.B., J.C.D., The Administration of Seminaries, VI-124 pp., 1931.
68. GREGORY, REV. DONALD J., J.U.D., The Pauline Privilege, XV-165 pp., 1931.
69. DONOHUE, REV. JOHN F., J.C.D., The Impediment of Crime, VII-110 pp., 1931.
70. DOOLEY, REV. EUGENE A., O.M.I., J.C.D., Church Law on Sacred Relics, IX-143 pp., 1931.
71. ORTH, REV. CLEMENT RAYMOND, O.M.C., J.C.D., The Approbation of Religious Institutes, 171 pp., 1931.
72. PERNICONE, REV. JOSEPH M., A.B., J.C.D., The Ecclesiastical Prohibition of Books, XII-267 pp., 1932.
73. CLINTON, REV. CONNELL, A.B., J.C.D., The Paschal Precept, IX-108 pp., 1932.
74. DONNELLY, REV. FRANCIS B., A.M., S.T.L., J.C.D., The Diocesan Synod, VIII-125 pp., 1932.
75. TORRENTE, REV. CAMILO, C.M.F., J.C.D., Las Processiones Sagradas, V-145 pp., 1932.
76. MURPHY, REV. EDWIN J., C.PP.S., J.C.D., Suspension Ex Informata Conscientia, XI-122 pp., 1932.
77. MACKENZIE, REV. ERIC F., A.M., S.T.L., J.C.D., The Delict of Heresy in its Commission, Penalization, Absolution, VII-124 pp., 1932.
78. LYONS, REV. AVITUS E., S.T.B., J.C.D., The Collegiate Tribunal of First Instance, XI-147 pp., 1932.
79. CONNOLLY, REV. THOMAS A., J.C.D., Appeals, XI-195 pp., 1932.
80. SANGMEISTER, REV. JOSEPH V., A.B., J.C.D., Force and Fear as Precluding Matrimonial Consent, V-211 pp., 1932.
81. JAEGER, REV. LEO A., A.B., J.C.D., The Administration of Vacant and Quasi-Vacant Episcopal Sees in the United States, IX-229 pp., 1932.
82. RIMLINGER, REV. HERBERT T., J.C.D., Error Invalidating Matrimonial Consent, VII-79 pp., 1932.
83. BARRETT, REV. JOHN D. M., S.S., J.C.D., A Comparative Study of the Third Plenary Council of Baltimore and the Code, IX-221 pp., 1932.
84. CARBERRY, REV. JOHN J., PH.D., S.T.D., J.C.D., The Juridical Form of Marriage, X-177 pp., 1934.
85. DOLAN, REV. JOHN L., A.B., J.C.D., The Defensor Vinculi, XII-157 pp., 1934.
86. HANNAN, REV. JEROME D., A.M., S.T.D., LL.B., J.C.D., The Canon Law of Wills, IX-517 pp., 1934.
87. LEMIEUX, REV. DELISE A., A.M., J.C.D., The Sentence in Ecclesiastical Procedure, IX-131 pp., 1934.
88. O'ROURKE, REV. JAMES J., A.B., J.C.D., Parish Registers, VII-109 pp., 1934.

89. TIMLIN, REV. BARTHOLOMEW, O.F.M., A.M., J.C.D., Conditional Matrimonial Consent, X-381 pp., 1934.

90. WAHL, REV. FRANCIS X., A.B., J.C.D., The Matrimonial Impediments of Consanguinity and Affinity, VI-125 pp., 1934.

91. WHITE, REV. ROBERT J., A.B., LL.B., S.T.B., J.C.D., Canonical Ante-Nuptial Promises and the Civil Law, VI-152 pp., 1934.

92. HERRERA, REV. ANTONIO PARRA, O.C.D., J.C.D., Legislacion Ecclesiastica sobra el Ayuno y la Abstinencia, XI-191 pp., 1935.

93. KENNEDY, REV. EDWIN J., J.C.D., The Special Matrimonial Process in Cases of Evident Nullity, X-165 pp., 1935.

94. MANNING, REV. JOHN J., A.B., J.C.D., Presumption of Law in Matrimonial Procedure, XI-111 pp., 1935.

95. MOEDER, REV. JOHN M., J.C.D., The Proper Bishop for Ordination and Dimissorial Letters, VII-135 pp., 1935.

96. O'MARA, REV. WILLIAM A., A.B., J.C.D., Canonical Causes for Matrimonial Dispensations, IX-155 pp., 1935.

97. REILLY, REV. PETER, J.C.D., Residence of Pastors, IX-81 pp., 1935.

98. SMITH, REV. MARINER T., O.P., S.T.Lr., J.C.D., The Penal Law for Religious, VII-169 pp., 1935.

99. WHALEN, REV. DONALD W., A.M., J.C.D., The Value of Testimonial Evidence in Matrimonial Procedure, XIII-297 pp., 1935.

100. CLEARY, REV. JOSEPH F., J.C.D., Canonical Limitations on the Alienation of Church Property, VIII-141 pp., 1936.

101. GLYNN, REV. JOHN C., J.C.D., The Promoter of Justice, XX-337 pp., 1936.

102. BRENNAN, REV. JAMES H., S.S., M.A., S.T.B., J.C.D., The Simple Convalidation of Marriage, VI-135 pp., 1937.

103. BRUNINI, REV. JOSEPH BERNARD, J.C.D., The Clerical Obligations of Canons 139 and 142, X-121 pp., 1937.

104. CONNOR, REV. MAURICE, A.B., J.C.D., The Administrative Removal of Pastors, VIII-159 pp., 1937.

105. GUILFOYLE, REV. MERLIN JOSEPH, J.C.D., Custom, XI-144 pp., 1937.

106. HUGHES, REV. JAMES AUSTIN, A.B., A.M., J.C.D., Witnesses in Criminal Trials of Clerics, IX-140 pp., 1937.

107. JANSEN, REV. RAYMOND J., A.B., S.T.L., J.C.D., Canonical Provisions for Catechetical Instruction, VII-153 pp., 1937.

108. KEALY, REV. JOHN JAMES, A.B., J.C.D., The Introductory Libellus in Church Court Procedure, XI-121 pp., 1937.

109. McMANUS, REV. JAMES EDWARD, C.SS.R., J.C.D., The Administration of Temporal Goods in Religious Institutes, XVI-196 pp., 1937.

110. MORIARTY, REV. EUGENE JAMES, J.C.D., Oaths in Ecclesiastical Courts, X-115 pp., 1937.

111. RAINER, REV. ELIGIUS GEORGE, C.SS.R., J.C.D., Suspension of Clerics, XVII-249 pp., 1937.

112. REILLY, REV. THOMAS F., C.SS.R., J.C.D., Visitation of Religious, VI-195 pp., 1938.
113. MORIARTY, REV. FRANCIS E., C.SS.R., J.C.D., The Extraordinary Absolution from Censures, XV-334 pp., 1938.
114. CONNOLLY, REV. NICHOLAS P., J.C.D., The Canonical Erection of Parishes, X-132 pp., 1938.
115. DONOVAN, REV. JAMES JOSEPH, J.C.D., The Pastor's Obligation in Prenuptial Investigation, XII-322 pp., 1938.
116. HARRIGAN, REV. ROBERT J., M.A., S.T.B., J.C.D., The Radical Sanation of Invalid Marriages, VIII-208 pp., 1938.
117. BOFFA, REV. CONRAD HUMBERT, J.C.D., Canonical Provisions for Catholic Schools, VII-211 pp., 1939.
118. PARSONS, REV. ANSCAR JOHN, O.M.Cap., J.C.D., Canonical Elections, XII-236 pp., 1939.
119. REILLY, REV. EDWARD MICHAEL, A.B., J.C.D., The General Norms of Dispensation, XII-156 pp., 1939.
120. RYAN, REV. GERALD ALOYSIUS, A.B., J.C.D., Principles of Episcopal Jurisdiction, XII-172 pp., 1939.
121. BURTON, REV. FRANCIS JAMES, C.S.C., A.B., J.C.D., A Commentary on Canon 1125, X-222 pp., 1940.
122. MIASKIEWICZ, REV. FRANCIS SIGISMUND, J.C.D., Supplied Jurisdiction According to Canon 209, XII-340 pp., 1940.
123. RICE, REV. PATRICK WILLIAM, A.B., J.C.D., Proof of Death in Prenuptial Investigation, VIII-156 pp., 1940.
124. ANGLIN, REV. THOMAS FRANCIS, M.S., J.C.L., The Eucharistic Fast.
125. COLEMAN, REV. JOHN JEROME, J.C.L., The Minister of Confirmation.
126. DOWNS, REV. JOHN EMMANUEL, A.B., J.C.L., The Concept of Clerical Immunity.
127. ESSWEIN, REV. ANTHONY ALBERT, J.C.L., Extrajudicial Penal Powers of Ecclesiastical Superiors.
128. FARRELL, REV. BENJAMIN FRANCIS, M.A., S.T.L., J.C.L., The Rights and Duties of the Local Ordinary Regarding Congregations of Women Religious of Pontifical Approval.
129. FEENEY, REV. THOMAS JOHN, A.B., S.T.L., J.C.L., Restitutio in Integrum.
130. FINDLAY, REV. STEPHEN WILLIAM, O.S.B., A.B., J.C.L., Canonical Norms Governing the Deposition and Degradation of Clerics.
131. GOODWINE, REV. JOHN, A.B., S.T.L., J.C.L., The Right of the Church to Acquire Property.
132. HESTON, REV. EDWARD LOUIS, C.S.C., Ph.D., S.T.D., J.C.L., The Alienation of Church Property in the United States.
133. HOGAN, REV. JAMES JOHN, A.B., S.T.L., J.C.L., Judicial Advocates and Procurators.
134. KEALY, REV. THOMAS M., A.B., Litt.B., J.C.L., Dowry of Women Religious.

135. KEENE, REV. MICHAEL JAMES, O.S.B., J.C.L., Religious Ordinaries and Canon 198.

136. KERIN, REV. CHARLES A., S.S., M.A., S.T.B., J.C.L., The Privation of Christian Burial.

137. LOUIS, REV. WILLIAM FRANCIS, M.A., J.C.L., Diocesan Archives.

138. McDEVITT, REV. GILBERT JOSEPH, A.B., J.C.L., Legitimacy and Legitimation.

139. McDONOUGH, REV. THOMAS JOSEPH, A.B., J.C.L., Apostolic Administrators.

140. MEIER, REV. CARL ANTHONY, A.B., J.C.L., Penal Administrative Procedure Against Negligent Pastors.

141. SCHMIDT, REV. JOHN RUGG, A.B., J.C.L., The Principles of Authentic Interpretation in Canon 17 of the Code of Canon Law.

142. SLAFKOSKY, REV. ANDREW LEONARD, A.B., J.C.L., The Canonical Episcopal Visitation of the Diocese.

143. SWOBODA, REV. INNOCENT ROBERT, O.F.M., J.C.L., Ignorance in Relation to the Imputability of Delicts.

144. DUBÉ, REV. ARTHUR JOSEPH, A.B., J.C.L., The General Principles for the Reckoning of Time in Canon Law.

145. McBRIDE, REV. JAMES T., A.B., J.C.L., Incardination and Excardination of Seculars.

CPSIA information can be obtained
at www.ICGtesting.com
Printed in the USA
BVHW031526260319
543744BV00003B/50/P